Praying the Language of Enmity in the Psalter

Praying the Language of Enmity in the Psalter

A Study of Psalms 110, 119, 129, 137, 139, and 149

ARAN J. E. PERSAUD

Foreword by James M. Houston

WIPF & STOCK · Eugene, Oregon

PRAYING THE LANGUAGE OF ENMITY IN THE PSALTER
A Study of Psalms 110, 119, 129, 137, 139, and 149

Copyright © 2016 Aran J. E. Persaud. All rights reserved. Except for brief quotations in critical publications or reviews, no part of this book may be reproduced in any manner without prior written permission from the publisher. Write: Permissions, Wipf and Stock Publishers, 199 W. 8th Ave., Suite 3, Eugene, OR 97401.

Wipf & Stock
An Imprint of Wipf and Stock Publishers
199 W. 8th Ave., Suite 3
Eugene, OR 97401

www.wipfandstock.com

PAPERBACK ISBN: 978-1-4982-8961-0
HARDCOVER ISBN: 978-1-4982-8963-4
EBOOK ISBN: 978-1-4982-8962-7

Manufactured in the U.S.A.   07/21/16

Contents

Foreword by James M. Houston | ix
Preface | xi
Abbreviations | xiii

Chapter 1
Introduction | 1
    The Problem of the Language of Enmity in the Psalms | 1
    Synecdoche as a Way to Understand Moral Evil | 3
    Some Preliminary Matters of Methodology | 3
        Determining the Nature of the Psalmist's Perceived Suffering and the Meaning of the Response | 4
        Investigating Expressions of Enmity in the Light of Previous Commentators | 8
        Prayer as the Basis for the Inclusion of Non-lament Psalms | 12
        The Extent of Book V and Its Meaning for this Study | 15
        Selection of Psalms to be Studied | 21

Chapter 2
An Exegetical and Historical Study of Psalms 110, 119, 129, 137, 139, and 149 | 25
    Exegesis of Psalm 110—Yahweh's "lord" and Unrestrained Evil | 25
        Establishing the Nature of the Text and Clarifying the Difficult Verse Three | 26
        Structural Implications for Understanding Psalm 110 as a Messianic and Royal Prophecy | 28
        The Perceived Suffering of the Psalmist | 31
        The Meaning of the "lord's" Response | 34
        Conclusion of Exegesis | 35
    A Select Historical Survey of the Interpretation of Psalm 110 | 36
        The early Post-exilic Restoration | 36
        The NT—Christ's Role as Judge and Priest | 38

    The Pre-Nicene and Post-Nicene Fathers—Literal and Spiritual Tensions | 40
    Augustine— Christ's Session | 42
    Psalm 110 in the Reformers | 44
    Comparison with the Exegetical Findings of Psalm 110 | 48
Exegesis of Psalm 119: Overcoming Injustice through the Pursuit of the Law | 49
    Verses One to Eight as the Psalmist's Orientation and Verse Seventy–eight | 50
    Artistic Unity | 51
    The Psalmist—A Member of the Early Post-exilic Community | 53
    Identifying the Enemies—A Weakness of the Form-Critical Approach | 54
    The Perceived Suffering of the Psalmist—Diverse and Intense | 55
    Dedication to Torah as a Response to Suffering. | 56
    Conclusion of the Exegesis | 60
A Select Historical Survey of the Interpretation of Psalm 119 | 61
    Psalm 119 and an Early Post-Exilic Ethos | 61
    Psalm 119 in the New Testament—The Law as a Window into the Inseparability of
        Yahweh's Character and Judgement | 63
    Psalm 119 in the Ante-Nicene and Post-Nicene Fathers | 65
    Psalm 119 in Augustine | 67
    Psalm 119 in the Reformers | 72
    Comparison with the Exegetical Findings of Psalm 119 | 78
Exegesis of Psalm 129:The Severity of Agricultural Curses | 81
    An Agrarian MT or the War Text of the LXX? | 82
    Maintaining the MT's Agrarian Images | 84
    The Enemies and the Translation of the Verbs in Verses 4–7 | 85
    A History of Suffering | 88
    Withering Grass—A Symbol of Utter Destruction | 90
    Conclusion of the Exegesis | 93
A Select Historical Survey of the Interpretation of Psalm 129 | 93
    Post-Exilic Interpretation—A Mitigation of the Curses? | 94
    The NT—Agriculture as an Image of Severe Judgment | 94
    The Ante-Nicene and Post-Nicene Fathers | 97
    Augustine | 98
    Calvin | 99
    Comparison with the Exegetical Findings of Psalm 129 | 100
Exegesis of Psalm 137: The Problem of Dashing Little Ones Against the Rock | 102
    Establishing the Text: When was Babylon Destroyed? | 102
    Structure, Unity and Setting as Bases for Interpretation | 104
    What the Text Says about Suffering | 107
    A Metaphorical–Historical Meaning of the Response | 108
    Conclusion of the Exegesis | 113

A Select Historical Survey of Psalm 137 | 113
    A Post-Exilic Perspective | 113
    The NT—Historical Judgment and Fixed Memory | 115
    The Ante-Nicene and Post-Nicene Fathers | 116
    Augustine | 121
    Calvin | 123
    Comparison with the Exegetical Findings of Psalm 137 | 125
Enemies, Obligation, and Sin: Keys for Understanding
   the Imprecations in Psalm 139 | 127
    A Unified Text | 128
    Structure and Form—A Unified Literary Petition | 131
    Identification of the Enemies as a Clue to the Setting | 133
    Perceived Suffering | 136
    Meaning of the Response | 138
    Conclusion of the Exegesis | 139
A Select Historical Survey of the Interpretation of Psalm 139 | 140
    Psalm 139 in the Post-Exilic Restoration | 140
    The NT—Spirit of God and the King of the Nations | 141
    The Ante-Nicene and Post-Nicene Fathers | 143
    Augustine | 147
    John Calvin | 149
    Comparison with the Exegetical Findings of Psalm 139 | 151
Exegesis of Psalm 149: Praising with Violent Images of War | 154
    The MT—A Praising Tone | 155
    Structure, Form, and Setting | 156
    Perceived Suffering | 159
    Meaning of the Response | 161
    Conclusion of the Exegesis | 164
A Select Historical Survey of the Interpretation of Psalm 149 | 165
    Post-exilic Restoration—Another Perspective | 165
    The NT—Psalm 149 and the Book of Revelation | 166
    The Nicene and Post-Nicene Fathers | 167
    Psalm 149 in Augustine | 169
    John Calvin | 171
    Comparison with Exegetical Findings of Psalm 149 | 173

CHAPTER 3
Towards Developing an Understanding of the Language of Enmity as Prayer and God's Just Dealings with His People | 176

Analysis of Findings | 176
    Suggesting an Appropriate Way to Understand the Images of Enmity | 176
    A Comparison of the Different Responses to Adversity in Pss 110, 119, 129, 137, 139 and 149 | 177
    Images of Judgment | 183

Understanding the Language of Enmity as Normative Prayer | 186
    Prayers as Normative Scripture | 186

Towards a Spiritual Understanding of the Images of Enmity | 188
    The Language of Enmity | 193
    Psalm 137 as an Example | 194

The Canonical Context and God's Just Dealings with His People | 195
    Psalmist, Enemy, and God and the Developing of a Theology of God's just Dealings with his People | 195
    Psalm 110: Unrestrained evil and Yahweh's "lord" | 198
    Psalm 119: Torah as Yahweh's Presence and Judgment | 199
    Psalm 129: Yahweh's Righteousness, Agency, and Agricultural Imagery | 202
    Psalm 137: Memory, Violence and the Extent of Judgment | 205
    Psalm 139: Creator and Sustainer of all People and Avenger of Blood | 206
    Psalm 149: Praise, Violent Judgment and Universal Reign | 207
    How God Engages Moral Evil and its Nature | 209

CHAPTER 4
Conclusion | 212

Summary of Investigation and Findings | 212
    Implications of this Study | 214

Bibliography | 219
Subject Index | 233
Ancient Authors and Personalities Index | 243
Scripture Index | 245

Foreword

I AM PRIVILEGED TO be asked to write this foreword for my good friend Aran Persaud, for a number of reasons. First of all, because as one of my former students, I have watched him with great tenacity and deepening scholarship pursue the Hebrew misunderstood psalms of the Psalter, "the imprecatory psalms." He completed his "Master of Theology thesis on Psalm 109, which is often rejected or only partially recited in our church lectionaries. He then pursued this Ph.D. on six other imprecatory psalms – Psalms 110, 119, 129, 137, 139 and 149. The inclusion of Ps. 119 is surprising to some scholars, as it is not usually investigated with 'imprecatory' psalms. While its length is so daunting that even the Church's great psalm expositors – Augustine and Calvin – hesitated until late in life to plunge into its intensity and length. Altogether, this book is the fruit of over twenty years daily perusal upon this most difficult challenge of Biblical scholarship.

The author's own personal life is expressive deeply of inner sufferings, giving him resonance as "deep unto deep" of the sufferings being expressed by the Psalmist. As Athanasius pointed out in the late fifth century. The uniqueness of the Psalms is that while all the other Scriptures are God's voice speaking *to* us, the Psalms articulate our voice before God.

A third reason why I gladly endorse this book, is because it is 'prophetic' in a way that the past generation of scholars would never have recognised. We are now 'post-modern' for many reasons, certainly because as Charles Taylor calls it "the malaise of the modern," that reason is no longer enough, or that hyper-cognitive scholarship and behavior is no longer adequate to voice what is 'human'. We have moved forward to what is also 'emotional intelligence', and the Psalms voice many emotions. But a new era of historical and multi-cultural studies, is given voice to suppressed peoples, like African slaves, peasants grinded by poverty and starvation, to explore new unheard voices of human consciousness for the first time!

Now we can appreciate, instead of being embarrassed by the violence voiced in these imprecatory Psalms. God who created all humankind in his "image and likeness," hears the voices of all humanity, as we can never do. In turn, we need not only a framework of 'sound doctrine', but a much deeper 'Biblical consciousness', which rules sovereignly over all the hidden recesses of our hearts and minds.

It is our prayer then, that this study of the imprecatory Psalms will help you, the reader, to overcome the hurdles of theodicy, shallow views of the mystery of evil, the cultural blinkers of the use of language, and even personal prejudices, to value this important book, as a new guide. WE can anticipate that the Psalter will be recovered to become once more, the Church's prayer-book, as it once was, Israel's prayer book. Putting yourself in the place of the imprecator, you may hear your own voice expressing what you have never been able to express before, now no longer "a stranger to yourself." For our God – 'a very present help in time of trouble' – is sovereign over every human emotion, however fearful and violently evil they can become. He can redeem even the inner fears of the terrorists, terrorising the civilised world to-day!

James M. Houston

Preface

PSALMS USING THE LANGUAGE of enmity present a challenge for Christians who wish to use these psalms as prayer. Christians struggle to hold in tension the New Testament ethic to love one's enemies and these graphic prayers which seek for the enemies' utter destruction. This present age of "terror" has heightened this tension. This work tries to address this challenge in a way that recognizes the normative value of these texts. It is essentially my PhD thesis, but edited so that those without a specialist background can read and interact with it more easily. I have also had the benefit of further feedback on my exegesis of Psalm 110, which is incorporated into this version. In particular, my view on the eschatological nature of the text is presented more clearly. Another significant change is the reworking of my argument on sacred language. My main point is that even in a theocratic society, the meaning inherent in language used in the Israelite cult has the capacity to function differently than that used in a non-cultic setting. I had originally framed this from the modern perspective of a religious—secular dichotomy. Additional changes include adding indices of general keywords, early church writers, and scriptural references. The overall effect of these changes is to maintain the substance of my thesis, but make it more readable and hence more accessible to those who are interested in the issues raised when Christians pray these texts.

I originally began my look into the language of enmity through the imprecations or curses in Psalm 109 as part of my Theological Master's degree. I had originally wanted to do a thesis in the context of pastoral theology. However, Dr. James Houston at that time suggested that I ground my studies in the discipline of the Old Testament. For my purposes, he was right. However, I hope that my pastoral concerns are evident in my approach to this present work, especially in the last section which looks at the psalms as prayer. I have really tried to get at the basis for praying this language, which

I believe in the long run will allow people to pray them in authentic, efficacious, and therapeutic ways.

There are many people who stood behind this present work in hidden ways. I would like to thank Jim Houston and the Christian Culture Foundation whose scholarship went a long way in helping me to meet the financial obligations of this thesis. My deep gratitude also goes to Dr. Houston for writing the forward to this book. I also must remember those who helped me get orientated towards the Old Testament as a young boy: Lyle and Florence Jeffrey, who ran Frontier Ranch, the place where my own faith took root, and Vincent Craven (Cobber), chaplain and friend to many.

I would also like to thank my promoters, Dr Kathleen Rochester and Dr Herrie Van Rooy. Thank you both for dedicating so many years to my studies. Further, thank you to Ms Hester Lombard and the library staff at North-West University whose help went beyond the normal bounds of service. I also would like to thank Peg Evans and the staff of GST.

I would also like to thank the very small Men's Bible study group and small Wednesday night prayer group in Arnprior, Ontario. Thank you to my wife, who has patiently borne with me and this project. I am especially grateful to my daughters Sophie and Hannah, who brought much needed balance to this work. Lastly I would like to thank B. P. and Guinevere Ann Persaud, whose support, especially in the summer of 2014, allowed me to get to the finish line. I close with a reference to the song of the Lamb, "Great and marvellous are your deeds, Lord God Almighty. Just and true are your ways, King of the ages."

Abbreviations

AT	*Acta Theologia*
ASV	*American Standard Version*
BAGD	*A Greek English Lexicon of the New Testament and Other Early Christian Literature*
BEATAJ	*Beitrage zur Erforschung des Alten Testaments und des antiken Judentums*
BCP	*Book of Common Prayer*
BDB	*The New Brown-Driver-Briggs-Gesenius Hebrew and English Lexicon*
BHS	*Biblia Hebraica Stuttgartensia*
BZAW	*Beihefte zur Zeitschrift für die alttestamentliche Wissenschaft.*
CBQ	*Catholic Biblical Quarterly*
ESV	*English Standard Version*
FC	*Fathers of the Church*
FOTL	*Forms of the Old Testament Literature*
GES	*Gesenius' Hebrew Grammar*
GIND	*Shorter Lexicon of the Greek New Testament*
GNT	*Greek New Testament*
HAT	Handbuch zum Alten Testament
HALOT	*Hebrew and Aramaic Lexicon of the Old Testament*
IBHS	*An Introduction to Biblical Hebrew Syntax*
JBL	*Journal of Biblical Literature*

JSNTSup	*Journal for the Study of the New Testament Supplementary Series*
JSOT	*Journal for the Study of the Old Testament*
JSOTSup	*Journal for the Study of the Old Testament Supplemenatary Series*
KJV	*King James Version*
MT	*Masoretic Text*
NAB	*New American Bible*
NASB	*New American Standard Bible*
NEB	*New English Bible*
NICNT	*New International Commentary on the New Testament*
NIDOTTE	*New International Dictionary of Old Testament Theology and Exegesis*
NIGTC	New International Greek Testament Commentary
NIV	*New International Version*
NKJV	*New King James Version*
NETS	*A New English Translation of the Septuagint and Other Greek Translations Traditionally Included Under That Title*
NLT	*New Living Translation*
NRSV	*New Revised Standard Version*
OTL	*Old Testament Library*
RSV	*Revised Standard Version*
SBLDS	*Society of Biblical Literature Dissertation Series*
STDJ	*Studies on the Texts of the Desert of Judah*
TDOT	*Theological Dictionary of the Old Testament*
TOTC	*Tyndale Old Testament Commentaries*
VT	*Vetus Testamentum*
WBC	*Word Biblical Commentary*
WMANT	*Wissenschaftliche Monographien zum Alten und Neuen Testament*
WUNT	*Wissenschaftliche Untersuchungen zum Neuen Testament*
ZAW	*Zeitschrift für die Alttestamentliche Wissenschaft*

Chapter 1

Introduction

THE PROBLEM OF THE LANGUAGE OF ENMITY IN THE PSALMS

IN CERTAIN PSALMS LANGUAGE which consists of images/motifs of enmity and which calls on God to punish enemies or depicts God or people acting in a hostile way towards others presents a challenge for those who wish to use these psalms as prayer both in private use and in public worship in the Church. Perhaps the unique interplay between prayer, belief and action, expressed by the phrases *lex orandi*, *lex credendi*, and *lex agendi*, is nowhere more pronounced than when one is praying these psalms.[1] If these psalms as prayer are to be appropriated by the Church in every age, then understanding how they can be used as prayer and inform the Church's theology of God's just dealing with humankind and, in particular, his people in the midst of unjust suffering, is challenging.

A general survey of the study of violence and vengeance in the Psalms shows that the approach of recent biblical scholars has been to study these troubling texts through the form critical category of lament, mainly in the category of lament of the individual.[2] There have been some exceptions to

---

1. For the relationship between ethics and the uniqueness of the psalms as prayer, see Wenham, *Prayer and Practice*, 279–295. For a look at some "violent psalms" in relationship to the principle of *lex orandi*, *lex credendi*, and *lex agendi* see LeMon, "Saying Amen to Violent Psalms," 95–109.

2. *Volksklagelieder* and *Klagelieder des Einzelnens*, Brongers, *Die Rache und Flchpsalmen*; Laments as a category of Psalms of Disorientation, Brueggemann, *Message of*

this trend, for example, Alex Luc investigates expressions of enmity through the category of *prophetic judgment oracles* and Joel M. LeMon examines expressions of enmity through the mutually dependent relationship of prayer, belief and practice.[3] At the beginning of the form critical enterprise, Gunkel investigated the notion of "curse" independently of form category, which was consistent with his understanding of how psalms were composed of mixed genres.[4] Weiser also considered the curse to "appear in different contexts and in different psalm types."[5] Nevertheless, the main approach of recent scholarship remains to study these disturbing texts through the category of individual lament.

However, lament psalms and imprecatory psalms can provide only a partial understanding of what the psalms have to teach about the language of enmity used as prayer and its relationship to the concept of justice. First, images and motifs of enmity occur in psalms not typically assigned to this form category.[6] Psalm 149, for example, falls into the category of Hymn[7] and accordingly implies that the execution of *vengeance* on the *nations* (Ps 149:7) is a matter to be celebrated in communal worship. Why should a psalm like Psalm 149, a Communal Hymn, be less problematic for those wishing to make sense of the psalms with language of enmity as prayer? Second, expressions with images or motifs of enmity are not the only response to the hostility of an adversary, as is the case in Ps 119:78. This verse suggests that wishing for shame on one's enemies and "meditating on statutes" can both be appropriate responses to adversity. If images and motifs of enmity can be examined in the larger context of other responses to distressing situations in the Psalms, then a more accurate picture may be obtained as to what they have to say about how these images function as prayer and how the psalmist(s) perceived justice.

Recently, some Old Testament scholars have tried to reclaim a normative function for the imprecatory psalms in the liturgical life of the Christian church.[8] The results reflect various understandings as to how the texts

---

the Psalms; Individual and Communal Laments, Zenger, *A God of Vengeance?*; Individual Laments, Firth, *Surrendering Retribution*. Nancy de Claissé-Walford (*Theology of Imprecatory Psalms*, 76, 86) adds Pss 94 and 129 to Zenger's list of imprecatory psalms, but only makes one minor reference to Ps 129 in her article.

3. Luc, *Interpreting the Curses*; LeMon, *Saying Amen to Violent Psalms*.

4. According to Gunkel, "The goal of the curse is to cause pain, and to hamper and destroy life." Gunkel and Begrich, *Introduction to the Psalms*, 231.

5. Weiser, *Psalms*, 86.

6. Luc, *Interpreting the Curses*, 395; LeMon, *Saying Amen to Violent Psalms*, 98.

7. Firth and Johnston, *Interpreting the Psalms*, 300.

8. Imprecatory psalms are one type of psalms belonging to the larger category of

function as the Word of God and how these psalms are thus to be understood and used in Christian worship. None of these approaches, however, has as a basis for its proposal a satisfactory explanation of the imprecatory psalms both as normative, revelatory scripture and as functional for ongoing prayer. Unlike some narrative portions of scripture which portray acts such as war and violence without censure, and which allow the reader to develop a descriptive hermeneutic without consenting to the morality of those acts, praying psalms with language of enmity requires a particular assent to the message of these words on the part of the person who prays them. An understanding of the message of these psalms and how they function as prayer forms the basis for speaking about God's just dealing with people in the Psalms.

SYNECDOCHE AS A WAY TO UNDERSTAND MORAL EVIL

In this study, I will argue through an exegetical and historical investigation of the language of enmity in Psalms 110, 119, 129, 137, 139 and 149, beyond the limitation of the form critical category of lament of the individual and in the larger category of responses to perceived suffering at the hands of an enemy, that the language of enmity in these psalms is best understood as reflecting the true nature of moral evil and best described by the rhetoric of synecdoche. Further, the psalmist or psalmists were expressing a peculiar way of understanding victim, perpetrator and God. These psalms as prayers, when viewed from the perspective of the modern pray-er, form the basis for formulating a theology of God's just dealing with all people and in particular his people. It is hoped that this investigation can contribute to a clearer understanding of moral evil and the Church's participation in its eradication through prayer, as well as contribute to the larger theological understanding of the Psalms.

SOME PRELIMINARY MATTERS OF METHODOLOGY

This investigation will focus on the perceived suffering and responses to that suffering in Psalms 110, 119, 129, 137, 139, and 149 of the *BHS MT* text. This suffering originates from an evil moral enemy and in this regard I will not

---

psalms which contain motifs of enmity. For different proposals see Brueggemann, *The Message of the Psalms*; Firth, *Surrendering Retribution*; Zenger, *A God of Vengeance?*; deClaissé-Walford, *Theology of Imprecatory Psalms*; and LeMon, *Saying Amen*.

investigate responses to suffering caused by natural evil. I will first exegete these psalm texts as independent integral units in their canonical context using commentaries from the nineteenth century to the present time. Then, I will investigate how these psalms have been used and understood by a selection of commentators throughout Church history and synthesize these findings with the first section. Next, I will compare the findings between these psalms to better understand how the language of enmity is functioning. Finally, I will integrate the findings in the first three sections from the perspective of the Psalms as public and private Christian prayer in order to contribute towards a theology of God's just dealing with humankind and in particular his people.[9]

Determining the Nature of the Psalmist's Perceived Suffering and the Meaning of the Response

The exegesis or the critical reading of these psalm passages in their canonical context will follow what Waltke calls an accredited exegesis, that is, one which investigates the plain sense of the text while judiciously employing the grammatico-historical, form-critical, rhetorical-critical, cult-functional and canonical-Messianic approaches.[10] Using these exegetical tools, I will seek to reconstruct the nature of the psalmist's[11] perceived suffering at the hands of an enemy and determine the meaning of the responses given to these sufferings.

Such a task raises at least two questions. First, to what extent can these poetic texts portray a historical enemy and situation?[12] On a literary level, the answer seems to lie in the capacity of biblical poetry to portray historical events according to the constraints of its genre and purpose. A comparison

---

9. Dorothea Erbele-Küster (*Lesen als Akt des Betens*, 51) argues that a critical reading of the Psalms and reading the Psalms as prayer are not mutually exclusive.

10. Waltke and Houston, *Psalms as Christian Worship*, 112.

11. I use the singular psalmist, but in actuality it may be psalmists.

12. '*ōyḇ* and *rš'ym* are the two main Hebrew words for the enemies in the Psalms. Van Rooy ("Enemies in the Headings," 41–58) has provided a helpful overview of how scholars from the time of Franz Delitzsch to the present have understood the term *enemies* in the Psalter and specifically in the headings of the Psalms. Stephen Croft's (*Identity of the Individual*, 11–48) study identifies the enemies in the Psalms based on a temple-cult setting as the text-generating context. Gerald Sheppherd ("Enemies and the Politics of Prayer," 61–68) provides an overview of the enemies from a social-scientific perspective.

of the narrative and poetical accounts of Israel's encounter with Pharaoh at the Sea of Reeds in Exodus 14 and 15 serves as an example.[13]

This type of direct historical reference may not always be present, but even as poetry, the approach taken here is that the psalms bear witness to divine-human relationships in specific contexts, including the text's generating history. By the generating context I am referring to the historical events which lie behind the text at the non-cultic level, although for those scholars who follow Sigmund Mowinckel, the generating context is solely the cult of Israel.[14] Other scholars, such as Childs, downplay the generating context because they believe it moors a text in the past, preventing its actualization in the present.[15] However, it seems intuitive to me that a morally evil adversary, who evokes a response with images of enmity, suggests some form of original historical setting.

Second, since at one point in their existence many of the psalms were clearly used in the cult of Israel, what is the relationship between the cultic setting and the historical references in the texts? Roy Melugin recognizes that the original referent does not exhaust a text's meaning, that is, a text's generating history does not necessarily lock the text into the past, inaccessible to the modern reader.[16] Melugin gives as an example the promise of land, of which the original fulfillment is not exhausted, but can function once again as a promise for the return from exile in Babylon.[17] Similarly, Jeremy D. Smoak has shown through using inner-biblical discourse on an ancient Israelite wartime curse that the imagery of the curse, which was attached to ancient siege warfare, resonated over two centuries, the eighth to sixth centuries B.C.E.[18] The point is that historical indicators in the text do not necessarily need to be conceived of in terms of static reference with

---

13. Grisanti, "Old Testament Poetry," 172–177.

14. "The Psalms should not be seen as autobiographical accounts of personal experience but liturgies composed for the use of certain categories of person in certain types of situation in the temple cult . . . must be seen as confirming Mowinckel's view" (Croft, *Identity of the Individual*, 12). However, note: "Some non-cultic poems do appear to have been included in the Psalter; we would suggest Pss 1; 19B; 34; 37; 49; 78; 105; 106; 111; 112; 127" (Mowinckel, *Psalms*, vol 2., 111).

15. Childs, *Introduction to the Old Testament*, 79.

16. Melugin, "Canon and Exegetical Method," 55. Melugin states the contexts of theologically orientated exegesis as "(1) the text itself as a synchronic entity, (2) the generating contexts that the texts reflect, and (3) the context of the interpreter and the interpreter's community" (Ibid., 51). These correspond roughly to what I call (1) canonical exegesis, (2) historical-grammatical exegesis, and (3) liturgical exegesis.

17. Ibid.

18. Smoak, "Building Houses," 35.

regards to the cultic *Sitz im Leben*. The text's original generating setting may be helpful in understanding later meaning, rather than preventing it.

In other words, a cult-historical method of interpretation alone, as defined by Mowinckel, cannot provide the basis for a complete understanding of the generating context of the psalms.[19] Mowinckel acknowledges historical allusions to real events behind some of the psalms:

> In spite of a definite and fundamental cult-historical view we shall, in what follows, resist the one-sided exaggeration of this view which has cropped up in certain quarters lately, where it has even been suggested that all the psalms and all details in them allude to cult-mythical happenings and experiences, leaving no room for an historical background or for allusions in any of the psalms to historical events. This can be understood as a reaction against older interpretations which paid no heed to the cultic side.[20]

Nevertheless, Mowinckel's comments on Psalm 137 are indicative as to how he saw the relationship between the cult-composed documents and the events to which they allude. Psalm 137 has "sprung out of a genuine poetical ability to identify oneself with the former time of enslavement, with its bitter experiences, burning longings and savage thirst for revenge . . . Just so, he himself, the player of harp and composer of psalms in Zion, could imagine that he might have been sitting, if he had been one of them."[21] Mowinckel's corporate identification of the congregation with the speaker in the cult and his focus on the creative aspect of the cult leave the questions of historiography unclear. Did the composer of Psalm 137 receive his material from oral tradition or was he privy to some other written source? The historical events are clearly subsumed to the "cultic personality."[22]

Another factor when considering the historical nature of the cult, as Kidner has articulated it, "is the concept of actualization which is bound up with the cultic understanding of the Psalms."[23] Do the Psalms encourage a focus on the events in the context of being actualized in the cult? Or do they

---

19. Mowinckel, *Psalms*, vol. 1, 23–41.

20. Ibid., 37.

21. Mowinckel, *Psalms*, vol. 2, 130.

22. Mowinckel developed a theory of "cultic personality" based on a cultural and historical understanding of the relationship between corporate Israel and the individual in society (Mowinckel, *Psalms*, vol. 1, 42–46). It should also be noted that Mowinckel believed that the suffering in national psalms of lament, and I-laments (Royal) which are also national represent "real historical troubles, . . . actual political conditions . . . sometimes it may be a genuine case of illness" (Ibid., 246).

23. *Psalms 1–72*, 27.

preserve a distinctness with the cultic acts in which they were recited in such a way that indicates they

> ...were not the means, *ex opera operato*, of annihilating time or of renewing the potency of the past: they were kept 'that you may remember the day when you came out of . . . Egypt', and '*remember* that you were a slave in Egypt' (Deut. 16:3, 12), and 'that your generations may *know* that I made the people . . . dwell in booths when I brought them out of . . . Egypt' (Lev. 23:43). This is the language of conscious, rational response, not mystical experience.[24]

Kidner, in my opinion, correctly suggests that the recollection of the traditions and history of Israel's dealings with Yahweh should form the actual basis for understanding cultic content. Even for post-cultic compositions of which Gunkel suggested there were many,[25] or of pre-cultic compositions of which Gerstenberger believed provided the basis of the later cultic forms,[26] the pious individuals who composed these psalms were not living in a cultural and religious vacuum. Weiser's suggestion of the covenant renewal as the central act of Israel's cult helps to highlight Israel's own contribution to its cult. That is,

> 'History and Law' as the two foundation-pillars of the self-revelation of Yahweh determined the nature of the cult of the Covenant Festival just as it did that of the tradition of the Hexateuch, for which that cult had provided the setting in which it developed.[27]

In other words, the uniform "features of cultic tradition . . . are strikingly parallel to the same basic elements which are to be found in the narrative and in the prophetic literature."[28] Even if Weiser's proposal of the Covenant Renewal Festival to explain the cultic setting of some of the psalms is set aside, his proposal is helpful in that it suggests there is more

---

24. Ibid., 29.
25. Gunkel and Begrich, *Introduction to Psalms*, 13.
26. "...they believe in a slow process of democratization of cult practices (Mowinckel, *W* I:78ff.). I argue that just the opposite occurred. Prayer rituals were used, long before any kind of kingdom existed, within and for the benefit of small groups. Only much later did developing tribal and state societies formalize their own ritual systems, more often than not on the basis of small-group ceremonies. In this view, royal ceremonialism is ultimately an adaptation of popular rites and prayers to the needs of the court" (Gerstenberger, *Psalms Part 1*, 19).
27. Weiser, *The Psalms*, 32.
28. Ibid., 25.

involved in understanding the context of the psalms than the cultic setting as it came to be institutionalized during the time of temple worship. The historical and ethical basis for understanding the content of the psalms is related to the narrative of Israel's relationship with Yahweh. So it may be true to say that the forms of Israel's worship share similarities with the forms of worship of the other nations with which they coexisted. However, Israel's relationship with Yahweh provides the main historical and ethical setting for understanding the psalms.[29] The documents, whether used in the cult or collected and edited into a "Book of David," point back to this relationship with Yahweh as the basis for their understanding. It is hoped that through a broad range of investigative tools the perceived suffering of the psalmist and the meaning of the response will become clear.

Investigating Expressions of Enmity in the Light of Previous Commentators

When I examine the use made of Psalms 110, 119, 129, 137, 139 and 149 in the Christian tradition,[30] I will try to understand how Christian scholars throughout Church history have understood the perceived suffering and responses in these psalms. The results will be compared with my exegetical work to help clarify and correct my own findings. I will not offer an analysis of the differing hermeneutical methods since my purpose is practical, although the differing hermeneutical methods will be recognized. Houston lists some of the difficulties in attempting a historical commentary.[31] In general, some apply to the task at hand: 1) not all commentators completed work on all 150 psalms, and some parts may not have survived (e.g., Hilary's *Tractatus super Psalmum*; Theodore of Mopsuestia's extant psalms consist of Pss 1–81); 2) some commentators changed their views over the course of their lives; 3) some commentators are inconsistent in their methodology

---

29. The lack of clear explanation of ritual cautions against isolating the cult as the sole focus of meaning. Weiser noted that the absence of any preserved ritual for the Covenant Festival stands in contrast to the preserved ritual in the Babylonian New Year Festival and the Akitu Festival at Uruk. Weiser believed that in the OT cult ritual was probably passed on "by the priests by means of oral tradition, as is still evident from the history of the origin of the Targum" (Ibid., 35). Nevertheless, one is left wondering, if the psalms were meant to be defined solely as cultic documents, why there were no detailed instructions for their cultic use as found in these other coexisting festivals.

30. My own perspective is from a Protestant tradition. For an example of a liturgical investigation of the Psalms in the Roman Catholic tradition, see Braulik, "Psalms and Liturgy," 309–332.

31. Waltke and Houston, *Psalms as Christian Worship*, 14.

(e.g., this is especially true until the time of Constantine [c. 272–337] after which Augustine [c. 354–430] had a platform to spread his allegorical method to the *totius Christi*); 4) the definitions of what is literal, and/or historical, as well as what is prophecy, have changed; 5) there are different purposes in the writings (e.g., the emphasis of Theodoret of Cyrus [c. 396–460] was on the household, whereas Justin Martyr [c. 100–165] was interested in an apologetic use against Jewish opponents). Clearly all of these factors make asserting that any one commentator represents a particular period difficult and limit the selection of commentators. Scholars will be chosen from different historical periods on the bases of relevance, availability of materials and space limitations. The selection, therefore, will be based on availability and relevance to this study.

Besides the above challenges, perhaps some of the assumptions of this investigation also present a challenge to understanding and using these earlier commentators. As will be seen, many of the earlier commentators, especially of the Alexandrian school, did not seek to explain the violent images in the selected psalms from the same modern perspective that I bring to the text. Augustine, for example, believed that the meaning of imprecations was hidden and fulfilled in the future and did not reside in the sentiments of the psalmist.[32] An assumption of my approach is that the sentiments of the psalmist are in and of themselves essential to the interpretation of the language of enmity. In this regard, I am to a certain degree following the Antiochene understanding of *theoria* (see below). Nevertheless, the questions that most pre-nineteenth-century interpreters bring to the text might be different in approach, but their interpretations are not necessarily different in substance from the present approach. There seems to be a convergence of understanding with some interpretations when looked at in the larger picture of God's rule through Christ (Ps 110). Therefore, although having a different focus, earlier commentators can provide further insight into the questions of my investigation.

I begin my investigation with the early stages of the post-exilic restoration period where relevant. As I argue below, the editor(s) seem to have intended Book V to be understood from the perspective of the early post-exilic restoration period. The post-exilic community's understanding of the images of enmity is important because it represents a canonical perspective (intra Book V) before the time of Christ. This view of the exilic/post-exilic setting (not necessarily editing) of the Psalms is not a modern perspective. For example, Theodore of Mopsuestia of the Antiochene school of exegesis connects the historical setting of certain psalms to the time of

---

32. Luc, "Interpreting the Curses," 398.

the Babylonian exile, even suggesting that some originated in the time of the Maccabees. Unfortunately, his extant psalms consist of only Psalms 1–81.[33]

The New Testament investigation is included in the historical survey, but in actuality the use of the psalms in the NT provides the true *skopos* by which the psalms can be understood as Christian scripture. The NT perspective is investigated separately as part of the historical survey in order that the plain meaning of each OT text in its immediate canonical context can be thoroughly examined.[34] The connections between the Psalms and the NT will be based upon quoted references or allusions and verbal parallels given in the Greek New Testament.[35] In addition, the links Augustine sees between Psalm 129 and the NT will be noted. Such a methodology is open to some criticism about its subjectivity, especially since none of the modern scholars who contributed to the Greek New Testament project noted any connections between the agricultural imagery in Psalm 129 and the NT. Augustine, however, perceptively did. All that can be said is that I have approached the NT section as a non-specialist without a preconceived agenda and have let modern scholars suggest the connections.

In general, the Psalms account for two-thirds of all Old Testament quotations in the New Testament.[36] The purpose here will not be to analyze the various theories of NT use of the OT or to enter into the debates (Did the Psalm maintain its OT perspective or was it used mainly as a proof-text? What type of exegetical method was being used—Pesher? Midrashic? What source was the NT writer quoting? etc.). Nevertheless, many of these questions lie behind how scholars determine the meaning of the text in its NT context.

---

33. Theodore believed that the psalms were the prophetic words of David, but saw the headings as later additions and so removed them. In their place he gave an introduction to each psalm which scholarship has shown to have been retained to a certain degree in the headings to the East Syriac translation of the Psalms (Van Rooy, *The East Syriac Psalm Headings*, 218–219).

34. To a certain degree, this study would be aided by an investigation of the psalms in the context of other OT texts. However, where it has been relevant, e.g., Jeremiah, I have made mention in the exegesis. I am working from the assumption that these other texts would be supplementary to the findings in the NT and the Psalms themselves. The guiding hermeneutical principle for this work is that the texts of the OT can only be understood through their appropriation in the person and work of Jesus Christ (Lk 4:21; 24:44–45; Heb 1:2, etc.). This appropriation, however, differs from the allegorical Christ-centered approach of Augustine, which relies only on orthodox belief as a control for the range of possible interpretations.

35. Aland et al., *GNT*.

36. For a specific list of all the psalms quoted with correlating NT verses based on United Bible Society lists see Daglish, "Use of the Book of Psalms," 26–27.

For an examination of the use of the Psalms in the history of the Church, Houston's division of Church interpretation into four "hinge" points can serve as a helpful framework: Pre-Nicene and Post-Nicene Fathers; Augustine and Medieval Monastic exegesis; Christian Hebraism and Scholasticism in the High to Late Middle Ages; and the Reformers.[37] These hinge points serve as a reminder that different principles of exegesis dominated different localities and periods in the history of the Church. My goal will be to determine a deeper understanding of the expressions of enmity, which it is hoped will act as a supplement and/or a corrective to my exegetical work.

Of particular diversity, and so worth further comment, are the writings of the early Church fathers. Generally the early Church fathers are categorized as the Apologists, the Antiochene school, the Alexandrian school, the Cappadocian fathers, and the Western Church commentators.[38] It would be overly simplistic to state that the Antiochene school followed a literal exegesis, whereas the Alexandrians followed a figural exegesis. In actuality there is some fluidity between the two schools, as will be evident in some of the discussion.[39] For the Antiochenes, though, to say something else than what is intended in the text (or its *theoria*) was allegory, and allegory was an overthrow of the obvious sense of the text.[40] Another case in point is that the Alexandrian school did not deny a literal interpretation. In fact the Alexandrian school did not distinguish between *theoria*, *allegoria* and *anagoge*, a feature which was extended to the Cappadocian Fathers.[41] They merely

---

37. Waltke and Houston, *Psalms as Christian Worship*, 37–79. Due to length restrictions and availability of resources this study will be limited and not quite as ambitious as needed to cover all of Houston's divisions. For Medieval Monastic exegesis I will use only Cassiodorus and for the Reformers I will use only Luther and Calvin. Luther's first lectures on the Psalms consist of Pss 1–126. According to Houston (Ibid., 60–61) Luther met Christ in the Psalms by the time he had reached Psalm 51 and in 1515 his appraisal of this commentary was rather negative. He began a second commentary on the Psalms (*Operationes in Psalmos*) which was published in 1519–20, but stopped at Ps 22 as he was caught up in the crisis of his excommunication. Furthermore, I will not attempt to investigate scholars from the period of Christian Hebraism and Scholasticism in the High to Late Middle Ages.

38. Gillingham, *Psalms through the Centuries*, 24–39.

39. So John Chrysostom's overall reading of the OT is literal, but he occasionally takes the approach of the Alexandrian school, as is the case in Ps 7:12 and 13 (Heine, *Reading the Old Testament*, 148–51). The same can be said of Diodore in his interpretation of Ps 30:1. Our discussion below will also evidence this flexibility on the part of some of the Antiochene commentators.

40. Hidal, *Exegesis of the Old Testament*, 548.

41. Ibid.

subsumed the literal sense to the text's figural interpretation, as for example Origen did, in order to produce ideas which are appropriate to God.[42]

Within each of the schools there are also differences between commentators, so Theodore was more interested in arguing against the Jews whereas Theodoret was interested in the Psalms as prayers in the household of faith.[43] Another distinction between the commentators arises in terms of how they viewed the Psalms as prayer. Athanasius, Diodore of Tarsus, and John Chrysostom all saw the Psalms as the voice of the Christian. In contrast, Origen, Jerome, and Augustine identify various speakers in the Psalms, in particular Jesus Christ and his body the Church.[44] The perspective towards the Psalms as prayer taken in this study is akin to the former group. The Psalms as the voice of the Christian will be discussed in Chapter Four.

In the historical survey I will discuss the commentators to a certain degree according to the same pattern of investigation in the exegesis. That is, I will seek to see what the commentators have to say about the suffering of the psalmist and then what they have to say about the response. At times, as is the case for Psalm 110, I will follow this pattern loosely and allow the commentators to speak for themselves. Again, this recognizes the different hermeneutical perspectives and concerns which the commentators bring to the text. I will for the most part follow a chronological order according to when the commentators lived. This structure rather than grouping according to major interpretive schools prevents lopsidedness when one school does not have many comments which pertain to my investigation, as is the case with the Alexandrian commentators on Psalm 149. Further, it allows Augustine as the vanguard commentator on the Psalms to be investigated independently. Pertinent comments about the different schools will be made as necessary.

Prayer as the Basis for the Inclusion of Non-lament Psalms

In the third movement of this thesis, I will try to compare the findings to clarify how psalms which contain language of enmity can function as prayers in the life of faith and to make some proposals in explaining God's just dealing with humankind and in particular his people. Particular attention will be given to the Psalms as a genre of prayer.[45] Wallace suggests that

42. Heine, *Reading the Old Testament*, 148.
43. Gillingham, *Psalms through the Centuries*, 33.
44. Heine, *Reading the Old Testament*, 146–74.
45. Once again, my own perspective is from a Protestant tradition. For a liturgical

the whole Psalter has been edited to draw participants in to making the Psalms their own prayers.[46] This genre of prayer is unique in OT scripture because of the powerful "commitment . . . that the Psalms demand of their users."[47] Indeed, the "authors and editors of the Psalter clearly recognized that ethics are linked inextricably to the forms and content of prayer."[48]

Furthermore, the genre of prayer plays a central role in allowing the language of enmity to be investigated beyond the constraints of laments of the individual or community.[49] Throughout its history, the Church has maintained the dual tradition of the Psalms as prayer and song to God and the use of the Psalms for the instruction and guidance of the faithful.[50] This dual capacity is a unique feature of the Psalms and suggests that the pray-er's role should be central in any investigation. As Brueggemann has noted,

> Thus the question of function is put as a hermeneutical issue. The question concerns both the use in ancient Israel, which admits of some scholarly analysis of the Psalms, and the contemporary religious use of the Psalms by practitioners of faith.[51]

Of particular interest, then, is how the contemporary religious use of the Psalms as prayer pertains to the selection of psalms for this investigation.[52]

Exegesis which focuses on the voice of the psalmist without regard to the voice of the modern worshipper tends to limit the number of psalms which are considered prayer. This is so because such a perspective sees prayer as implying "address to God in the vocative sense, as well as the use of pronouns and verbal forms in the second person plural, particularly the imperative."[53] Some scholars also include in the definition of prayer the third person subjunctive.[54] Outside of these linguistic markers, the speech of the psalmist is not considered conventional prayer.[55] Thus, for some, prayer is

---

investigation in the Roman Catholic tradition, which sees the Psalms functioning in a different manner, cf. Braulik (2003, 309–32).

46. Wallace, "King and Community," 271.

47. Wenham, "Prayer and Practice," 294.

48. LeMon, "Saying Amen to Violent Psalms," 95.

49. Nasuti's (*Defining the Sacred Songs*, 52) insight that genre is defined as those elements a reader sees as common to certain texts applies here.

50. Wallace, *Words to God*, 3. In Chapter Four I will return to Wallace's notion of the Psalms as prayer.

51. Brueggemann, *The Psalms and the Life of Faith*, 3.

52. The language of enmity as normative prayer will be discussed in Chapter Three.

53. Aejmelaeus, *Traditional Prayer*, 10.

54. Gerstenberger, *Der bittende Mensch*, 121.

55. I believe this is the implicit assumption guiding many studies which focus only

limited to only those psalms in which modern worshippers can identify their voices with the voice of the psalmist. The expressions of enmity in the second person vocative or jussive forms become a challenge to use, while phrases of enmity in a different form such as third person descriptive are considered troublesome but not as prayer.

However, the literary nature of the psalms cautions against a hermeneutic of function that limits the selection of psalms to that of similarity between ancient and modern voice. Those who participated in the cult were also the recipients and users of these literary documents. That is, the documents which they used were carefully composed literary units, a claim which is supported by many rhetorical and structural studies on the psalms.[56] Psalm 137, for example, has an intricate literary form and allusions which suggest that it was a prayer written to help focus the uncontrolled rage from military humiliation and to seek for true justice. The Psalms portray enmity and violence, not as *ad libitum* expressions of uncontrolled human feelings, but as carefully constructed literary documents which were at one particular stage used in the cult but now have been edited to become canonical literature.

Since we have received the psalms as literary documents, as did those who used them in the pre-exilic cult and those who used them at the beginning of the post-exilic restoration, we would expect to find indications in their present literary structure which infer parameters for their use. Mays proposed that changes in the idea and use of genres opened the psalms to new uses different from what might be expected based on their original classification.[57] For our purposes of examining the psalms as liturgical prayer documents it may be more helpful to talk about disassociating the voice of the psalmist from the voice of the worshipper. Mays used Psalm 30 to make his point, where a thanksgiving song for an individual was taken and then edited for group use as a psalm for the dedication of the temple.[58] This move is important because it suggests that the experience portrayed in

---

on Individual and Communal Laments. There are exceptions where this has not been the case. Mowinckel (*Psalms*, vol. 1, 203) labelled Ps 149:7 as a *"prayer for revenge."* LeMon ("Saying Amen to Violent Psalms," 98) likewise considers Ps 149:6–9 as prayer.

56. See the review of psalm research in Howard, "Psalms in Current Study," 31–33.

57. Mays, "Question of Context," 17.

58. It may not always be possible to indicate the extent of this editing. It may be that an individual lament or other type of psalm genre was used unchanged in the cultic setting. Such a use would have been part of the oral tradition that accompanied the psalms in their cultic use, but was never recorded. Such a use, then, would be similar to the appropriation of the psalms by modern worshippers.

the psalm does not necessarily need to be the immediate experience of the worshippers, but can function as a secondary one.[59]

Embedded in the literary nature of some psalms, then, is an indication that the use of certain psalms as prayer is independent of the voice in which the psalm has come to the worshipping community. The psalms are no longer prayer only if the immediate voice of the *persona*, whether historical or hypothetical, is in the second person direct address or third person jussive. A liturgical reading of the psalms as prayer, which I am suggesting, is one in which all of the psalms can be offered as prayer directly to God, whether the voice is first, second or third person and whether it is addressed to God or to someone else.[60] In terms of exegesis, this means that investigation of expressions of animosity as prayer cannot be limited to laments of the individual or community. The words in the psalms which represent many voices become the prayers of those who use them, independent of the voice in which the psalms were first written.

The Extent of Book V and Its Meaning for this Study

To limit the scope of this study, Book V will form the basis of an inter-textual reading as it is generally recognized as the last stabilized part of the canonical Psalms.[61] Indeed, this claim is supported by the Qumran Hypothesis,[62] which concludes that Books IV and V should be considered the last stabilized part of the Psalter.[63] Further grounds for this selection result from Book V's distinctive hymn-like nature and theological profile.[64]

---

59. Weiser (*Psalms*, 95) points to a comparison of Ps 102:18 with its superscript: "Stating the way in which the psalm was to be used shows that these superscripts were attached to the psalms subsequently."

60. According to Wallace, the voice of the psalmist can vary and be directed to different people. The psalmist addresses God directly in half of the psalms, but in another major grouping addresses "enemies," "the congregation," "the king," "the faithful" or "Israel." In a third major grouping, most of which are hymns of praise or thanksgiving, the psalmist speaks to parties other than God. Variety in voice can also be seen within psalms (*Words to God*, 21). The voice in Psalms 34 and 35 alternates between first and third person. We must consider this alternation as purposeful because of repeating patterns. For example, Erbele-Küster notes that in these psalms the righteous are always referred to in the third person (*Lesen als Akt des Betens*, 111–112).

61. Zenger, "Composition and Theology," 81.

62. Whether one concurs or does not concur with the Qumran Hypothesis does not change the integrity of Book V as a distinct unit.

63. Flint, *Book of Psalms*, 460–461.

64. See Zenger, "Composition and Theology."

That Book V exists as a self-contained unit in the Psalms is not contested by scholarship and has been firmly established in tradition. However, the exact extent of Book V has not been agreed upon. Some scholars see the last five psalms as an ending to the Psalter as a whole. Patrick Miller, for example, sees Psalms 146–150 acting as a coda to the whole Psalter.[65] The problem is further complicated because the doxology which ends each of the first four books is missing from the end of Book V.

Wilson proposed that Psalm 145 was the last psalm of Book V. He saw Psalm 145:21 as providing a liturgical motivation for Psalms 146–150 which form the closing to the whole Psalter.[66] However, Wilson's argument that in Book V an *inclusio* is formed by the wisdom verses of 107:42, 43 and 145:19, 20 may not be as conclusive as first appears.[67] Wisdom refrains involving Yahweh's punitive actions against the "wicked" (*rš'ym*) also occur at Psalms 146:9 and 147:6. The wisdom refrain in Psalm 145, then, is not exclusive in its connection to 107. Another problem that weakens Wilson's argument is that it is hard to know what weight to give this wisdom element in determining the connection with Psalm 107. In terms of genre, Gunkel, Sabourin, Day, Bellinger, Gillingham and Lucas, as cited in the appendix of Firth and Johnston, all assign Psalms 145–150 to the category of Hymn.[68] Wisdom psalms and psalms influenced by the wisdom tradition do not seem to carry the same weight of evidence. With the smaller wisdom units one must be even more skeptical as to whether any connection is coincidental or purposeful. Wilson's suggestions provide an inconclusive basis for ending Book V with Psalm 145.

Like Wilson, Zenger also sees the fifth Book of Psalms ending at Psalm 145.[69] According to Zenger, Psalms 107 and 145 form an *inclusio* through several connections. Both psalms celebrate YHWH's universal greatness and goodness for the purpose of making it known *before the sons of mankind*,[70] (*lbny 'dm*), contain the same key words "steadfast love" (*ḥsd*), "wonderful works" (*npl'wt*), "save" (*yš'*), and praise for the duration of "eternity" (*l'lm*). In addition, both contain a wisdom frame in their conclusions and Psalm

---

65. Miller, "End of the Psalter," 105.

66. Wilson, *Editing of the Hebrew Psalter*, 189.

67. Wilson, "Shaping the Psalter," 78–79.

68. Klaus Seybold categorizes Psalm 145 as both a Hymn and a Wisdom Psalm. Firth and Johnston, *Interpreting the Psalms*, 300.

69. Zenger, "Composition and Theology," 88–89.

70. The meaning in modern English might be better captured by the gender-neutral phrase *before humankind*. When translations are given, I will stick to the Hebrew gender distinctions unless it is necessary to emphasize some aspect of meaning. This approach should help make the Hebrew text more transparent.

145 seems to extend the theme of salvation found in Psalm 107. Although Zenger's observations are astute, his proposal is open to the same type of subjective bias that was levied against Wilson's proposal. To what extent are the key connections based on clear observations of the purposeful work of an editor? Perhaps a better case can be made for extending the end of Book V past Psalm 145.

Koch is one of the few scholars who consider Psalms 146–150 to be part of Book V. First, Koch's division of Book V recognizes the parallelism between the Davidic Psalms 138–145 followed by the Hallelujah Psalms of 146–150 and the Davidic and Hallelujah Psalms (107) 108–118.[71] Similar to Wilson's proposal, which sees Psalms 146–150 as a response to "Ps 145:21," Koch sees Psalms 146, 147 and 148 as answering Psalm 145:2, 21.[72] Furthermore, for Koch the thematic connection of the *new song* (144:9) between the fifth Davidic Psalter and Psalm 149 of the Hallelujah hymns suggests a close association:

> [Psalm 149] picks up the "new song" from 144:9 on and leaves the children of God exulting in their king, 'praising God with their throats and a double-edged sword in their hands.[73]

Moreover, Koch's observation, "Apart from Psalm 145, the [last] Davidic group of psalms progresses to a war song with the blessing of God [Psalm 144:15]," also suggests a close association between the Davidic Psalms and the Hallelujah Psalms.[74] Koch's observations, although convincing, are also susceptible to the same challenges that were levied against Wilson and Zenger.

I propose that a structural *inclusio* exists between Ps 107 and Ps 149 and that Ps 149 is best considered the close of Book V with Ps 150 acting as a doxology. To begin with, although Ps 149 belongs to the final Hallelujah Psalms, it differs from Pss 146 to 148:

> Each Psalm except Ps 149 contains a double theology of God as creator—or, more often, maintainer of the created order—and as patron of Israel in a covenant relationship; Ps 149 offers only the later perspective.[75]

---

71. Koch, "Der Psalter," 255.

72. Wilson, "Structure of the Psalter," 232; Koch, "Der Psalter," 255.

73. Ibid., 256. "Er [Psalm 149] greift das "neue Lied" aus 144:9 auf und läßt die Kinder Zions über ihren König (vgl. Schon 145:1; 146:10) jauchzen, "Ruhmungen Gottes in ihrer Kehle und ein zweischneidiges Schwert in ihrer Hand" 149:6.

74. "Sieht man von 145 ab, läuft die vorgegebene Davidsgruppe auf ein Kriegslied zu mit der Segnung des Gottes." Ibid., 225.

75. Allen, *Psalms*, 76.

If Psalm 149 were to have a particular function in addition to its role as one of the final Hallelujah Psalms, we would expect it to be distinct from the other Hallelujah psalms. Secondly, the thematic *inclusio* between Pss 107 and 149, which is developed on the basis of the historical people mentioned in these psalms, seems to provide a stronger link than speculating about word connections. The "redeemed of the Lord" *g'wly yhwh* (107:2), the "upright" *yšrym* (107:42), and "his faithful ones" *ḥsydyw* (149:9) are the same people, those who stand in a special relationship to the Covenantal God, Yahweh. What has changed between Pss 107 and 149, however, is their reversal in fortune. In Psalm 107 the *redeemed of the Lord* are depicted as encountering all types of distress, even being "prisoners (*'syr*) in misery (*'ny*) and in irons (*brzl*)" (Ps 107:10). While in 149:8 it is the "faithful/saints" *ḥsydym* (Ps 149:5), who "bind (*'sr*) their [nations] kings with fetters and their nobles with chains of iron (*brzl*)" (Ps 149:8). The *saints* exact "vengeance," *nqmh* (Ps 149:7), on the nations and their kings. This reversal in fortune provides a strong link through which to understand the context of Book V.

Similarly, Joseph Brennan suggests connections between Psalm 2 and Psalm 149 which form an *inclusio* and set off Psalm 1 as a prologue and Psalm 150 as an epilogue to the Psalter as a whole:

> The *nations, peoples* and *kings* who seek to throw off Yahweh's authority in 2:1–2 become the object of his retribution in 149:7–9... The divine promise in 2:9 to break the rebels with a rod of *iron* is paralleled in 149:8 by the binding of the princes with fetters of *iron*. Also worth noting is the similarity between the *bonds* and *cords* which the kings attempt to throw off in 2:3, and which are replaced in 149:8 by *chains* and *fetters* of iron. There is also a close similarity between the *princes* and *rulers* who are warned of Yahweh's wrath in 2:2,10 and the *nobles* who are the object of the divine judgment in 149:8.[76]

This mention of the *saints* and the *nations* and the reversal in roles of fortune is substantial in recognizing the connection between Psalms 2, 107 and 149. Psalm 149, then, as the last concrete psalm of the Psalter, and not Psalm 145 or Psalm 150, forms the strongest structural *inclusio* with Psalm 107. Furthermore, the theme of this reversal in roles created by this *inclusio* presents a picture of justice being obtained for the people of God.

It is probably not coincidental that an *inclusio* also occurs within the concluding Hallelujah Psalms (146–149). As Allen has noted, Psalms 146 and 149 form a connection where,

---

76. Brennan, "Psalms 1–8," 26.

The overall parallelism of present and future covenant perspectives is enhanced by an inclusion in the four hymns. In 146:7 Yahweh even now "carries out justice (עשׂה משׁפט) for the oppressed" and in 149:9 the divine intent is "to carry out justice" (לעשׂות משׁפט) against Israel's foreign rulers.[77]

These paralleling *inclusios* which center on the theme of justice within Book V and within these concluding Hallelujah Psalms cannot be dismissed as coincidental.[78]

The usefulness of this *inclusio* in determining editorial intent goes beyond assuming connections based on individual or phrasal word links (so Zenger and Miller's bases for the *inclusio* between Psalms 107 and 145) which may or may not be coincidental. We can take this connection of these historical themes one step further. The fact that they are the first and last psalms of Book V might suggest that the editor is reinforcing a Book-wide perspective through the technique of *inclusio*. If *inclusio* can emphasize closure we can surmise that in using it to close the Psalter the editor places his perspective as the overarching editorial perspective of Book V. The people are those who have been restored in Psalm 107 and are now the ones who will exact revenge (*nqmh*) on the kings and nations who have bound them. The historical setting established by the editor, which is the historical point of view of the returnees, is therefore meant to reflect a time at the beginning of restoration, but which does not yet seem to be complete. What is of concern at this point is the editor's perspective as the Psalms were arranged or incorporated into the canon of scripture.

It is not an uncommon view for modern OT scholars to assume the final literary setting of Book V as occurring during this time period.[79] Goulder thinks "Book V as a whole belongs after the exile."[80] Zenger sees Book V as representing a perspective of "the end of the exile and the beginning/ already begun restoration of Zion/Israel."[81] Wilson believes that the "final

---

77. Allen, *Psalms*, 77.

78. It should be noted that Bernard Grosse, like Brennan, sees Ps 149 as clearly forming an *inclusio* with Ps 2: "Par ailleurs l'inclusion du Psautier entre les Ps. ii et cxlix apparait clairement si l'on compare Ps. ii 1–3 et Ps. cxlix 7–8." Grosse, "Le Psaume cxlix," 259. According to Grosse, the expression of vengeance against the nations plays an important role in the redaction of the Psalter and in particular Isaiah: "L'expression de la vengeance du Seigneur contre les nations joure un rôle rédactionnel très important dans la redaction des livres prophétiques, particulierement le livre d'Isaie." Ibid.

79. Nor was it uncommon for those of the Antiochene School; see Van Rooy, "Reading the Psalms Historically."

80. Goulder, *Psalms of the Return*, 17.

81. Hossfeld and Zenger, *Psalms 3*, 2.

form of the Psalter reflects the period of the exile."[82] Mitchell suggests the Psalms were "fashioned in a single redaction, under the hand of an all-controlling redactor, in the early post-exilic period."[83] Consistent with this view, he locates Book IV as reflecting the time of the exile. Mitchell's explanation of the dearth of references to the king of Israel in Book IV is the "reason why Book IV does not refer to the king of Israel. Exiled Israel is kingless (Hos. iii 4; Ezek. xxi 25–27; Zech. xiii 7)."[84] His understanding of Book IV being linked to the exile is consistent with the dearth of superscripts, especially Davidic superscripts, in Book IV. The editor was reflecting in Book IV the history of the exile not only explicitly (Pss 103–106), but implicitly in the superscripts as well.

Further, the editor chose pre-existing psalms and purposefully incorporated them into the book of Psalms based on the needs of the worshipping community at a particular time and under specific historical circumstances. For example, Burnett has shown that the Elohistic Psalter (Pss 42–83) has been arranged to reflect a plea "to the divine for the reestablishment of David and Zion."[85] The implications are that this arrangement reflects a period of exilic (Ezekiel) or post-exilic (Haggai and Zechariah) concern.

However, the editing of Book V does not necessarily have to reflect the historical period of the editor (i.e., for Wilson first century C.E., for Goulder and Mitchell before the translation of the LXX), but it does lend credibility to the idea that the editor would reflect a specific historical setting in the structural editing of Book V, the history of the beginning but not completed restoration. Since the exile appears to be one of the main defining events in their own theological understanding for the people of God before the time of Christ, as is evident by the amount of canonical literature centered around the exile and restoration, it should not be considered novel that this would be a central perspective of an editor. The canonical setting of the Psalter then accords with what the editor appears to have established through the use of structural and thematic *inclusio* in Book V.

The implication for this study is that if we can understand the perspective of the restoration community in their interpretation of the psalm, we can determine a pre-Christian interpretation. Although this is speculative and so is relegated to the historical survey of the psalms investigated, how this community interpreted the language of enmity in some of these psalms

---

82. Wilson, "Structure of the Psalter," 235. Wilson's position highlights the tension that exists between the editor's point of view and the point of view which the editor wishes to project in the editing of the Psalms.

83. Mitchell, *Message of the Psalter*, 532.

84. Ibid., 539.

85. Burnett, *Plea for David*, 113.

can allow insight into the true meaning behind the use of this language and contribute to better developed parameters in order to understand it.[86] That is, if their interpretation evidences a "sacred"[87] understanding of the use of this language of enmity, we will be on surer ground to interpret it as such. In other words, we can distill spiritual insights which arise in a particular historical frame of reference but are not bound to that historical frame of reference.

Selection of Psalms to be Studied

Before I begin the exegesis of selected psalms, it will also be helpful to examine several other works which investigate, from some particular perspective, motifs of enmity in the Psalms. Although the purpose of each of the studies differs, it will be helpful to look at the criteria employed for the selection of psalms in each work. The first scholar, David Firth, has attempted to address the issue of violence theologically by determining how the content in lament psalms of the individual offers a response to violence.[88] He approaches the question by exegeting individual lament psalms using a synchronic and canonical approach,[89] which gives the texts a new function, namely as texts of prayer for those who suffer from violence.[90] He selects individual lament psalms based on "those psalms that contain at least two non-parallel verbal terms depicting violence" within the categories of physical, psychological and structural violence.[91] Studying responses to violence through the category of individual lament limits his investigation by reducing the range of psalm texts which can be investigated, something which Firth acknowledges:

> Although one also finds references to violence in other *Gattungen*, such as individual thanksgivings [for example, Psalm

---

86. This historical perspective which reflects the desire for restoration is not the only perspective for viewing the psalms. The editor has left other indicators in place to aid the worshipper in the use of the psalms. Seeing and praying the psalms through the eyes of David, according to a Davidic reading suggested by the *inclusio* in Book V (Pss 108–110 and 138–145) may be another purposeful way the editor intended the psalms to be understood.

87. The term "sacred" is discussed in Chapter Four.

88. *Surrendering Retribution*, 3. In the category of false accusation, Pss 7, 17, 109, 139; in the category of prayers of protection, Pss 3, 27, 35, 55, 56, 64, 143; in the category of psalms of sickness, Pss 38, 69 (Ibid., ix-xi).

89. Ibid., 7.

90. Ibid., 3.

91. Ibid., 11.

92], these psalms do not record a response to violence, and their place as prayers of the individual are open to question. They therefore are not treated in this study.[92]

A further criticism of Firth's study is that the exact nature of the violence is not always explicitly stated, but implied, and so limiting the study to psalms with specific verbs may limit any study as well.

Zenger has tried to make sense of the psalms of divine wrath for the modern Christian.[93] The basis for his selection of seven imprecatory psalms is that they provide multiple perspectives on speaking of the God of vengeance and violence in the book of Psalms. These texts are "difficult, awkward, and resistant texts" to those who read them.[94] They have been dropped from the Roman Catholic liturgy (Pss 58, 83, 109) or ecclesiastical censorship has dropped verses (Pss 137, 139). However, Zenger also includes two psalms which provide Israel's statement and refinement of the problem of violence (Pss 12, 24). His choice of psalms is limited, like Firth's, in that Zenger stays within the category of individual and communal lament,[95] although his choices are essentially guided by what psalms contain the most offensive language to modern readers. His ultimate goal behind his selection, however, is to remove misunderstandings for the modern user of the psalms and to "make them comprehensible as *authentic prayers* of Biblical people."[96] Perhaps Zenger's strength of selection is that his discussion of Psalms 12 and 44 shows how the problem of God's wrath in the psalms, which repulses the modern Christian, must have a larger context to be properly understood.

Another approach to explain the troublesome expressions of enmity in the Psalms is Alex Luc's proposal. He suggests interpreting the troubling imprecatory psalms as *prophetic judgement speeches* which are "futuristic statements concerning the destiny of the wicked, whether stated in form of a divine oracle or from the psalmist's confident perspective," for example, "his enemies I [God] will clothe with disgrace" (Ps 132:18).[97] According to Luc, there are at least 27 psalms that contain this type of judgment prediction. Luc's proposal is not without its drawbacks. If it were to be accepted it would only displace the ethical issues of these texts to the future at the expense of the historical setting in which they arose and the present setting in which

---

92. Ibid., 15.
93. Zenger, *A God of Vengeance?*, 26.
94. Ibid., 25.
95. It is clear that Zenger does not see Ps 139 as a Hymn. Ibid., 30–31.
96. Ibid., 63.
97. Luc, *Interpreting the Curses*, 401– 402.

they are used. However, his recognition that the proper interpretation of the imprecatory psalms must go beyond their form-critical structure and cultic use is helpful.

Therefore, in view of what this investigation hopes to achieve, I will proceed in the following manner. I will exegete psalm texts as complete integral units in themselves. Psalms may be a combination of mixed genres as Gunkel described,[98] but I will assume that their canonical meaning comes from the meaning of the text as a whole. Using the methodology outlined above and in light of the investigations mentioned, I will use the following criteria for the investigation of psalms in Book V in this study. I will investigate categories outside of individual lament and only include other form categories (110 Royal; 119 Mixed Genre; 129, 137 Communal Laments; 139 Royal Petition, and 149 Hymn).[99] The psalms I will investigate in Book V cover all the categories of violence which Luc proposes (physical infliction, shame, death, suffering of family members, and unspecified retributive violence), as well as two psalms in Zenger's investigation (Pss 137 and 139) which have been censured in the Liturgy of the Hours, and one psalm which Firth classifies as a lament of the individual and reflects the psychological violence of false accusation. I will investigate Ps 149, which none of the three include in their studies. Ps 119 and Ps 149 will especially be useful because they offer responses to adversaries which are unexpected.

In short, I will investigate the language of enmity in Psalms 110, 119, 129, 137, 139 and 149. I will use the *NRSV* translation as a basis for investigating the psalms, noting any differences from my own translations based on the *BHS MT*, which are pertinent to my investigation. The focus of this study is on the response to situations of distress caused by an enemy in the category of moral evil. It is hoped, however, that although this approach is not exhaustive, this cross-section of psalms examined will allow enough of a diverse perspective to determine what the psalmist's responses to perceived suffering at the hands of an enemy have to say about the use of this language of enmity in prayer and God's just dealing with humankind and in particular his people.

---

98. Gunkel and Begrich, *Introduction to Psalms*, 306–318.

99. The classification of these psalm types will be discussed in the individual exegesis. Ps 119 can possibly be considered an individual lament, but it contains no language of enmity. Firth considers Ps 139 to be a lament of the individual (*Surrendering Retribution*, 43–50).

Imprecation	Content of imprecation/Prophetic Judgment Speech (Luc)	Firth Individual Laments	Zenger	My Selection
110:5-6 (P.J. speech)	Shame, Death			Royal Psalm
110:12	Shame			
119:78	Shame			Mixed genre
129:5-8	Shame, Death			Communal lament
137:7-9	Physical infliction Family members suffer Retributive punishment		Censured in the Roman Catholic Liturgy	Communal Lament
139:19-22	Death	Psychological violence of false accusation of a capital crime	Censured in the Roman Catholic Liturgy. Restoration of the order of justice (p. 49)	Protective Psalm of the King/ Communal Lament
149				Hymn

Table 1 A comparison of relevant psalms in Book V investigated by Luc ("Interpreting the Curses," 410), imprecations and the dominant elements; Firth (*Surrendering Retribution*, 5–6), categories of violence; Zenger (*A God of Vengeance*), psalms of divine wrath; and psalms to be investigated in this study.

Chapter 2

An Exegetical and Historical Study of Psalms 110, 119, 129, 137, 139, and 149

EXEGESIS OF PSALM 110—YAHWEH'S "lord" AND UNRESTRAINED EVIL

PSALM 110 IS OF special interest to this study because it falls outside of the category of individual lament, being categorized by most modern scholars as a Royal Psalm.[1] On a linguistic level the psalm presents many semantic and syntactical challenges. On a theological level, the psalm becomes problematic once the specific imagery of hostile acts of war is taken over as the basis of prayer.[2] Yahweh is portrayed as violently judging the nations through the means of his throne partner who is both David's "lord" (*ădōnî*)[3] and Melchizedekian Priest. Yahweh's throne partner "heaps up" (*mālē'*) "corpses" (*gᵉwiyyôṯ*) and "shatters" (*māḥaṣ*) the "heads" (*rōš* "over the wide earth" (*'al—'ereṣ rabāh*).[4] Despite these images, Psalm 110 is the

---

1. Königslied" (Gunkel, *Die Psalmen*, 481). For some examples of scholars who interpret it this way see Firth and Johnston, *Interpreting the Psalms*, 299.

2. Once again, I am assuming that the psalms can function as prayer in the tradition of Athanasius, Diodore of Tarsus, and John Chrysostom who all saw in the use of the psalms the voice of the Christian.

3. The term can refer to people or God in the MT of the Old Testament, although this pointing with the first common singular suffix was used by the Massoretes to indicate a non-divine use (BDB10). On the other hand, the pointing of (*ădōnāy*) which is found in v. 5 always refers to God (HOLL 4).

4. Zenger (Hossfeld and Zenger, *Psalms 3*, 145) on the contrary suggests that

most frequently quoted and alluded to OT text in the NT.[5] Furthermore, the *lord* who is addressed in the text has traditionally been understood as the Messiah[6] whom Christians identify as Jesus. The notion of a warrior-God who sanctions violence in overcoming enemies becomes directly connected to Jesus, which confronts the Christian who wishes to understand what it means to pray these violent images. The goal of this section will be to determine the meaning of these expressions of hostility by determining the perceived suffering of the psalmist as it is portrayed in the text of Psalm 110. These findings will later be correlated with selected interpretations which have been understood by the Church throughout its history.

Establishing the Nature of the Text and Clarifying the Difficult Verse Three

> 1. <Of David, a Psalm>[7]
>   An oracle[8] of the LORD to my lord,
>   "[9]'Sit at my right hand
>   until I put your enemies as your footstool.'
>
> 2. The LORD sends out from Zion your mighty scepter.
>   'Rule in the midst of your foes.'

---

whereas in Psalms 18 and 21 the king acts as warrior, here it is Yahweh who is the warrior. Scholars come to no consensus for who is the subject of these actions (see below). Nevertheless, whether Yahweh is the primary acting agent or acting through the king he both sanctions the military activity and ensures its success. The sole agency of Yahweh does not preclude the involvement of the Israelite army according to the Hebrew concept of holy war (Allen, *Psalms*, 115).

5. Houston (Waltke and Houston, *Psalms as Christian Worship*, 484) suggests 25x; Guthrie ("Hebrews," 943) suggests 22x.

6. This appears to be true even for those scholars like Allen who do not hold to an original Messianic intent.

7. The NRSV is used as a base translation.

8. NRSV uses the term *says*.

9. NRSV marks off with quotation marks "Sit. . .footstool," which limits the prophetic utterance to the end of verse 1. The grounds for this are prosopological—the apparent change of voice from 1st person to 3rd person in v 2. However, as Hilber ("Psalm CX," 359) and Waltke and Houston (*Psalms as Christian Worship*, 499) have noted, in the Old Testament prosopological change can indicate change in perspective rather than change in the nature of the speech, as is the case in Isa 3:1–4, Hos 5:1–7, Amos 3:1–7, Mic 1:3–7. Hilber ("Psalm CX," 359) also notes that short Assyrian oracles can display a rapid shift in voice, although "the entire speech was conceived as the word of the divinity."

3. Your people will offer themselves willingly[10] on the day of your battle.
Arrayed in holy garments,[11] from the womb of the dawn
is the dew of your youth.[12]

4. The LORD has sworn and will not change his mind.
'You are a priest forever
according to the order of Melchizedek.'

5. The *Lord* is at your right hand;
he will shatter kings on the day of his wrath.

6. He will execute judgment on the nations; he will heap up corpses.[13]
He will shatter the heads[14] over the wide earth

7. He will drink from the stream by the path;
Therefore, he will lift up his head."

---

10. I am choosing to follow the *MT* in v. 3, although semantically and syntactically the verse has been the subject of many revisions. The Septuagint (*LXX*) has *meta sou ē archē* which is retroverted in Hebrew to *imm^{e}kā n^{e}dibōt*, and can be translated into English as "with you is nobility." This translation has the advantage of maintaining consistency within the context of the psalm (so Kissane, "Interpretation of Psalm 110," 192). With the resonating between Yahweh and his throne partner in the rest of the psalm, the mention of *your people* here seems out of place. However, if the *LXX's* translation of the last word in the verse *y^{e}lidtîkā* "I have begotten you" is rejected (see below) the MT text provides a consistency within the verse (Your people ... your youth, i.e., young men).

11. *Arrayed in holy garments* can be accepted over some MSS, the Targum, Symmachus, Jerome and the NRSV's translation, which has *biharrê* "in the holy mountains." Kissane (Ibid.,192) argues that accepting the MT would place the Messiah under the Aaronic priesthood. However, if one follows the accenting in the MT, *arrayed in holy garments* describes the youthful warriors who rally to this throne-partner of Yahweh. Furthermore, the reference to Melchezidek places the psalm in a pre-Aaronic time frame before the concept of priesthood was limited to the tribe of Levi.

12. The *LXX* reads *y^{e}lidtîkā* translated "I have begotten you," which as Zenger (Hossfeld and Zenger, *Psalms 3*,142) notes becomes problematic if preceded by the words *l^{e}kā ṭal* "to you" and "dew" respectively, as are found in the MT but not in the *LXX*. Since these two terms add complexity to the text, they most likely were not added at a later time and should be kept.

13. NRSV uses the phrase *filling them with corpses*. The English verb *heap up* eliminates the need for a double object and so better reflects the MT. Proposals which conflate Symmachus, Aquila (Greek: *pharangges*; Hebrew: *gēāyôt*) "valleys" and Jerome (*valles*) with the *MT g^{e}wiyyôṯ*, "corpses," translated into English as *he will fill the valleys with corpses*, provide a more concrete image, but do not lessen the violence in the image.

14. MT is singular. However the plural is attested to in some Medieval Hebrew manuscripts. For the singular *rō'š* used as plural see Ps 68:22.

Structural Implications for Understanding Psalm 110 as a Messianic and Royal Prophecy

The structure of Psalm 110 has generally been thought to reflect two distinct sections each beginning with an oracular introduction (vv. 1 and 4) followed by expansions.[15] This position is well supported by reference to the same number of colas in both oracles and the same number of colas in both of their amplifications (2 and 8 respectively), stylistic use of Yahweh (vv. 1a and 4a) and Lord (vv. 1b and 5a).[16] Further support of two distinct sections comes from the use of volitional verbs in vv. 1–3, *šēḇ* "sit," *yišlaḥ* "[Yahweh] sends out," and *rᵉḏēh* "rule," and in vv. 4–7 the use of perfective *nišba'* "has sworn," *māḥaṣ* "will shatter," *mālē'* "will fill/filling," and non-perfective verbs, *yāḏîn* "he will execute judgment," *yišteh* "he will drink," and *yārîm* "he will lift up." The use of three of each type of verb should probably not be considered coincidental.

However, suggesting that the psalm has two parallel units or strophes can act to downplay the importance of any dominant element. On closer examination it may be possible to suggest a central emphasis in the psalm. Auffret proposed a double concentric structure of Psalm 110, one of which centered on 4aα, the oath formula.[17] Zenger also makes the comment: "Without v. 4 there would be a coherent textual and historical continuum."[18] Further evidence for the importance of the oath formula comes from reconstructing what the hypothetical prophetic oracle may have looked like in its pre-liturgized form. That is, if the oracle formula and oath formula were separated from their expansions and combined according to the principles observed when they occur together in the book of Jeremiah (see below), then the emphasis would fall on the content of the oath formula and serve to highlight v. 4, the Melchizedekian lineage of this person.

The structural location of Melchizedek at the center of the psalm is significant in this regard. Structurally, the placement of v. 4 in the middle of Psalm 110 parallels its placement in the middle of the narrative account of Abram's defeat of the Canaanite kings in Genesis 14, which strengthens the allusion. I suggest that in Genesis, Abram's encounter with Melchizedeck functions, in one regard, to legitimate the claim that Abram has to wage war against the Canaanite kings. The covenant had not been ratified as of this time and so this is a pre-ratified legitimation of Abram's right to possess

---

15. Allen, *Psalms*, 113; Waltke and Houston, *Psalms as Christian Worship*, 500–501.
16. See Allen, *Psalms*, 113.
17. "Note sur la Structure," 83–88.
18. Hossfeld and Zenger, *Psalms 3*, 146.

the land. But it should be noted that the psalm portrays the Messiah's right to rule beyond any right to rule according to pre-exilic boundary markers and includes the whole earth. In the Genesis text, Abram acknowledges Melchizedek's sovereign right by paying tithes.[19] We may conclude that the legitimacy of Abram's military conquest is then sanctioned by Melchizedek's blessing.[20] Such an idea of legitimacy is then appropriated through the Messiah on whom this priestly title is conferred by Yahweh.

The traditional Christian interpretation of this psalm until the early nineteenth century categorized it as a messianic prophecy. Waltke and Houston note that Delitzsch (1830–90) was one of the last German scholars to interpret Psalm 110 in a conservative orthodox way as a prophetic and messianic psalm.[21] J.M. Neal (1818–1866) and Bishop Perowne (1823–1904) were his English counterparts. Kraus suggests that form-critical research has contributed to the rejection of traditional messianic interpretations in Psalm 110.[22] Yet, according to Gunkel, classification of Royal Psalms, unlike other psalm types, is based on "their different causes."[23] In the case of Psalm 110 the different cause seems to be tied into understanding the implications of the phrase, n^{e}'um yhwh, "an oracle of Yahweh."[24] So caution must be exercised in making any assumptions based on what can be understood

---

19. Von Rad, *Genesis*, 180.

20. The function of such an allusion in Ps 110 would work on an argumentative justification, but not necessarily as a theological basis acknowledging any form of Canaanite pantheon, just as, for instance, the statement in Ps 136:2, *Give thanks to the God of gods*, would not necessarily be a concession for any Israelite to the existence of other gods. This idea of divine mandate was common in the ancient world, for example, it was believed that "Cyrus received his rule from the hands of the Babylonian gods" (Herrmann, *History of Israel*, 295).

21. Waltke and Houston, *Psalms as Christian Worship*, 74–75.

22. Kraus, *Psalms 60–150*, 353.

23. Gunkel and Begrich, *Introduction to Psalms*, 103.

24. Psalm 110, as an "oracle of Yahweh" (n^{e}'um yhwh) has no other comparable psalm. In the Psalms, the term, n^{e}'um, occurs only here and in Ps 36:1, where "transgression" (*peša'*) is personified. The *TNIV* translates Ps 36:1 as "I have a message from God in my heart" which captures the divine implied subject of the oracle. Waltke (Waltke and Houston, *Psalms as Christian Worship*, 502) notes that the term n^{e}'um occurs 375x in the OT and is used exclusively of divine speech. Gerstenberger (*Psalms, Part 2*, 266) contests whether Pro 30:1, 2 Sam 23:1, and Ps 36:2 represent divine speech. However, see Waltke (Waltke and Houston, *Psalms as Christian Worship*, 502) for arguments to suggest that even in these cases the n^{e}'um can be understood as divine speech. For example, the term n^{e}'um is used of David in 2 Sam 23:1 where it is clear that David is speaking through *the Spirit of the Lord* (2 Sam 23:2). According to Bible Works 9, n^{e}'um only occurs approximately 20 out of 377 times in non-prophetic books (Gen 22:16, Num 14:28, 24:3 (2x), 24:4, 24:15 (2x), 24:16; 1 Sam 2:30(2x) 2 Sam 23:1 (2x); 2 Kgs 9:26 (2x), 19:33, 22:19; 2 Ch 34:27; Ps 36:2, 110:1, Prov 30:1.

from the general knowledge of Royal Psalms. Some modern scholars follow the New Testament witness to David as the author and speaker in this psalm and categorize it as a messianic prophecy.[25] However, the general tendency can be seen in Allen's statement that restricting the psalm to an original messianic intent "hardly accords with the pattern of historical and theological development discernible in royal psalms in general and with the ancient cultural and historical royal references within Ps 110."[26] Waltke is correct in noting that academics who deny Davidic authorship reach no consensus about the date of Psalm 110.[27]

Comparison with similar prophetic oracles in Jeremiah shows that the psalm-form is a liturgical modification of the pure prophetic form. The phrase *nᵉ'um yhwh* occurs 167 out of 267 times in Jeremiah.[28] According to Rendtorff, in Jeremiah when the phrase stands alone it functions as a conclusion to divine speech. However, when it is placed with another speech formula, such as an oath formula *nišba'*, a *niphil* form of "to swear," it is displaced from this concluding function and stands in an introductory position.[29] This later situation is the one we find, albeit in a modified form, in Psalm 110. When it occurs, for example, in Jeremiah 22:5 and 49:13 (also found outside of Jeremiah, e.g., Gen 22:16) with the term *nišba'tî* "by myself I have sworn," the phrase *nᵉ'um yhwh* succeeds the *nišba'tî* formula without intervening words. In this function it still introduces divine speech, but in a secondary manner serves to highlight the distinct function of the oath formula. In Psalm 110 the oracle formula *nᵉ'um yhwh* in v. 1 is parallel to the oath formula, *nišba'*, "[the LORD] has sworn" in v. 4. Possibly, the altered placement of the terms in Ps 110 and the expansion of the oracle before the oath formula may be due to the liturgical shaping of the psalm. The evidence for this modification of a pure prophetic oracle to a liturgical form is supported by comparison of Ps 110 with Assyrian enthronement oracles.[30]

It is hard to know for certain to what extent David is responsible for the final form of the psalm.[31] As Delitzsch points out, David had known

---

25. Kidner, *Psalms 73–150*, 427; Kissane, "Interpretation of Psalm 110," 106.

26. Allen, *Psalms*, 113.

27. Houston and Waltke, *Psalms as Christian Worship*, 502.

28. See Holladay ("Indications," 245–261) for an example of how some scholars approach the issue of the literary dependence between the Psalms and Jeremiah. The very nature of this debate itself suggests that understanding the function of a particular form in one book can illuminate its use in the other.

29. Rendtorff, "Zum Gebrauch," 28.

30. See Hilber, "Psalm CX," 353–366 and *Cultic Prophecy*, 76–88.

31. Furthermore, if David were carried away in a state of uttering prophecy as Perowne (*Book of Psalms*, 288–289) noted, we cannot be sure as to how he perceived the

of egregious sin in the midst of his military campaign against Ammon.[32] Such a crisis could have been the impetus for his prophetic oracle, which was later reshaped into a liturgical psalm.[33] Perowne suggests that it was composed to accompany the bringing in of the Ark, of which David acted both as king and priest.[34] Regardless as to its provenance, the poem's close structural affinity to Assyrian royal prophecies suggests that it functioned as part of royal prophecy in Israel's coronation ritual.[35] Weiser suggests that it was probably used at the "festival of the king's enthronement" and reflects a courtly style which was "composed at a time when under the kings of Judah national enthusiasm was still a national and unbroken force."[36] According to Mowinckel, "the kings must be real Judean or Israelite kings in these psalms."[37] Allen tentatively suggests "the psalm was composed to celebrate David's earlier conquest of Jerusalem."[38] The ideal of a co-regent with Yahweh, expressed in the term "my lord" (la'ḏōnî) in v. 1 became the benchmark by which Israelite Kings were to measure up.

The Perceived Suffering of the Psalmist

When we talk about the perceived suffering of the psalmist in this instance we mean the suffering of the *lord*[39] or Messiah of this psalm. In the first part of the psalm (vv. 2–3) it seems fairly clear that the *lord* is the subject of the actions. However, regarding vv. 5–7 scholars are divided as to who the subject of the actions is. The closest antecedent to the subject of verse 6 is the ʾăḏōnāy "Lord" of verse 5, and in v. 7 difficulties arise in assigning to the *Lord* the anthropomorphic language of drinking from a stream. Zenger on a linguistic basis believes there is no indication in the sequence of clauses

---

exact meaning of ʾăḏōnî. The inherent semantic range of the term ʾăḏōnî always involves deference to the one who is addressed.

32. Delitzsch, *Psalms, Vol 3*, 187.

33. The details of this ceremony would be open to speculation and are not necessarily important to our understanding of the meaning of Ps 110. For a review of possible suggestions of the King's role prior to the exile in such a ceremony see Shirley Lucas' chapter entitled "Kingship in the Hebrew Scriptures: The Psalms." Lucas, *Concept of the Messiah*, 66–93.

34. Perowne, *Book of Psalms*, 299.

35. Hilber, *Cultic Prophecy*, 76–80.

36. Weiser, *Psalms*, 693.

37. Mowinckel, *Psalms, Vol. 1*, 48.

38. Allen, *Psalms*, 113.

39. The use of the term *lord* corresponds to the Masoretic pointing of ʾăḏōnî, whereas the term *Lord* corresponds to the Masoretic pointing of ʾăḏōnāy.

(vv. 5–7) to infer a change of subject.[40] So the 'ăḏōnāy "Lord" is the acting subject in the campaign against the enemies. Kissane, by interpreting 'al as a conjunction (*because*) in v. 5 instead of as the preposition *at* insists that it is the *lord* who is the acting subject of all three verses.[41] Waltke keeps the subject of v. 5 as the Lord, but on the basis of semantic pertinence believes the subject of vv. 6–7 to be the *lord*.[42] The structure of the psalm may lend support to Waltke's position. If we remove the kernel of the oracle, we find that the psalm contains parallel ideas.

v 1aβ	'ăḏōnî (*lord*) is seated at the right hand of *yhwh*	v 5a	'ăḏōnāy (*Lord* i.e., Yahweh) is at the right hand of this "*lord*-priest"
v 1b	Subjugation of enemies by Yahweh	v 5b	Subjugation of *kings* by Yahweh
v 2a	Symbol of might from Zion (the *lord's* mighty scepter)	v 6a	Judgment of *nations* (*He will judge*)
v 2b	Subjugation of enemies	v 6b	Subjugation of *heads*
v 3	Exaltation of the speaker's lord	v 7	Symbolic exaltation of the subject, *He will lift up his head*

Table 2. Identification of the subject of vv. 5–7 based on the structure of Psalm 110.

The parallel ideas in the table suggest that the subject of vv. 6 and 7 can be regarded as the *lord* of the first half of the psalm and not the Lord. The *lord* then is the object of the foe's hostility and engaged in a campaign against them

If we assumed that originally David had been "prophesying" it would be difficult to determine the exact meaning he had for the terms for enemies, 'ōyēḇ "enemy" (vv. 1bα and 2aβ), *mᵉlāḵîm* "kings" (v. 5), *gôyim* "nations" (v. 6) and *rōš* "head(s)" (v. 6).[43] From a form critical perspective, according to the inner logic of the psalm, the 'ōyēḇ of v. 1 are the *gôyim* of v. 6.[44] Thus the general term for *enemies* is given a more specific designation in vv. 5–7 as

---

40. Hossfeld and Zenger, *Psalms 3*, 151.

41. Kissane, "Interpretation of Psalm 110," 194.

42. Waltke and Houston, *Psalms as Christian Worship*, 509. Kirkpatrick (*Book of Psalms*, 669) suggests that in v. 6 the subject is the Lord because of the use of the term *yāḏîn* "he will judge." This term is used of Yahweh in Pss 7:8, 9:8, and 76:9. However, if the *lord* is the throne partner of Yahweh, the collation of the verb *judge* with the *lord* as subject should not be considered unusual.

43. The implied eschatological argument is not dependent on the extent to which David is responsible for the written text of Psalm 110, or whether it is indeed David prophesying.

44. Croft, *Identity of the Individual*, 36.

the *kings*, *nations* and *heads*. The setting is a battle sequence. To begin with, the *lord* is enthroned at the right hand of Yahweh. The *enemies* surround the *lord* and hence *Zion* on every side. Zion is the place where Yahweh resides with his throne partner. The enemies' attack on *Zion* reveals their complete antagonism to the rule of Yahweh and his throne partner. As in Psalm 2 the *foes* are positioned as the instigators. The "mighty scepter" *maṭṭēh-'uzzᵉkā* (v. 2) is a symbol of the Messiah's right to rule, to fulfill Israel's covenant mandate to subdue enemies and bless respectful nations.[45] At other times it is a symbol of Yahweh's justice (Ps 45:6; Isa 10:5). In contrast it can be inferred that the enemies are unjust in their cause. The reference to the *mighty scepter* coming forth from Zion may indicate hostility against the Messiah in a manner similar to Psalm 2 (a Royal Psalm) where the nations plot and conspire against the king whom Yahweh installs on Zion.

The subduing of the enemies, symbolized by placing the enemies as *your footstool*, shows the determination of the enemies. Such behaviour is only used to humiliate those who have been conquered. The battle sequence continues as the *lord* who was enthroned at the right hand of Yahweh now finds Yahweh standing at his right hand helping him in battle. The term *'ap* "wrath" (v. 5) is used in Psalm 2:5 to indicate God's wrath directed against his enemies to quell wilful resistance.[46] Zenger notes that the notion of God's wrath is not only an emotional category but a philosophical category directed towards kings and rulers who flout the universal order.[47] Perhaps Zenger's placement of emphasis on God's wrath as a philosophical category makes the notion of God's justice seem disassociated from his character. However, Zenger's suggestion is important in understanding the relationship between the moral world order God has created and God's wrath. We can infer that the term must carry the same range of meaning for the co-regent.

The picture of the enemy is that of a purposeful resistance to what the Messiah enthroned on Zion symbolizes. On the basis of Ps 2:1–2 and Eph 6:10–20, Waltke suggests that the rulers are empowered by demonic forces.[48] The term *yādîn* "he will judge" (v. 6) means to give right and just verdicts in contrast to the term *špṭ*, which carries the notion of righting wrongs.[49] The implication of this is that the cause of the *nations*, *kings* and *heads* is unjust, just as was their conspiracy recorded in Psalm 2. The aftermath of the in-

---

45. Waltke and Houston, *Psalms as Christian Worship*, 505.
46. Allen, *Psalms*, 118.
47. Hossfeld and Zenger, *Psalms 3*, 150.
48. Waltke and Houston, *Psalms as Christian Worship*, 510.
49. Ibid., 511.

tense battle is that corpses are heaped up. The inference is that the enemies have been in active opposition to the Messiah meeting him on the field of battle in intense warfare. Thus, the picture given in the psalm indicates that the enemy is antagonistic to all that *Zion* and hence the rule of God stands for. There is no middle ground. The images are strong and decisive. The enemies appear as conquered, unjust aggressors in the military action.

The Meaning of the "lord's" Response

The focus of Psalm 110 is on the utter defeat of the enemies by means of Yahweh's throne partner, which results in his world-wide universal rule. Although the battle begins with *ōyēḇ* surrounding *ṣiyyôn* "Zion" (v. 2), it moves to the subjugation of the *heads* over *the wide earth* (v. 6). The aggression of the enemies is firmly responded to, as is seen in the symbols (*enthronement, footstool, mighty scepter, wrath*) justifying the right of the Messiah to utterly defeat them in battle. As mentioned above, justification for the Messiah's military action also comes from the allusion in v. 4 to his priestly endowment by Yahweh *according to the order of Melchizedek*. In the Genesis account Melchizedek blesses Abram before God ratifies his covenant with Abram, as mentioned in Genesis 13:14–17, and before the limitations on priesthood imposed by the Aaronic order.[50] The allusion creates a chronological frame of reference which moves the reader from a pre-covenantal time frame to *Yahweh's* throne partner's reign over the whole earth, supported by a nation of priests who are symbolized by their apparel, *arrayed in holy garments*.

Whether the text was originally understood as eschatological by the communities, which first used it in the cult, cannot be proved for certain.[51] Eschatological perspective can be communicated through various emphases.[52] In Psalm 110 neither the motifs of the ingathering of Israel, nor the

---

50. Gillingham's ("Messiah in the Royal Psalms," 228) suggestion that the eschatological focus in Psalm 110 functions by reflecting on the past Davidic dynasty in order to "uphold the legitimacy of the Temple, and with that, the worship of God there" does not take into account the different focus to which the reference to Melchizedek draws the reader. The reference to Melchizedek takes the reader outside of the historical reference frame of the theocratic state established by David.

51. Zenger (Hossfeld and Zenger, *Psalms 3*, 149) comments: "It is rather doubtful that here, as throughout Psalm 110, a concrete historical situation is in view." Gillingham ("Messiah in the Royal Psalms," 224) opposes viewing this or any of the psalms eschatologically because there appears to be very little Messianic awareness in other pre-exilic material. Such a position *a priori* does not take into consideration the uniqueness of the phrase *nᵉʾum yhwh*.

52. According to Mitchell (*Message of the Psalter*, 151–152), a tripartite eschatological

universal peace portrayed in the ingathering of the nations, is of primary focus. Yet, removing the focus from pre-exilic land boundaries is of particular importance. The conflict now becomes centered on the defeat of the enemies, who are opposed to and seek to exterminate the rule of *Yahweh's* throne partner enthroned on Zion. Without concrete historical referents for these enemies, the older commentators may be understood for interpreting the singular *rōš* (v. 6) symbolically as the "head" or "chief" adversary, namely Satan, or, as Zenger suggests, figures of a universal power of chaos which must be combatted and destroyed by Yahweh and his *lord*.[53] The Messiah's defeat of the enemies establishes Yahweh's universal rule, which is grounded in the Messiah's pursuit of justice.[54] The last verse of the Psalm captures the completeness of his success: *therefore he shall lift up his head*. The complete earth falls subject to his rule.

Conclusion of Exegesis

The hostile images of war are best understood in the context of the eschatological framework within the psalm. The nations are portrayed as actively and antagonistically engaged in battle against Yahweh and his throne partner, the *lord*. The imagery reflects the scope and underlying reality of the battle. The complete subjugation of the enemy is justified on the basis that the enemy has engaged willfully with the intention of, not only throwing off Yahweh's rule, but of destroying the place from which Yahweh rules, namely Zion. In the context of this eschatological profile the incorrigible and recalcitrant nature of the enemy is overcome according to Yahweh's right to establish his universal reign through his Messiah the *lord*.

---

schema is found in Ezekiel, Zechariah, Joel and also in the structure of the Psalms. This schema consists of the ingathering of scattered Israel, the gathering of the nations against Jerusalem, and the ingathering of Israel and the nations to worship on Zion. I am working from the position that the psalms must have integrity as individual units, because they are used as such. In this instance then Ps 110, by itself, does not contain the full-fledged eschatological programme that Mitchell sees in the over-arching structure of the Psalms. However, the lack of certain images does not mean that the psalm is not eschatological in its framework.

53. Hossfeld and Zenger, *Psalms 3*, 150.

54. Perhaps the mandate in v 2b, *r^{e}dēh* "rule," also alludes to that given in Gen 1:26 and 1:28.

A SELECT HISTORICAL SURVEY OF THE INTERPRETATION OF PSALM 110

The early Post-exilic Restoration

During the post-exilic restoration, Psalm 110 might have been used in a liturgical ceremony, possibly even at the time of the restoration of the temple. Since under Persian rule it could not have been used overtly in an actual royal coronation, it is most likely that it became symbolic, somewhat similar to how the crowning in Zechariah 6 must in some way have been considered symbolic.[55]

How it was understood and used may be open to conjecture, but, based on biblical witness, it seems unlikely that the post-exilic community saw any of their leaders fulfilling the unified regal and priestly theme. Goulder, working from a presupposition that the psalms in Book V were composed by Asaphites at the time of the return from exile, suggests that Joshua ben Jehozadak is the *lord* being referred to in Ps 110.[56] His argument is based on Zechariah's account (3:8; 6:12) which mentions that Joshua is the ṣemaḥ "branch." Two concerns arise in this identification. First, in the term's metaphorical use referring to a descendent of David (Ps 132:17; Jer 23:5, 33:15; Ezek 29:21) the name of David also occurs. However, David is not mentioned in the Zechariah passages.[57] Therefore there seems to be incompleteness in the allusions in Zechariah (3:8 and 6:12) to Joshua being the ṣemaḥ. He was not of David's line and could not have been considered the literal heir of David. In the eyes of the restored community Joshua ben Jehozadak may have satisfied the priestly requirements of the psalm, but could not satisfy the community's royal requirements.

The other choice that the exiles may have had in mind was Zerubbabel (Zec 4:6), grandson of Jehoiakin. He is recorded as the one who is to lay the foundation and build the temple (Zec 4:9).[58] But he conspicuously disappears from the spotlight.[59] In the dispensation of the old temple

---

55. Hays ("Use of Oracles," 81) insists that in Israel's use of foreign oracles against the nations, "Their function and importance were not dependent on the foreign powers' knowledge of or response to them." Nevertheless, any literal declaration of autonomous kingship, besides being impractical, would have had serious consequences for Israel's restoration (Neh 6:5–7).

56. Goulder, *Psalms of the Return*, 145.

57. See also the argument against associating Joshua with the ṣemaḥ put forward by Collins in "Eschatology of Zechariah," 77–80.

58. Apparently contradicted by Ezra 5:16.

59. Collins (Ibid., 77–82) argues for associating the ṣemaḥ with Zerubbabel based on his role in rebuilding the temple. However, it is uncertain as to whether Zerubbabel

it was the king's jurisprudence to be protector of the temple, but in the new political climate under the Persian kings, no exile could have conceived of Joshua as becoming the ruling king of Israel, which had been divided into Persian administrative units. Even at the time of Nehemiah (6:5–9) a kingly appointment was not in the minds of the leadership in Judah. So if the returnees considered Zerubbabel as the 'ădōnî, it was most likely not literally. Furthermore, the prophets Zechariah and Haggai seem to divide the role of priest and political leader into two distinct spheres assigning the political to Zerubbabel and the priestly to Joshua.[60] To the contrary, the roles of king and priest are unified in Psalm 110.

Overall, the post-exilic community was not engaged in any form of conflict that would have literally matched the foes, images and events given in Psalm 110.[61] Although the post-exilic community was ruled by satraps of the Persian kings, Cyrus is not looked upon as an enemy, but an instrument of the Lord.[62] There is no indication that any of the other Persian kings are considered enemies of the Israelites, and it is hard to think that the post-exilic community could have conceived Cyrus, Xerxes, Artaxerxes, or Darius as the "Kings" or "Head(s)" to be shattered. On the contrary, the Persian kings with their decentralized liberal governing policies are the safeguards against the local opposition to the building of the temple and the re-establishment of Jerusalem.[63]

In his assessment of Peter Ackroyd's[64] study of Hebrew thought in the sixth century, Kratz comments, "The handling of the exile is not therefore

---

is at the dedication of the temple. In the end, his disappearance from this portion of history precludes him from being the ṣemaḥ of David's line.

60. A cursory reading of Zechariah 6:13 might suggest that in some way Joshua was to unite the two roles. However, such a reading is based on presuppositions about the connotative meaning associated with ṣemaḥ (see ibid., 77–80).

61. Goulder assigns the context of the text to Nehemiah's time of restoration, when there was a threat of violence from the Persian governor, Sanballat, the Ammonites, Arabs and Ashdodites who sent groups to fight against Jerusalem. There was opposition from the Trans-Euphrates Satraps to the movement in Judah to re-establish the autonomy of Jerusalem, as seen for example in Tobai's attempt to prevent the building of the walls around Jerusalem. Yet, any correlation with the enemies and conflict portrayed in Ps 110 cannot be made on a literal level.

62. Scholars might find the phrase in Isa 45:1 controversial, but there is no denying that Cyrus and his successors implemented a generous and tolerant policy towards subjected nations (Bright, *History of Israel*, 362).

63. For a review of the different views on the style of Persian governance see Jigoulov, "Administration," 138–151.

64. One of Ackroyd's (*Exile and Restoration*, 13) main assumptions is that religious tradition had far greater weight on how the prophets understood the events than the impulses of the moment.

solely a problem of historical reconstruction; it is a matter of attempting to understand an attitude, or more properly a variety of attitudes, taken up towards historical fact."[65] How the members of the post-exilic community interpreted this psalm and so the images of enmity is open to speculation.[66] Perhaps as an insignificant community in the midst of world powers, the ruler in Psalm 110 became a symbol of future hope. The implication is that neither the enemies nor the ruler in Psalm 110 can be literally identified in the circumstances of the post-exilic community.

The NT—Christ's Role as Judge and Priest

Of importance to this study is the quotation of Psalm 110:1, which is the most extensively quoted section of Psalm 110 in the NT.[67] This verse captures two of the three central themes in the psalm: that of the *lord* (v. 1) as Yahweh's throne-partner and that of the violent defeat of the enemies which in its nascent form is expressed in the phrase *until I put your enemies as your footstool*. Five partial or complete quotations of Ps 110:1 are given in the gospels and Acts (Mk 12:36; Mt 22:44; Lk 20:42–43; Acts 2:34–35). The general thrust of these uses challenges the concept of Messiah which the Jewish leaders had. As Houston notes, Jesus' claim in Mk 14:61–64 is pivotal to the ensuing death of Jesus by the Jewish leaders.[68] But in Jesus' answer there is more than just a desire to correct assumptions about his nature. His session provides the very basis by which he claims the right to judge. As Watts notes, "if only the nature of Jesus' messianic identity were at stake, then the first strophe of 110:1 would have sufficed; however, the addition to make his enemies a footstool adds yet an even darker note. Jesus' enemies are God's enemies."[69] Furthermore, Watts goes on to explain that Jesus' claims in Mark meet with hostility, which sees the OT citations shift towards threats of prophetic judgments against a resistant leadership

---

65. Kratz, "Relation between History," 162.

66. Based on my analysis alone, it would be unfounded to say that the post-exilic community interpreted Ps 110 eschatologically, but since the text does not match the events surrounding the restoration as depicted in the biblical witnesses, it remains a possibility. Other studies such as Mitchell's (*Message of the Psalter*), which explore the eschatological program of the psalms, might provide insight in this regard.

67. The Greek New Testament (*GNT*, 898, 906) has Ps 110:1 quoted eight times and alluded to or containing a verbal parallel ten times.

68. Waltke and Houston, *Psalms as Christian Worship*, 484–485.

69. Watts, "Mark," 222.

(Mk 3:29, 4:12; 7:6, 10) and in a final transitioning pericope (Mk 8:17–18) directed at the similarly uncomprehending disciples.[70]

Watt's observation that the text speaks of prophetic judgment is reinforced in the Matthean and Lukan accounts. In each of the accounts (including Mark), in the immediately following pericope Jesus issues a form of judgment (condemnation) on the teachers of the law (Mk 12:38–40 and Lk 20:45–46), or the teachers of the law and the Pharisees (Mt 23:1–39). In Acts, after the Holy Spirit has come, Peter's preaching of the session leads to the repentance of the crowd. The gospel accounts and Acts, then, relate Psalm 110 to judgment as it pertains to one's understanding of who Jesus is.

Hebrews contains five references to Ps 110:1 explaining Christ's role as both judge and priest.[71] The use of the session provides a picture of the subjugation of the enemies as having begun but yet awaiting consummation through the bringing together of Ps 8:4–6 and Ps 110:1 in Heb 2:8–9. The quotation from Ps 8 suggests the subjugation of enemies is accomplished, whereas that from Ps 110 suggests it is a future event. In other words, the reality has been inaugurated, but its consummation will come at a time in the future.[72] Susan Docherty has noticed that the author of Hebrews' connection of Ps 110:1 with Ps 110:4 can be seen in Heb 1:3 where Jesus' purification of sins is hinted at prior to his ascension.[73] Furthermore, the connection is warranted because the author of Hebrews quotes this same verse at Heb 5:6, 7:17, and 7:21 and bases his identification of Jesus as priest on it.[74] So it is no surprise that this beginning but unconsummated rule (Ps 110:1) is joined together with Jesus' priesthood in Hebrews 10:12—10:14. Jesus' session as Melchizedekian priest provides the basis for mercy to be shown to those of the New Covenant as he waits for "his enemies to become a footstool at his

---

70. Ibid., 112. Moyise (*Jesus and Scripture*, ch. 1, par. 26) seems to downplay the theme of judgment of the second coming. He believes the quotation of Ps 110:1 in Mk 14:62 which is coupled to an allusion to Dan 7:13 "coming on the clouds of heaven" as most likely meaning to receive power and authority rather than to go anywhere. Further, he implies that the theme of suffering as means of triumph is indicated by vineyard workers killing the son and the ending in Mark which emphasizes suffering through quoting Ps 22. Although the theme of suffering is certainly central to how Jesus ushers in his Kingdom, Watts' contention is correct that the latter half of Ps 110:1 was included for a purpose. It seems possible that both views of triumph are in view.

71. According to Guthrie (*Hebrews*, 923–924) Ps 110 serves as a key to the structural development of the book, being quoted in 1:13 and alluded to in 1:3; 8:1; 10:12 and 12:22.

72. Ibid., 946. For an explanation of the anthropological interpretation of the bringing together of these two psalms and a critique of Guthrie's christological interpretation see Moyise, *Later New Testament*, 4.3.

73. *Use of Old Testament*, 169.

74. Mason, *You Are a Priest Forever*, 18.

feet." Finally, perhaps, there are echoes of the violent images from Ps 110 and their fulfillment in the final judgment from the apocalyptic NT images of judgment (e.g., Rev 17:14).[75]

The NT writers in general see Christ's ascension as fulfilling the *lord's* ascension to the throne of Yahweh. The second part of the phrase *until I put your enemies as your footstool* is seen as occurring but not as yet fulfilled. Thus, the NT portrays Ps 110 in an eschatological framework.[76] The notion of judgment portrayed in the gospels and Acts is directed towards those who have rejected Christ's claims about himself, whether the Jewish leaders or the general populace.[77] The book of Hebrews further spells out Christ's role as judge and as mediator (Melchizedekian priest) of the new covenant more distinctly. Judgment has been averted on those who were once enemies of the *lord* by the once and for all sacrifice of Christ which is superior to those offered in the Aaronic priestly order. Therefore, the session with its notions of judgment in the NT is concerned with one's relationship to Christ's rule and its relevance is specifically directed to those who were or are enemies, in order that they repent and no longer remain enemies. The violent images in Ps 110 of judgment against recalcitrant enemies are developed primarily in the apocalyptic violent images given, for example, in the book of Revelation.

The Pre-Nicene and Post-Nicene Fathers—Literal and Spiritual Tensions

Many of the early commentators understood Ps 110 with the focus of establishing the person of Christ as a coequal member of the Godhead. Hence some of the earliest writers known as the Apologists used Ps 110 to defend orthodox beliefs about the nature of Christ from heresy. In this context,

---

75. The violent images are generally associated with the concept of the Son of Man from the book of Daniel. However, Bloomberg ("Matthew," 84) in commenting about Matthew's account of the session suggests that Matthew draws out the concept of eschatological judgment through the Messianic connection with the theme of Son of Man, and that the future implementation of perfect justice throughout the universe, at the end of time, will occur through this priest and king.

76. "Usage of this text [Ps 110:1] may reflect a polemical purpose to support the Christian view that the coming of the Messiah falls in two stages, over against the messianic expectations of Judaism, and to explain the resultant interim period in scriptural terms" (Allen, *Psalms*, 118).

77. Although preaching to Jews in Jerusalem, the universal scope to whom the text applies implied by the text itself is most likely indicated, as Moyise (*Later New Testament*, 1.2) notes, in the fact that Theophilus would have understood references to phrases in Acts such as "everyone who calls," "all families," and "restores all things" as references to gentiles like himself.

however, there are some glimpses as to how these commentators understood Ps 110 as it pertained to the theme of judgment. So, for example, Clement identifies the enemies as all the wicked who oppose the will of God.[78] In contrast, Justin Martyr understands the enemies as devils.[79] He also sees the phrase "He shall send to Thee the rod of power out of Jerusalem" as referring to the word which the apostles who went out from Jerusalem preached everywhere. Nevertheless, it is clear from the warning that he gives his opponents to whom he is writing that he sees the punishment for sinners as an eternal one by fire. Tertullian sees the event of putting Christ's enemies under his feet as an eschatological event which will occur in the "day of the Lord."[80]

Origen, a younger contemporary of Tertullian, but of the Alexandrian school, gives a more detailed explanation. Origen, interested in the spiritual meaning of the text, allows leeway for dispute about the meaning of the subjection given in Ps 110:1. For Origen, the subjugation which is talked of is a spiritual one which has happened to those who have become subjects of Christ.[81] Jerome in his homily on Ps 110 (109) also uses prophetic allegory to interpret its meaning. He clarifies the word scepter (v. 2) with Isa 2:3 to mean "instruction" and notes, "The psalmist did not say, kill your enemies . . . [but] rule."[82] For Jerome, ruling over the enemies does not involve their violent death, but their conversion. He interprets the violent image in v. 6, *he will crush kings on the day of his wrath*, by linking the kings to the devil through Luke 4:5, 6. The day of wrath is further defined by "on the day of conflict and strife."[83] However, in contrast Jerome says that nations are judged. The violent image of *heaping up corpses* refers to unbelievers who have not believed the message of the apostles. The death, nevertheless, is an allegorical one where they "fall in the death of the desert of this world."[84] Therefore for Jerome the explanation of judgment in Ps 110 is soteriological and has to deal with one's ultimate relationship with Christ. Judgment is the withholding of God's presence and the benefits therein.

In contrast to Jerome, Gregory of Nazianzus of the Antiochene school sees the judgment as eschatological and since Christ has already brought

---

78. Clement of Rome, "First Epistle of Clement," 15. Clement of Rome (fl. c. 92–101) was part of the group known as the Apologists, whereas Clement of Alexandria (c. 150–215) was of the Alexandrian school of interpretation.

79. Justin Martyr, "First Apology," 178.

80. Tertullian, "On the Ressurection," 560–561.

81. Origen, "De Principiis," 260.

82. Origen, *Homilies*, 271.

83. Ibid.

84. Ibid., 276.

about submission in Christians, the final judgment does not refer to the submission of Christians.[85] Theodoret of Cyrus, also of the Antiochene school, suggests that "the foes are in particular the devil, the demons ministering to him, and in addition to them also those resisting his divine teachings, Jews and pagans."[86] *Rule in the midst of your foes* is interpreted soteriologically, where the majority are converted and led like captives to the king in embracing service.[87] Nevertheless, Theodoret is clear in his interpretation of v. 6 that judgment on the recalcitrant enemy is not only eschatological, but also occurs in the present time:

> Here he indicated more clearly the judgment, and the fact that on that day he will consign to manifold punishments those living a life of impiety. In the present life, of course, he often subjected them to many corrections, teaching the ignorant his peculiar force.[88]

John Chrysostom was a contemporary of Augustine, and although he was from the Antiochene school of exegesis, which was known for a more literal exegesis of the text, the tension that he had in balancing a spiritual and literal interpretation of the violent images can be seen in his interpretation of Ps 110:6. According to Stander, Chrysostom interprets the violent images spiritually in the sense that the images represent Christ doing away with folly, but in another sense they could also refer to the fate of the Jews.[89] Furthermore, the execution of harsh acts by God is qualified by his beneficent nature and so stands in contrast to people.[90] Chrysostom's tension between a literal and spiritual interpretation of Ps 110:6 epitomizes the range of interpretations in the Ante-Nicene and Post-Nicene Fathers.

Augustine— Christ's Session

In terms of writing about the priesthood of Christ, Augustine suggests that the gospel is the arm of his strength that has gone out from Zion,[91] whereas in *Our Lord's Sermon on the Mount: according to Matthew*, he states that the

---

85. Gregory of Nazianzus, "Oration 30," 311.
86. Theodoret of Cyrus, *Commentary on the Psalms*, 209.
87. Ibid., 210.
88. Ibid.
89. Strander, "Violence in Chrysostom's," 120–121.
90. Ibid., 121–122.
91. Augustine, *City of God*, 749.

image of the enemies under his feet is an image of eternal punishment.[92] Augustine, therefore, allows for Christ's priestly function as intercessor and his kingly function of judge, thereby allowing for both functions in his interpretation of Christ's session.

Augustine's comments from his classic work *Enarrationes in Psalmos* provide more detail. There are at least two points to keep in mind in order to understand his interpretation of this psalm. First, Augustine was working from a version of text substantially different from the present-day MT. So in v. 3 instead of *Your people will offer themselves willingly* Augustine has *with you is the beginning*,[93] and instead of *of the dawn is the dew of your youth* he has *before the morning star I begot you*.[94] Secondly, Augustine interpreted the psalms in light of their fulfillment in Jesus Christ. So, for Augustine the LXX heading εἰς τὸ τέλος[95] "to the end," which is found in 55 psalm headings, reinforces the idea that all the psalms find their intended meaning in Christ.[96] From this perspective proceed his allegorical interpretations.

As such, Augustine interprets the images of enmity in a soteriological framework. This is not to say that he does not see God's judgment as a horrific event. When speaking of the eschatological judgment in Ps 110 (109), he refers to the wicked burning in eternal punishment.[97] But the present judgment is given as relating to one's relationship with Christ. He defines the enemies as the nations, kings and rulers given in Ps 2, and then relates the enemies to all people: "You, whoever you are, were once his enemy."[98] Furthermore, the putting of his enemies as a footstool at his feet "is being visibly fulfilled" now and will continue until the end of time.[99] Augustine's spiritual interpretation is seen in v. 6. The judgment of the nations is made to mean a destroying of what a person used to be.[100] *He will shatter the heads* for Augustine means that Christ exercises judgment by transforming proud people into humble people. For Augustine the significance of the violent

---

92. Augustine, "Sermon on the Mount," 14.

93. Augustine, *Exposition*, 273.

94. Ibid., 278. The word *beginning* from the LXX ἡ ἀρχὴ and *before the morning star* from πρὸ ἑωσφόρου. See the exegesis for a discussion of the underlying Hebrew terms in the MT.

95. *lamnaṣṣēaḥ* in the MT. Found in 55 psalm headings in the MT, but only three occur in Book V (Pss 109, 139, 140).

96. Waltke and Houston, *Psalms as Christian Worship*, 212–213, 488.

97. Augustine, *Expositions*, 272.

98. Ibid., 270.

99. Ibid.

100. Ibid., 283.

images in Ps 110 lies in their spiritual portrayal of the conversion of the enemies of Christ into followers of Christ.

Psalm 110 in the Reformers

Martin Luther—Christ's Spiritual and Hidden Fulfillment

Martin Luther left a collection of eight sermons on Ps 110; they provide insight into how he understood the images of enmity. Central is Luther's understanding of Christ as fulfilling the prophecy in Ps 110 both as the King and as the Melchizedekian priest in a spiritual rather than temporal manner.[101] The image of Christ's session shows that he is no longer an earthly ruler.[102] Hence, the subjugation of all enemies is done in a secret way.[103] Christ's government is one in which He controls the hearts of all men.[104] Furthermore, Christ's kingdom must exist and remain here in a state of weakness and suffering.[105]

The nature of the expansion of his kingdom has two aspects to it. The first is explained through a metaphorical interpretation of the sending out of the scepter (Ps 110:2).[106] For Luther the scepter is the preaching of the gospel or the "Word." And from Ps 45:6 Luther recognizes that justice is closely related to the preaching of this gospel.[107] He explains the effect that Christ's Word will have: "It will be like a massive defeat in a huge battle, where the field is full of corpses."[108] Quoting 2 Cor 12:9, Luther suggests that the weakness of the kingdom is really a display of God's wisdom, authority and power.[109] So, God's *modus operandi* is not just to overcome the enemies by force, but God's plan is to overcome his enemies by "foolishness and nothingness in order to disgrace them."[110] For Luther, then, the postponement of justice on evildoers is so that the kingdom of Christ, which is an internal kingdom, can extend throughout the world.[111] Christ does not

---

101. Luther, "Psalm 110," 306.
102. Ibid., 233.
103. Ibid., 242.
104. Ibid., 241.
105. Ibid., 255.
106. Ibid., 269.
107. Ibid., 267.
108. Ibid., 342.
109. Ibid., 253.
110. Ibid., 254.
111. Ibid., 259.

bring to actualization his full reign here on earth because there are many others who are to come.[112]

But the other aspect of the establishing of the lord's kingdom, the subduing of incalcitrant enemies, does occur. The enemies in Ps 110 are those who are spoken of in Ps 2, the nations that rage and the people that plot against the Lord and his anointed.[113] This enmity and hatred of the Lord's *lord* is not of a natural or human kind but has its source from the devil.[114] The enemies of Christ are not only the world and the devil but also "death" (1 Cor 15:25–26).[115]

For Luther the enemies are both external and internal, that is, those who claim to belong to the kingdom.[116] In Luther's time this amounted to all those in the Roman Church who abused the true gospel. As examples of external enemies, Luther believed that through Mohammed and the Turks, the devil had subverted and exterminated the gospel in Greece.[117] Yahweh himself subdues the enemies under the lord's feet by miracle alone without the assistance of Christians or physical power.[118] But this is not to say that he does not operate through the affairs of the world. God can punish "one rogue by another."[119] God uses other enemies as he has used the Turks to devastate Greece and Asia Minor.[120] That is, Luther sees v. 6 as being fulfilled in the laying waste of Asia Minor, Egypt and Greece. Further historical examples of nations who have been recalcitrant as enemies to Christ and that have met with disaster are the Jewish people and Rome.[121] However, Christ himself openly destroying the enemy will occur only at the final judgment.[122]

Central to Luther's thinking, however, is the idea that the Kingdom is not to be ushered in by Christians with fist or with armed might.[123] Violence by Christians in establishing the kingdom of God was not an option. Unlike Müntzer and other Anabaptists he did not believe that all the enemies of the

---

112. Ibid., 260.
113. Ibid., 249.
114. Ibid., 251.
115. Ibid., 261.
116. Ibid., 273.
117. Ibid., 325. Luther uses the term *Greece* to mean the Byzantine Empire.
118. Ibid., 255.
119. Ibid., 274.
120. Ibid., 257–258.
121. Ibid., 256.
122. Ibid., 258.
123. Ibid., 255.

church would be physically exterminated before the Last Day.[124] Christians were not to physically resist their enemies as was part of the thinking of the Anabaptists of Luther's time.[125]

In conclusion, for Luther, as with the NT witness, Christ was the fulfillment of the prophecy in Ps 110 as the unified king and priest. But this raised questions about the nature of the Kingdom of God which Luther answered through a spiritual interpretation.[126] The entire psalm is a prophecy concerning the spiritual Kingdom of Christ. Everything must be understood spiritually.[127] Although Luther interpreted the *mighty scepter* in metaphorical language, Luther's historical examples show that he understood God as using violence and the means of war to punish those who opposed the *lord*. But until the last day, this would be both secret and mitigated because of the overriding concern of the expansion of the Kingdom of Christ, which involves the making of disciples. The end for the enemies is to be cast into the abyss of hell to be eternally damned.[128]

John Calvin's Pastoral Concerns

Calvin's main pastoral concern in his exegesis of Ps 110 was to provide comfort and encouragement to those who, like himself, were caught up in the religious and political turmoil of the Reformation. Since Christ in Matthew 22:41–46 applies Ps 110 himself, Calvin does not feel the need to "apply to any other quarter for the corroboration of this statement."[129]

Calvin sees that all people are opposed to God and must be brought to submission, but some of these God makes partakers in his glory while others remain forever in their lost estate and are the true enemies, the reprobate.[130] The sending out of the *mighty scepter* in v. 2 is the extension of

---

124. Ibid., 264.

125. Ibid., 279. The exact words of Luther are "Christ does not start this quarrel and enmity and discord. He must endure it from his enemies. However, it is not the meaning of this verse [110:2] that we physically resist our enemies, which is part of the thinking of the Anabaptists and other rebels." It must be remembered that Müntzer was an Anabaptist (see Ps 149 in this thesis). A discussion on early Anabaptist views on pacifism and physical resistance are beyond the scope of this thesis.

126. Luther uses spiritual and metaphorical interpretation. He uses allegory similar to Augustine to interpret v. 7. Once again the reader is referred to the comments about Luther's commentary on the Psalms given in the Introduction.

127. Ibid., 347.

128. Ibid., 348.

129. Calvin, *Commentary*, 295.

130. Ibid., 300.

Christ's Kingdom.[131] The effect of this extension is further explained by the connection between the "mighty scepter" in v. 2 and the "iron scepter" in Ps 2:9 and is meant to cause people not to provoke Christ's wrath with a rebellious spirit.[132] The spreading and prospering of Christ's rule is meant to provide comfort to Christians, even though the whole world might stand in opposition.

Calvin notes that Christ will execute vengeance through "the dreadful nature of that power which Christ possesses for the dispersion and destruction of his enemies."[133] In contrast to Luther's and Augustine's allegorical understanding of v. 7, Calvin interprets v. 7 as a military metaphor depicting the rapid approach of the enemies' impending disaster. But the actual working out of that judgment here and now as opposed to its eschatological working out is not expanded upon by Calvin in his comments on Ps 110.[134] He does, however, answer the questions as to how this militaristic picture can coexist with the "meekness and mildness with which scriptures elsewhere inform us he shall be endued."[135] In answering this question, he uses the metaphor of a shepherd who cares for the sheep but is fierce towards wolves and thieves.[136]

For Calvin there is a purpose in not eliminating all the enemies of Christ. The response of Christians to the kingdom of Christ being encompassed by many enemies is to be kept in a state of constant warfare where they maintain patience and meekness.[137] The enemies act as a means to the end of a more sanctified elect. For Calvin the complete subjugation of the reprobate symbolized by them becoming Christ's footstool will not be

---

131. Ibid.

132. Ibid., 310.

133. Ibid., 308.

134. This is not to say that in other passages in the Psalms Calvin does not comment on judgment. According to Herman Selderhuis (*Calvin's Theology*, 157) Calvin depicts God as "a judge who inspires awe without striking terror." In Ps 119:52 God carries out judgments daily but these are hidden and not perceptible without God's help. Calvin understood civil authorities as playing a role in meting out God's judgment (Barth, *Theology of John Calvin*, 210). The civil authorities reward the good and punish the bad (Ibid., 211). Furthermore, God commits to the state the execution of vengeance (Ibid). Calvin believed that the state has the right to enforce the death penalty and wage war. It would be beyond the scope of this paper to investigate how Calvin understood God's judgment through forms of government. For Calvin, the ability to see God's judgment is closely linked with his view of revelation and its relationship to history (Ibid., 1–2).

135. Calvin, *Commentary*, 309.

136. Ibid., 310.

137. Ibid., 301.

accomplished before the last day. Until then, the kingdom of Christ will be assailed by many enemies.[138]

Comparison with the Exegetical Findings of Psalm 110

The goal here will be to supplement the salient features of the exegesis with the historical survey. To begin with, almost all the approaches share the common perspective that all people are enemies of Christ at some point in their existence. The enemies are identified as the teachers of the law, but also the general populace (NT), the individual (Augustine), devils, demons, Jews and pagans (John Chrysostom); devils (Justin Martyr); all people (Calvin), originating from the devil and as nations (Luther). Calvin's plain approach to the interpretation of the text is helpful in clarifying the identification of the enemies into two distinct groups, those who become subjects of the kingdom and those who are the reprobate.

Some earlier commentators seem satisfied with interpreting the harsh images allegorically (so Jerome and Augustine). However, as is seen in the comments of Augustine, there existed a very real notion of a painful and horrific future punishment for those who oppose the will of God. Nevertheless, the effect of the allegorical and spiritualizing approaches seems to soften, if not mute, the violent images of judgment. It must be noted that the NT writers did not try to allegorize the images of judgment. Rather, the images of judgment were peripheral to their main concern of relating judgment to how one understood the person of Christ. The NT writers simply did not develop the violent images of judgment in Psalm 110 against a recalcitrant enemy outside of the apocalyptic images of the end times.

The utter defeat of the enemies of Yahweh's throne partner, resulting in his world-wide universal rule, is the focus of this psalm. The allusions to Ps 110 in the New Testament, especially in the book of Hebrews, help to set this psalm in an eschatological framework which has been inaugurated but as yet is unfulfilled. This understanding of time is already latent in the allusion in Ps 110 to Melchizedek (Gen 13:14–17), which stands outside of the timeframe of the Aaronic priesthood. In this regard, Christ is understood as the type of the Melchizedekian priest. All stand in opposition to Yahweh's throne partner, yet through the sacrifice of this Melchizekekian priest some of the enemies become subjects, whereas others remain recalcitrant. The lack of concrete historical references in the psalm, such as boundary markers, and the use of universals, *the wide earth*, also lend support to the understanding of many commentators that the devil is somehow included

138. Ibid., 299.

in this anti-Christ scheme. Furthermore, the enemies are portrayed in the imagery of Ps 110 as active agents of aggression who wish to exterminate all that Yahweh and his throne partner stand for. Therefore the extension of the kingdom and the establishment of justice by Yahweh and his throne partner are justified.

Overall, the NT witness to Ps 110 helps us to see the spiritual nature of the violent images. From its very inception in Book V, the violent images took on meaning beyond their intrinsic violence. The emphasis here is not on allegorical meaning without any parameters for interpretation. The images of violence were used because that was the frame of reference by which those who composed and edited the psalm understood the working out of justice. However, with the identification of Christ as the *lord* a more specific historical time frame is provided. For those who become subjects of the kingdom the images take on a metaphorical meaning. For those who are recalcitrant the images take on a meaning which is consistent with the nature of their aggressive and deceptive recalcitrance. The connection between these images of subjugation in Ps 110 and the actual working out in history of the subjugation of the enemies covers a wide range of possibilities which are dependent on the secret working out of the kingdom and hence the actualization of God's justice in history.[139] The response appeals for the complete rule of Christ which in its end is consummated eschatologically.

EXEGESIS OF PSALM 119: OVERCOMING INJUSTICE THROUGH THE PURSUIT OF THE LAW

A premise of this study is that an investigation of enmity cannot be limited to psalms which only contain explicit expressions of enmity against an adversary. Other psalms in which the psalmist responds without expressions of enmity can provide a different perspective on responses to adversity. Psalm 119 is one such psalm where the psalmist experiences the hostility of adversaries, yet in all but one verse responds with affirmations towards

---

139. Some in the Antiochene school, such as Theodoret, allow for an imminent judgment on those who remain enemies, but he does not expand on it. Luther and Calvin attempt to comment on this aspect of judgment. Both answer the questions why Christ does not always bring justice on the enemies now, why there are still enemies present, and why there appears to be a lack of judgment in general. Calvin also tries to reconcile the fiercely violent militaristic image of Christ as the *lord* of the OT with the gracious images of Christ in the NT through the image of the shepherd. Luther in particular gives suggestions about what the secret working out of the judgment of Christ might look like in history. Calvin does in other places but not in his commentary on Ps 110.

Torah rather than imprecations against his prosecutors. In v. 78 the psalmist wishes for shame on his adversaries. The form and length of Ps 119 also contribute to it being unusual for its selection. Its length raises questions about the unity of the psalm and the identification of the enemies. Furthermore, Ps 119 has no heading and contains various motifs. The goal here will be to determine the suffering of the psalmist and then how that suffering provides a context for understanding the psalmist's response.

Verses One to Eight as the Psalmist's Orientation and Verse Seventy-eight

> 1 Blessed[140] are those whose way is blameless,
>   who walk in the law of the LORD.
> 2 Blessed[141] are those who keep his decrees,
>   who seek him with their whole heart,
> 3 who also do no wrong[142]
>   but walk in his ways.
> 4 You have commanded your precepts
>   to be kept diligently.
> 5 O that my ways may be steadfast
>   in keeping your statutes!
> 6 Then I shall not be put to shame,
>   having my eyes fixed on all your commandments.
> 7 I will praise you with an upright heart
>   when I learn your righteous ordinances.
> 8 I will observe your statutes;
>   do not utterly forsake me.
>
> 78 Let the arrogant be put to shame, because they have subverted
>   me with guile;
>   but I[143] will meditate on your precepts.

---

140. NRSV has *happy*. But in my opinion *blessed* better captures the depth of the term *'ašrê* and is used by the *NIV, ESV, KJV, NKJV* and *NAB*.

141. *NRSV* has *happy*.

142. The *LXX* tries to maintain the masculine participle form from v. 2 and has the translation οἱ ἐργαζόμενοι "those who do," instead of the perfect form in the MT. The effect in the *LXX* is to introduce the enemies earlier than they are introduced in the MT (see Hossfeld and Zenger, *Psalms 3*, 285).

143. NRSV has *as for me*.

Artistic Unity

From a form-critical perspective, Gunkel classified this psalm as a "formless" mixed genre, which was "confusingly mixed together."[144] He was reticent about categorizing Ps 119 as exclusively an individual complaint song because it lacked the initial "*summons in the name of Yahweh*," even though he recognized that it uses the motifs of the individual complaint genre.[145] For Gunkel, the *Sitz im Leben* was the post-exilic liturgy.[146] Gunkel did believe, however, that the wisdom sayings found in the psalm—like sayings in all psalms—originally arose out of the context of a real life setting.[147]

Mowinckel understands Ps 119 to be a non-cultic psalm, but classified it as an individual psalm of lamentation.[148] He explains the numerous instances of the psalmist's own devotion to the law as motivations for the prayer. According to Mowinckel modern interpreters fail to understand mixed psalms because there is a "lack of consideration for this difference between Hebrew and modern ways of thinking and poetry and technique of composition."[149]

As is apparent, the mixture of genres in Psalm 119 presents a challenge to modern scholars who wish to classify it in a specific form-critical category, usually wisdom or lament. According to Allen the lament-orientated imperative and jussive petitions number forty-nine, whereas the number for Torah wisdom-orientated ones is twenty-nine.[150] Allen himself does not believe the hymn and wisdom elements can be subsumed under the genre of lament.[151] Neither does he see Psalm 119 functioning with a cultic purpose. Zenger concurs with a non-cultic setting and considers the psalm a work of Torah wisdom,[152] although "in terms of form criticism, Psalm 119 is a petition for rescue from manifold threats, or more precisely for rescue through YHWH's Torah."[153] Goulder on the other hand argues from internal evidence in the psalm that it was used in the cultic festival of Pentecost.[154]

---

144. Also included are motifs from the hymn, the thanksgiving song, wisdom poetry and the individual complaint song (Gunkel, *Introduction to Psalms*, 20, 305, 310).

145. Ibid., 153.

146. For Gunkel (Ibid., 330), around 500 B.C.E.

147. Ibid., 7–8.

148. Mowinckel, *Psalms, Vol 1.*, 78.

149. Mowinckel, *Psalms, Vol 2.*, 75.

150. Allen, *Psalms*, 181.

151. Ibid., 182.

152. Hossfeld and Zenger, *Psalms 3*, 263.

153. Ibid., 256.

154. Goulder, *Psalms of the Return*, 209.

The psalm is both "a prayer and instruction for his [the psalmist's] pupils."[155] Furthermore, "The insistent persecution theme fits better in the earlier part of the postexilic period."[156]

Despite the lack of consensus as to the form-classification and the setting, there are good grounds to suggest that the psalmist intended Psalm 119 to be understood as a prayer arising out of the experiences of a particular individual. In this regard, Eaton's criticism of Gunkel's assessment is *apropos*: "Gunkel does not consider the radial character, like spokes of a wheel, the unity being formed by the relation of each statement to the center in God."[157] The unity is reinforced by the poetic artistry behind the piece.

Psalm 119 is a carefully construed alphabetic psalm consisting of twenty-two sections of eight lines (distiches). Each section has lines beginning with the same letter, progressing through the twenty-two letters of the Hebrew alphabet. In addition there are only two verses (122, 132)[158] which do not mention a synonym for God's revealed word (*tôrâ* "torah," *dābār* "word," *'ēdût* "testimony," *mišpāṭ* "judgment," *ḥōq* "statute," *miṣwōṯ* "commandments," *'imrâ* "promise/word," *piqqûdîm* "precepts"). Furthermore, it cannot be coincidental that the term *Yahweh* occurs twenty-two times. Consistency is also achieved through the constant theme of suffering[159] in the psalm and the voice of the psalmist; each verse addresses Yahweh except vv. 1–3 and 115. Artistic unity does not of necessity imply the actual experiences of one individual as opposed to a literary anthology, but does suggest that the composer intended the psalm to be understood coherently.[160]

---

155. Ibid., 199.

156. Ibid., 207.

157. Eaton, *Psalms of the Way*, 32.

158. Verse 132 has *kᵉmišpāṭ* which is the relevant Hebrew word, although it is translated *as is your custom*.

159. The lament ethos of the psalm is reinforced by its similarity to Chapter 3 of Lamentations, the next largest alphabetic acrostic in the Bible. The content of Lamentations is generally understood to represent a lament over a fallen Jerusalem very soon after its destruction in the 6th century B.C.E. This form of poetry was thought fitting to portray the tumultuous events of the destruction of Jerusalem and its use during the exile would certainly not have been unreasonable.

160. Whether the psalm was composed as a literary anthology as suggested by Deissler (*Psalm 119*, 19–31), Levenson ("Sources of Torah," 563) and Allen (*Psalms*, 182–183) in my opinion cannot be answered for certain. Does a similarity in written expressions between Jeremiah and the psalmist (see Levenson, "Sources of Torah," 563) suggest literary dependency or speak of culturally-shared norms as means for expressing lament?

The Psalmist—A Member of the Early Post-exilic Community

Earlier commentators saw a single person who lay behind the artistry of Psalm 119. Delitzsch, basing his view on vv. 9, 99, and 110, saw the psalm as expressing the laments of a young man who was in prison during the Maccabean age.[161] He saw in the psalm a progression of the psalmist's thought through each of the successive strophes. Perowne, in the late nineteenth century, also viewed the psalm holistically, although Perowne disagreed with Delitzsch's understanding of vv. 9, 99, and 110 and in seeing a progression of thought in the arrangement.[162] Perowne believed that vv. 9, 99, and 110 represent the reflections of an older man looking back on his life.

Internal evidence in the Psalm suggests that the psalmist is most likely a member of the exilic community. Furthermore, indications in the text also point to an exilic composition. In verse 19 the psalmist refers to himself as a *gēr bāāreṣ* "an alien in the land," (v. 19); he does not have a permanent residence, but lives *beḇêṯ meḡûrāy* "wherever I make my home" (v. 54). We would not expect this language to express the sentiments of those who had returned to the land in the post-exilic restoration. But who in the exile would be important enough to become the object of the *slander*[163] of the *śārîm* "princes" (v. 23)? Or who would have the status to speak before *melāḵîm* "kings" (v. 46)? W.B. Soll has argued that the psalm was written in the exile, possibly by Jehoiachin.[164] In contrast, many scholars tend to see a post-exilic dating for the psalm.[165] The crux of this post-exilic argument depends on the definition of the term *torah* and its sequential relationship to other books such as Deuteronomy, Proverbs, Isaiah and Jeremiah. Further evidence of post-exilic composition is cited because of Aramaisms in the text, which is characteristic of late or post-biblical Hebrew.[166] However, if we assume that Ezra brought the Law with him when he returned with the exiles, we can assume that the Law was in circulation and in use by certain groups in the exilic community.[167] The Aramaisms in the text may be ex-

---

161. Delitzsch, *Psalms*, Vol. 3, 243, 245.
162. Perowne, *Book of Psalms*, 349.
163. NRSV—*plotting*
164. Soll, *Psalm 119*, 126–54.
165. Allen, *Psalms*, 183.
166. For a list of the Aramaisms see ibid., 183.
167. The dating of Ezra's journey to Jerusalem challenges scholars because it seemingly contradicts the dating of Nehemiah's stay in Jerusalem. See Grabbe (*Judaism from Cyrus*, 88–93) for a discussion of the various historical issues. I am assuming Ezra was a real person as described in the biblical accounts and that he first visited Jerusalem in the seventh year of Artaxerxes around 458 BCE.

plained as the result of later minor editorial changes.[168] A scribe might have replaced antiquated terms with more commonly used terms when the text was copied. Assuming the psalm was composed during the exile explains both the interest in the Law, which we know from Ezra (7:10) was a concern of certain exilic groups, and the overarching ethos of lament in the psalm. It is probably best to date the composition of Psalm 119 between the exile and the return of Ezra.[169]

Identifying the Enemies—A Weakness of the Form-Critical Approach

Positing the experiences of a single psalmist, whether according to the earlier patterns of seeing the psalm as the personal experience of a suffering individual or whether assuming the psalm was an anthological-literary composition composed in a cultic setting, does not simplify the identification of the enemies. Psalm 119 especially presents a problem for the majority of scholars who categorize the enemies in the Psalms from a form-critical perspective. Such a perspective sees the enemies divided into three groups according to whether the psalm can be classified as a communal lament, individual lament or royal psalm.[170] However, the mixed genres (lament, wisdom, hymn, thanksgiving), the length (176 verses) and the number of terms for enemies (6 identifiable groups) in Psalm 119 caution against the limitations of using only the form-critical approach.

The enemies can be divided into identifiable groups of persons: *śārîm* "princes" (vv. 23, 161); *mᵉlākîm* "kings" (v. 46); *zēdîm* "insolent" (vv. 21, 51, 69, 78, 85, 122);[171] *rᵉšāʿîm* "wicked" (vv. 53, 61, 95, 110, 119, 155); *ʾōyēḇ* "enemy" (v. 98), and *ṣar* "foe" (v. 139). Sometimes the enemy is also described using a participial form. At times this participial term refers to one of the identifiable groups of enemies and at other times it is uncertain. For example, in v. 21 the *zēdîm* are described by the participles *ʾărûrîm*[172] "accursed

---

168. Note, however, Dahood's (*Psalms III*, 173) comment relating to the numerous poetic usages that were not employed in the post-exilic period. Also see Waltke's (Waltke and Houston, *Psalms as Christian Worship*, 544) arguments for Ps 110 which caution against placing too much emphasis on using Aramaic forms to date texts.

169. Although a pre-exilic dating cannot be excluded either, see Dahood, *Psalms III*, 173.

170. Van Rooy, *Enemies in the Headings*, 41; Kraus, *Theology*, 125.

171. *zēdîm* occurs eight times in the Psalms and only five other times: Pr 21:24, Isa 13:11, Jer 43:2, Mal 3:15, Mal 3:19.

172. The *LXX* rendering of *ʾărûrîm* as a predicate adjective, ἐπικατάρατοι, which modifies v. 21b does not alter the fact that the *zēdîm* are the ones being referred to.

ones," and *haššōgîm* "who wander." However, in v. 42 the closest identifiable group to the *ḥōrpî* "those who taunt me" are the *mᵉlākîm* "kings" of v. 46. Positing that the two terms are the same group would be speculative.[173]

Another way to identify the enemy is according to their relationship to the law.[174] The *mᵉlākîm* (v. 46) are non-Israelite kings to whom the psalmist will speak of Yahweh's *ʿēdût* "testimonies." The *rᵉšāʿîm* "wicked" are described as those who *forsake your law* (vv. 53, 155). They are not only Israelites, but found all over the earth (v. 119). By means of comparison, the psalmist implies the *ʾōyēḇ* "enemies" (v. 98) do not have the *miṣwōṯ* "commandments," since the psalmist is made wiser than these enemies by means of the *miṣwōṯ*. In vv. 21 and 85 the *zēḏîm* "insolent" stray from the *miṣwōṯ* and flout the *tôrâ* respectively. The *ṣar* "foes" are those who forget Yahweh's *dāḇār* "words" (v. 139). There do not appear to be any implicit or explicit references in relation to the law for the *śārîm* "princes." In summary, then, there appear to be at least two different groups of enemies in Psalm 119, who can be grouped into those external to the nation and those internal. Even though this observation goes against seeing a unified enemy in the psalm, the totality of the experiences represented in the acrostic structure suggest that it might not be unreasonable to suggest the psalmist is dealing with various enemies.

The Perceived Suffering of the Psalmist—Diverse and Intense

In order to understand the meaning behind the response to adversity, we will first sketch a general picture from the psalm of the psalmist's suffering. After a general overview, we limit our investigation to several instances where the psalmist responds to adversity by appealing to the *Torah*. In the response we shall seek to understand the meaning behind the psalmist's use of *Torah* and the relationship it establishes between the psalmist, victim and Yahweh. We shall include in our picture of the general suffering of the psalmist any descriptions from any sources of the psalmist's distress including those originating from Yahweh, the psalmist because of his perspectives on Torah, and the enemies. Nevertheless, our main focus will be on the suffering caused by the moral evil of the enemies.

To begin with, the psalmist feels as if he has been *forsaken* (v. 8) by God. He is an *alien* (v. 19) without permanent abode (v. 54). He has not

---

173. The Masoretes pointed *ḥōrpî* as singular and *mᵉlākîm* as plural.

174. By law, I am referring to one of the eight synonyms mentioned above. Croft (*Identity of the Individual*, 43) suggests that in the Psalms the *rᵉšāʿîm* "wicked" are defined primarily in relation to God's judgment rather than by race."

been able practically to live up to the ideal of the law (vv. 4, 176), and so has experienced frustration. He sees God as the one who has afflicted him (v. 75). But it is unclear whether the psalmist means that God is responsible for all of his suffering portrayed in the psalm or whether there is a particular suffering that the psalmist believes that God is responsible for.

During the course of the psalm the psalmist mentions that he is *'ŏnî*, in "distress/misery," four times (vv. 50, 92, 153, 107). In verse 107 this is clarified with the adverbial modifier *'ad-mᵉ'ōd* "severely." He suffers from *mē'ōšeq 'ādām* "human oppression" (v. 134). His affliction is further described in the following ways: his soul clings to the dust (v. 25), his life melts from sorrow (v. 28), his soul languishes for salvation (v. 81), his eyes fail waiting for salvation (v. 82), he is a wineskin in smoke (v. 83), he has suffered for some time (v. 84), he has almost lost his life (v. 87), and trouble and anguish have come upon him (v. 143). At times his feelings are the result of his enemies' failures to keep Yahweh's law: *hot indignation seizes* him because the wicked forsake the law (v. 53). His eyes shed streams of tears because Yahweh's law is not kept (v. 136) and zeal consumes him because his foes (*ṣāray*) forget Yahweh's words (v. 139).

As for persecution identified as arising directly from the enemies, the *princes plot* against him[175] (v. 23) and *persecute him without cause* (v. 161). His *rōdēp* "persecutors" *are many* (v. 157); the *zēdîm* "insolent/arrogant" *utterly deride* him (v. 51), *smear him with lies* (v. 69), *subvert* [him] *with guile* (v. 78), *dig pits* to trap him (v. 85), and *oppress* him (v. 122). The *rᵉšā'îm* "wicked" *ensnare* him with cords (v. 61), *lie in wait* to destroy him (v. 95), and *set a snare* for him (v. 110). No description is given for what the *ōyᵉbîm* "enemies" have done, but the *ṣārîm* "foes" enrage him because they have forgotten Yahweh's laws (v. 139).

Dedication to Torah as a Response to Suffering.

In investigating the response of the psalmist there are several factors that can influence our understanding. First is the cause/effect relationship between the psalmist's statements of devotion to Yahweh's Torah[176] and his circumstances of adversity. Wisdom readings tend to emphasize the difference between the righteous and wicked using the technique of contrast. So, for example, verse 69, *The arrogant smear me with lies, but with my whole heart I keep your precepts*, in the wisdom tradition focuses on the contrast

---

175. Either translation *plot against* or *slander* may be acceptable, but if the psalmist is a member of the exile there would be no need for rulers to plot against him.

176. Including any synonyms.

between the psalmist's righteousness and the hostility of the *zēdîm* as a descriptive teaching tool. Or in the category of lament, this plea of devotion would function as part of a motivational prayer for Yahweh to act. But are there grounds to suggest that the psalmist's dedication to the Torah is a response to adversity? I believe the answer to be yes. The psalmist did not follow the Torah before his suffering,[177] but now he does (vv. 67, 71 and 75).[178] In other words, his affliction has been the means of motivating him to turn to the Torah. There is a discernible chronological progression then of the psalmist's experience in Psalm 119: the psalmist strayed[179] from the Torah before his suffering and now the psalmist seeks Yahweh's Torah during his suffering. The psalmist's resolute dedication to Torah as a response to his affliction stands behind an understanding of the psalmist and his responses. As Brueggemann noted, "To enter into the piety of this psalm we must break the stereotype of *retribution* regularly assigned here. It is not a psalm of bargaining, but a psalm of utter trust and submission."[180]

Another factor which influences how one interprets the responses of the psalmist to adversity is the hermeneutical key of the psalm. I suggest that the first three verses give the basis by which to understand the psalmist's use of Torah (or synonyms) when confronted with adversity. Structurally, the *'ašrê* "blessed" formula at the beginning of vv. 1 and 2 and the *'ap* "also" of v. 3 provide coherence for the unit.[181] Zenger divides this strophe, aleph (א), into two sections: vv. 1–4 and 5–8.[182] However, the shift in voice from third person in v. 3 to second person in v. 4 also serves to differentiate vv. 1–3. I propose that bicola 1a, 1b, 2a, 3a, 3b are metonyms for 2b which is the symmetrical center of vv. 1–3. Verse 1a speaks of *hahōlkîm* "those who walk" *bᵉtôrat yᵉhwāh* "in the Torah of Yahweh," and 3a states *hālākû* "they walk" *bidrākāyw* "in his ways." The parallelism and use of the term *hlk* suggest

---

177. In some way the psalmist sees God as responsible for his suffering (v. 75), although it is not clear the extent to which he sees God as responsible for the suffering he must endure at the hands of his enemies. However, it is clear through the tone and petitions of the psalm that he sees God's intervention as necessary for his rescue from his suffering.

178. Vv. 67 and 71 belong to the ט "taw" strophe and v. 75 belongs to the י "yod" strophe. Zenger (Hossfeld and Zenger, *Psalms 3*, 274–275) suggests a thematic link between the two.

179. The term for going astray *šōgēg* has connotations of being on a path of sin (Ibid., 273).

180. Brueggemann, *Message of the Psalms*, 41.

181. *'ašrê* finds its parallel as an introductory formula at the beginning of Psalm 1 which many scholars believe functions as a hermeneutical key for the whole Book of Psalms.

182. Hossfeld and Zenger, *Psalms 3*, 265.

equivalence between the two ideas. Likewise verses 1a, 2a and 3a are expressions of the same idea presented first positively, *completeness of way* (1a),[183] then as *those who keep his decrees/testimonies* (2a), and finally negatively as *they do no wrong*. In other words, these first six bicola are different ways of expressing the phrase *they seek him with their whole heart* (2b). As such they help the reader to understand the psalmist's expressions about Torah (1b), about sin (3a), and about walking in Yahweh's ways (1a and 3b as an *inclusio*) as expressions of his desire for the presence of Yahweh, epitomized in the last verse of the א "aleph" strophe: *I will observe your statutes; do not utterly forsake me* (v. 8).[184] Moreover, the term *lēḇ* "heart" in 2b, which defines the psalmist's intensity in his pursuit of Yahweh, with its phrasal variations, is a major theme in Ps 119, occurring more times than in any other chapter in the MT.[185] This theme is further reinforced at the beginning of Ps 119 in v. 5,[186] where the psalmist expresses his longing to be able to keep the *hukkîm* "statutes" of Yahweh and in the last verse, v. 176, where the psalmist has *gone astray like a lost sheep*, although he *does not forget your* [Yahweh's] *commandments* (176b). Further, the pursuing of the Torah as a means of seeking Yahweh is contrasted with the *zēdîm* who are described as *accursed ones who wander from your* [Yahweh's] *commands* (v. 21) and those under Yahweh's judgment are, *all who stray from your* [Yahweh's] *statutes* (v. 118).

The multifaceted meaning behind the use of the term Torah in Psalm 119 does not appear to be limited to this notion alone. P. J. Botha's study of the meaning of Torah in Pss 1, 37 and 119 and the book of Proverbs suggests that Torah functions as a metonym for true wisdom found in Proverbs, and also subsumed in the meaning of Torah is an understanding of the Promised Land.[187] The exhaustive nature of the repetitive mentioning of Torah in

---

183. NRSV has *blameless*. However, the Hebrew term has a positive nuance and is translated in English with a negative nuance in order to create a parallel with the idea of v. 3a.

184. If the chronological progression depicting the psalmist's suffering and his relationship to the law mentioned above is accepted, then the verbs may be translated into present or future. Translation of these verbs presents a perspective as to how one should understand the psalmist's devotion to Torah. It is also worth noting that many of the verbs used to express the relationship between the psalmist and Torah were used in other and earlier texts to describe the relationship between the Israelites and God (Hossfeld and Zenger, *Psalms 3*, 260).

185. Occurrence of *lēḇ* in Ps 119 (14 out of 176 verses); Deut 35 (9/35) and then Prov 15 (9/33). Psalms has 99 uses of the term *lēḇ* and Proverbs follows with 95 mentions. However, Proverbs has a greater concentration of usage when the number of verses is taken into consideration.

186. I am interpreting v. 4 as a *Janus* verse.

187. Botha, "Interpreting 'Torah,'"

Ps 119 without explicitly making reference to its content seems to support the fact that the theme is neither the nature nor the content of the Torah, but an individual who speaks of his relationship to Torah.[188] Furthermore, formulaic expressions are applied to Torah that are otherwise used only or mainly when addressing Yahweh.[189]

The psalmist's response to his adversity through his devotion to the Law is particularly clarified in v. 78 because here the psalmist responds to the *zēdîm* both by offering an imprecation *yēḇōšû zēdîm*, "may the insolent be put to shame" (v. 78a), and by *śîaḥ* "meditating" on Yahweh's *piqqûdîm* "precepts" (v. 78c). According to the psalmist both are valid responses.

The response of the psalmist in v. 78 is highlighted through the emphatic pronoun *'ănî* "I," *Let the arrogant be put to shame because they have subverted me with guile, but I will meditate on your precepts*. We can conclude that meditating on Yahweh's precepts and cursing his enemies are closely related for the psalmist. Meditation on Yahweh's law brings the psalmist into the *way of Yahweh* which is devoid of the *šeqer* "false/deceitful [ways]"[190] of the *zēdîm* (vv. 29, 104, 128 and 163). Imprecating against the enemies is the psalmist's way of calling on Yahweh to bring the psalmist's enemies in line with *the way of Yahweh*, which entails Yahweh's judgment (vv. 118). The psalmist loves Yahweh's decrees because (note the *lāḵēn* "therefore" at the beginning of v. 119b) Yahweh *discards*[191] *as dross all the wicked of the earth* (v. 119a). This understanding of Yahweh and his posture towards the *wicked* is reflected in the psalmist's own response, *Hot indignation seizes me because of the wicked, those who forsake your law* (v. 53; see also v. 139).

The psalmist is also resolute in his pursuit of the Torah while being persecuted. *The wicked lie in wait* to destroy the psalmist (v. 95a), but his response is to *consider your decrees* (v. 95); the wicked have set a snare to entrap him, but the psalmist has not strayed from Yahweh's precepts (v. 110). Even at his breaking point the psalmist continues to seek Yahweh's *precepts* (v. 87). It is his delight in Torah (v. 92a) which prevents him from perishing

---

188. Hossfeld and Zenger, *Psalms 3*, 256–257.

189. Ibid., 271. Zenger gives Ps 119:48 as an example, literally *I lift my hands to your commands*, but translated in the NRSV as *I revere your commandments*. He is basing his information on Y. Amir's (*Psalm 119*, 4–11) study, which is not available to me. N.T. Wright (*Case for the Psalms*, 113) makes the case that "the Temple theology that is so characteristic of the psalms had already developed in the direction of a Torah theology, in which the devout worshiper could be assured of God's presence and love in any geographical location."

190. *NIV* has "deceitful (ways)," which seems to be a more accurate reflection of the character of the *zēdîm*.

191. NRSV has *count as*

in his misery/affliction (v. 92b). In the midst of persecution by princes his heart is steadfast in the Law (vv. 23, 61).

If we assume that the psalmist's posture towards the Law is an actual response to the injustices that he has faced we can conclude several things. First, his perusal of the Law subsumes in it the notion that those who are far from the Law (the enemies) will experience Yahweh's judgment. Why would delight (v. 92) come to the psalmist unless Yahweh were to deliver him, that is, the psalmist delights in the Law because contained therein is the notion that Yahweh is just in punishing the wicked and exonerating the righteous. We can infer in the psalmist's responses that subsumed under the Law is the notion of Yahweh's justice.

Then again the connection can be further clarified. Curses are the tool of the powerless, so it is also in a state of powerlessness that the psalmist uses dedication to the Law as his response. Curses as a means of seeking justice turn outward, whereas dedication to the Law forces the psalmist to turn towards Yahweh. Nevertheless, both appeal to Yahweh. One asks for justice to be brought according to the constraints of the Law. The other turns to the aspect of Yahweh's presence, which guarantees justice. Merely seeing the psalmist's responses as expressions of steadfastness or bargaining pleas limits the range of meanings inherent in Torah's use in Ps 119. As a response to persecution the people understood that the Law must maintain a central place in their response to persecution. This is because the Law ensured with it an understanding of Yahweh's presence. In turn Yahweh's presence was a guarantee of victory over one's enemies. Undoubtedly, there is an implied exilic theology here relating to the king and the keeping of the Law.[192] More pertinent to our discussion, though, the Law is seen for what it is really meant to be and that is a guarantee of Yahweh's presence, which brings forth justice.

Conclusion of the Exegesis

In summary, Psalm 119 allowed the community to place together a renewed understanding of the Law coupled with lament. In other words, it allowed the community to start to redefine its identity, to come to grips with understanding the exile as a failure to keep the Law in the context of the new situation of suffering that exists in the post-exilic community. One aspect of that suffering in particular was the suffering caused by the persecution of enemies. One important response was walking in the way of Torah, a

---

192. Was there a particular message that the editor was trying to convey by placing a kingship psalm 118 before Ps 119 (so Grant, *King as Exemplar*, 240–251)?

guarantee for the presence of Yahweh, which would eventually bring about the rectification of all injustice.

A SELECT HISTORICAL SURVEY OF THE INTERPRETATION OF PSALM 119

We will investigate in this section what the commentators have to say about the suffering of the psalmist and his response to that suffering. In particular, in Psalm 119 there are several areas of note. As was mentioned above, the length of Ps 119 presents a challenge in identifying the enemies. How were the enemies identified by the commentators? Furthermore, given that the psalm talks about the psalmist's relationship to the Law, but not necessarily its content,[193] what was it the psalmist perceived in his meditation on the Law? And hence, what was the psalmist's motivation for pursuing the Law? Further, what did the commentators notice about how the psalmist understood justice and judgment from his meditation on the Law?

Psalm 119 and an Early Post-Exilic Ethos[194]

The formulaic language in Psalm 119 makes identification of the enemies of the post-exilic community speculative.[195] Nevertheless a general sense of the scope of meaning the terms may have had can come from the picture given of those who opposed the restoration project. The biblical picture of the restoration of the temple with cultic worship and the reestablishment of Jerusalem is that the post-exilic community met with resistance from the time of Cyrus (559–530 BCE) until the time of Darius (423–404 BCE).[196] The inhabitants of the land, along with bribed officials (Ezra 4:4–5), opposed the reconstitution of Jerusalem as an independently functioning district in the time of Cyrus. In the time of Ahasuerus (Xerxes, 486–465 BCE) the

---

193. Ps 119 does not focus on the nature or content of the Torah but on an individual who speaks of his relationship with Torah (Hossfeld and Zenger, *Psalms 3*, 271; Eaton, "Proposals in Psalms," 557; *et al.*).

194. The following identification of the enemies in the post-exilic period will form a general background for Ps 119 and the other psalms in this study, so it will not be reproduced for each psalm.

195. I am assuming the biblical dating of Ezra's arrival in Jerusalem (c. 538 BCE). For a range of the historical issues involved see Grabbe, *Judaism from Cyrus*, 88–93; for a canonical perspective see Childs, *Introduction*, 624–638.

196. Interestingly the biblical portrayal of the Persian kings is sympathetic to the plight of the post-exilic community, but the kings are uninformed regarding Cyrus' decree (Ezra 4:6 to 6:12).

people of the land wrote an accusation against the inhabitants of Judah and Jerusalem (Ezra 4:6).[197] In the reign of Artaxerxes I (464–424 BCE) "Rehum the royal deputy, Shimshai the scribe, and the rest of their associates, the judges, the envoys, the officials, the Persians, the people of Erech, the Babylonians, the people of Susa, that is, the Elamites" (Ezra 4:9) all appealed to have the restoration stopped. Furthermore, when Sanballat and Tobiah and the Arabs (led by Gesham) and the Ammonites and the Ashdodites heard that the repairing of the walls of Jerusalem was going forward and the gaps were beginning to be closed, they were very angry, and all plotted together to come and fight against Jerusalem (Neh 2:19). The enemies were also the Jewish kin themselves who practiced unjust servitude (Neh 5:1–5). Religious leaders are also depicted as the enemies of the restoration, the prophet Shemaiah (Neh 6:12) and the prophetess Noadiah (Neh 6:14) and priests (Eliahsab *et al.*, Neh 13:4, 28). In the reign of Darius, Tattenai the governor of the province "beyond the River" and Shethar-bozenai and their associates (Ezra 5:3) acted against Nehemiah's mission to build the wall.

The exact circumstances of how the psalm was used in the post-exilic restoration must remain speculative. Croft assumes that the length of the psalm precluded it from cultic use. Yet Ezra himself gave a reading of the law to all the people, who attentively listened, from "daybreak until noon" (Ezra 8:3).[198] As was pointed out in the exegesis, the psalm represents the lament of a man of standing, who else would have an audience of *princes* and *kings*. As such, it would have easily had credibility to be adopted into the liturgical reforms of the post-exilic community at the time of the restoration. The importance and support given to the reforms of Ezra (see the letter from Artaxerxes in Ezra 7:11–28) made clear that the identity of the restored community was to be associated with the implementation of the Law. Furthermore, the Law being brought to Jerusalem (Ezra 7) after the dedication of the temple (Ezra 6:13–18),[199] Yahweh's dwelling place, is in itself suggestive of the close relationship which existed between the Law and Yahweh's presence. Finally, the circumstances for lament closely coupled with rededication to Torah thoroughly fit the general ethos of the post-exilic restoration quite well.

---

197. Perhaps the lack of mention of Ahasuerus in Ezra 6:14 means that he was unsupportive?

198. As with later Jewish and Christian uses, it may have been divided into smaller units and used over a successive time frame.

199. As given in the biblical narrative.

Psalm 119 in the New Testament—The Law as a Window into the Inseparability of Yahweh's Character and Judgement

In investigating the psalmist's meditation on the "law" from a NT perspective I will reserve my comments to the verbal parallels with Ps 119 in the NT and some general perceptions of the law held by Jesus and Paul.

According to the Greek New Testament, Psalm 119 is not quoted in the NT, but it is alluded to or contains a verbal parallel five times (119:46[200] in Rom 1:16; 119:137 in Rev 16:5,7 and 19:2; 119:165 in 1 Jn 2:10).[201] In the first verbal parallel the term *statutes* from the psalms is syntactically equivalent to the term *gospel* in Romans. The implication from the collation of each term with not being ashamed (*bôš*, Ps 119:46; ἐπαισχύνομαι, Rom 1:16) is the utter trustworthiness which the psalmist and Paul attribute to God in how he has revealed himself. The point of reference for both is their unsympathetic audience.

The context for the second parallel (119:137) with its three parallels in Revelation suggests that God's judgments of wrath on the earth are just. The term in the MT is *mišpāṭîm* (NRSV: *judgments*; NIV: *laws*). However, when used to describe God's punishing acts, the term carries the notion of righting wrongs.[202] The terms in the Revelation passages (16:5 and 19:2)[203] are from the verb κρίνω "to judge," which is used nine times in the book of Revelation and here emphasizes the punishment which lies beyond the divine verdict.[204] In Ps 119:137 Yahweh is *ṣaddîq* "righteous" and his *mišpāṭîm* "judgments" are *yāšār* "right." In Rev 16:5 the Holy One is δίκαιος "righteous" (NRSV: *just*) *because* (ὅτι) he has judged. In Rev 16:7 the Lord God Almighty's *judgments are true and just* (ἀληθιναὶ καὶ δίκαιαι αἱ κρίσεις σου). In Rev 19:2 God's judgments are also *true and just* (ἀληθιναὶ καὶ δίκαιαι αἱ κρίσεις αὐτοῦ). In Revelation, then, we have the notion that God is righteous because he judges and that his judgments are just and true. In Ps 119:37 we have both ideas—that Yahweh is righteous and that his judgments are right. Depending on how strongly a case can be made for the connection between the passages, the idea of Yahweh's self-disclosure in the law as righteous is inextricably linked to the nature and actualization of his judgments upon

---

200. Also connected through the act of testifying before kings in Mt 10:18 and Acts 26:1–2.
201. *GNT*, 906.
202. Waltke and Houston, *Psalms as Christian Worship*, 511.
203. The term used for judgment in Rev 16:7 is from the noun form, κρισις.
204. *BAGD*, s.v. κρίνω 4b, 452.

the earth, which are *true* and *just*. Yahweh's character and his judgments become inseparable.

The connection between Ps 119:165 and 1 Jn 2:10 relates in verbal parallel those *who love your law* (119:165a) with *whoever loves his brother* (1 Jn 2:10).[205] In the psalm passage nothing can make them *miḵšôl* "stumble" and in Revelation there is *no cause for stumbling* (σκάνδαλον, 1 Jn 2:10; Ps 119:165 *LXX*). Furthermore, according to the parallel there is a connection between *great peace* (119:165) and *living in the light* (1 Jn 2:10). Moyise suggests that the similar use of the phrases in 119:65 and 1 Jn 2:10 is no more than a similarity in the use of biblical language.[206] However, this third parallel which relates the love of one's brother with the love of the Law resulting in a perfect life (i.e., σκάνδαλον and *miḵšôl* free) echoes Ps 119:1–3 which also expresses the same idea of a fault-free life. Furthermore, Ps 119:2 describes the relational nature of the Law by expressing the same idea positively as those who seek Yahweh with their whole hearts.

It will be worthwhile making some general comments about the Law[207] as it was understood by Jesus and Paul. First, both Jesus and Paul are not ambiguous about the central role of the Law as part of divine revelation, but challenge a misuse or misunderstanding of the Law. Of particular importance are Jesus' statements where he equates the fulfillment of the Law and prophets with himself (Mt 5:17–18; Lk 24:27; Jn 5:39, 46). His criticism of the Pharisees and teachers of the Law is that they misinterpret the Law (Mt 23:23–24) and burden others with their misinterpretation of the Law (Lk 11:52; Mt 23:13).

Paul writes about the Law not from the perspective of a first-century Jew under the Law or as a Jewish Rabbi, but as one whose whole understanding of the Law had been transformed by his Damascus Road experience. His general understanding was that the Law "revealed the will of God and showed what a right relationship with God was; but Israel failed to attain to that goal because they misused the law by making it a means of attaining righteousness by their own works instead of through faith (Rom 9:32)."[208] Important for Paul was the notion that the promise to Abraham (Galatians 3 and Romans 4) had preceded the giving of the Law and so even

---

205. The Law itself has the notion of love for neighbor (Lev 19:18).

206. Moyise, *Later New Testament*, 5.8.2.

207. According to Ladd (*Theology of the New Testament*, 547–548), the Torah is not the same as the Greek term νόμος which "is fundamentally 'custom' hardening into what we call 'law' and is human in perspective."

208. Ibid., 539.

before the time of Christ had defined the relationship of the Law to that of the covenant.[209]

Psalm 119 in the Ante-Nicene and Post-Nicene Fathers

Suffering in Psalm 119—Encouragement in the Midst of Suffering

For some of the commentators the term 'ašrê (*LXX* and NT: μακάριος) which begins verses 1 and 2 provides a key for interpreting the psalm. So Cyprian (fl. 248–258)[210] when writing about the benefits of martyrdom quotes Ps 119:1–2 alongside Mt 5:10. The suffering in Ps 119 is connected to the suffering of following Jesus from the connection with the term "blessed" also found in the Sermon on the Mount (Mt 5:10) where "the Lord in the Gospel, Himself the avenger of our persecution and the rewarder of our suffering, says: 'Blessed are they who suffer persecution for righteousness' sake, for theirs is the kingdom of heaven.'"[211] The *blessedness* of those who are undefiled, walk in the way of the Lord, and search his testimonies is used to describe those who keep themselves faithful after the manner of Paul (2 Tim 4:7,8; Rom 8:16, 17).[212] Psalm 119:1 and 2 provide motivation to be faithful "for the righteous and for martyrs after the conflicts and sufferings of this present time."[213]

The overall understanding seems to imply that the suffering has a purpose in God's scheme. Hilary of Poitiers interprets the psalmist's reference in Ps 119:50 to "his humility"[214] as the spurning, mocking, vexing by injustices and being dishonored by insults.[215] However, the second part of the verse responds that "his soul, renewed by the utterances of God, contains within it, so to say, the nourishment of eternal life." Ambrose (c. 333–397) interprets Ps 119:136, *Streams of tears flow from my eyes; for your law is not obeyed* as relating to the common experience of personal penitence which all saints have.[216]

---

209. See ibid., 550–552.

210. The fact that Cyprian, bishop of Carthage, would go on to martyrdom makes this insight remarkable in itself.

211. Cyprian, "Treatises of Cyprian," 506.

212. Ibid., 539.

213. Ibid., 506.

214. NRSV: suffering

215. Hilary of Poitiers, "Homily on Psalm 118," 322.

216. Ambrose, "Two Books Concerning Repentance," 357. Interestingly, Ambrose applies Ps 119:46, *I will speak of your statutes before kings and not be put to shame*, to his successful attempt to persuade emperor Theodosius that his decision to allow the

In contrast, the Antiochene, John Chrysostom, linked the "blessed" formula in 119:1 with other scripture containing the formula (including Ps 1:1, 94:12, 2:13, 33:12, 112:1 and Sirach 14:2) with the beatitudes in Mt 5:3–10 as part of his argument that hostilities, calumnies, contempt, disgrace, and torments, and all things without exception will be as pleasurable as riches for the person who has taken hold of virtue.[217] Chrysostom interprets Ps 119:71 to mean that tribulation is profitable for the saints so that they may exercise moderation and lowliness and not become puffed up by their miracles and good works.[218] He cites Paul as saying the same thing in 2 Cor 12:2, 4, 7.

The Psalmist's Meditation on the Law—Spiritual Benefits for Believers

There is an understanding that the meaning of "the way" in Ps 119:1 goes beyond a pathway marked out by written stipulations. Ignatius (c. 35–107/112) in his epistle to Ephesians equates the "way" in Ps 119:1 with Jesus' own declaration as the exclusive way to the Father in Jn 14:6.[219] Similarly, Athanasius (295–373) in his discourse against the Arians, links the expression *blessed are the undefiled in the Way* (119:1) with Mt 5:8, "Blessed are the pure in heart," and then further links the term *way* with Jesus' own claim in John's Gospel to be "the way."[220] The "blessedness" then is being able to understand the true nature of Christ. Ambrose links one's relationship to God closely to his precepts. That is, Ambrose equates Isa 54:17 with Ps 119:57 and v. 111. In doing so he equates "God is my inheritance" with *I have become an heir of your precepts*.[221]

Bede (c. 672/673–735)[222] takes an existential view towards the "blessed" formulas in vv. 1 and 2. Based on Jesus' saying, "you will be blessed if you do these things" (μακάριοί, Jn 13:17), he equates human happiness with doing the heavenly commands and not just knowing them. This is summarized in

---

restoration of a burnt Jewish synagogue would be perilous ("Letter 40," 440).

217. John Chrysostom, "Homily XIII," 462.
218. John Chrysostom, "Homilies on the Statutes," 337.
219. Ignatius, "Epistle of Ignatius," 53.
220. Athanasius, "Discourse Against the Arians," 314.
221. Ambrose, "Letter 82," 322.
222. Bede falls into the chronological category of Augustine and Medieval exegesis, but is included here.

the phrase "Blessed are they who search his testimonies and seek him with their whole heart."[223]

In Origen, Jerome, and Chrysostom's reflections on Psalm 119, there is inherent in meditating on the Law a sense of needing the aid of the Holy Spirit. Origen (fl. 200–254) interpreted Ps 119:18 as the basis for understanding "when Moses is read" since the Law as the written OT scripture is shrouded in mysteries.[224] For Origen this involved entreating the Holy Spirit to remove the darkness that obscures the vision of one's heart, which has been stained by sin.[225] Jerome, quoting Rom 7:14, insists that "'the law is spiritual', and a revelation is needed to enable us to comprehend it and, when God uncovers his face, to behold his Glory."[226] Chrysostom also recognized, on the basis of Ps 119:18, that the way to approach the scriptures was meditatively with "prudent reflection in order to understand God's word," and to seek for wisdom more than silver or gold.[227]

Psalm 119 in Augustine

Psalm 119 (118) was the last psalm on which Augustine expounded; he did this by sermon and dictation.[228] The reason for putting off this work was because of the profundity of Psalm 119 rather than its length.[229] Of importance in this investigation will be Augustine's understanding of the psalmist's meditation on the Law in Ps 119.

The Enemies and Different Types of Suffering

Some brief comments about how Augustine viewed the enemies and the suffering of the psalmist in Ps 119 will be useful. In v. 61 Augustine identifies the enemies as the devil, his angels and people.[230] However, Augustine's practical emphasis is evident. In 119:53 those who forsake the law are the large number of people joining the Church who show no signs of true faith

223. Bede, "Homilies on the Gospels," 314.
224. Origen, "Homilies on Genesis," 315.
225. Ibid.
226. Ibid.
227. John Chrysostom, "Homilies on the Gospel of John," 316.
228. Fiedrowicz, "Introduction," 342–496.
229. Augustine's work consists of 32 expositions. In addition to the *Enarrationes in Psalmos* (Expositions of the Psalms) he has 31 sermons or verses on the psalms. Furthermore, his *Confessions* has been described as an amplified Psalter (Ibid., 13).
230. Augustine, "Exposition," 415.

and who are "bad people."²³¹ The enemies of v. 98 are those who by their own efforts strive to establish a righteousness which, though conformed to God's law, is in essence their own.²³² The enemies show their hostility towards the psalmist in v. 139 for the reason that the psalmist wanted them to love God.²³³

Augustine gives the psalmist's suffering several different interpretations. In v. 67 Augustine interprets the affliction which the psalmist had as "best understood of the humiliation suffered by Adam, in whom the entire human creation was corrupted at its root and was subjected to futility."²³⁴ The psalmist's petition "Do not utterly forsake me" is interpreted as the Church who is praying this and it most likely refers to God in a sense abandoning the world because of its sins.²³⁵

The suffering of the psalmist is also linked to martyrdom in the Church.²³⁶ For example, in v. 107 Augustine interprets the psalmist's suffering for his oath (v. 106) and decision to observe the judgments of God's justice in this light.²³⁷ Nevertheless, there is a strong sense that God is in some way behind the suffering. In v. 71 the reason for the psalmist being humbled is in order that he would seek the Lord's justifying acts.²³⁸ Augustine links Ps 119:71 with Romans 8:28, seeing that God is purposeful and that "suffering is meant to jar the calm of treacherous prosperity which prevents the soul from pursuing the haven of true and certain safety."²³⁹ Persecution from the enemies is also attributed to the psalmist's self-deception in vv. 169 and 170. Through parallelism Augustine notes that "By being given understanding he is delivered, because when he did not understand he was self-deceived."²⁴⁰

---

231. Ibid., 322. In the context of the Donatist controversy.
232. Ibid., 444.
233. Ibid., 477.
234. Ibid., 421.
235. Ibid., 358.
236. The influence of the liturgical calendar and the practical nature of Augustine's sermons are reflected in his interpretation of the psalmist's persecution. In particular, the liturgical year is seen in Augustine's interpretation of the Psalms at the vigils and feast days of African martyrs, although Psalm 119 (118) is not listed as one of the seventeen expositions devoted to these occasions. It is also suggested that his endeavor to enhance these festivals was to form a polemic against the Donatists' cult of martyrs (Fiedrowicz, "Introduction," 17).
237. Augustine, "Exposition," 452.
238. Ibid., 412.
239. Augustine, "Letters of St. Augustine," 469.
240. Augustine, "Exposition, 493.

Meditating as a Response to Adversity—Knowing and Observing the Law as a Just Response

Augustine's understanding of the notions of the relational nature of the law and the concepts of justice and judgment as they pertain to Ps 119 is relevant to this study. In v. 119 Augustine attempts to explain how Paul's teaching on the law can be reconciled with the psalmist's understanding of the law in Ps 119. He understands the law as the Mosaic Law[241] but also recognizes a natural law for Jew and Gentile,[242] which was a law through the bonds of original sin.[243] Furthermore, "Not only does law bear witness to the justice of God to be revealed outside the law; it also turns those who know the law into law-breakers, to such a point that the letter is death-dealing."[244] According to Augustine the psalmist's statement "I have loved your testimonies" is because the testimonies tell of God's grace: "The function of the law is to send us Grace."[245] For Augustine, Jesus liberates the Christian from the thralldom of the law and in this way one can be without sin, that is, one can keep God's commands with the help of God.[246] However, Augustine believed that no one could be beyond praying the phrase "Forgive us our trespasses" (Mt 6:12), which is what the Pelagians opposed.[247] Augustine also understood the law to contain in it the notion of faith. Augustine interprets the *law* in the psalmist's request for God to be merciful according to his law (v. 29) as the law of faith as Paul uses the term in Rom 3:27.[248]

The relational nature of the law is clear for Augustine since true study of God's testimonies leads one to God.[249] In vv. 1, 2 and 3, "to search the Lord's testimonies carefully, seeking him with one's whole heart is the same thing as to be undefiled in the way and to walk in the law of the Lord."[250] The psalmist is able to love the commandments (v. 47) through the power of the Holy Spirit.[251] So it is God who not only is the one to be pursued, but aids

---

241. Ibid., 460.
242. Ibid., 462.
243. Ibid., 463.
244. Ibid.; 2 Cor 3:6.
245. Ibid.
246. Augustine, "Treatise on the Merits," 47.
247. Augustine, "Sermon on the Mount," 12.
248. Augustine, "Exposition," 385.
249. Ibid., 345.
250. Ibid., 344.
251. Ibid., 405.

in his own pursuit.²⁵² Furthermore, Augustine equates "in the way of God's testimonies" (*in via testimoniorum tuorum*) of v. 14 with Christ "in whom are hidden all the treasures of wisdom and knowledge" (Col 2:3).²⁵³ In v. 57, Augustine comments that the Lord is the portion of everyone who keeps his law,²⁵⁴ and from v. 163, the lovers of God's law are the lovers of God.²⁵⁵ In his interpretation of v. 34, Augustine suggests that when someone studies the law and obtains its lofty precepts on which the whole of it depends, it must mean that he loves God with all his heart and his neighbour as himself (Mt 22:37–40) because "on these two commandments depend the whole law and the prophets."²⁵⁶

For Augustine the psalmist's pursuit of the law convinces the psalmist of God's justice and judgment. Augustine defines the Latin term *iustificationes* as just actions performed with God's help, whereas he defines *iudicia* as the just sentences he pronounces.²⁵⁷ For example, the term *ḥuqqîm* (NRSV: statutes) is found in the *LXX* 119:5 as δικαίωμα²⁵⁸ which is taken into Latin by Augustine as *iustificationes*. So the English translation of v. 5 and 6 is "O that my ways may be directed toward observing your *ways of justice*! Then I shall not be put to shame, if I look carefully into all your statutes."²⁵⁹ For Augustine, "Ways of justice are not statements about justice but just deeds, the works performed by just people in obedience to God's commandments.²⁶⁰ They are said to be God's ways of justice because, although it is we who perform these actions, we can do so only by God's gift."

This theme of putting the commands into practice being of utmost importance is found throughout the composition at vv. 6, 12, 15, 34, 71, 135 and 145. God's ways of justice are just actions which can also be defined as righteous deeds.²⁶¹ For Augustine the purpose of performing the works prescribed in the law is a love of justice and not fear of punishment and this is the way of God's commands.²⁶² Furthermore, God's ways of justice can be

252. See also Augustine's (Ibid., 356, 472–473) comments at vv. 5 and 133.
253. Ibid., 365.
254. Ibid., 414.
255. Ibid., 489.
256. Ibid., 390.
257. Ibid., 355.
258. δικαίωμα is derived from δικαιόω which means "to act justly" (Louw and Nida, s.v. δικαίωμα, 33.334).
259. Augustine, "Exposition," 355. The *LXX* has τὰς ἐντολάς σου "your commandments" (*miṣwōṯ*) while the English translation of Augustine's Latin text is "your statutes."
260. Ibid., 363.
261. Ibid., 374.
262. Ibid., 388.

described as absent when they are known but not observed.²⁶³ From v. 26, it is only a person who acts justly who can be said to know justice.²⁶⁴

The psalmist's understanding of judgment is closely related to his understanding of the concept of justice. In v. 121 Augustine comments, "he [the psalmist] takes it for granted that it can only be called judgment if it is just. If unjust it is not judgment."²⁶⁵ Furthermore, for Augustine judgment is the mode of operation of the virtue of justice.²⁶⁶ In v. 43, Augustine sees the "judgments"²⁶⁷ of God towards the psalmist as his discipline. So the psalmist hopes in God's "judgment" (MT: mišpāṭ; LXX: κρίμα; Vul: iudiciis). However, God's judgments are also those pronouncements whereby he judges the world, both now and at the end of time.²⁶⁸ Yet he separates a time of mercy and judgment, with the present being the time for repentance and not judgment. Augustine interprets v. 113 to mean "what he [the psalmist] hates in unjust persons is not their nature, which makes them human, but the iniquity that makes them enemies of the law he loves."²⁶⁹ In 119:52 the psalmist takes comfort in God's justice, to which Augustine suggests that through judgments on the vessels of wrath God reveals the riches of his glory on the vessels appointed for mercy.²⁷⁰

Finally, Augustine provides some comments on the dynamic which is occurring when the psalmist meditates on the Law as a response to persecution. He interprets the actions of the psalmist in v. 23 who meditates on the Law as a response to persecution as a means of repaying evil with good, as defined by the next verse. Augustine intimates that the Church is praying this psalm and the testimonies are the acts of martyrdom (note the LXX term μαρτύριον; the MT has 'ēḏûṯ, which is translated testimonies by the NRSV). In this way the martyrs are rendering good for evil.²⁷¹

In v. 78, Augustine comments that the psalmist's meditation on the Law is a fostering of love, which will never grow cold regardless of the sinfulness of those around him.²⁷² One can only truly know the Law if one

---

263. Ibid., 376.
264. Ibid., 384.
265. Ibid., 466.
266. Ibid., 466–467.
267. Most English translations do not translate the MT mišpāṭ in v. 43 with the sense of judgment.
268. Ibid., 363.
269. Ibid., 455.
270. Ibid., 409.
271. Ibid., 380, 381.
272. Ibid., 431–432.

lives in accordance with God's ways of justice. The result is that love is born when a person finds God's ways of justice delightful.[273] Furthermore, in v. 92 Augustine interprets the law as the law of faith: "not an idle faith but the faith that is active through love" and "in response to such faith believers receive the grace that strengthens them in temporal troubles."[274] Furthermore, "teach me the ways of your justice" (*iustificationes*, v. 64) is growing in the knowledge of the grace of Christ.[275] Indeed in v. 40 God's justice (*LXX*: τῇ δικαιοσύνῃ σου; "your righteousness") is Christ.[276] God's law will be sought without end because God's law is his truth (vv. 119, 142).[277] Further, the psalmist's meditation is in itself a keeping of the law.

Psalm 119 in the Reformers

Calvin

Sources of Adversity—David as the Psalmist

Calvin, in general, recognizes David as the psalmist and sees in the events of David's life a correlation with the events in the psalm (e.g., vv. 54, 176). Calvin does not always make a direct connection, but his references to David intimate that this is the background he has in mind for the historical understanding of the psalm. Calvin does note that the sorrows of the psalmist (v. 83) must have been intense in severity and duration.[278]

Behind the psalmist's adversity lie two different sources. The wicked despise the psalmist because of his true godliness and observance of the law (v. 141).[279] But also behind these adversaries is the work of Satan. So in v. 11, Calvin suggests that the remedy to protect us from Satan is to have God's law deeply seated in our hearts.[280] In v. 35 Satan is seen as the enemy with the battle ground being the Christian life;[281] see also Calvin's comments on

---

273. Ibid., 422.
274. Ibid., 440.
275. Ibid., 417.
276. Ibid., 398.
277. Ibid.
278. *Commentary*, Vol. 4, 463.
279. Calvin, *Commentary*, Vol. 5, 20.
280. Calvin, *Commentary*, Vol. 4, 409.
281. Ibid., 426.

vv. 35, 43, 173). Satan never fails to place snares in the way of Christians (vv. 60, 69).[282]

At other times God is seen as the adversary. For Calvin, in v. 39 it is possible that the reproach originates from the calumniators or from God himself.[283] Calvin understands that God has brought adversity to the psalmist in order to bring grace. So in v. 67 we never yield obedience to God until we are compelled by his chastisements, which Calvin gives in more detail as poverty, shame, illness, domestic distress or painful labours.[284] Again in v. 71 we only submit to God when he "softens our natural hardness by the strokes of a hammer."[285] For Calvin (v. 153) God stands behind the adversity in some mysterious way: "we wrestle against temptations and seek him even when he seems purposely to drive us away."[286] The world is governed by the secret providence of God (v. 155).[287]

MEDITATION ON THE LAW AS A RESPONSE TO ADVERSITY— SUCCOURING THE BELIEVER

The Holy Spirit's aid is essential in understanding the true nature of the law. For Calvin this stood in contrast with the "papist" interpretation which suggested that "the saints, of their own free will, anticipated the grace of the Holy Spirit, and afterwards were favored with his aid."[288] Hence, an important theme in Calvin's exposition is that the only way for a person to understand the true nature of the law is to be completely dependent on the Spirit of God (see Calvin's comments at vv. 19, 26, 29, 33, 34, 64, 73, 102, 112, 125 and 133).

At the beginning of his exposition Calvin defines each of the synonyms for the term law, defining each term as signifying a different aspect of the promulgation of the law of God.[289] For Calvin (v. 18) the content of the law which stands behind the psalmist's meditation includes not only the Ten Commandments but "the covenant of eternal salvation with all its provisions, which God has made," and since Christ is the end of the law

---

282. Ibid., 445, 453.
283. Ibid., 429.
284. Ibid., 451. Calvin gives Jer 31:18 as a cross reference.
285. Ibid., 454.
286. Calvin, *Commentary*, Vol. 5, 30.
287. Ibid., 31.
288. Calvin, *Commentary*, Vol. 4, 408.
289. Ibid., 401.

(Colossians 2:3, Romans 10:4) the law contains sublime mysteries.[290] In v. 103 Calvin responds to what Paul says in 1 Cor 3:9, that the law strikes fear in men, by intimating that the psalmist can delight in the law because he is not thinking of the dead letter which kills those who read it, but the whole doctrine of the law, the chief part of which is the free covenant of salvation.[291] In other words, the psalmist is not opposing the law to the gospel. Furthermore, knowledge of the law is not just a head knowledge, but one that penetrates to the heart of a person (v. 11)[292] and issues itself in a willing obedience (v. 32)[293] from a pure heart (v. 80).[294] And from the coupling of vv. 153 and 154, Calvin understands the keeping of the law is to show that he is a servant of God not to insist that "God pay him wage for his service" (see also Calvin's comments at v. 160).[295]

With this in mind, we can understand how Calvin understood the benefits which the psalmist gained by his meditation on the law of God especially during times of adversity. Meditating on the law was a primary means of succoring the psalmist. That is, the word, through its insistence on the notions that God is just, that his righteousness lasts forever, and that he will protect his people, was meant to provide comfort (see Calvin's comments at vv. 28, 50, 142, 143, 150 and 165). Calvin notes that God's promise inspires us with courage in sorrow and distress (v. 107).[296] Another function of the psalmist's meditation on the law is to encourage Christians to bear up under their struggles, even when God does not seem to be acting to relieve them (v. 87).[297] Still another function of the psalmist's example of continuing to love the law when exposed "as prey to the ungodly" was to show by example true piety (v. 61).[298]

Furthermore, since contained in the law is true righteousness, meditating on the law keeps the psalmist from relying on worldly wisdom, including perverse counsel (v. 95).[299] For Calvin there was a danger for people to follow ungodly counsel when assailed by the wicked. The word of God was also a means to prevent the psalmist from following his own judgment

---

290. Ibid., 413–414.
291. Ibid., 477. See also Calvin's similar description of the law in vv. 143 and 168.
292. Ibid., 409.
293. Ibid., 423.
294. Ibid., 460.
295. Calvin, *Commentary*, Vol. 5, 30.
296. Calvin, *Commentary*, Vol. 4, 481.
297. Ibid., 466.
298. Ibid., 447.
299. Ibid., 472.

(v. 24),³⁰⁰ or acting in an unjust way to repay evil for evil (v. 121).³⁰¹ Under adversity it is difficult to persevere in integrity, and "we rather begin to howl among the wolves," but "whoever is persuaded that God will be his deliverer and who pillars and supports his mind on the divine promises, will endeavor also to overcome evil with good" (v. 157).³⁰²

For the psalmist (vv. 92, 95), there was "no other experience and no other remedy for adversity, but our reposing on the word of God, and our embracing the grace and the assurance of our salvation which are offered in it."³⁰³ The law was the guarantee that wickedness must and would be punished (v. 127).³⁰⁴ Furthermore, for Calvin when we do not subscribe to the law God is robbed of his praise because righteousness is found in the law (v. 137).³⁰⁵ Importantly, the psalmist understood that it is the Lord alone by his Holy Spirit who can provide the benefits of his word (vv. 116, 117).³⁰⁶

Finally, it will be helpful to look at the notion of judgment contained in Calvin's exposition of the law in Ps 119. Of particular importance are his references to *mišpāṭ*, which can have several different senses. Calvin attributes to the term a meaning of judicial ordinances and decisions or legal sanctions.³⁰⁷ In general, when the term is used the judgments refer to God's righteousness, that is, the precepts of the law and the promises (see Calvin's introductory comments to vv. 52, 75). But at times the judgments are "the examples by which God has made himself known as the righteous judge of the world" and are for the strengthening of our faith, as in the case of v. 52,³⁰⁸ or to stir us up to repentance (v. 75).³⁰⁹ These judgments have flowed from age to age.

God's commandments, by which he executes judgment on the wicked and reprobate, are meant as a warning for the righteous not to lapse into sin and that God will ultimately judge the wicked (v. 21).³¹⁰ When the psalmist seeks for vengeance, it is not according to the "corrupt affections of the

---

300. Ibid., 418.
301. Calvin, *Commentary*, Vol. 5, 2.
302. Ibid., 33–34.
303. Calvin, *Commentary*, Vol. 4, 471, 472.
304. Calvin, *Commentary*, Vol. 5, 7.
305. Ibid., 18.
306. Calvin, *Commentary*, Vol. 4, 491.
307. Ibid., 402.
308. Ibid., 438.
309. Ibid., 456.
310. Ibid., 415–416.

flesh," but it is suitable to God (v. 84).[311] When God does execute judgment his vengeance is not shown all at once, but God compensates the slowness with severity (v. 119).[312] God's judgments lead the psalmist to love the doctrine of the law more because they show that God governs the world in power. Conversely, when wickedness is allowed to continue for long periods of time a love for God's word languishes (v. 119).[313] Once again, God's judgments instruct us and strike such terror that will lead us to true repentance (v. 120).[314] The scope of God's judgments is so universal that in v. 91 the psalmist, by using the term "judgments," is making an allusion to the law, suggesting that even the elements obey the secret command of God.[315]

Martin Luther's Medieval Exegesis of Psalm 119

Luther's commentary on Psalm 119 must be kept in the context of his yet not completely developed theological thought and the crises occurring in his life.[316] As was mentioned in the Introduction, Luther considered his works on the Psalms inadequate, and he was still applying the four categories of medieval exegesis to his commentary, which makes a consistent interpretation slightly difficult to ascertain.[317] An example of the variety of applications using this methodology can be seen in his commentary to v. 17.[318]

His break with the traditional interpretation of Ps 119 can be seen in his introductory statement, "I have not seen this psalm expounded by anyone in the prophetic sense."[319] For Luther this "prophetic sense" is the literal sense, which is the key for interpreting the psalm. In essence, "the whole psalm is nothing but a petition that the spiritual law be revealed and the letter be removed, that the spirit be brought forth and the veil taken away and the face appear, that Christ come and Moses pass away."[320]

---

311. Ibid., 464–465.

312. Ibid., 493.

313. Ibid., 494.

314. Ibid.

315. Ibid., 470.

316. Luther's (*First Lectures*, 470, 480, 490) comments on v. 79, vv. 98–100, and v. 109 show that he is still firmly a supporter of the Roman Church at this point.

317. Luther's overall theme of seeing Ps 119 as spiritually fulfilled in the Gospel also leads him to the conclusion that individual verses do not depend on each other (see his comments on v. 46).

318. *First Lectures*, 422–426. Note Luther's (Ibid., 433) comments, "But every Scripture passage is of infinite understanding."

319. Ibid., 414.

320. Ibid., 422.

Judgments in general are the "words of reproof and of the cross of Christ, in which is contained what evils of guilt must be avoided for the purpose of preserving righteousness and which evils of punishment must be borne for the sake of righteousness and Christ."[321] So, for Luther there is a pietistic understanding of judgments as being good for the soul.[322] When God's judgments are avoided then he [God] flees, but when it is received he draws near.[323] But Luther is willing to admit that judgments can mean both punishment and salvation and refers to a "gloss" which defines judgments as a seizure of the righteous and the destruction of the ungodly.[324] Testimonies are spiritually understood as referring "to nothing but only the Christ who was to come."[325]

Luther interprets those who are cursed in v. 21 as the proud hypocrites whom God does not convert, but only reproves because "they are unteachable and incorrigible and of their own turn away from His commandments, therefore they are cursed."[326] In interpreting v. 23, which speaks of princes speaking against the psalmist, Luther notes that all who present the truth in humility will be the object of reproach by those who are wise in their own eyes.[327] Commenting on v. 40, the enemies are the Jews, heretics and the proud, of which he suggests the readers should make their own tropological application against the "suggestions, snares, and impulses of the flesh, the world, and the devil" because "these are truly the ones which seek to kill your faith in you and thereby you also."[328] But in contrast in v. 51 the proud can be either the iniquity of one's own righteousness or the iniquitous persecution of the Church.[329] When commenting on v. 60 and referring to Job 7:18, Luther suggests that for a "beginner" an adversary is raised up so that the Lord may test him.[330] The affliction and humbling of the psalmist leads to his arrival at the true knowledge of the law.[331]

---

321. Ibid., 421.
322. Ibid., 444, 486, 513, 524.
323. Ibid., 514.
324. Ibid., 454.
325. Ibid., 421.
326. Ibid., 429.
327. Ibid.
328. Ibid., 447.
329. Ibid., 453.
330. Ibid., 456.
331. Ibid., 464.

Luther does make the observation that those who persecute the truth also persecute its devotees because of it.[332] In commenting on v. 91 Luther suggests that all things serve Christ and that he uses evil for "the increase, strengthening, and firmness of His church.[333] For to the saints they work together for good, as is well known." Furthermore, the Word of God is the sole comfort in trials because it comforts, exhorts, stimulates and strengthens through the hope of things to come.[334] Luther recognizes that the ungodly will be punished in the future judgment.[335]

Comparison with the Exegetical Findings of Psalm 119

The conclusion in the exegesis of Psalm 119 was that in the face of suffering, the psalmist's meditation on the Law goes beyond mere expressions of steadfastness or bargaining. Affliction was seen as the means of motivating the psalmist to meditate on the Torah. Furthermore, seeking after Yahweh with one's whole heart was seen as the hermeneutical key to Psalm 119 and synonymous to meditating on the Law. Such meditation on the Law ensured Yahweh's presence, with which injustice cannot coexist. It was further determined that the psalmist loves the decrees of Yahweh because innate in them is disclosed a certainty that Yahweh will judge the wicked.

The findings in the historical survey for Psalm 119 are helpful in understanding, in greater detail, the dynamics of the adversity of the psalmist meditating on the Law and in clarifying his response. To begin with, the biblical data from the post-exilic period seems to support the proposition (contra form criticism) that more than one enemy is portrayed in Ps 119.[336] The post-exilic period also allows one to see the close and important relationship which existed between the Law and the re-establishment of the temple, Yahweh's dwelling place.

In the survey, the adversary which the psalmist incurs is considered in a more holistic way. Of course the traditional enemies are recognized and figural interpretations given. However, in general, Augustine identified the enemy as being the devil, demons and people. Calvin also believed that

332. Ibid., 473, 508.
333. Ibid., 478.
334. Ibid., 478, 516.
335. Ibid., 517, 529.
336. Most commentators up until the nineteenth century understood Ps 119 as related to David's life in some way. The events in David's life certainly could be seen as reflected in the range of experiences of the psalmist and the adversity of the different enemies represented in Ps 119: periods of great distress and adversaries who are kings and princes as well as those close to him.

behind the psalmist's adversaries is Satan.[337] The effect is to remove the focus from the immediate adversity of the psalmist and to see it from a cosmic perspective. Furthermore, the psalmist is despised because the adversaries despise the Law. Cyprian and Augustine bring out this dynamic of hostility through the example of the martyrs who repay the evil of their persecutors with the good of following the testimonies. Athanasius and Ignatius tie the term *way* to Christ's own claim to be the *Way*. In doing so there is a sense that a defining characteristic of the enemies is their hatred for God. In other words, there seem to be no motivating factors for the adversity besides a hatred of the "Way" as the enemies see it reflected in the psalmist's life and as it is embodied in the Torah. Calvin as well notes the connection between the psalmist's suffering and his observing God's statutes.

In my exegesis the psalmist's suffering was seen as purposeful (on the basis of vv. 67, 71 and 75) and his affliction has been the means of his following the law. Chrysostom, Hillary, Ambrose, Augustine and Calvin, despite their differing hermeneutical methods, also see the suffering of the psalmist as purposeful in some way. Perhaps this is no more clearly seen than in the use of the *blessed* formula as a key which, for many of the early church commentators, connects Psalm 119 to Matthew 5. Moreover, Augustine and Calvin both link the cause of some of the adversity of the psalmist to God. Augustine saw God as the source of some of the psalmist's distress through judgment, but this judgment was discipline. From the psalmist's life, Calvin understands that God can inflict poverty, shame, illness, distress and hardships, which can drive Christians away in their time of need. This infliction, however, is given to the psalmist in order to bring grace, and so is purposeful. Calvin understands God as adversary in the context of God's secret providence.

Important also is the relational dimension attributed to the law. It would be unfounded to insist that the detailed meaning given to the law in the NT is found in the psalmist's exposition on the Law in Psalm 119. However, it seems that the psalmist's focus on his relationship to the Law is akin to the emphasis that Jesus himself made and which Paul clarified through his explanation of the relationship between the promise given to Abraham and the giving of the Law. Augustine's own conclusion was that vv. 1 to 3, searching the Lord's testimonies and seeking him with one's whole heart, was the same thing as being undefiled in the way and to walk in the law of the Lord. So the study of the Law guarantees Yahweh's presence because study of God's testimonies leads one to God. The irony is that this is a spiritual act dependent on God.

337. Based on Eph 5:12.

Furthermore, meditating on the Law is not just knowledge about the Law, but involves an actualization. Indeed, meditation on the Law is dependent on the love of God and leads to the love of God and the love of one's neighbour (so Augustine). Ps 119:165 and 1 Jn 2:10 link the notion of love for one's brother and love for the Law with a perfect life (i.e., a life free of σκάνδαλον [skandalon] and *mikšôl*. The latter two notions are captured positively in Ps 119:2 as those who seek Yahweh with their whole hearts. Meditation on the Law contains within it ethical implications which are relational. This too, adds insight into the psalmist's meditation on the Law in response to evil. If Bede, Chrysostom, Augustine and Calvin are correct, then it would be more accurate to say the enemies despise the psalmist for the way he lives.

Important also is what is occurring when the psalmist is meditating on the Law. The post-exilic community saw the inextricable connection between the Law and the presence of Yahweh. The Law authenticates the cult and reinforces the notion of the temple as Yahweh's dwelling place for the restored community. The NT is sparse on direct links to Ps 119, but seems to equate the Law of the psalmist with the gospel (so Luther), both being trustworthy means in which God has revealed himself. Augustine notes that God's Law will be sought because it is truth. Origen, Jerome, Chrysostom, Augustine and Calvin all emphasize the need of the Holy Spirit in order to understand the true nature of the Law. Hence, the meditation on the Law is a spiritual act. But as was mentioned above, for Bede, Chrysostom, Augustine and Calvin, true knowledge of the Law entailed actualization of the law.

Meditating on the Law is also a means of repaying evil with good. The Law is righteous and so meditating on the Law prevents the psalmist from following bad counsel, even his own. As Calvin (v. 157) noted, there is a tendency for Christians when they encounter suffering to want to "howl among the wolves."[338] But there are also many forms of comfort the psalmist sees in the Law. Deliverance from his enemies could cause the psalmist to delight (v. 92). Another of these comforts is the knowledge that God is just and so are his judgments (so Calvin). The parallel with the book of Revelation suggests that God's revelation in the Law as righteous is on par with his revelation in history as judge. Righteousness is part of his character. So, Yahweh's self-disclosure in his Law as well as in history reflects his righteousness and is inseparable from his character. Augustine provides detailed comment on this aspect of Yahweh's self-revelation through his use of the terms *iustificationes* (just actions performed with God's help) and *iudicia*

---

338. Calvin, Commentary, Vol. 5, 33–34.

(just sentences God pronounces).³³⁹ The ways of justice are not statements about justice in the Law but just deeds from which love is born. And so for Augustine meditating on the Law is a form of repaying evil with good.³⁴⁰ Central to Augustine's hermeneutic is the theme of love, which was also suggested by the parallel between Ps 119 and 1 John. For Augustine the justice in the Law is Christ.

Furthermore, the judgment of God which is revealed in the Law is just because judgment is only judgment if it is just. Indeed, judgment is the mode of operation of the virtue of justice. As Augustine notes, the issuing of God's justice gives comfort because the judgment on the vessels of God's wrath reveals the riches of his glory to his people. Calvin also insists that the judgments in the Law act as a warning to the righteous. God's judgments also show that God rules the world in power. Conversely, when the Law is not subscribed to God is robbed of his praise. According to Calvin, even the elements obey the secret commands of God.

In Romans 2:1 Paul argues that "sin is humanity's ambition to put itself in the place of God and so be its own lord. This is what judges do when they assume the right to sit in judgment of their fellow creatures."³⁴¹ Perhaps the psalmist's emphasis on the Law rather than on cursing his enemies recognizes this innate concept of how the Law can be used wrongly. "He that forbade revenge now commands long-suffering; not as if just revenge were an unrighteous thing, but because long-suffering is more excellent."³⁴² From the psalmist's perspective in Psalm 119, the Law was a means of relationship with Yahweh that guaranteed Yahweh's presence.

EXEGESIS OF PSALM 129:³⁴³ THE SEVERITY OF AGRICULTURAL CURSES

Psalm 129 seems to be an unlikely candidate for an investigation into understanding more clearly the imprecatory psalms and God's just dealing with his people. Scholars have not come to a consensus regarding the

---

339. Augustine's use of the LXX as his basic text and his use of Latin to comment on that text means that the conclusions he comes to do not always correspond to straightforward interpretations of the MT. However, a thorough treatment here is beyond the constraints of this study.

340. Augustine's understanding of justice will be further commented on in Chapter 3.

341. Ladd, *Theology of the New Testament*, 548.

342. *Constitutions of the Holy Apostles*, 460.

343. The standard text is the *NRSV* with any changes being indicated.

classification of this psalm (see below), which is a reflection of some of the challenges in understanding the Hebrew text. Luc noted the meaning intended behind the imprecations in vv. 5–8 as indicating shame and death, but the agricultural metaphor seems to dampen their force.[344] If Luc's suggestion is correct, should a psalm that wishes for the shame and death of the enemies through agricultural images be any less problematic to pray? But Psalm 129 is also significant for our study because it is a psalm portraying adversity in some form throughout its entirety. The whole perspective in one sense is the demise of the enemies' past, present and future without any mitigating factors. Furthermore, understanding the agricultural metaphor in the form of imprecation can contribute to understanding the conceptual world of justice of the people who used this psalm.

An Agrarian MT or the War Text of the LXX?

1. A song of Ascents
Greatly[345] they have oppressed[346] me from my youth.
   Let Israel now say,

2. Greatly they have oppressed me from my youth,
   yet they have not prevailed against me.

---

344. "Interpreting the Curses," 410. For Luc, the curses or imprecations are *prophetic judgement speeches*.

345. Translated as an adverb of intensity (BDB, 912; s.v. *rab*, 1g. *much, exceedingly*) instead of an adverb of frequency (*NRSV, often*) because *ṣrr* better describes a state here (HOLL, 1997:311; s.v. *ṣrr, be hostile toward, be in a state of conflict*) and the image in v. 3 is severe. Zenger (Hossfeld and Zenger, *Psalms 3*, 406) suggests an adverbial usage entailing the notion of "very long and very hard."

346. *Oppress* instead of *NRSV attack*. In Num 10:9 the *NRSV* translates *haṣṣōrēr* as *the adversary who oppresses you*. The term *attack* in English is usually associated with warfare (note the use of πολεμέω, "to wage war" in the *LXX*), but if we keep the agricultural metaphors of the MT, then *oppress* has a less limiting connotation. Zenger (Ibid., 418) points out that vv. 1–4 in the *MT* text give a metaphor of distress, whereas the *LXX* gives an image of war.

3. The plowers[347] plowed[348] on my back;
They made their furrows[349] long.

4. The LORD is righteous.[350] He has cut[351]
the cords[352] of the wicked.

5. May they be put to shame and turned[353] backward

347. The *LXX* has οἱ ἁμαρτωλοί (Hebrew: *hārᵉšāʿîm*) "sinners" instead of the *MT*'s *ḥōršîm* "plowers." Zenger (Ibid., 418) suggests that this was done because in an urban-cultural context the agricultural imagery was "foreign and perhaps even incomprehensible." Yet, if this were the case, one wonders why the metaphor of withering grass in vv. 6–8 was not also changed. 11Psa contains the reading *ršʿym ḥršw* "sinners plowed," indicating a relatively early textual witness to *ršʿym*. However, the fact that Ugaritic bears witness to the term *ḥōršîm* seems to support Dahood's (*Psalms III*, 231) suggestion that the metaphor of the plowmen had become blurred by the time of the *LXX* and 11Psa, and the MT should be favored.

348. The *LXX* has the same underlying Hebrew verb *ḥāršû* as the *MT*, but offers a different lexical meaning for the word, *practicing their skill* (*NETS*, 612), *have forged/hammered/engraved* (Zenger [Hossfeld and Zenger, *Psalms 3*, 418]). Ironically the subject (*ḥršym*) of the verb in 6 of its 8 occurrences in the *MT* is pointed differently and refers to an *artisian* or *craftsman*, which would be the natural subject for the *LXX* translation of *ḥāršû*. This might further suggest that the translators of the *LXX* did not know the meaning of *ḥōršîm* "plowmen" or used a text which was emended to *hārᵉšāʿîm*. On the basis of the *LXX* having the agricultural metaphor in vv. 6–7, the *MT* should be favored because of its consistency throughout.

349. *LXX* has τὴν ἀνομίαν αὐτῶν (Hebrew: *ʿwnwṭm*) which is a derivative of *ʿwn* "guilt" or "sin." The *MT* use of *maʿănâ*, especially the *qere* reading, could be a word play on *ʿānāy* "poor, afflicted, humble." This might be supported by the Syriac, which has the underlying *ʿnwh*, translated as *submission* by Allen (*Psalms*, 246).

350. There is some debate as to how the syntax in this phrase works. The *LXX*, κύριος δίκαιος, and Kraus (*Psalms 60–150*, 462) have an adjectival phrase "righteous Lord," whereas Gunkel (*Die Psalmen*, 558) has an appositional relationship, *Yahweh, the faithful*. The Massoretes apparently read it as a noun clause.

351. Dahood (*Psalms III*, 231) translates the verb *qiṣṣēṣ* as a precative perfect because of the jussives that follow in vv. 5 and 6. He states that if a historical perfect is given, then the next verse does not make sense. Consequently, Dahood sees the prayer beginning in v. 4 and not v. 5. Allen, on the other hand, believes that the verbs in vv. 5–8a are statements of confidence based upon comparison with Ps 6:11 and 97:11. However, the choice of *piel* perfect may reflect the poet's desire to portray a state achieved (*IBHS*, 405, Par 24.3d), which would fit the context here. See "The Enemies and Translation of the Verbs in vv. 4–9" below.

352. The *LXX* has αὐχένας, "necks," but in Ps 2:3 the *LXX* translators translate the word *ʿăbōṯ* as ζυγὸν, "yoke" (Zenger [Hossfeld and Zenger, *Psalms 3*, 418]). The implication is that the translators of the *LXX* either had a different text or altered the word to fit its warfare imagery.

353. Translated and understood as a *hendiadys* as suggested by Dahood (*Psalms III*, 129). However, also fruitful might be translating the *waw* as an *epexegetical waw* (*IBHS*, 652, Par. 1.6.2c), which would render a consecutive jussive of explanation (e.g. Gen 28:3).

all who hate Zion.

6. Let them be like the grass on the housetops
that withers before it grows up,[354]

7. with which reapers do not fill their hands
or binders of sheaves their arms,

8. while those who pass by do not say,
"The blessings of the Lord be upon you!
We bless you in the name of the LORD!"[355]

Maintaining the MT's Agrarian Images

The structure of Psalm 129 is generally divided into two strophes, vv. 1–4 and vv. 5–8. Gunkel classified this psalm as a mixed genre, seeing vv. 1–4 as a communal thanksgiving and vv. 5–8 as a communal complaint.[356] Westermann categorizes it as a declarative psalm of praise of the people,[357] whereas Kraus sees it as a *community prayer song* on the basis of viewing vv. 5–8 as confident assertion.[358] One's translation of the verbs in vv. 4–8 is crucial in determining the structure and form of this psalm, as Allen points out.[359] Dahood translates the *piel* perfect in v. 4 as a precative, reasoning that the subsequent verbs in vv. 5–7 are jussive and the wishes against the enemy do not make any sense if the translation is in the past, *he has cut the cords of*

---

354. The LXX takes ḥāṣîr as the object of the verb šālap̄ and renders "before one plucks it up" (Brenton, *Septuagint*, 777); or Pietersma in a passive equivalent *before it was pulled out* (NETS, 612). This common transitive meaning for šālap̄ is to "draw out a sword or draw off a shoe" (BDB, 1025). However, most English translations, including the NRSV, translate the verb as an intransitive. Delitzsch (*Psalms, Vol. 3*, 300) translates with ḥṣyr as the subject of šlp̄, giving an intransitive signification meaning "to put itself forth." Driver ("Studies," 277) proposes that the term šlp̄ means to "produce a stalk," on the basis of an Akkadian cognate and the late Hebrew term šelep̄. On the basis of meter Gunkel (*Die Psalmen*, 560), Kraus (*Psalms 60–150*, 460) and Weiser (*Psalms*, 770) amend the text to šeqqād̄îm tišdōp̄ "which the east wind scorches" and delete yāb̄ēš "whithers." This should be rejected on the grounds that yāb̄ēš is attested to collocation with ḥāṣîr (occurs 6x within 6 words; 3x times yāb̄ēš immediately precedes, Isa 15:6; 40:7; 40:8) and more importantly the *inclusio* between yēb̄ōšû "may they be put to shame (v. 5) and yāb̄ēš (v. 6) would be affected (so Dahood, *Psalms III*, 233).

355. Allen (*Psalms*, 250) takes v. 8b as a benediction on the congregation by a priestly group, but see the discussion in the section "Structure and Form" which suggests it is an integral part of the poem.

356. Gunkel and Begrich, *Introduction to Psalms*, 44–45, 82.

357. Westermann, *Praise and Lament*, 81.

358. Kraus, *Psalms 60–150*, 461.

359. Allen, *Psalms*, 247.

the wicked.³⁶⁰ Accordingly, he structures the psalm with two different strophe divisions, vv. 1–3 (oppression and preservation) and vv. 4–8 (directed against the enemies), reinforcing this division by noting the *inclusio* in vv. 4 and 8 formed by *yhwh* "LORD." This structure allows him to classify the psalm as a communal lament.

The placement of the metaphors and the evoking verbal expressions may provide another way of understanding the structure of the poem.

vv. 1-2	The summons to praise *yō'mar—nā'* "Let (Israel) now say," with the repetition of content *ṣrr* "oppressed"(2x)	v. 8	Negative invocation of blessing *wᵉlō' 'āmrû* with the repetition of *brk* "blessings/bless" (2x)
v. 3	Agricultural metaphor of oppression	vv. 6–7	Agricultural metaphor of imprecation
v. 4	The Lord cuts the chords of the *rᵉšā'îm* "wicked"	v. 5	Imprecation against the *śōnᵉ'ê ṣiyyôn* "(all) who hate zion"

Table 3. A proposed structure of Psalm 129 based on the chiastic arrangement of similar content.

The chiastic structure of similar content seems to support two strophes. The two summonses to praise in vv. 1–2 are balanced by the two invocations to blessings, which suggest that both blessing formulas in v. 8 are integral to the poem and that 8c is not just a late addition.³⁶¹ Scholars tend to separate v. 8c on the basis of voice and assign it to a function as a priestly blessing for the congregation.³⁶² In addition, the two agricultural metaphors mirror each other, which may implicitly lend support to the superiority of maintaining the agricultural metaphor in the first strophe of the *MT* over the slightly altered *LXX* (see above). Finally, rather than one distinct center, vv. 4 and 5 parallel each other. This overall parallel structure, however, does differ in the total number of stichs and stresses included in each strophe, as do all of the proposals listed above.³⁶³

---

360. Dahood, *Psalms III*, 230–233.

361. A stichometric and stress analysis of v. 8 suggests a similar conclusion (see Botha, "Social Scientific Reading," 1403).

362. Van der Wall, "Structure of Psalm CXXIX," 364–365; Allen, *Psalms*, 248.

363. This is made difficult to determine because scholars do not always count the same number of stresses in each stich. For example, Botha ("Social—Scientific Reading," 1402) has v. 5b as containing three stresses, whereas Allen (*Psalms*, 246) counts only 2 stresses.

The Enemies and the Translation of the Verbs in Verses 4–7

Identification of the enemies is closely tied in to how one translates the verbs in verses 4–6. The following table indicates the possibilities.

		Dahood	Weiser, Anderson	Allen, Kraus, Gunkel	Perowne, Delitzsch
v. 4	*qiṣṣēṣ* "cut"	precative	perfect	perfect	perfect
vv. 5–6	(v. 5) *yēḇōšû* "be ashamed" *wᵉyissōg û* "turn away" (6) *yihyû* "be"	jussives	jussives	confident assertions	jussives
Enemies		foreign	1–4 foreign 5–8 internal	foreign	foreign

Table 4. Translation of the verbs in verses 4–6 and the identification of the enemies.

Dahood proposed that translating the verbs as wishes in vv. 5–6 does not make sense if one translates *qiṣṣēṣ* the *piel* perfect in v. 4 as a perfect tense.[364] However, his assumption is that the enemies of v. 4 are the same enemies the community is praying against in vv. 5–8. Allen, Kraus, and Anderson translate the verbs in vv. 5–6 as statements of confidence rather than as wishes, allowing *qiṣṣēṣ* in v. 4 to be translated as a perfect tense.[365] In this case the first strophe points to Israel's past and the second strophe asserts with confidence the inevitable demise which is to come to all of Israel's enemies. Allen's basis is that the only other occurrence in the Psalter of *all* (*kōl*) enemies being put to shame is found in Ps 6:11, which is an assertion of confidence. However, Botha rightly queries whether both instances must serve the same function.[366] In contrast, grounds for translating the verbs in vv. 5–6 as jussives comes from the volitional tone of Psalm 129, which is created by the *inclusio* between vv. 1, 2 and 8. Verse 1 begins with *yōʾmar—nāʾ*,[367] a summons, "Let Israel now say." The blessing formulas at the end (v. 8) also have a volitional tone, *not say . . . we bless you in the name of the Lord*. The overall mood is that of a petition and, as Zenger notes, one would expect

---

364. *Psalms III*, 231.

365. Allen, *Psalms*, 247–248; Kraus, *Psalms 60–150*, 461; Anderson, *Book of Psalms*, 871–872.

366. "Social-Scientific Reading," 1404.

367. Note the particle.

jussives in a petitionary prayer of Israel.³⁶⁸ The traditional way of viewing these verbs as jussives is well justified.³⁶⁹

Weiser suggests that the enemies are members of the covenant community, on the basis that a different description (vv. 5–8) would be expected for Gentiles and 8c would seem harmless applied to a foreign foe.³⁷⁰ But the use of v. 5a could be expected with foreign foes. First, the phrase *may they be put to shame and turned backwards* (*yēḇōšû weyissōḡû ʾāḥôr*) has a military connotation to it. The same phrase in different word order occurs in Isa 42:17, *they shall be turned back and utterly put to shame* (*nāsōḡû ʾāḥôr yēḇōšû*, where it is used to depict a military judgment³⁷¹ on those who trusted in idols, and is clearly implying the devastating effects of the exile.³⁷² But the idea of turning back can also be applied to the hostile nations (Ps 9:3 ff.). The phrase depicts the complete defeat and shame of those to whom the phrase refers. In the case of this psalm the foes are identified as *śōnʾê ṣiyyôn*, "those who hate Zion."³⁷³ Botha notes that *love* and *hate* are terms of the covenant and *those who hate Zion* (Yahweh) could not be members of the same covenant.³⁷⁴ Furthermore, the description for the enemies as *all* (*kōl*) *those who hate Zion* carries an eschatological nuance of the foreign enemies, which is further connected through the military nuance of 5a and the mention of *Zion*, which finds similarity with the Royal Psalms 2 (v. 6) and 110 (v. 2). This military notion may have influenced the translators of the *LXX*.

---

368. Hossfeld and Zenger, *Psalms 3*, 407.

369. Most English translations translate them as such (*ESV, NIV, NKJ, NLT, NRSV, KJV*, etc.).

370. *Psalms*, 771; so Anderson, *Book of Psalms*, 873. Van der Wall ("Structure of Psalm CXXIX," 364–367) also proposes, on the basis of how the enemies are linguistically portrayed differently in vv. 4–8b with vv. 1–3 and the phrase *śōnʾê yhwh* "those who hate the LORD" (2 Ch 19:2), that the enemies are from within. He sees vv. 4–8b as forming a subdivision of the main division vv. 1–8b. The argument that the metaphors seem awkward if applied to the same enemy—in v. 3 the enemies are merciless plowmen, whereas in vv. 6–7 they are those who wither away—is not convincing. First, the enemies are separated chronologically, and secondly the metaphors serve a different purpose.

371. *Yhwh* is a soldier (v. 13); the devastating effects of the exile are those of war victims (v22). So he (Yahweh) poured upon him (Jacob) the heat of his anger and the fury of war (v. 25).

372. A similar phrase in Ps 44:11, *tešîḇēnû ʾāḥôr minnî-ṣār*, "you made us turn back from the foe," has the connotation of military defeat being associated with the predicament of the exile.

373. Identifying the enemies is made more difficult because the phrase *śōnʾê ṣiyyôn* "those who hate Zion" is a *hapax legomenon*.

374. "Social-Scientific Reading, 1406.

Further reasons for Weiser's internal identification of the enemies comes from what he believes is the inefficacy v. 8b would have if applied to a foreign foe. However, the blessing formulas, at least 8b, seem to be part of an expansion of the metaphor of the withering grass.[375] Therefore its function within the metaphor should be the primary means of understanding it. The identification of the enemies in vv. 5–8 as foreign enemies and the assertion that the verbs in vv. 5–7 are more naturally translated as jussives does not limit the translation of *qiṣṣēṣ* "cut" to a traditional perfective sense. However, there are grounds to encourage translating it as such. First, Dahood's grounds for translating it as a precative were based on the premise that the enemies in v. 4 are the same as the enemies in v. 5.[376] Nevertheless, the structure of the poem places v. 4 in the first strophe and in terms of ideas seems more naturally identified with vv. 1–3. It would seem more consistent to translate the term *qiṣṣēṣ* in the same tense as the verbs in v. 3 (perfect 2x) since they all form part of the first strophe and relate to a similar plowing metaphor. In this case Yahweh's cutting the cords of the wicked would have occurred in the past. Lastly, the *piel* perfective sense (see above) of an achieved state fits well with the indications in the text of the national enemies' failure to succeed (vv. 2c, 4a). The psalm structure more clearly reflects foreign enemies viewed from two perspectives, those who were unable to subdue Israel in the past because of Yahweh's intervention and those which are a present or future threat to Zion.

A History of Suffering

In the first part of the psalm the worshippers recall a long and painful history. The repetition in vv. 1 and 2 speaks of the intensity of this oppression.[377] Youth (*neʿûrîm*) *is* used here as a metaphor which refers to the early stages of the nation (cf. Hos 2:15; Jer 2:2), to the time of the Exodus and wilderness wanderings. The emphasis, however, is not on the time of *youth*, but *from* the time of youth.[378] Through the Egyptians, Philistines, Arameans, Assyrians and Babylonians Israel had experienced successive forms of oppression. As Kraus notes, "The history of Israel is one single passion narrative."[379] Yet the suffering has not been absolute. It has been *rab* both long and severe, but the enemies have not been able to annihilate the nation.

375. So Perowne, *Book of Psalms*, 401.
376. *Psalms III*, 231.
377. Anderson, *Book of Psalms*, 872.
378. Hossfeld and Zenger, *Psalms 3*, 411.
379. *Psalms 60–150*, 462.

In the context of this limitation of the suffering the psalm moves into describing its severity through the metaphor of the plowmen. Plowing is elsewhere used as a metaphor of military judgment issued by Yahweh as a result of the injustice of the rulers of Zion (Mic 3:12; Jer 26:18). The plowmen here *make long* (v. 3) their furrows. The image is one of excessive harshness. There has been no part of the field left untouched. Anderson suggests that the plowmen are an allusion to the use of taskmasters' whips which would leave welts or weals resembling furrows.[380]

After a declaration that Yahweh is righteous, the psalm continues in its metaphor with the speaker representing the ploughed field.[381] Dahood suggests that, if the metaphor continues, the plowmen's harnesses are broken so they can no longer continue to plow, but if Israel becomes the ox, then the yoke represents servitude.[382] However, it is probably best not to make too linear a comparison of the metaphor and so reduce the effect of the images. Israel can remain the field plowed by its enemies without losing the symbolism of the yoke. The yoke still connotes subjugation and exploitation by foreign rulers. It is difficult to know for certain if the *cutting of the cords* refers specifically to restoration from the exile. But the image is that of liberation,[383] and the restoration would best fit such an image. Weiser suggests that the psalm does not refer to a specific event because it was composed in the cult.[384] Nevertheless, the time frame given in vv. 1–4 seems to be a panoramic history of the nation's suffering. Furthermore, the editing of Book V, I have argued, seems to support a post-exilic framework. The allusions would seem to cover the time from youth to the time of cutting of the cords, which would seem to be the restoration.[385]

In v. 5 the psalm changes focus from the external enemies who have subjugated and exploited the Israelites in the past to the enemies of the present and future. As the translators of the *LXX* noticed, the psalm supports a militaristic theme, something which they made explicit in their translation of vv. 1–4. This militaristic theme continues and is implicitly found in the imprecatory metaphor of vv. 5–8 with an eschatological nuance (see below "Meaning"). Furthermore, the hostility of *those who hate Zion* is given a theological emphasis because the term Zion entails in its meaning an

---

380. Anderson, *Book of Psalms*, 872.
381. So Allen, *Psalms*, 249.
382. Dahood, *Psalms III*, 232.
383. Kraus, *Psalms 60–150*, 462.
384. Weiser, *Psalms*, 771.

385. This statement is related to the dating of the psalm and the editing of Book V, the latter of which I have discussed in the introduction.

Withering Grass—A Symbol of Utter Destruction

According to the observations above, the psalm can tentatively be classified as a special form of communal lament or complaint, with vv. 1–4 acting in a double function as recounting the suffering and Yahweh's deliverance in the past, but also as a foundation for understanding the imprecations in vv. 5–8.[386] The congregation offers a petitionary prayer through the personified singular voice in the psalm against all their enemies. How the community understood the agency of the response to the adversity of the enemies depends to a large degree on how one interprets the verbs in vv. 5–8. If one interprets vv. 5–8 as statements of confidence then the agency of the working out of the curses remains unclear. The symbol of the *ḥāṣîr* "grass" on the rooftop which *yāḇēš* "withers" representing the enemies' demise could be the result of Yahweh's active judgment or the natural outworking of the self-demise of *those who hate Zion*.[387] However if vv. 5–8 are taken as imprecations expressing the speaker's volition, then the demise of the enemy is more naturally identified as occurring through the agency of Yahweh's active judgment. In Psalm 129 that judgment derives its meaning from the context of Yahweh's past dealings with Israel and the imprecations themselves.

The metaphor of the withering grass can be considered as consisting of vv. 5–8.[388] The image of grass withering on a mud-packed roof was readily observable. In the sweltering heat of the Middle East, the shallow-rooted

---

386. I thank Dr. Kathleen Rochester for suggesting another way of seeing the frustration of the enemies in not being able to overcome the Israelites. She suggests that in the first metaphor the enemies are the ones who plow and expect to reap. In the second metaphor the enemies are like the grass that is withered. But in both the plowman/reaper is bitterly disappointed by a loss of blessing of fruitfulness in his labor, which is reinforced by v. 8. The only weakness with this way of seeing the metaphors is that it confuses the focus on the enemies. The enemies are the plowmen in the first metaphor and the grass in the second, but it is the reaper in the second metaphor who is bitterly disappointed. According to the way I am reading the metaphors, the reapers in the second metaphor only play a supporting role to indicate the complete destruction of the wicked represented as the grass.

387 Delitzsch's (*Psalms, Vol. 3*, 300) translation of *ḥṣyr* "grass" as the subject of *šlp* with an intransitive signification meaning *to put itself forth* leads him to conclude that "their [enemies of Israel] life closes with sure destruction, the germ of which they (without any need of rooting out) carry within themselves."

388. In Perowne's (*Book of Psalms*, 401) words, "These two verses [7–8] are a poetic expansion of the figure, an imaginative excursus."

grass was bound to wither. But the metaphor continues, and the latter part in v. 7 is also significant in contributing to its meaning. Here, we find the relative particle *š* and a switch in verb stems (*piel-qal-piel*) indicating a distinction from the jussives of vv. 5–6, which seems to support its function as an explanation of the preceding wish. The grass has withered and it is dead, but now the focus becomes the lack of grass for the reapers to gather. The concept of harvesters reaping on a roof is a strange one since the normal place of harvesting would have been in cultivated fields. Consequently, the metaphor is not implying that harvesting occurs on the roof, but rather by degree of comparison, indicating the utter uselessness of withered grass on the roof.[389] It is completely destroyed, nothing is left to harvest. Perhaps this uselessness of the withered grass signifies an essential characteristic of the wicked as well.[390]

The image of withering grass is associated with that of divine judgment with all its nuances. Withering grass can represent the godless (Job 8:12) or the wicked (Ps 37:2). In Ps 37:2 the metaphor functions as a warning to the Israelites not to follow the wicked. It can also be used to signify the transitoriness of human life (Ps 103), but even in this regard the transitory nature of life can be conceived of as a category of God's wrath (Ps 90:5). Grass on the rooftop which is *šᵉdēpâ* "blighted" symbolizes the devastating effects on the victims of military invasion (2 Kgs 19:26; Isa 37:27).[391] Botha suggests on the basis of these two verses that the image of the withering grass also has the connotation of shame.[392] The community prays that the enemies not only fail in their attack on Zion, but that the defeat of the enemies will be such that they experience shame.

Verse 8, as a negative blessing formula, seems to continue the curse with its volitional tone. As Perowne noted, v. 8 functions as poetic expansion of the metaphor.[393] Therefore, Delitzsch's comment that the blessing formulas were not withheld from the heathen misses the point.[394] The grass on the roof has died. There has been nothing for the harvesters. Now, a

---

389. So the *LXX* transitive *before it is plucked* (*slp* is normally used in the transitive sense of drawing out a sword, shoe, or umbrella) presents an unrealistic picture of harvesting occurring on the rooftop, although the meaning does not alter the force of this metaphor.

390. Anderson, *Book of Psalms*, 872.

391. Withering grass can refer to either the Israelites or foreign nations. One sees how the nuance of this metaphor could be interpreted as supporting the LXX's military imagery in vv. 1–4.

392. "Social–Scientific Reading," 1410.

393. *Book of Psalms*, 401.

394. *Psalms, Vol. 3*, 300.

negative form of blessing, and hence a curse, will ensure that the process is not temporary. What we have is a threefold development of the metaphor: the utter devastation of the grass in terms of substance, quantity and time. Verse 8 b and c may be given in covenantal language, but that is most likely for the sake of those who use this prayer.

The concept behind the use of these "agricultural" blessings alludes to Boaz's exchange with the harvesters in Ruth 2:4. As in the book of Ruth, blessing is tied into the abundance-desolation theme. God's presence and favor is represented through the abundance of crops provided for Ruth and Naomi. A lack of blessing, as is depicted in Ruth 1—2:4 (before these words are spoken by the harvesters to Boaz and he responds in kind) is represented by the famine in the land and then the loss of husbands to provide. What the community was wishing on these enemies is for their utter demise, something which was represented in the covenantal language of the dying grass, the utter lack of crop for the harvesters, and withholding of any blessing which would reverse the situation.[395] The image then is the complete defeat of the enemies to such an extent that they cease to exist.

The Israelite's concept of Yahweh's righteousness in their deliverance as given in the panoramic history of vv. 1–4 also contributes to understanding these imprecations. Israel knew of unwarranted oppression in their youth, but they also knew of oppression in the form of judgment. In the context of the exile, the yoke was a symbol of the cruelty of the Babylonians, but it was also a symbol of divine judgment. So, in Hos 10:11 (also Deut 28:48 and Isa 9:3) Ephraim is put under the yoke of the nations as a judgment for its wickedness and injustice. The nation experiences *shame and is turned back* in defeat (Isa 42:17) because of its sin. The people were judged for not observing the commands and decrees of Yahweh.

In another episode, through Hezekiah's prayer (2 Kgs 19; Isa 37) they had come to a deeper understanding of the justice of Yahweh. It is clearly explained that Israel had sinned. The consequence was that the LORD had sent Sennacharib and his army as a form of judgment. Their repentance had caused Yahweh to deliver them from the very instrument he had set against them. In the context of this antinomy, their cry in Psalm 129 is *Yahweh is righteous*. The enemies with all their oppression have not been able to overcome Israel (v. 2). They understood that although Yahweh acted both as punisher and deliverer he was just in doing so. The enemies themselves are portrayed as oblivious to the plan of Yahweh. Yahweh's covenantal loyalty to

---

395. The final blessing formula in 8c most likely serves a double function as Allen (*Psalms*, 248–250) *et al.* suggest—it is a benediction to the congregation. But it also functions to heighten the severity of the negative curse in v. 8b. According to Gerstenberger (*Psalms, Part 2*, 354) the plurality of blessing people is unique.

Israel is the basis on which Israel prays for the destruction of its enemies. They could perceive their own history in terms of Yahweh's covenantal justice. How much more would he punish the foreign enemies! The psalm has a distinct chronological movement in it. The enemies are not able to prevail, Yahweh delivers Israel from the Exile, and then, in a petitionary prayer, all enemies are reduced to nothing.

Conclusion of the Exegesis

Finally, the image of this imprecation goes beyond the mere wish for physical death. The scope of the metaphor is the complete destruction of the enemy in manner, space and time. This lack of agricultural virility takes on a symbol of the eschatological judgment of Yahweh. This perspective is reinforced implicitly throughout vv. 5-8 through the military nuances attached to the phrase in vv. 5a and the metaphor of the withering grass. Furthermore, the scope of *all those who hate Zion* carries in it an eschatological perspective. As in the royal Psalm 2 and the royal messianic Psalm 110 the enemies are enemies of Zion and all that it stands for. Zion is the holy hill where Yahweh and his throne partner reign. These imprecations are tied into the covenantal worldview of the worshippers, a connection strongly implied in the negative covenantal blessing formulas in v. 8. However, unlike the depiction of explicit military victory, Psalm 129 approaches the demise of the enemies through agricultural imagery. One can only surmise that one type of imagery could not contain all the nuances of the eschatological imagination of the worshippers.

A SELECT HISTORICAL SURVEY OF THE INTERPRETATION OF PSALM 129

A quick survey of secondary literature in any major commentary reveals the fact that Ps 129 has not elicited as much academic writing as other psalms. This scarcity also holds true for ancient works on Ps 129. Nevertheless, it will be helpful to state what we are investigating in these commentaries on Ps 129. We are interested in how the commentators understood the adversity in the psalm. An observation in the exegesis was that this psalm portrays adversity across time in its entirety, vv. 1-4 relating to the past and vv. 5-8 relating to the present and future. We are also interested in how the agricultural imprecation was understood and the intensity the curse was perceived to have. It will be left to Chapter four to discuss how agricultural metaphors in the form of imprecations contributed to the conceptual world of justice of the people who prayed Psalm 129.

Post-Exilic Interpretation—A Mitigation of the Curses?

Goulder takes the main portion of the background to Ps 129 as the Chronicler's narrative told in Nehemiah 13:4–14.[396] Specifically, Ps 129 is a "dual response" which refers to thanks for deliverance seen in the re-establishment of the government in Jerusalem by exiles and cries of confusion and shame on the opponents who are presented as Tobiah and Eliashib.[397] Hence he sees the phrase "all who hate Zion" as referring to internal enemies. However, Goulder allows for the imagery in vv. 1–3 to refer not only to the deliverance seen in the cleansing of the temple, but also to the events surrounding Israel's slavery in Egypt.[398] The long furrows of the plowmen in v. 3 depict the harsh flogging (so Isa 50:6; 51:23). But the pressing concern of the defilement of the temple in the post-exilic restoration provides the primary context for the imprecations. Goulder believes the identification of internal enemies is supported by the "blessing" formula in v. 8 (but contra the exegesis above).[399] Perhaps this is why he can mitigate the force of the imprecations in vv. 5–7 by referring to them as the "mildest of maledictions."[400]

The NT—Agriculture as an Image of Severe Judgment

The Greek New Testament (1983) does not list any quotations, verbal parallels or allusions for Psalm 129. However, Augustine in his commentary on Psalm 129 seems to make connections with agricultural imagery from the NT, such as Mt 3:12 (Jesus as judge) and the parable of the tares in Mt 13:26, 39.[401] So, despite the lack of specific connections as defined by modern biblical scholars between Ps 129 and the NT, how certain agricultural imagery

---

396. For Goulder's (*Psalms of the Return*, 74–76) explanation of the apparent chronological inconsistencies in the Nehemiah narrative are due to the Chronicler's specific purposes while editing, see his commentary. Theodore of Mopsuestia considered the psalm as "spoken in the person of the righteous ones among the people in Babel" (Van Rooy, *East Syriac Psalm Headings*, 153).

397. Goulder, *Psalms of the Return*, 77.

398. Ibid., 78.

399. Ibid.

400. Ibid.

401. For an explanation and examples of Augustine's many differing interpretive methods see Fiedrowicz, "Introduction," 13–66.

is used in the New Testament may possibly add insight into the meaning of agricultural imagery as an imprecation in Psalm 129. The amount of agricultural imagery in the New Testament which can be investigated goes far beyond the constraints of this paper. Therefore, I will examine three uses of agriculture imagery in the context of judgment, predominantly from the perspective given in the book of Matthew (Mt 3:1–12; 13:24–30 and 21:18–21)[402] but also two images of grass (1 Peter 1:24 and James 1:10, 11).

The first passage is Mt 3:1–12 and the scene is John the Baptist's testimony of Jesus' role as judge. The first image of judgment is directed towards the Pharisees and Sadducees and is that trees not bearing fruit will be cut down with an axe and thrown into the fire. The second is the threshing floor where the wheat is gathered up, but the chaff is burned with "unquenchable fire." Mark's (1:3–8) rendering of John's testimony omits both images of judgment, whereas Luke (3:2–17) only has the cutting down of trees that do not produce fruit and which are thrown into the fire.

In the second passage, the Parable of the Tares (Mt 13:24–30), the enemy sows weeds among the wheat. At the time of harvest the weeds are tied in bundles and burned, whereas the wheat is gathered into the barn. In the third image, Mt 21:18–21, the barren fig tree is met with Jesus' words "May you never bear fruit again," and the fruit tree withers immediately. In the Mk 11:12–14, 20–24 passage it is the next morning that Peter discovers the withered fig tree. The cursing of the fig tree is probably prophetic action symbolic of the judgment which is about to befall the nation.[403] The fig tree has a background in OT passages such as Jer 8:13 and Hos 9:10. "The story of Israel told under the figure of a fig tree is a narrative of decay."[404]

The specific use of grass as an image occurs in 1 Peter and James. In 1 Peter 1:24 the reference is to "grass" (χόρτος) and the "flower of grass" (ἄνθος χόρτου). The *LXX* Ps 128:6 (129:6) uses the same term χόρτος. The usage in 1 Peter contrasts the transitoriness of human life with the word of God.[405] The connotative implication from Isa 40:6–8 and Ps 90:5 is that the transitoriness of human life is a form of God's judgment. The other usage is James 1:10, 11, where both verses have the terms χόρτος "flower" and ἄνθος "grass." In this instance the image of grass is used as a warning to rich people not to become proud because their lives will also fade away. Based on what James says in 5:1–6 about the torment awaiting the rich at the last judgment,

402. Matthew has the characteristic of being a written for a Jewish audience.
403. Charette, Theme of Recompense, 133.
404. Ibid., 135.
405. That this image of grass withering implies a judgment has already been mentioned in the exegesis and seems to be suggested by Isa 40:6–8, from which this passage seems to quote.

the scorching of the sun's heat is "indicative of God's judgment which will follow and turn the 'fading away' into an eternal fact."[406]

The following observations of the NT use are pertinent. The images in Matthew portray the harshness of the judgment in terms of degree and extent. In general, the image of the burning of the chaff, fruitless trees, and weeds is symbolic of complete judgment. It goes beyond the image of drying up and passively dying to an image of complete destruction. According to Mt 3:42, τὴν κάμινον τοῦ πυρός "fiery furnace," which here is a picture of *Gehenna*, appears in the OT as an image of captivity and exile (Deut 4:20; Jer 11:14; 1 Kgs 8:51). However, in the OT, the furnace is a "metaphor for an ordeal which tests and purifies the people; here it has become a metaphor for the final destruction of the wicked."[407] The duration in the images also contributes to the severity. The chaff is to be burned in an "unquenchable fire" in Mt 3. This is true also of the fig tree, which is prohibited from ever bearing fruit again. With this latter example, Matthew emphasizes the efficaciousness of Jesus' curse. The fig tree withered immediately. So the NT's use of agricultural images in the context of judgment portray a painful, complete and very long punishing judgment. There is a sense, though, in the Parable of the Tares that judgment will occur in the future. The two images of grass suggest that grass symbolizes the span of human life. These images do not seem to have the same severe connotation as the images of fire in Matthew. However, the idea of death being a judgment portrayed through grass regardless of the unsettling denotative meaning seems to be implicit rather than explicit.

Finally, although the images of judgment are directed towards the Pharisees and Sadducees (so internal enemies) in John the Baptist's speech, there is nothing in the texts to suggest that the judgments and curses were to be understood as directed exclusively to Israel alone. The repetition of John's words in Mt 3:10b by Jesus in Mt 7:19 suggest that John's words serve as more than a rebuke to Jewish impenitence. They serve as a warning to the church also.[408] Overall, "the recompense schema connected with the story of Israel in the Old Testament is presented as a paradigm for the recompense schema developed in his [Matthew's] Gospel."[409]

---

406. Davids, *Epistle of James*, 78.
407. Charette, *Theme of Recompense*, 146.
408. Ibid., 124.
409. Ibid., 164.

The Ante-Nicene and Post-Nicene Fathers

Suffering

Theodoret of Cyrus, in a more literal sense, relates the psalm to the Gentiles' assaults on the Jewish people after their return to the land.[410] As for application, Theodoret applied v. 3, "the sinners did their worst on my back," to "the scourges and abuses inflicted on the victorious martyrs."[411] Cassiodorus, writing in the monastic tradition, explains that the persecution by the enemies never comes to an end.[412] However, the Church "grows under the persecution of the wicked and grows through its grief." Further, the church may appear to suffer when it loses "holy ones," but those who lose their lives become part of the Church unseen in the "fatherland" and this is what "the enemies could not prevail over it" means.[413]

Meaning of the Response

Gregory of Nazianzus uses the image of vv. 5–7, "small and untimely sheaves, like those on the housetop, which do not fill the hand of the reaper, nor call forth a blessing from them which go by," to emphasize the ungodliness of the people when he began to work in his "field."[414] But Gregory applies the image to describe the external appearance of those who were perceived as "well-eared and fat in the eyes of Him Who beholdeth hidden things."[415] Besides softening the force of the imprecations, the implication is that all are enemies of God at some point in their existence.

Theodoret seems to understand the psalmist's imprecations in vv. 6–7 as prayer for the enemies' forays to come to an untimely end.[416] However, Theodoret does allow for strong images of violence in his translation of v. 4: "The righteous Lord cut the throats of sinners."[417] In contrast, Cassiodorus interprets the imprecations in vv. 5–8 figurally. He suggests that the death which is spoken of in the image of the grass dying is a spiritual one, "for

---

410. Theodoret of Cyrus, *Commentary on the Psalms*, 300.
411. Ibid.
412. Cassiodorus, "Exposition on the Psalms 128.2," 359–369.
413. Ibid., 360.
414. Gregory of Nazianzus, "Select Orations," 387.
415. Ibid.
416 Theodoret of Cyrus, *Commentary on the Psalms*, 301.
417. Theodoret was using a form of the LXX which differed from the MT.

they also often die off here before they are taken from this world's light."[418] Furthermore, the heights where the grass unsuccessfully sprouts is taken to symbolize pride.

Augustine[419]

Suffering from within the Church

Augustine's understanding of the suffering in the psalm is closely linked with his understanding of the composition of the Church.[420] The Church has consisted of select individuals from the time of Abel, but mixed within the Church are "bad people, people of wicked lives, whom the Church carries even to the end."[421] Even in the early stages of Israel's history, "Moses and the rest of the saints endured the wicked Jews."[422] In other words, there have always been those who have identified with the Church, but opposed it. Augustine explains the dynamic of persecution through the subtle idea that the enemy is aggressive and hates the word of God because the good person will not follow the bad into bad conduct.[423] Furthermore, Augustine explains v. 5 by showing the irrationality of the enemies' sin through the example of avarice.[424] The enemies cannot restrain their evil nature and so when a command comes such as "Do not be covetous" they respond that God should not make gold. The implication is that their sin is a result of God's creative acts. In response, Augustine affirms that God's creation is his good work and so the whole notion of hating Zion is shown to be irrational at its foundation.

Judgment—Spiritual and Eschatological

When discussing the imprecations it is important to keep in mind that Augustine suggests that the recalcitrant enemies may change.[425] So he in-

---

418. Cassiodorus, "Expositions of the Psalms 128.6," 360.

419. Augustine's *LXX* text is different from the *MT*.

420 Augustine, *Exposition of the Psalms, Vol. 6*, 117.

421 Augustine, "Explanations of the Psalms 129.2," 359.

422. Ibid.

423 Augustine, *Exposition of the Psalms, Vol. 6*, 119.

424. Augustine, "Explanations of the Psalms 129.5," 360. It appears that Augustine may have made a connection between this passage and James 1:10, 11 where grass is used as an image of judgment to warn the rich.

425 Augustine, *Exposition of the Psalms, Vol. 6*, 117.

terprets v. 4 to mean it is a righteous act to refuse the wicked but it is also a righteous act to bear with them. Augustine sees the angels as the harvesters (Mt 13:39) who will eventually knock these sinners (v. 3) off the psalmist's back.[426] As for the image of the imprecation in vv. 5–7, the high place where the grass withers signifies pride. Augustine seems to mitigate the force of the imprecations by suggesting that they have not been finally dealt with at God's judgment, but already they lack the sap needed for any green growth.[427] However, at the judgment which occurs at the end of the world, the enemies are thrown into the fire.

Calvin

The Church in Extreme Distress

Calvin begins the introduction to his commentary on Psalm 129: "This psalm teaches in the first place that God subjects his Church to divers troubles and affections, to the end he may the better prove himself her deliverer and defender."[428] The youth of vv. 1 and 2 refers not only to the time of Egypt, but stretches back to the time of Abraham and the patriarchs.[429] Calvin suggests that the psalm was written at the time when Israel had almost fainted under the tyranny of Antiochus Epiphanes.[430] He clearly sees the psalm as portraying not slight hurt but severe suffering when the Church was in "a state of extreme distress, or dismayed by some great danger, or oppressed with tyranny, on the verge of total destruction."[431] Behind these enemies lies the influence of Satan, who arms these "innumerable bands of enemies."[432] The enemies are not only external to the Church but of an internal kind who profess to belong to the Church.[433]

---

426. Augustine's (Ibid., 121) translation of v. 3a is "sinners have wrought upon my back."
427. Ibid., 125.
428. Calvin, *Commentary*, Vol. 5, 119.
429. Ibid., 121.
430. Ibid., 120.
431. Ibid.
432. Ibid., 121.
433. Ibid.

A Response for Comfort

Calvin gives the introduction to this section of the psalm: "Under the form of an imprecation, he shows that the divine vengeance is ready to fall upon all the ungodly, who, without cause, distress the people of God."[434] The first part of the psalm (vv. 1–4) stands as instruction for what is to be hoped for in the future.[435] Calvin indicates that v. 5 can be taken as a prayer or promise. He translates the verb in v. 6, *šlp* as *to be brought forth* or *to come forth*, and so the image in v. 6 is that of the grass not persisting, but withering as soon as it springs up. The height of the rooftops is a symbol of the enemies' pride. In v. 8, the reapers withholding their blessings is meant to suggest that the enemies deserve to be hated or despised.[436] The image is meant to bring comfort during times of persecution since the enemies "are but barren grass, on which the curse of heaven rests."[437]

Comparison with the Exegetical Findings of Psalm 129

There are several areas where the historical findings shed light on the exegesis. In the exegesis, the covenant terminology, *those who hate Zion*, and the structure of the psalm seemed to imply external enemies. However, the military connotation in the phrase used in v. 5a could suggest internal or external enemies. Of the commentators I examined, Augustine, Calvin and Gregory identify the true Israel with the Church. As a result the enemies can be external or internal (so Calvin). Augustine relates the true Church back to the time of Cain and Abel.[438] This notion of a remnant of faithful among unfaithful has always been a theme in the history of God's people. Given the above observations it is probably better to see the enemies as those who are outside of the remnant whether they appear to be internal enemies as Goulder describes or external gentiles as Theodoret suggests. On a spiritual and practical level, Gregory was correct in identifying all people before their conversion as being the enemies.

434. Ibid., 119.
435. Ibid., 125.
436. Ibid., 126.
437. Ibid., 127.
438. Calvin extends the meaning of "youth" back to the time of Abraham and the patriarchs, and Augustine to the time of Abel. These identifications may be correct. However, for structural reasons and intertextual witness it is better to associate the author's meaning here with the time of slavery in Egypt. It is only at this time that we have biblical witnesses which explain the agency of God in the punishment and deliverance of Israel.

Important also is Augustine's explanation of the dynamic of how these enemies function. Augustine's observations do not seem to derive from the text, but illuminate the text. They seem to answer the question of why these enemies hate Zion. Augustine explains that to hate Zion involves an irrational posture. He explains this theological precept through avarice, most likely because the term "grass" (χόρτος) is also found in James 1:10,11 in the context of judgment on the rich. There is an absurdity in hating Zion which Augustine captures theologically.

Another observation is the severity of the imprecation. One of the questions which was posed in the Introduction was whether imprecations in the form of agricultural images were severe. The investigation suggested the images of judgment associated with agriculture could indeed be severe. The NT images of agriculture used in judgment would support the severity. The image of fire and unquenchable burning has a fearsome connotation. Furthermore, the efficaciousness of Jesus' curse of the fig tree shows the power inherent in the words of Jesus. Even the grass (1 Peter, James 1) as a symbol of human lifespan implies that death is involved. Calvin also noted the severity in the imprecations in vv. 5–7, captured in his use of the phrases "divine vengeance" and "curse of heaven." Augustine allowed for a horrific final judgment, but his figural interpretation mitigated the strength of the imprecations. Gregory and Cassiodorus likewise mitigate the force of the imprecations with their figural interpretations. Grass may not have the paralyzing imagery of physical violence, but the image of grass is one of life and death and hence the denotative meaning is quite significant.

Another area of investigation in the exegesis was how the two stanzas, vv. 1–4 and vv. 5–8, are related. The finding in the exegesis was that the term *righteousness* stands at the heart of the psalm because it connects what Israel experienced in the past with what it can expect in the present and future. Calvin suggests that the term *righteousness* in v. 4 is meant to suggest that although God may dissemble for a time, "the welfare of the Church is inseparably connected with the righteousness of God."[439] In essence, both the deliverance and the punishment in the form of servitude were extensions of Yahweh's justice. If so, how much more could they expect Yahweh to judge those who were haters of Zion, the dwelling place of Yahweh! The commentators who understood Israel as the true Church are able to support such an interpretation because they see continuity in the past, present and future purposes of God.

---

439. Calvin, *Commentary*, Vol. 5, 125; 2 Thess 1:6, 7.

EXEGESIS OF PSALM 137: THE PROBLEM OF DASHING LITTLE ONES AGAINST THE ROCK

Psalm 137 needs little explanation as to why it is an appropriate choice for this study. The images ostensibly depict graphic violence against children as a legitimate means of exacting revenge. How are prayers that ostensibly take vengeance on one's enemies through their children to be understood? Furthermore, for the form-critical scholar, Psalm 137 defies straightforward classification.[440] Most interpretive issues relate to how one is to interpret vv. 8–9. A common way to understand these two verses is to assign them to the uncontrolled or morally unacceptable passion of the psalmist.[441] Additionally the theme of memory seems to be a major thread providing unity to the psalm. How does memory contribute to our understanding of the psalm and the imprecations? There also seems to be historically definable enemies, Edom and Babylon, which, as van Rooy notices, is unusual in the Psalms,[442] and a historically identifiable event, *yôm yᵉrûšālāim*, on which the imprecations are based. How do these historical events influence the interpretation of the imprecations?

Establishing the Text: When was Babylon Destroyed?

1.[443] By the rivers of Babylon –
   there we sat[444] down and there we wept
   when we remembered Zion.
2. On the willows there
   we hung up our harps
3. For there our captors
   asked us for songs
   and our tormentors[445] asked for mirth

---

440. Psalm 137 has been termed "stylized prose" by Seybold (*Die Psalmen*, 509) and noted for its lack of semantic features of parallelism by Alter (*Art of Biblical Poetry*, 19).

441. So Gunkel, *Die Psalmen*; Weiser, *Psalms*; Gerstenberger, *Psalms, Part 2*; Kidner, *Psalms 73–150*.

442. "Enemies in the Headings," 46.

443. The basic text is the *NRSV*. The *LXX* has the heading τῷ Δαυιδ. Some manuscripts of the Lucan texts have τῷ Δαυιδ δια ιερεμιου, "Of David through Jeremiah." It seems most likely that the gloss *through Jeremiah* was added as an attempt to explain how an exilic psalm could be ascribed to David.

444. Although the term *yāšaḇ* also means *to dwell* or *live*, the parallelism with *we hung up our harps* suggests that the specific verb *sit* is a better translation for the image here.

445. This word is a *hapax legomenon* and presents a challenge for translators. The

saying "Sing us one of the songs[446] of Zion!"
4. How could[447] we sing
   the LORD's songs[448]
   in a foreign land?
5. If I forget you, O Jerusalem,
   let my right hand wither.[449]
6. Let my tongue cling to the roof of my mouth,
   if I do not remember you,
   if I do not set Jerusalem
above my highest joy.
7. Remember, O Lord,
   against the Edomites
   the day of Jerusalem's fall,
   how they said, "Tear it down! Tear it down!
   Down to its foundations!"
8. O daughter Babylon,[450] doomed to be destroyed![451]

---

parallelism with *šōbênû* "our captors" suggests that a *qal* participle should be expected, but the MT has the noun *tôlâl*, which BDB suggests is a doubtful word (BDB, 1064). The AV and RV have *they that wasted* (plundered) which is a reading supported by the Targum, but read *wᵉšōllênû*. The LXX supported by the Syriac has the more prosaic καὶ οἱ ἀπαγαγόντες ἡμᾶς "and those who carried us away" which retroverted becomes *ûmôlîkênû*. Freedman ("Structure of Psalm 137," 192) proposed *htl* "mock, deceive" a unique *qal* form which is a secondary root of the *Hiphil* form *tll*. The mocking tone of the phrase "Sing us one of the songs of Zion" (see below) seems to support this proposal.

446. *šîr* is singular in form, but translated as a collective (Gunkel, *Die Psalmen*, 581).

447. Translated as a *non-perfective of deliberation* (IBHS, 508, Par. 31.4f); or modal imperfect (GES, 318, sec 107r-t).

448. *šîr* is singular in form, but translated as a collective (Gunkel, *Die Psalmen*, 581).

449. LXX has ἐπιλησθείη, "be forgotten." The parallelism with 6a suggests a verb with some form of physical restrictive movement, although the syntax is probably limited by what the fixed form of this Hebrew hand idiom was. The verb *šākaḥ* "forget" supports the theme of memory found throughout this psalm and could be the reason it was so easily kept as part of the *MT*. Apparently, the *NRSV* has adopted *wither* via the Ugaritic root ☒*kḥ* (Allen, *Psalms*, 302). Bradtke's (so Kraus, *Psalms 60–150*, 501) proposal in the *BHS* (1217) *tkḥš* "grow lean" requires the simple explanation of transposed letters. The word *wither* in English has the symbolic connotation of being devoid of strength and skill. Since the different proposals (see Allen, *Psalms*, 302) do not significantly affect the meaning intended, as a poetic device *wither* works well.

450. *NRSV* has *daughter of Babylon*. On the basis of Ps 9:15, Dahood (*Psalms III*, 273) suggests the genitives which follow the construct *bat* "daughter of" are explanatory or appositional (GES, 416, sec. 128k). The constructs in Ps 9:15 and Ps 137:8 are both formed with a *maqqep*.

451. *NRSV* has *you devastator*. The translation of this word is important for understanding the possible time frame and perspective being put forward in the psalm and the meaning of the imprecation (see below). The form of the MT is passive, *haššᵉdûdâ*,

Blessed[452] shall they be who pay you back
what you have done to us.
9. Blessed shall they be who take and shatter
your little ones against the rock.

Structure, Unity and Setting as Bases for Interpretation

Some scholars see a concentric pattern as the basis for the structure in Psalm 137.[453] On the outside, vv. 1–2 and 8–9 are linked by references to Babylon, followed by v. 3 and v. 7, which have quotations of the enemies. Next is 4 and 6aγb, which surround vv. 5 and 6aβ, a precise chiasm at the center.[454] Generally, however, scholars see a threefold or fourfold division, differing in opinion as to the status of v. 4, with some placing it by itself.[455] The majority of scholars favor a threefold division. Some prefer three strophes of four lines, vv. 1–3, vv. 4–6 and vv. 7–9.[456] Others prefer dividing the poem according to vv. 1–4, vv. 5–6 and vv. 7–9.[457] Zenger provides two reasons for including v. 4 with vv. 1–3 in the first strophe.[458] First, v. 1aα and the end of v. 4 form an inclusion "Babylon" and "foreign land." Secondly, v.

---

but if it is translated in the traditional attributive sense of a *qal* passive participle, it creates difficulties on historical grounds since Babylon was never "destroyed violently" (BDB, 994). Further, the imprecations in vv. 8–9 imply that the judgment is yet to come. The *LXX* has the adjective ταλαίπωρος, "wretched," translated in the *NETS*, *you wretch*. The adjective apparently provides a basis for the imprecations which follow. The Syriac, like the Targum (*bzwzyt'* and Symmachus (ἡ λῃστρίς), all use words which can be reverted back to the adjectival *haššādôdâ*. But, as Delitzsch (*Psalms, Vol. 3*, 336) points out, the meaning of these words in the original languages is *plunder* and *šdd* does not mean "to rob or plunder" but to "devastate violently." Delitzsch (Ibid., 336) suggested translating the *MT* in the prophetical sense of *vastanda*, the poet anticipating the future destruction as a realized fact. Since Babylon was never devastated according to the *MT* form of *šdd*, it must be related to the imprecations in a different way than merely historical.

452. *NRSV happy*. However, *blessed*, here and in v. 9, better captures the covenantal nature of this language, which I argue below imparts meaning to the imprecations.

453. E.g., Freedman, "Structure of Psalm 137," 205.

454. Letters refer to the division of the verse according to the MT accentuation. For example, v. 6 a has three parts (α,β,γ), whereas 6 b has only one part. For a criticism of this concentric proposal see Allen, *Psalms*, 305.

455. So Dahood, *Psalms III*.

456. Mowinckel, *Psalms, Vol. 1*, 102; Kissane, *Book of Psalms*, 285; Ogden, "Prophetic Oracles," 89–90.

457. Allen, *Psalms*, 303; Hossfeld and Zenger, *Psalms 3*, 513; Anderson, *Book of Psalms*, 896–897 and Gerstenberger, *Psalms, Part 2*, 394.

458. Hossfeld and Zenger, *Psalms 3*, 513.

4 maintains the speakers' identity as "we" which keeps the voice of vv. 1–3. To these reasons can be added the coherence created by the term *šîr*, which occurs between v. 3 and v. 4, three times in v. 3 and twice in v. 4.

Some scholars noticing the prominence of the terms Jerusalem/Zion see the psalm related to the "Psalms of Zion," although reworked to reflect the circumstances of lament and mourning.[459] This may be a valid way of understanding the psalm. However, Gerstenberger believes that Zion psalms such as 46, 48 and 122 differ in structure and are much more removed from the basic complaint outlook.[460] Even so, the terms Zion and Jerusalem play an important role in understanding the perspective put forward in the psalm. Zion only occurs in the first strophe in vv. 1 and 3 and is tied into the perspective of the community reflecting during its time of captivity. Jerusalem is found once in each of vv. 5–7. In vv. 5–6, a carefully constructed chiasm consisting of self-cursing formulas, v. 6b is highlighted, calling for the absolute loyalty of the psalmist (community) to Jerusalem. Verse 7 is a prayer against Edom for its participation in *yôm yᵉrûšālāim*, "the day of Jerusalem." Verses 8–9, which are imprecations in the form of blessing formulas, do not mention Zion or Jerusalem. Therefore we can assume that the use of the terms *Zion* and *Jerusalem* was more than just a stylistic issue.

Another important theme which creates coherence in the psalm is the notion of memory. *Zākar* "remember" occurs in vv. 1, 6 and 7, while the term *šākaḥ* "forget" occurs twice in v. 5.[461] Furthermore, the focus on memory introduces the imprecations beginning in v. 7, *zᵉkōr yhwh* "remember, O LORD." The use of memory carries the worshippers through a range of experiences from past reminiscence to present longing and then to present/future imprecations. Furthermore, the notion of memory is closely related to the concrete historical reality of the *yôm yᵉrûšālāim*, "the day of Jerusalem," which is found only here as a phrase.[462]

Generally, there are three main positions proposed for the setting of this psalm. The perfects in vv. 1–3 and the adverb *šām* in vv. 1, 3 suggest the speakers of the poem are removed in distance and time from captivity in Babylon. Kraus suggests that the psalm arose out of the observance of lament by the exiles, perhaps removed from the waters but not the rule of

---

459. Kellermann, "Psalm 137," 48–51; Kraus, *Psalms 60–150*, 501; Anderson, *Book of Psalms*, 303.

460. Gerstenberger, *Psalms, Part 2*, 395.

461. See the section on text notes above.

462. The phrase also occurs at 2 Sam 24:8, but in the context of meaning "twenty two days." The meaning of the phrase, though, is attested to in the context of the "day of Midian" (Isa 9:3) and the "day of Jezreel" (Hos 2:2).

Babylon.⁴⁶³ He understands v. 8 as indicating the Babylonian empire still exists (see above). However, others believe it was composed at a later date for cultic use, Mowinckel assigning it to cultic imagination, Gerstenberger suggesting that it was remembered in their present setting of being under pressure from majority groups, and Zenger suggesting that the Asaphite temple singers are the authors.⁴⁶⁴ Allen believes the second strophe vv. 5–6 reflects the psalmist addressing Jerusalem as present, but that the psalmist had experienced the exile.⁴⁶⁵ Similarly, Weiser suggests the exiles had just returned and saw their city in ruins.⁴⁶⁶ Arguments locating the composition of the psalm shortly after the arrival in Jerusalem of the exiles, based on the pathos of vv. 5–6,⁴⁶⁷ are strong, but in the end inconclusive. There are some wounds so egregious that time does not heal them or alter their memory. However, it makes sense to see the emphasis of the self-curse as indicating loyalty to the historical Jerusalem, which the exiles expressed either from their place of exile or shortly after their return while the city and temple were still in ruins. If *Oh daughter Babylon, doomed to be destroyed* in v. 8a refers to Babylon being destroyed in some way then the *terminus post quem* would be 516 B.C.E. when the walls of Babylon were partially destroyed.⁴⁶⁸ Anderson suggests sometime between 537 and 515 B.C.E. when much of the city and temple were still in ruins.⁴⁶⁹ Arguments for an early dating based on lack of explanatory comments about the exile in the psalm are strong.⁴⁷⁰ Nevertheless, the present form and content might reflect the needs and purpose of the worshipping community rather than the total sum of their theological understanding of the exile. The historical markers within the psalm make mention of Edom, Babylon and *the day of Jerusalem*, suggesting that the content of the psalm is very closely linked to the historical experience of the *day of Jerusalem* and exile.

---

463. *Psalms 60–150*, 501–502.

464. Mowinckel, *Psalms, Vol. 2*, 130, Hossfeld and Zenger, *Psalms 3*, 514, and Gerstenberger, *Psalms, Part 2*, 395.

465. *Psalms*, 304.

466. Weiser, *Psalms*, 794, and Dahood, *Psalms III*, 269.

467. So Allen, *Psalms*, 304.

468. See notes on text.

469. *Book of Psalms*, 897.

470. For example, John Ahn ("Psalm 137," 273–274) dates the composition between 587 and 582, on the basis of what is not mentioned about the third deportation of 582 BCE.

What the Text Says about Suffering

The uniqueness of Psalm 137 makes understanding its form and how it was originally used liturgically a challenge from a form-critical perspective, but there is no mistaking the suffering of the community portrayed in this psalm. The general exigencies of the exile are well known and do not need to be retold here. Rather the focus here will be on the indicators in the text that can provide a perspective of the suffering which arises out of this psalm. The pathos of the exiles' suffering in vv. 1–3 is reinforced by several features. The poet uses the first person common plural suffix *nû* "we" nine times, denoting collective identity, which gives a strong voice to the suffering. A vivid image of deep sorrow is inferred from the exiles sitting and weeping by the rivers of Babylon, a traditional posture for mourning, *bāḵîû* being a term used for both informal and ritual weeping.[471] The exiles hanging their harps on the willows is a picture of both loyalty to Zion and impotence.

The use of the term *Zion*, which is only used in vv. 1–3 in the perspective of the exiles' reflection during the exile, implies a meaning that is more than just geographical. Yahweh is the protector of Zion (Psalms 46 and 48), and Zion becomes a metonymy for everything that Yahweh stands for (*songs of Zion* v. 3 are the *songs of Yahweh* v. 4). The mocking of the captors by asking for songs of Zion was a form of humiliation. As Zenger states, "*the day of Jerusalem* in the eyes of the Babylonians was clear proof of the falsehood of YHWH's intimate relationship to Zion which was praised in those songs."[472] Marduk, the primary god of Babylon, was victorious over Yahweh the God of Zion. Whatever injustice, cruelty and shame the exiles had experienced in military defeat was compounded by the religious implications. To their captors' psychological oppression could be added their own interpretation of the meaning behind the exile. The hand of the living God was upon them in the form of punishment.[473]

The pathos of their suffering also finds voice in the longings expressed in vv. 5–6. Whereas memory was tied to Zion in vv. 1–4, in vv. 5–6 memory is tied to Jerusalem through self-cursing formulas. Jerusalem is found at the centre of this strophe and becomes the focus of longing. To consider Jerusalem above one's highest joy carries with it a notion which must be understood in the context of the *day of Jerusalem* in v. 7. Whether the psalmist is speaking from the perspective of the exile or early restoration in vv. 5–6,

---

471. Goulder, *Psalms of the Return*, 225.
472. *God of Vengeance?*, 48.
473. So Weiser, *Psalms*, 795.

the poet is expressing his longing for the restoration of everything which was destroyed on this tragic day.

Finally, we move to the imprecations in vv. 7–9. The psalmist was in no way ambiguous as to how he perceived Edom's role in the destruction of Jerusalem.[474] The poet tries to catch the severity of the destruction in the recoding of Edom's speech, *ʿārû ʿārû*, the guttural sounds adding to the tone of suffering. The poet moves on to Babylon. In the course of Babylon's devastation of Jerusalem, the exiles had seen the graphic horrors of warfare, where neither women nor children were spared (2 Kgs 8:12; Jer 6:11; Hos 10:14; Nah 3:10). As Kraus mentions, the use of the graphic metaphor in verse 9 is a reference to the cruelty of ancient warfare.[475] The Babylonian conquest of Jerusalem had been no different (Jer 6).

A Metaphorical–Historical Meaning of the Response

Memory provides a bridge by which one moves through this psalm. The memory of the suffering of the exile had been conceptualized through the use of the term Zion (vv. 1–4). Hence when Jerusalem lay in ruins the exiles wept when they remembered Zion. The use of Zion also hinted at the indestructible part of Jerusalem, the dwelling place of Yahweh who could not be deposed. Then memory expressed through longing (vv. 5–6) provides the link by which to reassert the psalmist's commitment to Jerusalem. These first two strophes provide the background for the poet's request for Yahweh to remember (*zᵉḵōr yhwh*) the destruction of Jerusalem. As Allen notes, in the movement from vv. 5–6 to v. 7 there is a type of bargaining.[476] If the psalmist remembers the suffering of the exile and the centrality of Jerusalem, will not Yahweh remember those who committed such atrocities? Hence if memory unifies the psalm the imprecations can be understood as a vindication of Yahweh. The reversal in fortune implies the restoration of Jerusalem, the outer reality to the never-changing hidden reality of Zion.

The charges brought against Babylon are implicitly brought through Edom's testimony. Anderson believes that *zkr* has associated with it the notion of punishment, as it does in Neh 6:14 and 13:29.[477] If this is the case, then the desire for Edom to be punished is implicitly expressed in the call

---

474. For an argument which believes there is no historical basis for associating Edom with the destruction of Jerusalem by the Babylonians, see Tebes, *Edomite Involvement*, 219–255.

475. Kraus, *Psalms 60–150*, 504.

476. Allen, *Psalms*, 308.

477. *Book of Psalms*, 899.

for Yahweh to remember. But there may be another way to view Edom's role, that is, the mention of Edom could provide a forensic perspective to the imprecations. Edom's role then would be both as a perpetrator/collaborator and witness. Allen suggests that the construction *zkr l* in its opposite sense of *remembering to someone's advantage* (Ps 132:1) entails a forensic notion with Yahweh invoked as a judge.[478] Since there are no specific imprecations against Edom, could Edom's placement in this psalm function as a witness against Babylon's violence? Edom thus is not only a collaborator, but also a witness to this calamity. After all, one would expect some form of imprecation against Edom as well (Lam 4:21; Obadiah; Ezk 25:12 ff, 35:5 ff; Jer 49:7–11).[479] In this way the mention of Edom, rather than appearing as an intrusion into the text, functions as testimony against the *daughter Babylon*, the recipient of the imprecations. The Edomite's own speech, *how they said, "Tear it down! Tear it down!"* is damning testimony not only to itself but to Babylon's cruelty on the *day of Jerusalem*.[480]

With a slightly different emphasis, Kidner provides a cogent way of understanding the imprecations through this type of juridical background based on *zkr l* "remember against."[481] In v. 7, Kidner sees a case made against the Edomites and then in vv. 8–9 a case against Babylon. Verse 8b expresses the principal of *lex talionis* which is applied to legal but not personal decisions. With this principle of justice established, Babylon is guilty of *what you have done to us*, v. 9 being the mirror of 8c. The conclusion that Kidner arrives at is that the imprecation in v. 9 is a "white hot" expression which in a "cooler moment" the psalmist would not have uttered.[482] This cogent explanation provides a way to understand vv. 7–9 as a unit, but the historical and covenantal features in the psalm need to be probed more carefully.

Zenger believes that since the psalm thinks of the complete destruction of daughter Babylon, the statement *daughter Babylon, doomed to be destroyed* (*baṯ-bāḇel haššᵉḏûḏâ*) in v. 8 is not a clue to a historical dating of the psalm.[483] I would concur to a certain degree with this position. Since Babylon never met with the fate of this imprecation—being violently

---

478. *Psalms*, 308.

479. Once again, I am working within the context of the MT. Some midrashic interpretations suggest that vv. 8–9 are directed towards Edom (de Wit, 2005:5).

480. It is interesting to note that in Zenger's (1996:49) earlier examination of this psalm, he believed the whole psalm to be shaped by legal categories. For example, the gesture of swearing in vv. 5–6 is formulated in the sense of *lex talionis*.

481. *Psalms 73–150*, 496; So Childs, *Memory and Tradition*, 32.

482. However, contra to Kidner, Ps 137 is a carefully composed literary unit.

483. Hossfeld and Zenger, *Psalms 3*, 519.

destroyed—we must look for a different understanding of the meaning.[484] It is my belief that the imprecation is a metaphorical expression of the exiles' desire for Yahweh's justice, which in this case is the complete elimination of the functional existence of the enemies of God, here the Babylonians. This seems to be an appropriate explanation since the only way that Babylon was destroyed was in the fact that it ceased to exist as a nation. Babylon never fell violently but was incorporated into the Persian Empire and remained an important city even until the time of Alexander. However, as a nation it ceased to exist after the Persian conquest of 537 BCE.[485] This is what I believe the metaphor is trying to get at. It is not a watering down of the violent war images, but rather getting to the essence of what lies behind the violent image. Babylon becomes as if it had been completely devastated.

But there are other clues to this modified understanding of the imprecations. First, the mention of *ōlālayik* "your little ones" (v. 9) differs from the pattern of war oracles in the prophetic literature. Jeremiah provides a similarity in outlook with the judgment expressed against Babylon in this psalm.[486] Jeremiah 50–51 and Psalm 137 both speak of the complete destruction of Babylon.[487] The normal military expression for total defeat in war oracles usually involves some type of merism such as in Jer 51:22 *man and woman, old man and boy, young man and boy*. Actually, *ōlāl* is not mentioned in Jer 50 or 51, but when it is used in Jer 6:11, 9:20 and 44:7 to describe the devastating effects of war, it occurs in a form of merism. Even the Isa 13:16 use of the term includes the mention of wives (hence mothers). The sole use of *ōlālayik* "your little ones" (v. 9) in an irregular pattern may be because the poet was restricted by the rules of parallelism with v. 8.

---

484. This, however, does not negate the fact that Yahweh can act in this world and within history in such a way, which is an assumption of both the OT and NT (I owe this comment to Dr. Kathleen Rochester). The judgment of Yahweh then can certainly occur through the most offensive violence. However, the notion of Yahweh's violence is closely tied to agency.

485. I am assuming that the Babylonian Empire did not continue on in the form of the Persian Empire. My basis for Babylon's end is on canonical grounds. First, the biblical texts portray Cyrus as being the deliverer of the exiles and the one who reverses the effects of the exile (Ezr 5:13–17); Second, because the historical mention of Cyrus in the texts of Isa 44 and 45 makes it clear that Cyrus was the deliverer; Lastly, because of the fixation of the memory of Babylon as the epitome of evil in the book of Revelation.

486. Cf. Jeremiah 51:56 where the roots *šlm* "repay," *gml* "deal out," *šdd* "destroy" also occur in Ps 137:8. The verb *npṣ* "shatter" in Ps 137:9 occurs 22x in the OT, 12 of which occur in Jeremiah (13:14; 22:28; 48:12; 51:20; 51:21 (x2); 51:22 (x3); 51:23 (x3). It also occurs in Psalm 2 where the LORD's king will *smash them in pieces*—the kings and nations which have set themselves against the Lord.

487. Hossfeld and Zenger, *Psalms 3*, 519.

However, the isolation of children as the sole focus of the war imprecation could be conspicuous as to how it should be understood.

According to Dahood those who believe that it is possible to interpret *daughter Babylon* to mean the ordinary citizens of Babylon ignore the witness of the eighth-century B.C.E. Sefire inscriptions.[488] There is some truth to this, but we cannot forget that Israel may have borrowed forms and then adapted them to their own needs. According to Zenger, the psalmist in Psalm 137 picks the image of children for two reasons.[489] First, it corresponds to *daughter Babylon*, so on a metaphorical level she is the mother. Second, it evokes the royal house in Babylon whose continuation is to be thwarted through the death of the children.[490] Anderson says of v. 9, "The whole verse may be taken figuratively; the dashing of the babes upon the rocks (scarce in Babylonia!)."[491] Ps 141:6 might also provide support for understanding "little ones" figuratively. There it is *šōpṭêhem* "their judges"[492] (of *those work iniquity*—v. 4) who are thrown over the cliff (*š'l*–same root as 137:9). This type of violent act directed towards the leaders is attested to as a symbol of judgment. There are good grounds then for appropriating the war imprecation against children as a metaphor for the complete ending of Babylonian ability to rule in both space and time. Such a notion goes beyond the *lex talionis* of repaying violent war acts in kind. Babylon as the super-power entity that had once wreaked havoc on other nations would never again exist. The notion of justice comes out much more clearly here, since there is a removal of the evil at the most fundamental level. The

---

488. *Psalms III*, 269. Dahood's point is that "To the psalmist the law of retaliation for cruelty seems only just, and the shocking form in which he expresses his desire for the extermination of his country's destroyer must be judged in the light of customs prevailing in his age." The Sefire treaties are vassal treaties made between kings and as such the curses are generally directed against the king and his nobles. In Sefire Inscription I, Face A, section IV, the curse for breaking a treaty extends to brutal treatment of the wives of the treaty breaker and his offspring's wives (Fitzmeyer, *Aramaic Inscriptions*, 15). Lines 9 to 17 of Face C of Sefire inscription II, when talking about the curses for anyone who effaces the inscriptions, reads "may he and his son die by oppressive torment" (Ibid., 83).

489. Hossfeld and Zenger, *Psalms 3*, 522.

490. Ending Babylon's "royal rule" is the central perspective of Isa 47:1–15 (esp. 47:1–8, 9).

491. *Book of Psalms*, 900.

492. Most English translations translate *šōpṭêhem* as "(their) judges" (*ESV, KJV, NKJ*), "rulers" (*NIV*), "leaders" (*NLT*). The *NRSV* is the exception. It is beyond the range of this discussion to pursue the *NRSV* translators' reasons for their difference. This verse merely shows the idea of judges (leaders/rulers) being singled out for punishment and the mention of *bîdê-selaʿ*, literally, "down/by/at/over the hand of the cliff" (Ps 141:6) "cliff" (*NIV*), "rock" (*NASB*) in conjunction with that punishment.

evil which is not an abstraction, but the action of agents working against Yahweh, is completely disabled.

But this concept of cursing needs to be seen in the context of the theme of memory in the psalm, which connects the cursing with the *day of Jerusalem*, the self-cursing oaths, and the tormenting of the captors. The reality of Babylon would cease to exist and so there would be no memory of it as an independent nation from that point onwards, whereas the psalmist pledges loyalty to Jerusalem and the never-ending memory of it. On another level it may be possible to say that an appeal is made to Yahweh the indeposable ruler of Zion who cannot tolerate the infringement of his own majesty by the enemy's mockery.[493]

The use of the covenantal language of the "blessing formulas" is another reason to interpret this war imprecation metaphorically.[494] By covenantal language here is meant the specific language of the Israelite community which functions to express religious ideas and understanding in the context of the cult.[495] The poet used imagery of war and violence, but infused them with new covenantal meaning through the covenantal perspective of the "blessing formula" 'šrê. This covenantal language of course is meant for the Israelites and has meaning in connection with their religious life. Zenger suggests that the beatitudes normally refer to men,[496] but that here it refers to God as the agent.[497] Regardless of the agency, it expresses in the language of faith Yahweh's role in the process of judging Babylon. The benediction carries with it the notion that Yahweh would implement it.[498] Further, there is finality in the irony of blessing one who brutally ends the life of children when children are usually associated with blessings.[499] Understanding the absoluteness of this judgment is therefore helped through the language categories of the covenantal community.

---

493. For Weiser (*Psalms*, 796) this idea would apply only to the implied imprecations of v. 7, since he holds that vv. 8–9 are the psalmist's uncontrolled outbursts.

494. This notion will be further discussed in Chapter 3.

495. My assumption here is that even in a theocratic society the cultic function of language allows for a different meaning than the non-cultic use of language.

496. So Allen, *Psalms*, 308.

497. Hossfeld and Zenger, *Psalms 3*, 520.

498. Allen, *Psalms*, 81.

499. Gunkel (Gunkel and Begrich, *Introduction to Psalms*, 224–226) relegates blessings introduced by the 'šrê formula to use by the laity. He sees behind the meaning of these formulas the notion of prosperity.

Conclusion of the Exegesis

It has been said that for Israel no distinction was made between the sacred and the secular and that Israel did not reflect after war on whether war was justified or not.[500] The proposed exegesis of Psalm 137 in this study suggests that beneath the common war imagery there was a deeper meaning for the Israelites.[501] The horrific war imagery of the murder of helpless innocents could be understood as a symbolic means of praying for the removal of Babylon's power base and any further influence for evil. In other words, the psalmist took war imagery and imbued it with a deeper meaning through carefully chosen imagery and by placing it within the covenantal framework of the blessing formulas. These covenantally understood features, which act as a roadmap for the people who use this psalm, indicate that the real focus lies beyond the ostensible violent images. What this suggests is that the imagery was loaded with more than one meaning, and the underlying meaning, even from cultic times, is also a valid one. Furthermore, there are eschatological tones in the imprecation. The war imagery is not in itself an eschatological perspective but the absoluteness of the judgment is. Such a wish is the ultimate form of judgment—the removal of the existence of evil.

A SELECT HISTORICAL SURVEY OF PSALM 137

Before I begin the historical investigation of Psalm 137 it will be helpful to restate particular areas of interest which arose out of the exegesis. We are interested in how the commentators understood adversity in the psalm, but specifically how they understood the images of violence against "the little ones." A further area of interest is how the commentators understood the relationship between memory and the imprecations. Finally, was their anything peculiar about the historical understanding of Psalm 137?

A Post-Exilic Perspective

The approach taken in the exegesis of Psalm 137 was from a post-exilic setting and so the results of the exegesis do not need to be reiterated here. Nevertheless, a few comments are in order to show how the possible historical

---

500. Scheffler, *War and Violence*, 5. This assertion tends to view Israelite society from the modern's perspective of church and state being two separate entities. I will suggest in chapter four that even within a "theocratic" society, cultic or "sacred" language had the potential to carry a different meaning than its use in a non-cultic setting.

501. This can also be said of Ps 110 and Ps 129.

setting and composition of the psalm are related. The exact dating of the psalm depends on how one interprets vv. 5–7 (the psalmist's oaths) and the word *haššᵉdûdâ* (v. 8). Allen sees vv. 5–6 as indicating that the psalmist has just returned to Jerusalem while it still lay in ruins.[502] In this case, Anderson's date of composition between 537 and 515 BCE is representative.[503] Goulder, however, holds to a date between 537 BCE and 400 BCE, but implies it was probably written later than 445 BCE when Nehemiah rebuilt the walls.[504] For Goulder, the three *š* (שׁ) particles in vv. 8–9 suggest a date in the fifth century.[505] Even so, those who suffered by the streams in Babylon are the ones who find themselves in Jerusalem.[506] He tentatively suggests Sheshbazzar's company (Ezra 1:11) or possibly Ezra (Ezra 7:1, 8:1), but settles with the possibility of the psalmist being unknown.[507]

Since Goulder's observations were not necessarily incorporated into the exegesis, a few of his points may provide a different perspective. The suffering portrayed in v. 1 was not personal weeping but a formal liturgical lament, a liturgical weeping.[508] The enemies were hostile local people who made derisive requests.[509] Their taunts by the poplar trees were a subtle way of asking where Yahweh was.[510] Besides the horrors of war experienced in the exile such as the slaughter of infants, Goulder notes that Edom's treachery was motivated by the desire to annex land in southern Judea.[511] The psalmist, within the historical time frame which Goulder establishes, takes an oath with the threat of a curse on himself to remember Jerusalem.[512] Finally, Goulder suggests the imprecations are meant to ask for condign punishment for the crimes committed by Babylon.[513]

---

502. *Psalms*, 304.
503. *Book of Psalms*, 897.
504. *Psalms of the Return*, 227.
505. Ibid. But see the exegesis.
506. Ibid., 228.
507. Ibid., 229.
508. Ibid., 227.
509. Ibid.
510. Ibid.
511. Ibid., 229.
512. Ibid., 228.
513. Ibid., 227.

The NT—Historical Judgment and Fixed Memory

The Greek New Testament lists two allusions/verbal parallels: Ps 137:8 with Rev 18:6; and Ps 137:9 with Lk 19:44.[514] The first allusion in Rev 18:6 refers to the phrase ἀπόδοτε αὐτῇ ὡς καὶ αὐτὴ ἀπέδωκεν, "pay her back as she herself has paid back others,"[515] which is a verbal parallel with *LXX*s 136:8, [μακάριος ὃς] ἀνταποδώσει σοι τὸ ἀνταπόδομά σου ὃ ἀνταπέδωκας ἡμῖν, "[happy shall they be who] pay you back what you have done to us."[516] Further similarity is drawn because both texts refer to judgment on Babylon.[517] "Babylon" occurs five times as a nominative, Βαβυλῶνος (Mt 1:11, 12; 17x2; Acts 7:43) where it refers to the country, and once in the dative, Βαβυλῶνι (1 Pet 5:13). In this latter passage, it may be a code word used by God's people in dispersion.[518] The term occurs six times in the genitive form, Βαβυλῶν (Rev 14:8; 16:19; 17:5; 18:2, 10, 21) where it is a symbol of demonic world power.[519] In Rev 18:6 the phrase occurs in the context of a judgment on "Babylon." Babylon is described as "a home for demons and a haunt for every evil spirit" (Rev 18:2). The latter part of verse 6 reads "repay her double for her deeds." This expression may be an idiom indicating the firmness of the punishment she is to receive or it could be a measured punishment which extends beyond the principle of *lex talionis*. In this latter case the punishment extends beyond the "commensurate punishment" mentioned in the first half of this verse. Further, in v. 24 "In her was found the blood of the prophets and of the saints, and of all who have been killed on the earth." Even in New Testament times Babylon had retained its image as the epitome of evil.

The other passage is Lk 19:44, which corresponds to Ps 137:9. The Luke passage has for its background the triumphal entry of Jesus. The response of the Pharisees in v. 39 can be interpreted as proleptic for the response of Jerusalem itself.[520] The text which Jesus pronounces is "They will crush you to

---

514. *GNT*, 906.

515. *ESV*, in order to highlight the similarities between Rev 18:6 and *LXX* 138:8 through the English verb *pay back*.

516. NRSV

517. It appears that John has taken Babylon's end-time judgment mainly from Jer 51:13 (Beale and McDonough, "Revelation," 1137). Beale and McDonough's discussion also emphasizes Isaiah and Ezekiel as primary sources for John's discussion of Babylon's judgment and make reference to Ps 137 at Rev 8:6. However, in Rev 8:6 they only make reference to the first half of the verse, stating that "Babylon's punishment is commensurate with its crime" (Ibid., 1140).

518. GIND, 32.

519. *GELNT*, 93.420.

520. Green, *Gospel of Luke*, 689.

the ground, you and your children within you."[521] In actuality, Lk 19:43–44a presents five images of military conquest and judgment.[522] "Jerusalem's rejection of Jesus is reminiscent of its historic betrayal of the covenant that led to the first destruction of Jerusalem and the exile. As Israel of old fell to its enemies on account of divine judgment for its unfaithfulness, so Jerusalem will be judged for its inconstancy."[523] It is noteworthy that Jesus is weeping when he pronounces this prophecy of judgment, which is not relayed in the form of an imprecation. The weeping itself is a prophetic image in the OT associated with the destruction of Jerusalem (2 Kgs 8:11; Jer 9:1).[524] The judgment to come is not just for the inhabitants' failure to recognize God's coming, but their hostility evidenced in their desire to kill the owner of the vineyard's son (Lk 20:9–10). Further, in the Lukan narrative the next thing that Jesus does is go into the temple and attempt to cleanse it of corruption.

The Ante-Nicene and Post-Nicene Fathers

Suffering in Psalm 137

Methodius interprets the reminiscing of the psalmist in Ps 137:1–4 allegorically to support the value of chastity.[525] The connection between this text and chastity for Methodius apparently comes because the flowers from the

---

521. "Luke's use of OT scripture underlies his conviction that Scripture prophetically announced Jesus' life and ministry (18:31–33; 24:26–27, 44–47), and that Scripture illustrates the story of Jesus' ministry, rejection, and death" (Pao and Schnabel, "Luke," 252). Allison ("Rejecting Violent Judgment," 459–478) makes the point based on a comparison of Lk 9:52–56 with several apocryphal texts (Acts of Phillip, Pseudo Clementine Literature, Testament of Abraham) for rejecting violent judgment. He argues that, in the OT texts of judgment alluded to in these texts, there was already an uneasiness towards the notion of violent judgment even among the ancients. However, in the case of Luke 9:52–56, Jesus' refusal to allow James and John to call down fire may be more indicative of their impropriety in knowing what just judgment was. The prophetic judgment against Jerusalem was not just for rejecting him, but as was explained in the parable of the vineyard for the hostility that is reflected in the parable of the tenants (Lk 20:9–19).

522. See Green, *Gospel of Luke*, 691. According to Pao and Schnabel ("Luke," 356) the allusions in these five descriptions of hostile activity are 1) Isa 29:3; 2) 2 Kgs 6:14; 3) Jer 52:5 (an allusion to the siege of Jerusalem by Nebuchadnezzar king of Babylon; 4) Ps 137:9; and 5) Mic 3:12.

523. Green, *Gospel of Luke*, 691.

524. See Pao and Schnabel, "Luke," 356.

525. Methodius (d. 311) was known as the chief antagonist of Origen (Methodius, 1987:307).

"willow" tree when mixed with water and drunk extinguish sensual desire.[526] Babylon is interpreted as "disturbance or confusion which signifies this life around which the water flows . . . the rivers of evil always beating upon us."[527] Also noteworthy is his understanding of the phrase "If I prefer not Jerusalem above my chief joy" where Jerusalem refers to the incorrupt souls, which God promises to place first after the resurrection.[528]

Ambrose, a commentator of the Western Church, interprets the weeping in 137:1 as an example of repentance to be followed "of those who, as a reward for sin, had been led into miserable captivity."[529] But his figural approach is seen in his interpretation of the strange land in v. 4 as the situation where "the flesh wars against the mind, and is not subject to the guidance of the Spirit . . . and so cannot produce the fruits of charity, patience, and peace."[530] This is part of his argument that in a state of sin one should not take the sacraments.

John Chrysostom, an Antiochene commentator, offers a perspective on both memory in the psalm and the harshness of the suffering.[531] In his exposition on Hebrews 11:20–22 he quotes Ps 137:1 and suggests that the reason that enduring hardship appears difficult is because we do not remember God as we ought to.[532] Chrysostom's analogy captures both his understanding of the relational aspect of memory with God and his practical but figural interpretation of Babylon:

> For these two things are involved in each other, yet are two. For great is the effect of God's remembrance, and great also of His being remembered by us. The result of the one is that we choose good things; of the other that we accomplish them, and bring them to their end. . . Therefore let us also, as being in Babylon, [do the same]. For although we are not sitting among warlike foes, yet we are among enemies.[533]

526. "Banquet of the Ten Virgins," 324.

527. Ibid.

528. Ibid., 325.

529. "Two Books," 358. According to Gillingham (*Psalms through the Centuries*, 37) Ambrose combined a more pragmatic reading of psalmody with a neo-Platonist and more allegorical approach.

530. Ambrose, "Two Books," 358.

531. Chrysostom's interest in Christian morality in the Psalms was a reaction to the more mystical and allegorizing approaches in the Alexandrian school (Gillingham, *Psalms through the Centuries*, 33). However, his interpretation of Babylon here is indicative that he used certain forms of figural interpretation.

532. Chrysostom, *Commentary*, 484.

533. Ibid., 484–485.

On a more literal level, Chrysostom sees the suffering of the exiles as God's way of making them "contrite."[534] Furthermore, the weeping of the exiles was not just "idle weeping" but the occupation of the exiles.[535] The refusal to sing songs of Zion was also an act of observing the Law.[536] Chrysostom is also able to explain the intensity of the hostility which was shown towards the Israelites. This is reflected through the speech of the Edomites in v. 7 where Chrysostom notes that the psalm proceeds in an escalating fashion.[537] The Edomites go beyond being satisfied with the captivity of Jerusalem and beyond the overthrow of Jerusalem: "Their [the Edomites'] desire, you see, was that not even a base be left for the city."

Jerome, a Latin Father of the Western Church, takes the suffering figuratively. Babylon, which means confusion, is a figure of the world, and captivity is taken to be the captivity of sin.[538] In contrast, symptomatic of the Antiochene school, Theodoret says that the captives wept many tears like currents of rivers when they contemplated the deprivation of Jerusalem.[539] The captors were humiliated, as the purpose for asking the captives to sing songs was in order to make fun of their situation.[540] Theodoret's understanding of the psalmist's oath in v. 6, of setting Jerusalem as the zenith of the psalmist's happiness, means the psalmist's sight of Jerusalem's restoration and the performance of celebrations in it.[541]

Allegory as a Solution to Loving One's Enemies

Most of the commentators in this section try to address the tension which exists between a NT ethic to love one's enemy and the imprecations

534. Ibid., 242–243.

535. Ibid., 243.

536. Ibid., 242.

537. Ibid., 244.

538. Jerome, *Homilies*, 357–358. According to Gillingham's (*Psalms through the Centuries*, 37) analysis of Jerome's comments on Ps 1, Jerome avoids the Alexandrian reading which identifies the ideal figure as Jesus and the Antiochan reading which suggests the ideal figure might be King Josiah. For Jerome the ideal figure in Ps 1 is anyone and everyone who has been saved by Christ.

539. Theodoret of Cyrus, *Commentary on the Psalms*, 323. As mentioned previously, it would be a mistake to assign uniformity to all the commentators of a particular school. For example, Theodoret differed with Theodore of Mopsuestia in that Theodoret believed the Psalms should be interpreted as prayers and prophecies for the household of faith and not as a means to argue against the Jews (Gillingham, *Psalms through the Centuries*, 33).

540. Theodoret of Cyrus, *Commentary on the Psalms*, 323.

541. Ibid.

presented in Ps 137. We begin with Origen, an Alexandrian commentator of the Western Church, whose spiritualizing approach is seen in his own words:

> For "the little ones" of Babylon (which signifies confusion) are those troublesome sinful thoughts which arise in the soul and he who subdues them by striking, as it were, their heads against the firm and solid strength of reason and truth, is the man who "dasheth the little ones against the stones" and he is therefore truly blessed.[542]

More than a century later, and also writing from the context of the Western Church, Ambrose interprets the self-condemning speech of the Edomites in v. 7, "Tear it down! Tear it down!" as "the words of some who want to deprive the soul of protection when it has yielded to the flesh."[543] Regarding the imprecations involving the dashing of the little ones, Ambrose writes:

> David . . . calls for a healer for her, and says: "Blessed is he who shall take thy little ones and dash them against the rock." That is to say, shall dash all corrupt and filthy thoughts against Christ, Who by His fear and His rebuke will break down all motions against reason, so as, if anyone is seized by an adulterous love, to extinguish the fire, that he may by his zeal put away the love of a harlot, and deny himself that he may gain Christ.[544]

The Cappadocian father, Gregory of Nyssa also allegorizes v. 9 by having "the little ones" refer to Eunomius's (leader of the anomoean Arians) heretical manifesto:

> While we, seeking the blessing in the prophet ("Blessed shall he be who shall take thy children, and shall dash them against the stones") are only eager, now that it has got into our hands, to take this puling manifesto and dash it on the rock, as if it was one of the children of Babylon; and the rock must be Christ; in other words, the enunciation of the truth.[545]

---

542. Origen, "Against Celsus," 620–621. "Origen's real gift is his ability to combine a textual, philological approach . . . with a philosophical, Logos-based doctrine which was a development of Clement's allegorical approach" (Gillingham, *Psalms through the Centuries*, 28).

543. Ambrose, "Two Books," 358.

544. Ibid.

545. Gregory of Nyssa, "Dogmatic Treatises," 36. According to Gillingham (*Psalms through the Centuries*, 30), Gregory's use of the Psalms is close to Origen's use. However, Gregory saw the *skopos* of the Psalms as the ascent of the soul to God, whereas

Chrysostom, in a more literal interpretation, which marks the Antiochenes, says that the imprecations "are the expression of the captives' feelings in demanding heavy retribution."[546] The psalmist appears to be governed by the stipulations of justice in Ps 7:4, but when he tells of the sufferings of others he depicts their anger and their pain.[547] Nevertheless, Chrysostom sees the imprecations as contradictory to the NT injunction given in Lk 6:28.[548] Theodoret writes of the imprecations in vv. 7–9 that "the inspired author prophesied the like punishment for them."[549] Historically, though, Theodoret mistakenly suggests that "consequently Cyrus is declared blessed for punishing them and freeing these [i.e., the Jews]."[550]

Jerome's use of a prosopological approach, made popular by Origen more than a century earlier, presents the adversity in a different perspective. Jerome interprets Edom ("earthly," "bloody") in v. 6 to be the devil.[551] Adam, therefore, is speaking of the devil, "the devil-serpent recognized in Nabuchodonosor [sic]" who thrust him out of Paradise. Therefore, the psalmist asks God to punish the devil for his malice of dragging him to Babylon. Further, the daughter of Babylon is the soul that is ever restless.[552] For Jerome the little children to be dashed upon the rock are symbolic of the sensual passion which the sexually chaste must dash against the rock which is Christ.[553] In his homily he gives his own example of being filled with desire for a woman and the consequence that if he does not take that sinful desire by the foot and "dash it against the rock" it will be too late.[554]

Augustine

Suffering—The Spiritual City

To begin with, we are interested in how Augustine understood the adversity resulting from "the day of Jerusalem" and the captivity. For Augustine "the

---

those who influenced him (Origen, Basil, and to some extent Athanasius) expressed the *skopos* of the Psalms in relation to the person and work of Christ.

546. Chrysostom, *Commentary*, 244.
547. Ibid., 244–245.
548. Ibid., 245.
549. Theodoret of Cyrus, *Commentary on the Psalms*, 324.
550. Ibid.
551. Jerome, *Homilies*, 359.
552. Ibid.
553. Jerome, "Letters of St. Jerome," 24.
554. Jerome, *Homilies*, 360.

disasters which befell that city in a literal sense were types of what was to happen to us."[555] The devil and his angels led us into captivity, but they could not have done it without our consent. Furthermore, when we are solicited by people through whom the devil is working, it is he himself who is soliciting us.[556] However, in seeing the Church composed of the weak and the strong, those who are strong sit above the rivers of Babylon.[557]

In terms of the enemies, Augustine describes them through geographical analogy. He suggests that there are some who do not live in the city centre and so are not completely overwhelmed by the lusts and pleasures of the world, but others are "very bad indeed and live in the center of Babylon."[558] When it comes to applying v. 6 and the Edomites to the Church, Augustine's words are quite strong:

> What fierce persecutions the Church has endured! The sons of Edom are carnally-minded men and women, dominated by the devil and his angels, worshiping stones and wooden idols and pursuing the lusts of the flesh. How often have they shouted, "Stamp out those Christians! Get rid of them, don't let even one remain."[559]

Augustine also provides commentary on memory in Ps 137. He steps out of his figural interpretation to say of the psalmist, "Hemmed in by crowds of such people [evil-filled people] he seemed to sense the peril, so he raised his mind to the memory of Zion."[560] Augustine ties in with memory the notion that Zion is the true source of joy for the psalmist. The rivers of Babylon are the things which people love in this world and Babylon symbolizes the desires on every side which snatch people.[561] Sadness comes from seeing the things one thinks brings joy slipping away, and so Augustine can say by comparison that "he will indeed sit and mourn, if he remembers Zion."[562] For Augustine it is important how we remember Jerusalem, "for we remember some things with hatred and others with love."[563] Furthermore,

---

555. Augustine, *Exposition*, Vol. 6, 229.
556. Ibid.
557. Ibid., 231.
558. Ibid., 228.
559. Ibid., 239.
560. Ibid., 233.
561. Ibid., 224. It seems that from Augustine's emphasis on wealth that he is setting up wealth as a rival to the true Jerusalem for the Christian.
562. Ibid., 227.
563. Ibid., 236.

"supreme joy is found where we delight in God."[564] By extrapolation, memory is also seen as an aid for the Christian to resist temptation: "If you want to be armed against temptations in this world, let desire for the eternal Jerusalem increase and grow strong in your hearts."[565]

A Spiritual Response

We are interested here in how Augustine interpreted the responses to the enemies given in vv. 7–9. In his analysis of v. 6 Augustine interprets Edom (although see above) as Esau and then from Rom 9:12 and 13 goes on to suggest that Edom is the Jewish people who are elder and the Christian people are the younger.[566] But this contrast between the elder and younger can also be applied to carnal humanity and spiritual humanity. Edom then is carnal people and this is what the prayer in v. 7 is asking for, to be delivered from carnal people.[567]

The day of Jerusalem is the day when the enemies wanted to overthrow Jerusalem. However, interestingly, Augustine equates Babylon with daughter of Babylon, citing Jerusalem and daughter of Jerusalem as being an equivalent example.[568] Augustine, as predicted, interprets the violent images in the imprecations figurally. The infants of Babylon who will be dashed against the rock are "evil desires newly come to birth" and "the rock is Christ (1Cor 10:4)."[569] Augustine notes that the original populace of Babylon did not survive when it was overthrown, but that its successors, those who oppose God, are called the city of Babylon.[570]

Calvin

An Historical Approach to Suffering

Calvin begins his commentary by recognizing the historical nature of the psalm rather than assigning it as a prophecy of David.[571] The circumstances

---

564. Ibid., 237.
565. Ibid., 241.
566. Ibid., 237.
567. Ibid., 238.
568. Ibid., 239.
569. Ibid., 240.
570. Ibid., 239.
571. Calvin, *Commentary*, 189.

of the exile left the people in danger of being thrown into despondency because of the cruel bondage and indignities they had to endure.[572] Calvin sees two purposes that the psalmist had: (1) by giving expression to their sufferings in prayer they may keep alive the hope of the deliverance that they longed for, and (2) the people would have acquiesced in the corrupt practices unless endued with mental fortitude through a period of 70 years.[573]

Calvin also comments on the indicators of suffering in the text. He notes that sitting on the ground is a posture which "indicates mourning and deep distress."[574] However, tears are also the expression of humility and not just distress. So the tears are evidence that the exiles recognized in their calamities the deserved chastisement of God.[575] The tears represented that they "were cut off from the worship of God, upon which they were wont to attend, and felt that they were torn from the inheritance of promise."[576] Furthermore, the reason they hung up their harps was that the "grief was too deeply seated to admit of common consolations or refreshment."[577] The enemies' purpose in mocking the captives was to cast blasphemies upon God, as if to say, "Your God is dead."[578] Calvin understands the psalmist's oaths in v. 5 as God's people declaring that the remembrance of the holy city would forever be on their hearts, and as instructive for the Lord's people to be more affected by public calamities which affect the Church than by their own personal trials.[579]

A Just Judgment

Calvin understands v. 6 to imply that "vengeance is to be executed upon other neighbouring nations."[580] That is, under Edom are to be included all the neighbouring nations which conspired to destroy Jerusalem. Calvin suggests that Edom is specified because it showed more hatred and cruelty than the rest (cf. Deut 2:4–6).[581] In his imprecation, the psalmist is only

---

572. Ibid.
573. Ibid.
574. Ibid., 190.
575. Ibid.
576. Ibid., 191.
577. Ibid., 192.
578. Ibid.
579. Ibid., 195.
580. Ibid.
581. Ibid., 195–196.

confirming former prophecies that God would punish Edom, given in Ezekiel 25:13, Jeremiah 49:7, Lamentations 4:21, 22, and Obadiah 1:1–11.[582]

Calvin comments on the call by the psalmist to "Remember, O Jehovah":

> [This was] to remind God's people of the promise to strengthen their belief in his avenging justice and make them wait for the event with patience and submission. To pray for vengeance would have been unwarrantable, had not God promised it, and had the party against whom it was sought not been reprobate and incurable; for as to others, even our greatest enemies we should wish their amendment and reformation.[583]

In terms of the imagery of children being "dashed and mangled upon the stones," the psalmist does not speak with the impulse of personal feeling, "and only employs words which God had himself authorized, so that this is but the declaration of a just judgment."[584] The psalmist, Calvin suggests, most likely is aware of the prediction in Isa 13:16 ff.[585]

Calvin does offer a solution to the conundrum that Babylon was "doomed to be destroyed" but never met with the literal fate portrayed in vv. 7–9. He proposes that it was Cyrus and Darius who were supposed to carry out the judgment, but since they had done it negligently they would be cursed.[586] The psalmist most likely knew about the prediction in Jer 48:10.[587]

Comparison with the Exegetical Findings of Psalm 137

Once again my goal here is to use the insights from the survey to supplement the exegesis I have done. In the exegesis I suggested that the historical events surrounding Psalm 137 may hint at a metaphorical interpretation for the imprecations, although somewhat qualified. The predominantly allegorical interpretations of the commentators stand in contrast to a metaphorical interpretation.[588] Metaphoric and allegorical interpretations are both tropes. However, as Brown explains, for a metaphor to work "There must be a cor-

---

582. Ibid., 196.
583. Ibid.
584. Ibid., 197.
585. Ibid., 197–198.
586. Ibid., 197.
587. Ibid.
588. In Chapter 3 of this thesis I will argue that synecdoche best describes what is occurring in the images of enmity.

respondence between the metaphor and its target domain that is recognized by both poet and reader; otherwise, the metaphor remains idiosyncratic and indecipherable."[589] Allegory is idiosyncratic in that it is unrestrained in imagining correspondences.[590] The metaphorical interpretation I offered is closely linked to the historical events. For example, the metaphor still talks about the destruction of the real historical Babylon, but the images of violence are taken to refer to the symbolic elimination of the nation.[591]

One of the conclusions which led to my metaphorical interpretation was the historical anomaly created by the *qal* passive participle form of *šādad* (see exegesis) in v. 7. However, Calvin offers a plausible explanation for this conundrum: the imprecation was to be carried out through the agency of Darius and Cyrus but they were negligent.[592] Calvin's theory also depends on the date of composition being earlier than the defeat of Babylon. However, it is possible that the psalmist saw the image as a qualified metaphor and understood the deeper truth beneath the literal meaning of the imprecation as a reflection of the true justice of God.[593]

Memory was also an important observation in the exegesis, being seen as the thread which held the psalm together. Memory of the suffering of the exile, conceptualized through the use of the term Zion, and memory expressed in the commitment of the returnees in the term Jerusalem, were even seen to be the foundation of the imprecations. With regards to memory, Chrysostom is particularly helpful. Although he might not have been exegeting the psalm in a way that would gain consensus from modern scholars, his observations are connected to the exile's experience in Babylon. Memory of God (Zion) is done in the context of God's memory of us. For without the latter we would choose good things but never do them. Augustine helps us to understand what the psalmist does when he remembers Jerusalem. When the psalmist is remembering Jerusalem he is remembering where supreme joy is found. Memory allows one to see through the illusions and troubles of this world. For the exiles it allowed them to bear the peril of the crowds

---

589. *Seeing the Psalms*, 6.

590. Waltke and Houston, *Psalms as Christian Worship*, 9.

591. This is in itself a severe form of punishment. Although the violent images are shocking to most readers, the idea that a nation would cease to exist and be silenced forever so that there would be no future to create memory may lack the gratuitous violence, but seems to be as severe on a different level.

592. This may be analogous to the way in which some interpret the prophecy in Ezekiel 26 of the destruction of Tyre. To comment on the prophecy in Ezekiel would go beyond the purpose of this study. I only offer it as an example to show that Calvin's proposal is not unique.

593. See the exegesis for my supporting arguments. Furthermore, see Chapter 3 for a discussion of synecdoche.

of evil-filled people. For Christians it will allow them to overcome the sadness from seeing things they think will bring joy slip away. For Calvin the oaths taken in remembrance of the Holy City were an example to place the Church's well-being above one's own.

The commentators are helpful in providing perspective to the hostility shown towards Israel. Goulder and Calvin both note the treachery involved in Edom's part, whereas Chrysostom shows the intensity of their hostility. Nevertheless, most commentators show a struggle to interpret the imprecations of violence. It must be pointed out that Jesus quoted this imprecation as a prophetic judgment on Jerusalem for more than failing to recognize him. Jesus' acknowledgement that such violence was part of the historical judgment on Jerusalem is suggestive about the way God in his sovereignty may choose to work in the world. Furthermore, Jesus does not show any indication of there being any contradiction with his new Kingdom message.[594] However, his tears at this pronouncement does symbolize the tension that exists between the love of God and the justice of God. The commentators Ambrose, Origen, Gregory of Nyssa, Jerome and Augustine all use allegorical approaches to interpret the violent images in v. 9. Chrysostom and Calvin take the imprecations in a literal way and struggle to explain the uneasiness that the images have for Christians. Calvin is especially helpful in the parameter which he sets up around the use of the imprecations.

Finally, we must note the significance that Babylon took on in the Church's history. The evil perpetrated by Babylon in the early 6th century B.C.E. was a significant event not only in the life of the Israelites, but also for the NT Church. Babylon becomes symbolic in the NT of everything that is opposed to God. Specifically, in Revelation it is associated with demonic world power and described as the haunt of demons and the place of the slaughter of prophets and saints. Through its actions in the "day of Jerusalem" the memory of Babylon came to be understood and fixed as the epitome of evil. Consequently, the psalmist's imprecation for Babylon to cease to exist as a nation is certainly suitable.

---

594. Later in Luke 22:48–53, Jesus will instruct his disciples on the nature and ethic of his kingdom, which excludes violence. That other parts of the NT clearly teach that the Church is to have no role in any violent form of vengeance, retaliation or expanding the Kingdom of God lies behind the NT teachings. Nevertheless, the picture of Jesus weeping (so also the cross) becomes a symbol of the complexity of the issue of the justice and the love of God in ostensible tension.

ENEMIES, OBLIGATION, AND SIN: KEYS FOR UNDERSTANDING THE IMPRECATIONS IN PSALM 139

Verses 19-22 of Psalm 139 are often met with aversion by the modern reader. The psalmist asking for God (*ĕlôah*) to kill the enemy and stressing his own hatred of the enemies makes these verses difficult to interpret for those who believe such a prayer is incompatible with the New Testament ethic to love one's enemy. Moreover, the apparent contrast between the providential intimacy shown in vv. 1-18 and the ostensible vengeful request in v. 19a, which is expanded by a tirade expressing the psalmist's solidarity with Yahweh in hatred, seems to further exacerbate this hermeneutical difficulty.

There has been no consensus in understanding the enmity in the psalm. Gunkel is representative of a Marcionic understanding of this psalm, which suggests that vv. 19-24 represent the underdeveloped and unbalanced religion of the Israelites.[595] Firth categorizes the suffering as psychological violence done against the psalmist, the psalmist having been charged with a capital crime, and proposes that the psalmist's response represents a self-curse.[596] Zenger believes the bloodthirstiness in v. 19 represents not the acute threat from an enemy, but the structural violence in the society of the wicked.[597] Goulder believes that the *rāšā'* "wicked" (v. 19) is the governor of the province.[598] The approach taken here sees the interpretation of the suffering and expressions of enmity dependant on one's reading of the form and setting of the psalm.

A Unified Text

> 1. <To the director of music.[599] Of David. A Psalm.>
>   O Lord, you search me and know me.[600]

---

595. Gunkel, *Die Psalmen*, 586, 589. These last four verses of Psalm 139 have often been excised from prayer books. The online *Book of Common Prayer* (http://www.bcponline.org, p. 795) contains them, but printed versions (BCP Canada, 1962) in the past have omitted them. The most recent online version of *The Liturgy of the Hours Psalter* (http://www.liturgies.net/Prayers/lohpsalter.htm#Psalm 139) includes them, but they have often been omitted during the actual recital of the Liturgy of the Hours (Zenger, *God of Vengeance?*, 30).

596. Firth, *Surrendering Retribution*, 46-49.

597. Zenger, *God of Vengeance?*, 32.

598. *Psalms of the Return*, 246.

599. NRSV has *To the leader*. The exact phrase occurs elsewhere in Ps 40:1; 68:1; and 109:1. The implication is that the leader was a musical leader.

600. The NRSV translates these perfective and *waw* imperfective verbs into English with the present perfect. But in English the present perfect denotes an unspecified time

2. You know when I sit down and when I rise up;
   You discern my thoughts from far away.
3. You search out my path and my lying down
   and are acquainted with all my ways.
4. Even before a word is on my tongue,
   O LORD, you know it completely.
5. You hem me in, behind and before,[601]
   and lay your hand upon me.
6. Such[602] knowledge is too wonderful for me;
   it is so high that I cannot attain it.
7. Where can I go from your spirit?
   Or where can I flee from your presence?
8. If I ascend into heaven, you are there;
   if I make my bed in Sheol, you are there.
9. If I take the wings of the morning,[603]
   and settle at the farthest limits of the sea,
10. Even there your hand shall guide[604] me,
    and your right hand shall hold me fast.
11. If I say,[605] "Surely the darkness will seize[606] me

---

in the past, or a present state resultant upon a past action. Translating according to a gnomic perfective (so Waltke and Houston, *Psalms as Christian Worship*, 534) better catches the universal nature of God's omniscience and accounts for the later part of the psalm, which indicates a present situation (Booij, "Psalm CXXXIX," 2).

601. *You hem me in, behind and before*, begins verse 5 in the *MT*. However, the *LXX* links this phrase with 4b.

602. The word, *such* is not found in the Hebrew. The *LXX* and Symmachus read ἡ γνῶσίς σου, which has the addition of a 2nd person pronoun, σου "of you," and makes explicit that the knowledge is Yahweh's. The need for the translation *such* captures the ambiguity in the *MT* as to what the antecedent of *daʿat* "knowledge" is. Booij ("Psalm CXXXIX," 3) thinks that *daʿat* refers to Yahweh's nearness in v. 5 and that *daʿat* influenced by the context of 6b should be translated *understanding*. But *daʿat* can be considered all that the psalmist mentions about Yahweh's knowledge between the *inclusio* formed by the idea of "knowledge" in v. 1 and v. 6.

603. The *LXX* and Syriac have *kᵉnāpay* "my wings" as the direct object (*MT*: *kanpê* "the wings of").

604. *NRSV* has *lead*. The Syriac has *tiqqāḥēnî*, "shall seize me," but the *LXX* supports the *MT*.

605. Interpreted as a conditional according to GES (330, 111x), Jerome, and Symmachus. For a slightly modified view see Waltke and Houston, *Psalms as Christian Worship*, 537. For a position which rejects a conditional interpretation see Booij, "Psalm CXXXIX," 4.

606. The emendation *yᵉśûkēnî* "cover me" suggested by *BHS* (1218) and supported by Symmachus does not need to be adopted according to *HALOT*, *Vol. 1* (1146b–1447, s.v. שׁוף) which suggests "grip hard."

and the light become night around me,"[607]
12. Even the darkness is not dark to you;
the night is as bright as the day,
for darkness is as light to you.
13. For it was you who formed my inward parts;
you knit[608] me together in my mother's womb.
14. I praise you for I am fearfully and wonderfully made.[609]
Wonderful are your works;
that I know very well.
15. My frame was not hidden from you
when I was being made[610] in secret,
intricately woven in the depths of the earth.
16. Your eyes beheld my embryo.[611]
In your book were written all the days
which were formed for me
when none of them as yet existed.[612]
17. How precious[613] to me are your thoughts, O God.
How vast is the sum of them.
18. Were I to count them—they would be more than sand.[614]

---

607. Or *the night is light around me* which more accurately represents the syntax in the MT. *laylâ* "night" is construed as the subject on the basis that in a nominal clause the subject precedes the predicate (so Booij, "Psalm CXXXIX," 4) and on the basis of semantic pertinence with v. 12b (so Waltke and Houston, *Psalms as Chrisitian Worship*, 537).

608. The Hebrew root *śākak* is a homonymous form which can mean "to cover" or "to weave together." Here the sense of "weave together/knit" is preferred as in Job 10:11.

609. Scholars point out (Allen, *Psalms,* 319; Booij, "Psalm CXXXIX," 6; Waltke and Houston, *Psalms as Christian Worship,* 538) that the verb *niplêtî,* literally, "I am wonderful" by itself does not include the notion of "made." However, the preceding word *nôrā'ōt* "I am fearfully" suggests an adjectival substantive functioning as an accusative of manner, which describes the way an action is performed (Ibid.). If the context of v. 15 is also considered, then the idea of "made" does not seem unreasonable.

610. Instead of the *pual* form found here in the MT, the LXX, Vulgate, Syriac and Targum have second person active verbal forms. There is no reason, though, to reject the MT.

611. BDB (166) and HALOT, Vol. 1 (194) propose *embryo*. The NRSV has *my unformed substance*.

612. Verse 4 might give additional support to favouring the *Ketiv* form *weʹlō'* "not" over the *Qere* form *weʹlō* "to him" (See Allen, *Psalms,* 319).

613. NRSV has *weighty*. Based on structural parallelism with vv. 6 and 14 *plʾ* "wonderful," the Hebrew stative verb *yāqar* "to be precious" may have the Aramaic sense of "be difficult" (Ibid.). The LXX has ἐμοὶ δὲ λίαν ἐτιμήθησαν οἱ φίλοι σου ὁ θεός, "but to me your friends were honoured, O God."

614. NRSV has *I try to count them—they are more than the sand*. In my opinion, the above translation portrays the subjunctive mood better.

I wake up[615]— I am still with you.
19. Oh that you would slay[616] the wicked,[617] O God.
    Bloodthirsty men, depart from me![618]
20. Those who speak of you maliciously,
    your enemies who speak in vain![619]
21. Do not I hate those who hate you, O LORD?
    And do I not loathe those who rise up against you?
22. I hate[620] them with complete hatred;
    I count them my enemies.
23. Search me, O God, and know my heart;
    try[621] me and know my thoughts.
24. And see if there is any way of idolatry[622] in me,

615. *BHS* and some scholars (Ibid.; *et al.*) favour emending the *MT* to *hăqiṣṣôtî* "come to an end," but the root *qṣṣ* is not found elsewhere in the *hiphil* stem. Furthermore, the *LXX* has ἐξηγέρθην, which seems to support the *MT*. The root *qyṣ* of the *MT* is a biform of *yqṣ* "to wake up." Waltke and Houston (*Psalms as Christian Worship*, 539) suggest the *hiphil* may indicate an internal notion, "I wake myself up."

616. *NRSV* has *kill*.

617. A singular form, but a collective meaning because the other enemies are plural. Contra Goulder (*Psalms of the Return*, 246) who believes the *wicked one* here is the governor of the province.

618. *NRSV and that the bloodthirsty would depart from me*. *NRSV* is following the Syriac and Targum which appear to support the third person imperfect form, *yāsûrû* "they should leave." However, as Waltke and Houston (*Psalms as Christian Worship*, 539) note, transition to direct speech is noted elsewhere, in Pss 6:8; 119:15. The *LXX*, Symmachus and Jerome all omit the copula.

619. *NRSV* has *and lift themselves up against you for evil*, which involves understanding the *qal* perfect *nāśu'* "lift" as reflexive and emending *'āreykā* "your enemies" to *'lyk* "against you" (so Gunkel, *Die Psalmen*, 593; NEB). Many English translations (*ASV, ESV, KJV, NASB, NIV, NKJ, NLT*) and Targum refer to variations of *your enemies take your name in vain*, a reading which is reminiscent of Ex 20:7 and Deut 5:11. However, this involves an ellipse of "your name." The above translation follows Allen's (*Psalms*, 318, 320) proposal based on parallelism, suggesting that an ellipse of *qôl* "voice" is assumed as in Isa 3:7; 42:2, 11.

620. *NRSV* has *perfect*.

621. *NRSV* has *test*.

622. The root *'ṣb* can be translated with a meaning derived from the sense of *pain* (BDB, 780). So the *NRSV* has *wicked way*. But as Allen (Ibid., 320) points out, the ambiguity of who the object of the pain is is removed when *'ṣb* is translated according to its homonym form meaning of *idolatry* (BDB, 781) (so Kraus, *Psalms 60-150*, 511; Würthwein, "Erwägungen," 173-174). The author may have used this expression to sharpen the contrast between the religion of Yahweh and the religious myths which are alluded to in the poem. Furthermore, this expression does not have to be considered a protestation of innocence, but can be considered a petition by the psalmist for Yahweh to test his integrity, which has become a matter of concern due to the hostility he is encountering.

and lead me in the way of everlasting.

Structure and Form—A Unified Literary Petition

The psalmist communicates his message through four carefully balanced strophes (vv. 1b–6; 7–12; 13–18; 19–24). However, the carefully placed *inclusio*, found between vv. 1b and 23 via the words *ḥqr* "search" and *yd'* "know"; vv. 2 and 23 via *rē'î* "my thoughts" and *śar'ppāy* "my anxious thoughts"; and vv. 3 and 24 via *drk*, indicates a unified perspective from which the message of the psalm should be derived. Allen suggests a slightly different structure based on the direct praise found in v. 14 (1b–6; 7–14a; 14b–18; 19–24).[623] In this case all three strophes would end in either wondering praise (v. 6) or hymnic phrasing (vv. 14a, and 17, 18). However, conceptually v. 13 seems to contribute to the theme of omnificence (v. 14 can also be interpreted in this manner)[624] and forms a unified theme of omnificence with vv. 14–18, and so v. 14 can properly be considered part of a third strophe which includes vv. 13–18. In this case in v. 14, the psalmist, in an atypical response, breaks out in praise for Yahweh's creation of himself.[625]

The first three strophes each successively build the psalmist's perspective on Yahweh's involvement in the world from different angles leading up to the final strophe which contains the petition; the structure is: strophe 1, God's omniscience; strophe two, God's omnipresence; strophe three, God's omnificence.[626] Each strophe consists of a quatrain of two couplets, beginning with a summary verse (1, 7, 13, 19) followed by three expanded verses (vv. 2ff, 8ff, 14ff, 19ff) and finally a lone couplet (vv. 5–6; 11–12; 17–18; 23–24).[627] This unity reinforces the need to understand the petition in strophe four as part of the whole psalm.

Besides the *inclusio*, the poet creates the unity of his theme through other rhetorical skills. He uses merisms to highlight the notion of Yahweh's omniscience in the first strophe (vv. 1, 2, 3, 5), each merism representing completeness and so implicitly contributing to Yahweh's complete

---

623. *Psalms*, 321.

624. Allen (Ibid., 319) proposes emendations to v. 14 and translates differently.

625. Atypical because none of the eleven other uses of the form *'ôdkā* "I praise you" in the Psalms refers to creation (*yādāh* "to praise" occurs 67 times in the Psalms out of 114 occurrences in the OT).

626. So Waltke and Houston, *Psalms as Christian Worship*, 541, and Dahood, *Psalms III*, 284–285, although Dahood structures the latter part of the psalm vv. 13–16, vv. 17–22 and vv. 23, 24.

627. Waltke and Houston, *Psalms as Christian Worship*, 541–542.

knowledge. He uses a symmetrical rhetorical question (v. 7),[628] the subjunctive mood (vv. 8–12), and geographical opposites (e.g., *šāmayīm* "heaven"—*šš^e'ôl* "Sheol") to highlight God's omnipresence. The subjunctive mood provides the hypothetical conditions by which to highlight the impossibility of escape from Yahweh. Furthermore, in strophe three the theme of omnificence is reinforced through the mention of body parts: v. 13 *kilyâ* "kidneys," *beṭen* "womb"; v. 14 *nepeš* "person?"; v. 15 *'ōṣem* (bones/frame);[629] v. 16 *gōlem* "embryo," *'ayīn* "eye"; v. 17 *rēa'* 'thoughts?,"[630] and *rōš* "head."

Another technique which the author uses to disclose his perspective is the distribution of divine names. The Psalm begins in v. 1 with the psalmist evoking *yhwh* (also v. 4), the covenantal name for the God of Israel, to speak of God's omniscience. The psalmist then uses *ēl* in v. 17, which is the name which signifies Yahweh's transcendence.[631] Then in strophe four the psalmist alternates between the use of *ĕlôah* (v. 19), *yhwh* (v. 21),[632] and *ēl* (v. 23). This latter use with the verbs *ḥqr* "search" and *yd'* "know" forms an *inclusio* with *yhwh* in v. 1, where the same verbs occur. One possible reason may have been polemical, to reinforce that Yahweh was this *ēl*. In doing so, the psalmist relates the transcendent nature portrayed in the term *ēl* with the covenantal name by which *yhwh* was known to his people. There is also a switching of the terms for God when dealing with the enemies. It is *ĕlôah* (v. 19) whom the psalmist asks *qāṭal* "to slay" the *rāšā'* "wicked," but it is *yhwh* who is the object of the enemies' hatred.

Understanding the Psalm's message also depends on determining its form. Gunkel classified Ps 139 as a mixed genre consisting of the hymn of an individual (vv. 1–18) with an individual complaint added on (vv. 19–24).[633] Mowinckel, seeing the individual's voice in the psalm representing the whole nation, considered the psalm a communal lament.[634] More specifically he classified it as a "protective psalm" which was composed in the middle of or before some threatening danger. Westermann makes sense of the different elements under the classification of praise focusing on the motif of creation.[635] Other variations are also found, for example, Allen, indi-

---

628. verb + preposition—preposition + verb
629. Note the homonym in v. 17 *'āṣam* "many, much."
630. An anthropomorphism rather than an actual body part.
631. Ibid., 541.
632. BHS notes a few manuscripts do not contain *yhwh* in v. 21, but other ancient versions (LXX, Targum) have it.
633. Gunkel and Begrich, *Introduction to Psalms*, 306, 46, 121.
634. *Psalms, Vol. 1*, 220.
635. *Praise and Lament*, 219.

vidual lament; Kraus, an individual psalm of thanksgiving.[636] Gerstenberger suggests that the common salient features of the different elements of this psalm are the sapiential language and reflective mood and so he styles this psalm a meditation.[637] Hossfeld concurs with Gerstenberger's designation.[638]

Helpful is Waltke's classification of Ps 139 as a petitionary psalm, although in unusual order: v. 1a address; vv. 1b–12 confidence, although atypical; vv. 13–18 praise; vv. 19–22 lament; and vv. 23, 24 petition.[639] For Waltke the confidence section is atypical because the psalmist mixes confidence and anxiety.[640] The nuance of anxiety comes from the hostile military metaphors in vv. 5–7.

Identification of the Enemies as a Clue to the Setting

A popular proposal for a legal–ritual setting has been suggested on the basis of v. 24 *derek-'ōṣeb* literally "way of idolatry" (or way of pain),[641] but often glossed in English as *wicked way* (KJV and NRSV), *offensive way* (NIV), *grievous way* (ESV) etc. Würthwein, Weiser, Kraus, and Dahood all suggest that the psalmist has been accused of idolatry at a religious court and calls upon Yahweh to protest his innocence.[642] Consequently, Dahood believes the reference to the enemies is to religious leaders.[643] But perhaps the enemies being described as enemies of God rather than of the psalmist should caution against too literal an interpretation of the language as representing an actual cultic trial.[644] Even if the enemies are associated directly with the

636. Allen, *Psalms*, 324; Kraus, *Psalms 60–150*, 513, 517.
637. *Psalms, Part 2*, 405–406.
638. Hossfeld and Zenger, *Psalms 3*, 539.
639. Waltke and Houston, *Psalms as Christian Worship*, 543.
640. Ibid., 549–552. Gunkel (*Die Psalmen*, 587) had recognized that the psalm was unusual because it did not have an introduction and because of the subjectivity of treatment.
641. Both translations seem to have a point of convergence if the translation "pain" refers to the pain his sin inflicts upon him (so Waltke's interpretation of pain [Waltke and Houston, *Psalms as Christian Worship*, 569]) and if "way of idolatry" is taken as a metonymy for sin.
642. Würthwein, "Erwägungen," 165–182, Weiser, *Psalms*, 802, Kraus, *Psalms 60–150*, 513, 518, and Dahood, *Psalms III*, 284. Gunkel (Gunkel and Begrich, *Introduction to Psalms*, 140) suggested that the term *rāšā'* "wicked" (v. 19) originally belonged to the legal realm and designated the guilty party, and only later did it take on the general meaning of wicked or godless.
643. *Psalms III*, 284.
644. Which is the reason that Beyerlin (*Die Rettung*, 11) did not include this psalm as "an enemy psalm of the individual" in his study.

psalmist as Allen suggests,[645] the psalmist identifies them as Yahweh's enemies and in his second petition in an unusual manner does not ask to be delivered from them.

Croft sees the enemies as evildoers within Israel.[646] His identification of the enemies as internal enemies is tied to a cultic–legal setting, but there may be grounds to question whether the enemies can only be identified as internal enemies. The enemies are explicitly identified by the following terms: v. 19 *wicked*,[647] and *men of blood*; v. 20 *those who speak of you maliciously*; v. 21 *those who hate you*; and v. 22 *[my] enemies*.

From the unity of strophe four, all the terms for enemies appear to be representing the same group. Furthermore, the enemies are substantial: "Only in a communal context is Yahweh's confrontation with hostile groups thematized."[648] This does not necessarily mean that the enemies must be external, but it does indicate that the scope from which to identify the enemies should be considered on more than only a private individual level. For Croft, both of the terms used for enemies in Ps 139, *rāšā‘* "wicked" and *’ôyēḇ* "enemy," can refer either to external or internal enemies.[649] Croft allows that "foreign enemies and armies can be described as *rš‘ym* by reason of their opposition to Yahweh or his anointed."[650] The *’ôyēḇ*, Croft suggests, represent a threat to the psalmist and in about two-thirds of the psalms in which the term appears represents foreign enemies.[651] However, the language used by the psalmist to describe the enemies as *those who hate you* (v. 21) is covenantal language.[652] As was discussed in Ps 129 the word *hate* when used as an expression towards Yahweh (v. 21 *those who hate you, Lord*) is almost always used to identify those outside of the covenant and hence

---

645. *Psalms*, 324.

646. *Identity of the Individual*, 46, 81, 90.

647. The term *rāšā‘* "wicked" is construed as a collective singular because the other enemies are identified in the plural. Goulder (*Psalms of the Return*, 241) takes the *rāšā‘* as singular, and identifies him as the governor of Judea.

648. Gerstenberger, *Psalms, Part 2*, 404.

649. For Croft (*Identity of the Individual*, 47) the *rš‘ym* are classified by being under Yahweh's judgement. Likewise, Croft (Ibid.,) categorizes the *’ôyēḇ* as those who represent a threat to the psalmist.

650. Ibid., 32.

651. Ibid.

652. Gerstenberger (*Psalms, Part 2*, 404) to the contrary says, "By way of this declaration of solidarity (not by covenant formulas) the alliance of the believers with Yahweh is made perfect (cf. Ps 69:10 [RSV 9])." Is Gerstenberger making too much of a difference between the two?

external to Israel.⁶⁵³ Could the polemical tone of the psalm also mirror non-covenantal enemies?⁶⁵⁴

Is it possible to be more specific with the categorization of this psalm? It is partially on the basis that the enemies are God's enemies that Eaton identifies the psalmist as a king who is under attack.⁶⁵⁵ Eaton suggests that the psalmist is a king by comparison with psalms 16, 17 and 63; the enemies who beseech the psalmist are also God's foes; and the psalmist claims merit in his total opposition to the enemies, and wants to be led in the total way of eternity, cf. 21:2ff; 45:6; 61.7ff; 72:5; 110:4.⁶⁵⁶ Although this categorization has not garnered much following, Eaton finds support from Croft and Goulder. Croft understands Ps 139 as a psalm intended for the ritual preparation of kingship.⁶⁵⁷ Goulder agrees that the psalm must speak of some national leader, but believes the language dates it later.⁶⁵⁸ The arguments for a late dating are based on the Aramaisms in the text.⁶⁵⁹ However, some of

---

653. Botha, "A Social-Scientific Reading, 1406. The term *śn'* "hate" occurs four times in vv. 21 and 22. The suggestion that the enemies can be internal because of the use of the phrase *ûlᵉśōnĕ yhwh* "and to those who hate the LORD" in 2 Chr 19:2 may be questionable. The phrase is spoken by Jehu the seer to Jehoshaphat and it is unclear who the subject of the phrase is. If it is Ahab, he was only a nominal member of the covenant community at most. Furthermore, how did Jehoshaphat help? Did he help Ahab by wearing the royal robes of Israel? Ahab was still killed. Or did he help the Aramites by indicating he was not the king of Israel? Most likely the reference is to the former, although the context of the use of the phrase *those who hate the Lord* is a battle with Aram.

654. It is beyond the scope of this study to investigate these allusions, but it is generally recognized that the psalmist makes allusions to the pagan myths of the solar deity, the Mother Earth goddess, and the Tablet of Destiny (see Waltke and Houston, *Psalms as Christian Worship*, 534–572). There are further indications of a polemical tone: "Ea is the wise lord of the depths, Marduk is the battler against primeval Chaos, and Shamash drives away all darkness. Yahweh's activity embraces all these aspects (cf. Ps 139)" (Keele, *Symbolism*, 49). Further, in the practice of haruspicy in Babylon, the liver was believed to be a microcosm of the whole body (Ibid., 184–185). In Ps 139 Yahweh is the creator and determiner of human life. To these examples can be added the contrast between *the way of idolatry* and *the way everlasting* and the use of the various names for God (see above).

655. *Kingship*, 83, 84.

656. Eaton, *Psalms*, 459. Further evidence is the intimacy of the relationship of Yahweh with him and the regal allusions inferred from creation (Eaton, *Kingship*, 84).

657. *Identity of the Individual*, 46, 81, 90. He finds similarities with the Babylonian Akitu festival.

658. *Psalms of the Return*, 242.

659. See Allen, *Psalms*, 326 and Waltke and Houston, *Psalms as Christian Worship*, 544. Dahood (*Psalms III*, 284–299) has presented linguistic arguments based on similar lexical links with the book of Job, inscriptions, mixed dialects, Northwest Semitic vocabulary, Ugaritic, etc. as a means of suggesting an earlier pre-exilic date.

the ideas contained in Ps 139 appear to have an early provenance by comparison with the Amarna texts (fifteenth century BCE) and the biography of Hattusillis (Hattusillis the 3rd ruled from 1298–1260 BCE).[660] Perhaps at this stage in research it is best to hold with Weiser a tentative dating of the psalm.[661] I will consider the psalm as a protective psalm composed for the king under attack from significant enemies.

Perceived Suffering

The caesura between vv. 18 and 19 indicate that the king's meditation about God's active and relational presence stands in contrast with the hostile reality he faces. In v. 19b the psalmist transitions to direct speech and commands *men of blood* to depart from him. This phrase *men of blood* occurs four times in the Psalter and once in Proverbs. It has the meaning of those under Yahweh's judgement (Ps 26:9); those who will not live out half of their days because of Yahweh's judgement (Ps 55:24); those who are out to kill the innocent psalmist (Ps 59:3);[662] and those who hate the blameless and seek the life of the upright (Prov 29:10). Although the term *dām* "blood" has semantic multivalence,[663] the ethical implications are that those who are identified by this term have taken innocent blood, or in the case of Ps 59:3 and Prov 29:10 there is an intention to take innocent life. In the context of enemies arrayed against the king we can see this opposition as part of an historical process. "The word [*dām*] occurs frequently in the theological interpretation of a historical process which may often look like a series of bloody wars."[664]

The psalmist's *anxious/disquieting thoughts* (v. 23b) provide a wider context for the psalmist's disposition because they appear to be related to all that is included in the *inclusio* between vv. 1b and 23a. In the immediate context 23b refers to the hostility of the enemies with emphasis primarily as God's enemies. However, *the disquieting thoughts* must also be understood in the context of strophes one, two and three. Yahweh, who discerns the psalmist's *rēaʿ* "thoughts" from afar (v. 2a), and whose *rēaʿ* "thoughts" are *yāqar* "precious" to the psalmist (v. 17a), is intimately present in the

---

660. Young's ("The Background of Psalm 139," 101–110) purpose is to show the distinctness of the concept of the omniscience of Yahweh in Israel, but the comparison shows that the concepts existed and were in use relatively early.

661. *Psalms*, 802.

662. Possibly from v. 5 identified by foreign nations, but note the heading.

663. *TDOT*, 244–245.

664. Ibid.

psalmist's existence. This notion of presence stands in distinction to the notion of Yahweh's presence expounded in Ps 119 as presence through Torah, or the presence of place identified in Ps 110 as Zion. The contrast between what the psalmist has adumbrated about Yahweh's intimate knowledge and care and the psalmist's present reality of hostility becomes the basis for him to petition Yahweh to search and know his heart. While in v. 1b the psalmist is stating a habitual fact that Yahweh searches and knows him, here the psalmist uses the imperative mood.[665]

In the psalmist's worldview, he cannot reconcile the disparity between the presence of Yahweh and the presence of the enemies, whose immediate threat is captured in the psalmist's direct speech (v. 19b). Consequently, the psalmist turns to self-reflection to determine whether the cause may be his own shortcomings. Like the prophet Jeremiah (Jer 17:9) the psalmist knows that *the heart is deceitful above all things*. In vv. 5–7 the psalmist's choice of verbs reflects the anxiety that he feels. Now in strophe four, rather than protesting his innocence, the psalmist is asking God to test his mettle. The psalmist is implicitly formulating the problem of God's just dealing with his people. How can those who are enemies stand if God is present and fulfilling his obligations? The psalmist is worried that unknown sin is the cause. Perhaps the second petition (v. 24b) reinforces the psalmist's focus. The psalmist's ultimate concern is not framed in terms of deliverance from the enemies, but rather being led in the way everlasting.

Meaning of the Response

The crux of the issue is how to make sense of the psalmist's petition in v. 19, *Oh that you would slay ('im–tiqṭōl) the wicked, O God*.[666] The '*im* is the marker of the optative mood,[667] and the second person direct address to ĕlôah (v. 19) ensures that the expression is understood as a request and not just a soliloquy. The word *qāṭal* in its biblical use refers to the intentional taking of life. When used to describe a person's actions (only once, in Job

---

665. Dahood (*Psalms III*, 225) believes the imperatives in v. 23 are grounds for translating the same verbs in v. 1 as precative perfects, but this misses the nuance which the author creates. It is because Yahweh knows him that the psalmist is anxious about some unknown wicked way in his life. Further, it is better to translate the two verb forms in v. 1 as a merism in which the totality of God's knowledge is being reinforced not only by content but by rhetorical style.

666. It occurs four times in the OT: Job 13:15; 24:14; Oba 1:9; and Ps 139:19. The Aramaic form *qᵉṭal* also meaning *kill* occurs five times in the book of Daniel (2:13 x 2; 2:14; 3:22; 5:19).

667. GES, 477, s.v. 151e.

24:14) it carries with it an immoral characterization intensified by the object of the action, in this case the "poor." When Job uses the verb in Job 13:15 with God as the subject and himself as object it serves a rhetorical function. In Oba 1:9 it is used in the context of a prophetic judgment of Yahweh (*neʾum yhwh*), literally "an oracle of the LORD," but translated *declares the LORD* (Oba 1:8), against Edom for Edom's participation in the sack of Jerusalem and will occur on the *day of the LORD* (Oba 1:15). This last example, then, provides the closest similarity to Ps 139.

Furthermore, by referring to the enemies as *men of blood* the psalmist is implicitly remarking on the obligation that Yahweh has as the *dōrēš dāmîm* "avenger of blood" (Ps 9:13). Bloodshed pollutes the land and atonement cannot be made for the land on which blood has been shed except by the blood of the one who shed it (Num 35:33; Ps 106:38). God is the ultimate avenger of murder, cf. Deut 32:43; 2 Kgs 9:7; Ps 9:12.[668] Perhaps one function of the psalmist's portrayal of Yahweh as omniscient, omnipresent, and omnificent in vv. 1–18 is to remind Yahweh of his obligation to avenge the innocent shedding of blood. Yahweh is the creator of both those who murder and the innocent who are murdered. By virtue of his obligation to account for innocent blood, the enemies can be identified as Yahweh's enemies. The enemies in accordance with their characterization find their consequential end in opposing Yahweh himself via his representative the king. The king and the community rally in prayer that asks Yahweh to remember his obligations according to who the enemies are.

At times, Yahweh is portrayed as helping the righteous get revenge on the evildoer (Ps 58:11; Ps 68:24), but here it is Yahweh who is called on to act. The question of agency is left at its primary level. The king and his army would be the natural agency through whom Yahweh would work out his justice, but the king does not formulate this aspect of agency in his prayer. The response to the injustice of the bloodthirsty begins with developing a Yahweh-orientated perspective.

But there is another aspect to this prayer, that is, the psalmist's apprehension with whether there is an offensive way in his life. His direct speech to the enemies, "Bloodthirsty men, depart [*sûr*] from me" provides another perspective from which to see his dilemma. This juxtaposition of two very different approaches to the enemies makes sense if we see them in terms of the removal of the enemies as a sign of God's presence. In other words, whereas the first petition for the death of the enemies holds Yahweh to his obligations as creator, the direct speech for the removal of the enemies can

---

668. *NIDOTTE*, 963–966.

be seen in terms of Yahweh's presence. The psalmist has a worldview[669] that understands the unjust enemies and Yahweh's presence as incompatible. So now the psalmist turns from Yahweh's obligations to his own. Like Jeremiah he recognizes that the heart is evil and so he looks to see if there is any sin in his life. This apprehension is portrayed both in the psalmist's anxiety inferred in vv. 1–18 and in his second petition in vv. 23, 24. That the second petition (v. 24) does not further deal with the enemies by asking for deliverance serves to highlight the psalmist's understanding of the conundrum. To request to be led in the "way of everlasting" returns the focus to the psalmist's reliance on Yahweh's leading. The everlasting way is "the path of unbroken communion and life with the Lord."[670]

Conclusion of the Exegesis

In summary, Psalm 139 deals with the problem of God's justice as represented by his presence as maker and sustainer of life apart from expressions related to the Law and the cult.[671] The meaning of the imprecation comes from the perceived obligation of Yahweh as the *avenger of blood* and the psalmist's inability to reconcile the success of the wicked and the presence of Yahweh. The psalmist, which evidence suggests is the king:

> presents them [the enemies] (vv. 20f.) as hostile to God himself, somewhat as the enemies of God's kingdom in the royal Psalms 2, 101 and 144, planning rebellion, uttering arrogance. And like the anointed in Psalm 2, the psalmist would make the Lord's cause his own, utterly opposing the enemies of the Lord.[672]

The psalmist appeals to Yahweh's omniscience, omnipresence and omnificence as the basis for Yahweh's obligation to account for innocent blood being shed. Furthermore, the psalmist's own fear that there may be sin in his life is evident from the nuance of his plea in verses twenty-three and twenty-four. The poetic artistry of Psalm 139, suggests that verses 19 to 24, rather than standing in stark contrast with the apparently more enlightened poetry of verses 1 to 18 is thematically consistent. The God who knows, who

---

669. The historical narratives of both the judges and the kings would serve to reinforce such a worldview.

670. Eaton, *Psalms*, 461.

671. The use of the psalm in the cult and possibly the allusions of *dām* "blood" to cultic sacrifices might infer a cultic use (see also above, the modern commentators who propose a legal cultic setting). However, in a straightforward reading the content of the psalm does not include the Law or the cult *per se*.

672. Eaton, *Psalms of the Way*, 460.

A SELECT HISTORICAL SURVEY OF THE INTERPRETATION OF PSALM 139

In the context of the findings in the exegesis, it will be helpful to state what our particular focus will be in this section. We will be interested in how the commentators understand the adversity of the psalmist and what meaning they attach to the psalmist's response in vv. 19–24. Since some scholars attach a negative connotation to God's omniscience, omnipresence, and omnificence (see exegesis), how did the commentators understand these images in vv. 1–18? Also of interest will be how the commentators understood the relationship between the two sections vv. 1–18 and vv. 19–24.

Psalm 139 in the Post-Exilic Restoration

One of the proposals in the introduction was that in the editing of Book V, the editors presented a historical perspective which reflected the post–exilic restoration period.[673] This, however, does not mean that the individual psalms were composed in the post–exilic period. Rather, the editor considered the restoration as the central focus by which to arrange the psalms. The conclusion reached in the exegesis was that Psalm 139 was originally a protective psalm for the king under attack from significant enemies. Since the kingship did not exist in the restoration, one possible interpretation is that it took on an eschatological meaning at the time of the restoration. Nevertheless, its use during the restoration might be treated from a different viewpoint, which sees Ps 139 from the perspective of being composed in the post-exilic restoration.

Goulder takes Ps 139 to have been written when Jerusalem was only partially rebuilt.[674] The speaker is a reformist Jewish leader, and Goulder understands the *wicked man* in vv. 19a and 20b to refer to the governor of Judea, who, with his associates, are nominal worshippers of Yahweh.[675] This

---

673. Once again, this is irrespective of the date of composition of the individual texts and is not the only perspective which may have been intentionally incorporated during the editing of Book V.

674. *Psalms of the Return*, 241.

675. Ibid.

governor wants to impose an alien religious law on the cities in the land.[676] In this context, the religious leader is praying for the death of the "law-breaking governor and his men."[677] The psalmist does not feel God's hand to be hostile (vv. 1–6) or oppressive (vv. 7–12).[678] Goulder also sees evidence of a prophetic vocation from the imagery in vv. 7–12.[679] Furthermore, the governor and his armed retinue of "men of blood" hate Yahweh and rise up against him.[680] Jeremiah's prayer was more powerful than the psalmist's because in Jeremiah's case Hananiah the son of Azzur actually did die (Jer 28:17).[681] Goulder makes a tentative suggestion that Ezra is the religious leader and that Johanan (Neh 12:22) was the wicked man who did not follow God's true law.[682]

The NT—Spirit of God and the King of the Nations

The Greek New Testament (1983:906) lists no quotations of Ps 139 in the NT, but lists three occurrences of allusions/verbal parallels: Ps 139:1 with Rom 8:27; Ps 139:14 with Rev 15:3; and Ps 139:21 with Rev 2:6.[683]

In the Rom 8:27 passage[684] the larger context is the future glory of Christians at the resurrection, but the immediate context is of prayer. The general thrust of the passage is that the Holy Spirit aids the Christian in prayer, but that God himself searches the heart and knows the mind of this Spirit. It should also be noted that it is in the context of suffering (Rom 8: 17 and 18) in which this passage of prayer occurs. The searching effect of God then is one which aids the believer, who does not have the depth of knowledge of himself to know what to pray. The Spirit, in a way, reveals to God only what God can know because of the limitation of human self-knowledge.

The Rev 15:3 passage follows the mention of the last seven plagues symbolizing the completion of God's wrath (Rev 15:1).[685] "The deeds" (15:3,

---

676. Ibid.
677. Ibid., 242.
678. Ibid., 243.
679. Ibid.
680. Ibid., 246.
681. Ibid.
682. Ibid., 247.

683. For a discussion of whether John's use of the OT in Revelation was rhetorical, mystical, or scribal see Moyise, *Later New Testament*, 5.7.

684. Chrysostom (*Commentary*, 252) also notes this connection between Ps 139:1 and Rom 8:27.

685. Blount (*Revelation*, 285) notes that although Revelation is filled with hymns,

τὰ ἔργα; Ps 138:14 *LXX*) here, then, are related to the defeat of the beast, his image and the number of his name (Rev 15:2). Although John appeals to the "song of Moses,"[686] the new song presented in 15:3-4 is based on "a broad cross-section of OT texts that heralds a consensus about God's almighty and salvific nature."[687] Importantly, in the final words of verse 3, "John identifies the almighty judging God as the King, not of Israel or the conquering witnesses, but of the nations."[688] As Moyise notes, since the nations have been the subject of judgment in Revelation in chapters 6 to 14, the inclusion of a hymn that proclaims their salvation must be purposeful.[689] The connection is implied in Ps 139, where God is portrayed as the creator of all and hence the sovereign of all. A further point that Blount brings out about the "metaphor of singing" in 15:3 is that its connection with the plagues of wrath (15:1, 5-8) re-establishes "a focus on the realization of God's rule through the execution of God's justice/judgment."[690] The "song of the lamb" explains that Jesus will lead the deliverance of the saints from the beast.[691]

The last passage where a link is presented is in Ps 139:21 and Rev 2:6. The context for the Revelation passage is the message of John's vision to the Church in Ephesus. In the passage, the Church at Ephesus has lost its first love, but is commended by the risen Jesus because they hate (μισέω; also *LXX* Ps 138:21) the practices of the Nicolaitans which Jesus also hates. The solidarity of hating the enemies of Christ, then, is commended in this vision given to John.

---

only three times does John use the actual vocabulary of singing (ᾄδω), at Revelation 15:3; 14:3; and 5:9. Rev 15:3 relates to Ps 139, whereas Rev 5:9 and 14:3 relate to allusions in Ps 149, the last psalm in my investigation. Given the nature of the Psalms, such a connection should not be thought of as coincidental. "The central focus that joins both prior singing episodes [with 15:3] is celebration prompted by the realization of God's rule" (Ibid., 286).

686. Beale (*Book of Revelation*, 358) relates the "song of Moses" to Ex 15 and Deut 32, and notes that the "song of Moses" in Deut 32 ends with "he will avenge the blood of his servants." The idea of "bloodthirsty" (men of blood) in Ps 139:19 and its relation to Yahweh being the creator of all people was commented upon in the exegesis.

687. Blount, *Revelation*, 287.
688. Ibid., 288.
689. *Later New Testament*, 5.6.
690. *Revelation*, 286.
691. Beale and McDonough, "Revelation," 1133.

The Ante-Nicene and Post-Nicene Fathers

Suffering

The commentators have various opinions as to the impact that God's omniscience, omnipresence, and omnificence had on the psalmist.[692] Writing in the first century, the apologist Clement of Rome suggests that God's omnipresence (139:7-8) should lead to the fear of God and the abandonment of "the abominable lusts that spawn evil works."[693] A sense of not being able (or not wanting) to completely know oneself comes out in the Cappadocian father, Basil.[694] Basil, in speaking about God's omniscience (v. 6), suggests that "even our mind, which contemplates intently another's sin, is slow in the recognition of its own defects."[695] For Basil, by contemplating ourselves we can understand the superabundance of wisdom in God. The Antiochene, Theodoret of Cyrus, sees the expression from v. 6, "Truly your knowledge was wonderful to me: I was overwhelmed and could not reach to it" as words which should lead to praising of the "Benefactor" with all one's might.[696] Chrysostom sees v. 6, "Your knowledge is too wondrous for me," and v. 14, "I will give you thanks for you are fearfully wondrous: wondrous are your works"[697] as causing the psalmist to "shudder" and to be "deeply frightened."[698]

Peter Chrysologus interprets vv. 7-10 in the context of the fact that sin cannot be hidden from God.[699] That is, sin stands exposed to the eyes of God. Ps 139 is also used apologetically. Basil uses v. 8 in his argument

---

692. The discussion follows a sequential ordering of the verses as opposed to a purely chronological one.

693 Clement of Rome, "1 Clement," 385. In his *First Epistle,* Clement uses the paranetic approach of Philo to highlight the moral teachings of Jesus (Gillingham, *Psalms through the Centuries,* 25).

694. According to Gillingham (Ibid., 30) Basil has a more practical appeal to the Psalms and his 15 homilies on the Psalms have much in common with Athanasius. In his homilies, Basil is not so concerned with heresies as were the Alexandrian writers on the Psalms. A further characteristic of Basil is that he differs from his brother Gregory in that Basil sees the *skopos* of the Psalms in relation to the person and work of Christ rather than the ascent of the soul to heaven.

695 Basil, "Homilies on the Hexaemeron," 384.

696 Theodoret of Cyrus, "Discourse," 385.

697. The text here differs from the MT.

698 John Chrysostom, "Homilies on the Gospel of John," 385.

699 Peter Chrysologus, "Sermon 2," 386-387. Peter Chrysologus (c. 380-450) was the Latin archbishop of Ravena.

refuting any insubordination of Christ to the Father.[700] Augustine interprets vv. 7–8 to suggest that if God is everywhere his Spirit is everywhere.[701]

The sense of God's penetrating searching in the context of judgment comes across in Cyprian.[702] In the context of Christians who had taken *libelli* (certificates issued by Roman officials during the Decian persecution as proof that they had renounced their faith), he interprets v. 16 to mean that they will not escape judgment. Also interesting is the way he introduces the quotation of v. 16 by saying, "The Holy Spirit says in the Psalms." The penetration of God's searching is captured in "He sees the hearts and breasts of each one, and, when about to pass judgment not only on our deeds but also on our words and thoughts, he looks into the minds and the wills conceived in the very recess of a still closed heart."[703]

Meaning of the Response

Again, rather than following a chronological order in this section, we will begin by looking at how commentators viewed vv. 19–20 and then move on to vv. 21 ff.

In his commentary on the Psalms, Chrysostom says the psalmist does not ask for people to be killed but for sinners, and the meaning is to change people from sin to righteousness.[704] Further, by commanding bloodthirsty men to depart from him, the psalmist is pursuing a path to growth in virtue by shunning and departing from the company of such people.[705] The "particular marks of friendship" are solidarity with God in the hating of enemies and the opposing of opponents.[706]

Another literal interpretation is given by Theodoret, who believed that David was prophesying of Josiah in Ps 139: "Consumed with divine zeal, he disposed of all the priests of the idols, whereas on those embracing piety he lavished all attention."[707] The enemies, then, are the priests of the idols, and he consigns them to death and has their bones burned (1 Kgs 13:1, 2). For Theodoret, in v. 19 it is characteristic of good people to love good people

---

700 Basil "On the Spirit," 387.

701 Augustine, "On the Trinity," 387. This reference to Augustine does not come from his commentary and is included in this section for convenience.

702. Cyprian, "The Lapsed," 388–389.

703. Ibid. 388–389.

704. John Chrysostom, *Commentary*, 261.

705. Ibid.

706. Ibid.

707. Theodoret of Cyrus, *Commentary on the Psalms*, 329.

and detest the other kind, "Since you [God] in your loving-kindness do away with the sinners, much more shall I avoid their company."[708] The motivation for God to kill them comes from v. 20 based on the translation "They will take your cities,"[709] which means "not unjustly but because they will inhabit the cities to no good purpose, reaping no benefit from your laws"[710]

In contrast to the Antiochene school, Cassiodorus offers a figural interpretation of v. 19.[711] He understood this psalm to be recited by the mouth of Christ. Hence the psalm is interpreted prosopologically within a Trinitarian framework, with the fourth section describing the "pre-eminence of the faithful in spite of their enemies."[712] Cassiodorus suggests that if we analyze v. 19 in a spiritual sense all the difficulties are removed.[713] The meaning is that God kills the sinners when a person dies to sin and lives for the Lord. The words "bloodthirsty men, depart from me" are directed towards the unfaithful and stubborn who refuse to believe.[714] According to Cassiodorus, these people are "men of blood" and they "live according to the flesh, and perform bloody deeds."[715] However, Cassiodorus does not explain what the bloody deeds are.

The commentators offer various perspectives on the call to show solidarity with Yahweh by hating those whom Yahweh hates. The writer of the *Constitutions of the Holy Apostles* uses Ps 139:21 in his exhortation to Christians to avoid communion with impious heretics:

> Charge the faithful to abstain entirely from them, and not to partake with them either in sermons or prayers: for these are those that are enemies to the Church, and lay snares for it; who corrupt the flock, and defile the heritage of Christ, pretenders only to wisdom, and the vilest of men.[716]

---

708. Ibid., 334.

709. Theodoret's text may be different from the MT. The term *'r* "enemies" of the *MT* is translated as "city."

710. Ibid.

711. Cassidorus (c. 485–580) is representative of the monastic authors. According to Gillingham (*Psalms through the Centuries*, 56–57) Cassiodorus was influenced by Augustine and used an Alexandrian reading of the Psalms within a Latin setting. Also remarkable is the contribution to "gloss" which Cassiodorus made and his novel approach of identifying twelve Christological categories (around the two natures of Christ) with the psalm headings.

712. Waltke and Houston, *Psalms as Christian Worship*, 527.

713. Cassiodorus, *Eplanation of the Pslams*, 382.

714. Ibid.

715. Ibid.

716. "Book VI," 450.

Similarly, in the context of the Origenist controversy, the anti-Origenist bishop, Epiphanius, uses v. 21 to support arguments for actions he had taken to root out Origen's teachings:

> Origen's words are the words of an enemy, hateful and repugnant to God and to His saints; and not only those which I have quoted, but countless others... deceived by his persuasive arguments, and made by his most perverse teaching the food of the devil.[717]

Ironically, Houston suggests that Origen may have had Ps 139 in mind when he argued, against Celsus, for the compassion shown to humankind when the Word became flesh.[718] Houston concludes that it is Ps 139 which "holds these two aspects in remarkable tension: ineffability and intimacy."[719]

Chrysostom, while giving a homily on 1 Cor 13:4, sees a tension between Ps 139:22, which speaks of a perfect hatred, and the qualities of love exposited in 1 Cor 13:4. He thinks that in order for the Christian to evangelize, hating is not possible. He argues that David did not pen Ps 137 and by implication he did not pen these words in Ps 139 either. He exhorts Christians, "But now because he hath brought us to a more entire self-command and set us on high above that mischief, he bids us rather admit and soothe them."[720] And to the question whether Christians should hate the heathen and the enemy Chrysostom replies, "One must hate, not them but their doctrine: not the man, but the wicked conduct, the corrupt mind. For the man is God's work, but the deceit is the devil's work."[721] According to Basil, the psalmist's expression of solidarity with Yahweh in v. 21 is praiseworthy because God gives all power to the rational soul to love virtue and justice but to hate iniquity and vice.[722]

Theodoret shows the tension that exists in a literal interpretation of vv. 21–22:

> I hate them, but I continue grieving at them and wasting away: as sinners I hate them, but as human beings I pity them, obliged

---

717. "Letters of St. Jerome: From Epiphanius," 87. For a background to this dispute see the introduction to *To Pammachius Against John of Jerusalem* ("Letters of St. Jerome: To Pammachius," 424).

718. Waltke and Houston, *Psalms as Christian Worship*, 520–521.

719. Ibid., 521.

720. Chrysostom, "Homilies on 1 Corinthians," 199.

721. Ibid., 198.

722. Basil, "Homilies on the Psalms," 389.

to mourn for them out of natural fellow-feeling but in turn detesting them for their great wickedness.[723]

This appears to be a more nuanced form of the cliché, "hate the sin, but love the sinner," which Chrysostom (above) and Augustine (below) present. Theodoret closes his commentary by commenting that the psalmist's prayer "Examine me and lead me in the way" has to do with personal piety.[724]

Cassiodorus has a slightly different perspective on vv. 21–22.[725] He begins his explanation of v. 21 by pointing out that there are two reasons that our enemies rise up against us. The first is that we have offended them through some fault of our own. The second reason for enemies rising up is because of their own obduracy and arrogance, and such men are rightly to be regarded with disgust, for they were unmindful of God's great kindnesses. However, Cassiodorus defines perfect hatred in v. 22 as "loving men and always loathing their vices."[726]

Augustine

The occasion for Augustine's sermon on Ps 139 (138) was somewhat unexpected for Augustine. He had intended to speak on Ps 138 (137), but the speaker read 139 (138) instead and Augustine took it as a sign of the will of God to provide an exposition on it instead.[727]

Suffering

Augustine spells out clearly his understanding of Christ speaking in the psalm in unity with the Church.[728] It is this prosopolgical reading which provides unity for reading the psalm rather than the psalmist's experience. Augustine interprets much of vv. 2 to 6 through the illustration of the parable of the Prodigal Son, whose life represents a fleeing from God and who was "pursued by the righteous punishment of God."[729] Augustine interprets "lay your hand upon me" (v. 5) as "a punishing hand that lies heavy on the

---

723. Theodoret of Cyrus, *Commentary on the Psalms*, 334.
724. Ibid., 334.
725. Cassiodorus, *Explanation of the Psalms*, 382.
726. Ibid., 383.
727. Augustine, *Exposition, Vol. 6*, 256, 270.
728. Ibid., 256–259.
729. Ibid., 260.

proud."[730] God's knowledge is too wonderful and incomprehensible for the psalmist (v. 6) because of his sin.[731] In v. 7, Augustine suggests the psalmist is looking for a place where he can go to escape God's anger.[732] The imagery of fleeing on wings in v. 9 is "to flee from your [God's] avenging Spirit, from your stern, menacing countenance."[733] Furthermore, although Augustine is using a text different from the MT, he interprets v. 14 to mean "God shows himself as terrible."[734] Verse 15 seems to be a turning point in Augustine's exegesis. However, the general connotation of Augustine's interpretation up until v. 14 suggests that God's knowledge exposes sinfulness.

Meaning of the Response

Augustine sees vv. 19–22 very much relating to the bad people who are born within the Church. Christ is suffering through his body the Church as he is still with the Father. According to Augustine, "these sufferings are caused by the presence of sinners in the midst of the Church and by the heretics who separate themselves from it."[735] Furthermore, Augustine explains the psalmist's passionate expression in v. 19 as "Sinners are slain because, when they become puffed up with pride, they lose the grace which was their true life . . . This is how sinners are slain: darkened in their understanding, they are alienated from the life of God."[736] The heretics are spoken to in the exhortation, "bloodthirsty men depart from me," but there is also a warning for the "wheat."[737] The good people must not openly separate themselves from the wicked before the final winnowing at the end.[738] Good people, through their "praiseworthy conduct" and their different way of life, tacitly say every day, "Men of blood depart from me."[739]

For Augustine it is not possible to separate from the wicked before the end harvest because the wheat would be uprooted with the weeds.[740] Augustine makes sense of the apparent disparity between Jesus' exhortation

730. Ibid., 261.
731. Ibid., 264.
732. Ibid.
733. Ibid., 265.
734. Ibid., 272.
735. Ibid., 277.
736. Ibid., 277–278.
737. Ibid., 278.
738. Ibid.
739. Ibid.
740. Ibid., 279.

to love one's enemies and this verse to hate them by noting the meaning of the term "perfect hatred." For Augustine perfect hatred is hatred that "hates everything in them that makes them sinful and at the same time loves them because they are human beings."[741] Moses is held up as a figural example because he showed loved when he interceded for sinners (Ex 32:11–13), but also showed hatred in that he killed them (Ex 32:26–28).[742] In commenting on the last verse (24), Augustine says that to be led in the way of everlasting is to be led in Christ (Jn 14:6).[743]

John Calvin

Suffering

Calvin begins his introduction to this psalm thus:

> Quickened by this meditation to a due reverential fear of God, he declares himself to have no sympathy with the ungodly and profane, and beseeches God in the confidence of conscious integrity, not to forsake him in this life.[744]

Calvin then goes on to explain what this quickening means. He takes v. 1 to mean that it is impossible to deceive God.[745] In v. 6, God's knowledge is seen to be wonderful in forming humankind.[746] But then in v. 7 Calvin insists that it is "impossible that men by any subterfuge should elude the eye of God" with the face of God meaning knowledge or inspection.[747] Calvin sees God's hand in v. 11; if one were to attempt to withdraw from God's observation God would easily "draw back and arrest the fugitive."[748] Verses 11 and 12 are also seen to reflect the position that although we are ashamed to let others see our iniquities, we are indifferent to God, supposing our "sins were covered and veiled from his inspection."[749] Nevertheless, in v. 14 the knowledge which the psalmist is talking about is "simply the religious attention

---

741. Ibid., 280.
742. Ibid.
743. Ibid., 281.
744. Calvin, *Commentary*, 206.
745. Ibid., 207.
746. Ibid., 210.
747. Ibid., 211.
748. Ibid., 212.
749. Ibid., 213.

to the works of God which excites to the duty of thanksgiving."[750] Calvin interprets God's knowledge of the psalmist being formed in his mother's womb as indicating that the psalmist could not now "elude his observation" since all things "were written in his book."[751] Verse 17 is taken as speaking of the excellence of divine providence.[752] Calvin concludes this section of the psalm by saying that nothing can escape God and those who think they can commit a crime and try to hide will be found out.[753]

Meaning of the Response

Calvin does not believe that verse 19 should be interpreted as being connected with v. 18.[754] Neither does he think it expresses David's wish or that David is congratulating himself for "the wicked being cut off."[755] Rather, the vengeance taken on the ungodly would make clear the "divine judgments, and advance in godliness and fear of his name."[756] God punishes in this way so the elect will "withdraw themselves from their [ungodly] society" (Isa 26:9).[757] The psalmist is also presenting himself to God as having integrity because he has come to God's "bar" not as the wicked, nor does he have any connection with them.[758]

Calvin offers an explanation as to why God must judge the wicked. In verse 20 the psalmist describes the extent to which the wicked will go when God spares them and does not visit them with vengeance. They not only think they can commit any crime with impunity, but "openly blaspheme their judge."[759] Further, when the wicked take God's name in vain they are conceiving of God according to their own fancies.[760] The wicked are further characterised by their own pride and their forgetfulness of the Lord's power.[761]

---

750. Ibid., 215.
751. Ibid., 217.
752. Ibid., 218.
753. Ibid., 219.
754. Ibid., 220.
755. Ibid.
756. Ibid.
757. Ibid.
758. Ibid.
759. Ibid., 221.
760. Ibid.
761. Ibid.

Calvin suggests that the meditation up until this point serves as a basis for the psalmist to understand vv. 21 ff.[762] Verses 21 to 24 express the psalmist's resolution to live a holy life. The attachment to godliness generates an abhorrence of sin, "For whoever connives at sin and encourages it through silence wickedly betrays God's cause, who has committed the vindication of righteousness into our hands."[763] However, Calvin recognizes that the hatred spoken about in vv. 21–22 is not absolute. He states, "The hatred of which the Psalmist speaks is directed to the sins rather than the persons of the wicked."[764] For Calvin, "we are to seek the good in all, and, if possible, they are to be reclaimed by kindness and good offices."[765]

Finally, v. 23 serves to indicate that the psalmist is sincere in his religion, although not sinless, and that he is a genuine worshipper of God. This is why he has opposed the wicked.[766] As an example, he gives David who, although he was a man subject to sin, he was not devoted to the practice of it. Ultimately, the reason for opposing the wicked was that the psalmist was a true worshipper and desired others to be so as well.

Comparison with the Exegetical Findings of Psalm 139

The goal here is to use the findings in this historical survey to supplement my exegetical findings. In the exegesis, I suggested that there was a relationship between vv. 1–18 and vv. 19–24. The psalmist appeals to Yahweh's omniscience, omnipresence, and omnificence as the basis for Yahweh's obligation to account for innocent blood being shed and the psalmist's own apprehension that there may be sin in his life. In the NT allusion to Ps 139:1 in Rom 8:27, the context for the Holy Spirit's deep knowledge of the individual is his or her suffering. But this occurs in the time of the New Covenant when God has poured out his Spirit into the hearts of people (Acts 2:17; Jer 31:31–34).

Most of the commentators in this study see God's intimate knowledge of the psalmist as eliciting a self-consciousness of sin. Basil suggests that there is an unwillingness to search ourselves for sin. Chrysostom saw the knowledge of God's creation (v. 14) as eliciting a type of deep fear. Peter Chrysologus also explained vv. 7–10 in the context of how sin cannot be hidden from God. Cyprian, as well, can interpret the penetrating search of God in v. 16 in the context of God's judgment. Augustine from vv. 1–15

---

762. Ibid., 221–222.
763. Ibid., 222.
764. Ibid., 223.
765. Ibid.
766. Ibid.

would seem to make the same link between God's knowledge and sin with all its connotations. Calvin, in a similar manner, looks at this knowledge as indicating that it is impossible for those who do wrong to escape from God. On the other hand, Theodoret looked on God's penetrating knowledge as grounds for doxology. Some of the commentators mentioned above allow for a doxological perspective to a certain degree as well, but their focus seems to be with sin, judgment and purity (Augustine, Calvin, *et al.*).

Calvin interprets the psalmist's pleas for the wicked to depart (v. 19) as the psalmist presenting himself to God as having integrity, but besides Calvin, the commentators in this study do not make any explicit reference to the connection between vv. 1–18 and vv. 19–24.[767] However, this does not mean that they did not see the composition of the psalm from a holistic perspective. Augustine creates unity in the psalm through his prosopological interpretation. Perhaps the other commentators betray an implicit view as well when they emphasize God's intimate knowledge leading to a self-consciousness of sin. This type of reading follows the theme of verses 19–24 which speak of the sinfulness of the enemies as "bloodthirsty haters of God" and the psalmist's desire to go in the "everlasting way" (vv. 23–24). Without an explicit connection it is not possible to say whether the commentators believed the psalmist was approaching God from a position of confidence as grounds for his prayer to be heard (so Calvin) or a position of uncertainty about hidden sin in his life.

The interpretation of the psalmist's acclamation of God's wondrous works (deeds) in v. 14 also seems to be significant. This was brought out by the connection of v. 14 with Rev 15:3. In Revelation, the term ᾄδω "sing" occurs only three times (Rev 15:3; 14:3; and 5:9) with the latter two occurrences being linked to the last psalm in this study, Ps 149. The praise for Yahweh's deeds in Rev 15:3 is connected with the plagues and suggests the realization of God's rule through the execution of God's justice/judgment. Furthermore, John identifies the judging God as king of not only Israel, but all nations. Additionally, God's "works" of human creation in reference to "bloodthirsty men" in Ps 139 may stand in an analogous relationship to the ideas of the praise and judgment in Rev 15. Brown's comments are propitious here: "Personal creation is the divine charter of life and loyalty by which God becomes bound to a particular life, ensuring that the individual flourishes within the protective sphere of righteousness."[768] The other point worth pondering is whether Ps 139's connection with the book of Revelation (Rev 2:6 as well) betrays a similarity in eschatological genre and perspective.

767. Ibid., 220.
768. Brown, "Creatio Corporis," 124.

The psalmist's response that God would slay the wicked and his solidarity in completely hating the wicked was one of the key focuses of the exegesis. The commentators offer a range of interpretations. The request by the psalmist that God would "slay the wicked" and for "bloodthirsty men" to depart from him can be divided into figural and literal interpretations. In the figural interpretations the commentators justify the problem text by pointing out indicators in the text. For example, Chrysostom and Augustine both explain the text as calling for "sinners" to be slain. Chrysostom sees this as the process by which people become spiritually alive, whereas Augustine sees the death as representing the life void of God.

The literal interpretation presents a more substantial challenge. Theodoret interprets this wish of the psalmist as part of the descriptive narrative of King Josiah, the ones he killed referring to the priests whose bones Josiah burned (1 Kings 13:1,2). Calvin does not question the morality of the divine vengeance, but rather focuses on the effects particularly with reference to the godly. Vengeance on the wicked advances the fear of God and acts as a warning for the elect to separate themselves from the company of the wicked. Of particular interest is the insight Calvin offers into the nature of the wicked. God must judge them because if he does not they will think they can commit any crime with impunity and "openly blaspheme their judge."[769]

Almost all the commentators recognize as a type of hyperbole the psalmist's solidarity with Yahweh to hate the enemy with perfect hatred. The *Constitution of the Holy Apostles* using this text identifies heretics with whom Christians are to avoid communion. Origen is also considered to be an enemy, yet ironically, as Houston points out, the benefit the Church gained from Origen's understanding of Ps 139 is clear from Origen's debate with Celsus.[770]

Nevertheless, several commentators seem to understand "hating them with complete hatred" by distinguishing the person from that person's sin (Chrysostom, Augustine, and Calvin). However, in Theodoret's holistic approach we see the moral tension unresolved: "as sinners I hate them, but as human beings I pity them."[771] Cassiodorus presents a nuanced approach distinguishing between those who are hostile to Christians because of the faults of Christians and those who are hostile because they are arrogant and stand opposed to God. The latter should arouse a sense of disgust. However, he eventually resolves the tension by exhorting Christians to love people but to hate their vices.

---

769. Calvin, *Commentary*, 221.
770. Waltke and Houston, *Psalms as Christian Worship*, 521.
771. Theodoret, *Commentary on the Psalms*, 334.

If the psalmist is using hyperbole in vv. 21–22, then is he using hyperbole in v. 19 as well? In the exegesis it was determined that the verb *qāṭal* "to slay" can be used in a rhetorical way (Job 13:15), but its other two uses seem to be literal (see exegesis). The use in Obad 1:15 is prophetic and seems to be the closest in similarity to Ps 139. Perhaps the psalmist's assertion of perfect hatred is in keeping with the absoluteness of wisdom language, where there is no portrayal of the wicked person as a composite of good and bad. Calvin in the exegesis of Ps 139 comes to the conclusion that the wicked become worse if they are unchallenged. The answer to the question has to do with the nature of Ps 139 as a religious prayer text and so what the psalmist means when he uses these images as prayer will be taken up in Chapter 3.

EXEGESIS OF PSALM 149: PRAISING WITH VIOLENT IMAGES OF WAR

Whereas some of the violent images in the psalms have been the subject of theoretical musings, historical examples of the use of Ps 149 show the potential consequences of such. Caspar Sciopius in his book *Clarion of the Sacred War* (*Calssicum Belli Sacri*) inflamed the Roman Catholic Princes to the Thirty Year's War, and on the Protestant side a century earlier, Thomas Müntzer encouraged the War of the Peasants with this psalm. Although it might seem obvious that this kind of interpretation is a misuse, with its drastic consequences, one of the goals here will be to see if such an interpretation is indeed congruent with the meaning of the psalm. It will not be possible to answer this question completely until I have finished the historical survey and the NT understanding of the violent images in Ps 149. However, the answer begins with understanding Ps 149 in its immediate context. From a form-critical point of view, Ps 149 is generally regarded as a type of hymn (see below), which adds complexity to understanding the perceived suffering and interpreting the meaning of the responses. The harshness of the imprecations in lament psalms is often mitigated by stressing the helplessness of the victims,[772] but the tone of praise in Ps 149 makes the violent images of war seem even more vindictive. Ps 149 is also pertinent from an editorial perspective. The recognition of *inclusio* with Ps 107 and even Ps 2 can aid in understanding the psalm. The goal here will be to use the text and its location in Book V to understand the perceived suffering of the community and the meaning of the response.

---

772. So, Zenger (*God of Vengeance?*, 48) says about the sufferers in Ps 137 that the imprecations are the "passionate outcry of the powerless demanding justice."

The MT—A Praising Note

<Hallelujah>[773]
1. Sing to the Lord a new song,
    his praises in the assembly of the saints.[774]
2. Let Israel be glad in its maker;[775]
    let the children of Zion rejoice in their king.
3. Let them praise his name with dancing,
    and make[776] melody to him with tambourine and lyre.
4. For the Lord takes pleasure in his people;
    he adorns the lowly[777] with salvation.[778]
5. Let the saints[779] exult in glory;
    let them sing for joy on their couches.[780]
6. Let the high praises of God be in their throats
    and two edged swords in their hands.
7. To execute vengeance on the nations
    and punishment on the peoples.

773. NRS has *Praise the Lord*.

774. NRS has *faithful*. I prefer to retain the KJV and NKJV rendering of *saints* because I feel it better captures the distinction as a particular people that is implied in the term *ḥăsîdîm* as it is used in Ps 149. Kidner (1975:110–111, 116) suggests some considerations for translating the term *ḥăsîdîm*. Likewise translated in vv. 5 and 10.

775. The LXX and Syriac have the singular form of 'śh "to do/make." The plural form in the Hebrew is usually explained as a plural of majesty (so GBH, 470, 136e) or an older form that retained a *yod* before a suffix (GES, 399, 124k).

776. NRSV has *making* which reads smoothly, but can hide the fact that $y^e zamm^e rû$ is a jussive.

777. NRSV has *humble*.

778. NRSV has *victory*. The use of the translation *victory* can be inferred from the tone of celebration in vv. 1–6 and the subjugation of the nations and their kings in vv. 7–8. However, the normal meaning of the term $y^e šû'â$ describes Yahweh's saving intervention or help (Zenger [Hossfeld and Zenger, *Psalms 3*, 642]).

779. NRS has *faithful*.

780. The BHS and Kraus (*Psalms 60–150*, 566) propose *mišpᵉḥôṯām*, "their families"; Gunkel (*Die Psalmen*, 621): *m'rkwṯm*, "their battle ranks"; Briggs (*Critical and Exegetical Commentary*, 543): *mšknwṯm*, "their great tabernacle." Given the praising tone of vv. 1–6a and the minor modification needed (ב "*b*" to נ "*n*"), Briggs' suggestion seems the most probable except that the term *miškān* is only used with Yahweh as the referent for the pronominal suffix. Allen (*Psalms*, 396) opposes emendation based on the assonance of vv. 5a and 5b with v. 8. Accordingly, he translates the term as *places of lying* from which can be inferred the meaning of *prostrate* (so Anderson, *Book of Psalms*, 953). However, the problem with Allen's proposal is that *škb* is not used this way anywhere else. If *couches* is retained the meaning could be construed as a metonymy referring to the post-exilic resettlement of the people in their homes. This proposal also seems like an intrusion into what seems to be a cultically transpiring event, but might fit into the theme of *salvation* as being restoration.

> 8. To bind their kings with fetters
> and their nobles with chains of iron.
> 9. To execute on them the judgment written.[781]
> This is glory for all his saints.[782]
> < Hallelujah >[783]

Structure, Form, and Setting

Generally three structures present themselves for this psalm.[784] According to strophic divisions the psalm can be divided into three sections: vv. 1–3, 4–6 and 7–9. This gives a balanced strophic structure of three strophes with three bicola. The difficulty with placing structural emphasis on regularity in the poetical pattern is that the content gets subsumed under the form. Gunkel observed that when an author wished to begin new paragraphing he used the same forms which structured the beginning of a psalm.[785] Hence, the most common way to view the structure of Ps 149 is a twofold division of vv. 1–4 and vv. 5–9. In this accounting, both sections begin with a summons to praise (vv. 1–3; vv. 5–6) followed by a motivation for that praise, in v. 4 indicated by *kî* "for" and in vv. 7–9 by the prefix *l* plus infinitives. Further indications of two distinct units come from the following *inclusio*: vv. 1/4 *qhl* "assembly" and *'m* "people"; vv. 5a/9b *ḥsdm* "saints"; and vv. 5a/9b *kābôd* "glory" and *hādār* "glory/honor." This proposal, however, does not account for the change in theme that occurs between vv. 6a and 6b, which Prinsloo has proposed.[786] In his proposal vv. 1–5 constitute praises, and the nominal clause of v. 6a looks back to praise Yahweh, whereas the nominal clause of v. 6b looks forward to the theme of judgment expounded in vv. 7–9. Zenger responds that Prinsloo's proposal trivializes the significance of verse 4.[787] Those who support the structure of vv. 1–4 and vv. 5–9 must account for the uneven distribution of theme, whereas those who follow Prinsloo's assessment must account for the significant grounds for praise given in v. 4.

---

781. *NRSV* has *decreed* but the literal word is *written*.
782. *NRSV* has *faithful ones*.
783. *NRSV* has *Praise the Lord*. It is lacking in the *LXX* and Syriac.
784. See Zenger (Hossfeld and Zenger, *Psalms 3*, 643–645).
785. Gunkel, "Psalm 149," 51.
786. Prinsloo, "Psalm 149," 395–407.
787. Hossfeld and Zenger, *Psalms 3*, 645.

The setting of the psalm is open to various proposals. Gunkel thought Ps 149 was borrowed from the prophets and is an "eschatological hymn" when the "great Yahweh battle will take place and Zion be redeemed."[788] The psalm shows that:

> YHWH defeats the nations, and is called out as king. Now his entry is prepared, his majestic entrance and thus the beginning of a just kingdom.... Now the victors, holding the blood-drenched sword, stand and sing the victory song to their God. The manacled kings and princes of the nations are before them, those against whom the judgement shall be completed.[789]

Hence, the poem is a post-exilic composition for the future when Israel would humiliate its enemies. Kraus on the other hand believes that Gunkel laid too much stress on the eschatological element within the composition at the expense of the cultic. Kraus suggests that Ps 149 is a slightly modified communal hymn, based on two traditions in which either Jerusalem is attacked (Ps 46) or the kings and nations revolt against Yahweh's rule (Ps 2).[790] Kraus does allow for an older date for the composition of the psalm, but prefers to assign it to the time of Nehemiah.[791] Anderson considers Ps 149 a post-exilic hymn with a cultic setting being the more likely place of use.[792] The psalm presents the salvation history of the nation with the portrayed events also having present and future significance. Gerstenberger proposes that the psalm has not shaken off its original cultic setting and historical associations and represents a group under economic, political or religious pressure.[793]

The praise in the psalm is an expectation for the turning of fates of the oppressed Israelites. In terms of pre-exilic interpretations, Dahood believes the psalm was sung and performed in the religious assembly on the eve of a battle against the foreign nations.[794] Weiser considers Ps 149 a hymn performed at a pre-exilic cult festival with the covenantal armies present.[795] As the above proposals show, the setting of the psalm is open

---

788. Gunkel and Begrich, *Introduction to Psalms*, 22, 55.
789. Ibid., 273.
790. Kraus, *Psalms 60–150*, 566.
791. Ibid., 567.
792. Anderson, *Book of Psalms*, 951–952.
793. Gerstenberger, *Psalms, Part 2*, 456–7. Contra to Prinsloo, "Psalm 149," 407
794. Dahood, *Psalms III*, 356.
795. Weiser, *Psalms*, 839.

to much speculation. However, the placement of Ps 149 in Book V may provide further insight into identifying the context of the psalm.[796]

Further support for this method of approach comes from Zenger who suggests in his own exegesis that the psalm must be read in reference to the "pre-texts" Ps 1 and 2, which Ps 149 takes up and "eschatologizes."[797] One of the difficulties in making connections between different psalms through word similarities, though, has to do with the subjective nature of the task. However, as argued in the introduction and recapitulated here, the themes of Psalm 107 and 149 suggest that the purposeful use of *inclusio* cannot be overlooked. In these two psalms, the connection is based upon the people mentioned in the psalms and reversal of fortunes, rather than speculation about grammatical connections not necessarily dependent on the content and contextual meaning those words have. First, the *redeemed of the LORD* (107:2), the *upright* (107:42) and the *saints* (149:9) are the same people. Furthermore, in Psalm 107 the *redeemed of the Lord* are depicted as encountering all types of distress, even being *prisoners suffering in iron chains* (Ps 107:10, NIV). In 149:8 it is the *saints* (Ps 149:5), who *bind their* [nations] *kings with fetters and their nobles with chains of iron* (Ps 149:8). The *saints* exact n^eqāmâ "vengeance" (Ps 149:7) on the nations and their kings. This reversal in fortune provides a strong link within the context of Book V. The fact that Ps 149 reverses the fortunes of those who had been oppressed in Ps 107 would seem to suggest that the editor had a particular understanding of the meaning of justice in Ps 149.

Furthermore, there seems to be a connection between Ps 2 and Ps 149.[798] The *nations, peoples* and *kings* who seek to throw off Yahweh's authority in 2:1–2 become the object of his retribution in 149:7–9. The holy mountain of *Zion* where the *king* is anointed by Yahweh in 2:6 becomes the parent whose children rejoice in their *king* in 149:2 (although in the latter passage the parallelism of the verse suggests that the *king* is Yahweh himself, not a member of the Davidic dynasty). The divine promise in 2:9 to break the rebels with a rod of *iron* is paralleled in 149:8 by the binding of the princes with fetters of *iron*. Also worth noting is the similarity between the *bonds* and *cords* which the kings attempt to throw off in 2:3, and which are replaced in 149:8 by *chains* and *fetters* of iron. There is also a close similarity between

---

796. See the Introduction above on the editing of Book V.

797. Hossfeld and Zenger, *Psalms 3*, 646. According to Zenger, this is only one of four pre-texts that Ps 149 takes up. For the other three see ibid. Zenger also sees an inter-textual connection with Ps 107.

798. Brennan, "Psalms 1–8," 26. Kraus (*Psalms 60–150*, 566–567) also sees a connection between Ps 2 and Ps 149, with Ps 2 being a tradition which has influenced Ps 149.

the *princes* and *rulers* who are warned of Yahweh's wrath in 2:2, 10 and the *nobles* who are the object of the divine judgement in 149:8. This mention of the *saints* and the *nations* and the reversal in roles of fortune is substantial in recognizing the connection between Psalms 2 and 149.

We can tentatively suggest the following from the editorial links among Ps 149, Ps 2 and Ps 107. First, the psalm is in an eschatological category, as is Ps 2. Secondly, although the psalm's process of composition most likely extends back to pre-exilic times,[799] Ps 149 has been edited into the Psalter as a post-exilic psalm on the basis that Ps 107 is recognized as a post-exilic psalm. The psalm functions then as a hymn pertaining to the future.

A further observation on the author's development of the themes of praise and judgment can be made. The author reinforces the theme of escalating praise through his choice of verbs. He begins with *sing* in v. 1 and moves to *be glad* and *rejoice* in v. 2. Verse 3 begins with *praise*, but moves to *make music* with instruments v. 3. In v. 5 there is a further intensifying of the praise through the verbs *exult* and *sing for joy*, literally *give a ringing cry*.[800] Verse 6b ends the praise with the noun *high praise*. From v. 6b onwards, the poet develops the theme of judgment through the use of the *l*-prefix of purpose and infinitives. Verses 7a and 9a form an *inclusio* with *to execute vengeance* v. 7a and *to execute judgment* v. 9a. Verse 8 gives a picture of that *vengeance* and *judgment*.

Perceived Suffering

The nature of the setting and function of Ps 149 as a variation on the hymn adds different perspectives to the perceived suffering behind the psalm. Kraus rejected Gunkel's eschatological emphasis in interpretation because he felt it was too disconnected with the cult.[801] However, the placement of Ps 149 in Book V could have resulted in a modification of its original cultic emphasis. In terms of determining the perceived suffering behind Ps 149, Mowinckel is helpful in his perception that Ps 149 represents a mingling of the motives of lament with the genre of hymn.[802] These motives of lament are clues to the perceived suffering of the community. Whether em-

---

799. The lack of a messianic figure, the notion that Yahweh himself is king, and the war imagery are all reasons to suggest that the origin of Psalm 149 is quite old. And as Dahood (*Psalms III*, 357) points out, in terms of linguistic similarities with Isaiah, it is hard to determine the direction of influence.

800. BDB, 943.

801. Kraus, *Psalms 60–150*, 566.

802. Mowinckel, *Psalms, Vol. 2*, 30.

phasis is placed on past events, cultic events, or on future eschatological events, all three emphases assume that there is some form of adversity to the community.

The beginning-but-not-yet-completed restoration period perspective suggested in the introduction to this work seems to fit the dual themes of praise and judgment: praise for their return and judgment reflecting the feelings aroused for the recent experiences of the exile and the present hostility which the people continue to face during reestablishment. The perceived suffering behind the psalm blends the euphoric optimism of eschatological victory with the real circumstances of the suffering community. The *inclusio* between Ps 107 and 149 as part of Book V suggests that the optimism in the praise of vv. 1–6a could result from the restoration of the community or that some reversal of misfortune has occurred. Perhaps the difficult term *miškāḇ* "couch," portrays the community as being able to lie down without fear.[803] On the other hand, the term *'ănāwîm* "lowly" in v. 4b identifies all of Israel by its parallelism with *bᵉ'ammô* "in his people," in v. 4a. The Israelites are a helpless group of people assembled on Zion.[804] Gerstenberger suggests that the war imagery of vv. 6b to 9a speaks of their oppression by a superior oppressive force in the Near East.[805]

However, in the post-exilic understanding of the psalm, Cyrus and the other Persian leaders were not portrayed as oppressors. In contrast, the nations and kings in Ps 149 are portrayed as hostile to Zion (note the use of *bᵉnē-ṣyyôn* "children of Zion" in v. 2). The idea of the *kings* (v. 8) and *nobles* (v. 8), who represent the *nations* (v. 7) being bound suggests that the adversaries resist Yahweh's rule to the end. But if the psalm does represent an eschatological perspective, then the suffering under the enemies is probably best summed up by Zenger: "The event has been in progress since the rescue of Israel from the exile and will be 'hastened' by Israel's praise, which hymnically anticipates the completion of the event."[806] The post-exilic setting linked to historical enemies may not identify the original historical setting which gave rise to this psalm. However, the severity of the Babylonian exile must have formed part of the historical context for the editors.

---

803. Kidner, *Psalms 73–150*, 527.
804. Kraus, *Psalms 60–150*, 567.
805. Gerstenberger, *Psalms, Part 2*, 456.
806. Hossfeld and Zenger, *Psalms 3*, 643.

Meaning of the Response

A general tendency (so Delitzsch, Perowne, Kraus, Kidner) in the interpretation of Ps 149 suggests that this psalm cannot be prayed literally by those who come after Christ. Usually an allegorical reading related to 2 Cor 10:4 is given as an interpretive key. Uncommon is Gersetenberger's position which allows for the "propagation of violence" under certain conditions of survival.[807] My concern here will not be with the hermeneutical shift which might occur when the Christian prays Ps 149,[808] but rather how the psalm can be understood in its canonical placement within Book V.

The identity of Israel as a nation is central to understanding the horizon portrayed in this psalm. Whereas Ps 139 dealt with the creation of the individual, Ps 149 takes as its premise the creation of the nation is done by the LORD, $b^e\bar{o}\acute{s}\bar{a}yw$ "its maker" (v. 2). In vv. 1–4 the recipients in the psalm are the *assembly* (v. 1), *Israel* (v. 2), *children of Zion* (v. 2), *his people* (v. 4), the *lowly* (v. 4), and *saints* (v. 5)—all terms which describe the unique relationship Yahweh has with his people. After v. 5 there is no mention of the people except the repetition of the term *saints* in v. 9b. The use of the term *saints* in vv. 1, 5 and 9 provides coherence to the psalm. It is probably the notion of the special relationship between Yahweh and his people which is emphasized in the use of *saints* here rather than the notions of doing kindness or being loyal, which are usually associated with the word.[809]

In the larger context, the meaning of Psalm 149 derives from its function as an eschatological hymn. As mentioned above, authors may disagree on the historical nature of this hymn, whether it is based on a purely cultic composition (so Kraus) or whether it represents a purely eschatological form[810] or whether it reflects a conventionalized re-presentation of historical experiences projected into the future.[811] Zenger's understanding, that Yahweh alone is the agent who carries out the acts of war and that Israel merely offers songs of praise with metaphoric war images, does not seem to be the normal understanding of Yahweh's agency.[812] At times, as Zenger suggests, Yahweh acts in holy war as the sole agent, but more common are the

---

807. Gerstenberger, *Psalms, Part 2*, 457.

808. This will be examined during the look at the Psalms as prayer in Chapter 3.

809. BDB defines as *pious, the godly* who are faithful to God's service and notes the term is found only in the Psalter (339).

810. Gunkel and Begrich, *Introduction to Psalms*, 55, 263.

811. So Anderson, *Book of Psalms*, 952. For Gunkel ("Psalm 149: An Interpretation," 364) this is the meaning of "new song." Since Yahweh had done a new deed a new song was prepared.

812. Hossfeld and Zenger, *Psalms 3*, 646.

examples where Yahweh can be understood as the giver of victory through the agency of the people.[813] Therefore, the congregation of the saints who used this psalm most likely understood Yahweh's eschatological intervention as occurring through the community of the Israelites who were the "organs of Yahweh's governing and judging."[814] Perhaps this also explains the interpretive hermeneutic of Sciopius and Müntzer.

In v. 4 the grounds for the praise of Yahweh in vv. 1–3 is given as *he adorns the lowly with salvation*. That salvation, however, is in the very actions which are portrayed in vv. 7–9. The connection occurs through the term *pāēr* "adorn" (v. 4), which is linked through the term *kāḇôḏ* "glory" (v. 5) and picked up in the term *hāḏār* "glory" (v. 9, NRSV) in the phrase *this is glory for all of the saints*. The implication is that the agency of this universal salvation is via the covenantal people. The actions of the covenantal people are given in the three infinitive phrases of purpose. The unity of these three phrases is created through parallelism, and in the case of vv. 7 and 9 *inclusio*, and suggests that it is best to understand v. 9b as coordinate to the preceding v. 8.[815] That is, the *judgment written* (v. 9) is the *binding* of *kings* and *nobles* rather than their execution.[816] This latter meaning would require subordinating v. 9b in relation to v. 8. The distinction may be small, but it suggests that the defeat of those who oppose Yahweh's rule is in view and that any gratuitous violence done is secondary to this end.[817]

It is worth noting that the two themes of praise and judgment are unified in the psalm. Unity is created through the distribution of the name *saints*. Also noteworthy is the fact that the escalating praise in vv. 1, 2, 3, 5 and 6a finds a natural link to 6b by means of the alliteration and assonance of the body pairing *bigrônām* "in their throats" (v, 6a) and *bᵉyāḏām* "in their hands" (v, 6b), an intentional connection between the subjects. The overall effect is to show the intentional unity between praise and judgment. The

---

813. So, for example, the story of Joshua's defeat of the Amalekites through the intercession of Moses, Aaron and Hur in Ex 17:8–16.

814. Kraus, *Psalms 60–150*, 567.

815. Delitzsch, *Psalms*, 413.

816. Execution of the kings is how Gunkel (1926:621–622) and Gerstenberger (2001:455) understand this phrase based on the past examples of the killing of captured kings (Num 31:8; Josh 10:24–27).

817. This is not to say, as I have argued above, that the covenant community would have understood the war imagery and imprecations in a non-literal way. I am merely suggesting that beyond that literal reading there was already in place a deeper understanding to these psalms that lay beneath the violence. I will argue below that it is this innate deeper understanding which allows some of the psalms of enmity the capacity to be understood, without using the technique of allegorization, in a way that provides a spiritually accurate perspective and use of the images of enmity.

implication is that in the adorning of the lowly with salvation (v. 4), the praise (vv. 1, 2, 3, 5, 6a) and the judgment (vv. 7–9) carried out through military conquest form an intricate and mutual relationship. As Weiser says, "by the means of the execution of the judgment on the pagan nations the glory of the people of God is also made manifest [and] is to be understood exclusively on the assumption that it is the glory for God which is the real subject throughout."[818]

The exact identification of the *written* (v. 9a) source which legitimates the *vengeance* (v. 7a) and *punishment* (v. 7b) on the nations also has not been agreed upon. Gerstenberger, Dahood, and Weiser believe it might refer to the deuteronomistic descriptions about annihilating the inhabitants of the promised land (Deut 20:13, 16–18) and might reflect one of the first allusions to the Torah tradition.[819] Anderson suggests that the allusion is to the heavenly books where all the deeds of men are recorded, similar to that portrayed in Ps 51:1.[820] In any case, judgment occurs early in scriptures where memory exists independently of any prophetic writings.[821] Hence the judgement written need not refer to the prophecies of the earlier prophets as Kissane suggests it does.[822] If comparison is made with the book which records the destiny of each human being in Ps 139, on the basis that Yahweh is the creator of each individual, and that in Ps 149 He is referred to as the creator of the nation, perhaps the judgment written is on a national level rather than a personal level.[823]

The scope of the judgment depicted—the binding of kings and nobles—is symbolic of the utter defeat of the *nations* (v. 7). This picture is a quantified reversal of what Israel experienced in its exile. On the basis of coordinating ideas supported by parallelism, the *vengeance* (v. 7) and the *punishment* (v. 7) can be more clearly defined in the context of the defeat of the nations. Importantly, the term $n^e q\bar{a}m\hat{a}$ "vengeance" in its five uses in the psalms (18:48; 79:10; 94:1 x 2) always refers to the nations.[824] If the

---

818. Weiser, *Psalms*, 840.

819. Gerstenberger, *Psalms, Part 2*, 455; Dahood, *Psalms III*, 337; Weiser, *Psalms*, 838.

820. Anderson, *Book of Psalms*, 954.

821. As is the case with the judgment on the Amalekites (cf. Ex 17:14 with Deut 25:17 ff).

822. Kissane, *Book of Psalms*, 655.

823. The NT idea and also accounted for in the OT is that judgment is primarily on an individual level. The emphasis here may be on the universal rule of Yahweh over all nations and powers.

824. The headings in Ps 18 and Ps 79 may influence the understanding of the content of those psalms, but such an investigation would be beyond the scope of this study.

notion of *nᵉqāmâ* only meant to pay back hostility in the sense of *lex talionis*, then there would be no greater purpose for Israel but to merely punish the specific nations which have harmed them. The hostile nations had devastated and humiliated them, and according to this interpretation the same can be expected in turn if not to a greater degree. However, in Ps 149 it is not just the restoration of the people of God and the defeat of the oppressing nation, but the complete universal rule of *king Yahweh* over all nations. As an eschatological form of judgment this goes further than repayment of wrongs done only to Israel. The *nᵉqāmâ* can be understood in the context of the purpose of establishing the created order as it was meant to be under Yahweh's rule (*let the children of Zion rejoice in their king*, v. 2). The term *vengeance*, as it is used here, is not just an expression of the hostile feelings of those who suffered the cruelty of the exile. Rather, the acts of the nations, portrayed in Ps 149 as their hostility to Israel, Babylon included, were acts against God's sovereign rule over the earth. There is a broadening of the concept of vengeance to extend to the greater cosmic plane of all time. Furthermore, the *judgment* (v. 9) is from a written source, which is portrayed as originating as part of divine revelation. This is no regular war but a holy war where the players are God, the covenantal partners and all the enemies of the earth.

Conclusion of the Exegesis

The editing of Psalm 149 into Book V of the Psalter suggests that the circumstances surrounding the exile are important in understanding the images of violence and praise. The oppression that the Israelites experienced at the hands of the Babylonians is understood eschatologically as the subjugation of all nations which are opposed to King Yahweh's rule. Theologically, there is a mystery here which reveals itself in the idea that Babylon was both the means for God's judgment and to be judged as well (Isa 5; Jer 32, 51, 52; Ps 137, etc.). In other words, the exile also indicates Israel as failing to submit to Yahweh's rule. Israel's reversal of fortune then becomes a picture of the nations' judgment for failing to submit to Yahweh's rule. For the Israelites this rightful rule was portrayed through their special calling as the covenantal people in which they participated—both with exclamation of praise and a double-edged sword—in the larger issue dealing with Yahweh's legitimate claim as ruler of all the nations of the earth.

A SELECT HISTORICAL SURVEY OF THE INTERPRETATION OF PSALM 149

Besides investigating commentators on Ps 149 for how they understood the context and the meaning given to the violent images, it will be helpful to restate the particular areas of interest from my exegesis. One question posed was whether the use of Ps 149 as a text to incite a just war was congruent with the meaning of the text. Other areas of interest were whether the hymnic elements (or lack of lament) in Ps 149 influence the interpretation of the violent images, and whether an eschatological outlook is supported. The goal here will be to supplement my exegesis by determining whether the commentators address these issues and what they have to say.

Post-exilic Restoration—Another Perspective

Predominantly in the discussion on methodology in the introduction to this study, but also in the exegesis of this psalm, I presented my view that Ps 149 was edited into Book V of the Psalter through its *inclusio* with Ps 107. I suggested that Ps 150, the last psalm of Book V, was a doxology to Book V, a type of coda for Book I, and a conclusion of unmitigated praise for the whole Psalter. Although my conclusions may be debatable, it is this post-exilic perspective which stands behind the way I have investigated Ps 149 in its present placement in the canon. Several comments on how Ps 149 may have been understood in the post-exilic restoration were made in the exegesis and need not be repeated here. However, since Goulder believes the psalm was composed in the time of the restoration, he may provide a foil to think about how it may have been understood from a different perspective.

Goulder believes the psalm was sung at the "festal gathering of all Israel at Tabernacles."[825] The setting seems to be the time of Ezra and Nehemiah which is implied by the present *rôṣeh* "one who takes pleasure" in v. 4.[826] He implies that the psalmist saw in the turn of his country's fortune an opportunity for revenge on the nations.[827] Further, he interprets v. 9 to indicate the execution of the kings and nobles.[828] In my exegesis, I suggested that indicators in the text might add support to an eschatological perspective with emphasis being placed in the religious text on the subjugation of the nations rather than on gratuitous violence.

---

825. Goulder, *Psalms of the Return*, 298.
826. Ibid.
827. Ibid., 300.
828. Ibid.

Lastly, the psalm was interpreted as post-exilic by Theodore of Mopsuestia, whose introduction to the psalm states, "He admonishes the people that they should praise God unceasingly for their return from Babel and their victory over their enemies."[829] Unfortunately, Theodore's explanation of how this victory over their enemies relates to the violent images does not survive.

The NT—Psalm 149 and the Book of Revelation

The Greek NT does not list any quotations for Ps 149 in the NT, but it does suggest that Ps 149:1 is alluded to or supports a verbal parallel with Rev 5:9[830] and Rev 14:3.[831] In the first passage Jesus is depicted as the lamb who has taken the scroll. The picture is of the four living creatures and the twenty-four elders worshipping Jesus in the context of the prayers of the saints. The prayers in 5:8 appear to be a call for God to act in judgment and vindication.[832] The content of the "new song" is the worship given to Jesus for his crucifixion and the priesthood he has conferred on the people he has redeemed along with their reign over all the earth. In the OT the "new song" always expresses God's victory over the enemy and sometimes includes thanksgiving for God's work of creation.[833] Blount notes that all the hymns which contain a new song, OT and NT, "anticipate God's impending judgment against those who have persecuted God's witnesses."[834] Furthermore, a causal relationship exists which shows that Jesus is the one who is worthy to open the scroll.[835] In other words, Jesus has become the worthy judge.

829. Van Rooy, *East Syriac Psalm Headings*, 168. I am using Van Rooy's English translation of manuscript 6t1. For a discussion of the complex issues involved from the various transcripts see Van Rooy's work.

830. According to Moyise (*Later New Testament*, 5.2.2) most scholars consider Rev 5:5-6 as the most important passage in Revelation because it is placed here as an interpretive key to the book. The juxtaposition of lion and lamb in Rev 5:5-6 is to "reinterpret the traditional Christian image of Christ as lamb. John's hearers know that Christ died for their sins (Rev 1:5; 5:9); what John wishes to tell them is that he is also the powerful conqueror who will defeat their enemies and win the final victory." For Moyise's discussion of other views on the constrast of the lion and lamb see Moyise (Ibid., 5.2.2).

831. Despite the many hymns, John uses the actual vocabulary of singing (ᾄδω) only three times, in Revelation 5:9, 14:3 and 15:3. Rev 15:3 relates to Ps 139:14, whereas Rev 5:9 and 14:3 allude to Ps 149:1.

832. Blount, *Revelation*, 113.

833. Beale, *Book of Revelation*, 358.

834. Blount, *Revelation*, 114.

835. Ibid.

In the second passage, Rev 14:3, we again have the lamb symbolizing Jesus, and the 144,000. The mark on these 144,000 counter the mark given by the beast to those in Revelation 13. The song is exclusive—only those who were redeemed could learn the song. The "new song" as per above was an expression of praise for God's victory over the enemy and sometimes included thanksgiving for his work of creation.[836] Interestingly, the description of Babylon's defeat comes very soon in 14:8 and the idea of smoke of torment rising forever in 14:11.[837] Rev 14:2–3 celebrates God's universal rule which is seen in the judgment of those who reject his lordship and the redemption of those who give witness to it.[838]

The Nicene and Post-Nicene Fathers

Suffering according to the Antiochene School

Given the hymnic nature of Ps 149, it is not surprising that the Alexandrian commentators with their predominantly figural interpretations have little to say about an historical situation of suffering. However, this is not true for those of the Antiochene school. Chrysostom implies a historical connection of the psalm with the Maccabees: "it is the famous and remarkable song they were due to sing for the victories, the doughty deeds, the trophies."[839] Chrysostom also suggests that "they will rejoice on their beds" shows "the complete safety from the problems he thus led them from, the great relief, the great joy, the great satisfaction."[840] Theodoret says that this psalm tells of the returnees "who triumphed through divine aid" but suggests that it is also a prophecy of the Maccabees.[841] Further, Yahweh as King defines the peculiar relationship of the Israelites with God.[842] Theodoret goes on to suggest that those "bereft of help and practicing good behaviour" God will lift up.

---

836. Beale, *Book of Revelation*, 736.
837. See ibid.
838. Blount, *Revelation*, 267.
839. Chrysostom, *Commentary*, 376.
840. Ibid., 378.
841. Theodoret, *Commentary on the Psalms*, 370.
842. Ibid.

Meaning of the response

There are two ideas in the psalm we will comment on in determining the meaning of the response. First is the understanding of the "new song" (and praise) and then the images of violence.

Cyril of Jerusalem interprets the "new song" as indicative of the emergence of the new Churches of Christ which consist of gentiles.[843] Jerome as well focuses on the idea of the "new song" in his interpretation of the text. A new song is indicative of a new people, so the Church rejoices in its new king, Christ.[844] Cassiodorus, in the monastic tradition, sees the "new canticle" as referring to the secret of the incarnation, the nativity, the teaching, the suffering, and the resurrection of Christ who now sits at the right hand of God the Father Almighty.[845]

The praise in vv. 5 and 6a is predominantly given a Christian interpretation. The Cappadocian father, Gregory of Nazianzus places the exaltations of v. 6 on the mouths of Christians: "Let us adore the One Godhead in the Three; not ascribing any name of humiliation to the unapproachable Glory, but having the exaltations of the Triune God continually in our mouth."[846] In the Western Church, Jerome takes the injunction of Paul in Gal 6:14 to "glory in the cross of Jesus Christ" as the proper manner to understand the call for the faithful to "exalt in glory."[847] Sulpitius Severus uses v. 5 on the mouth of David in the context of the return of Christ in the last judgment, where David stands up and declares that only the name of the Lord was to be worshiped.[848]

In terms of the more literal interpretations of the Antiochene school, Chrysostom notes that in vv. 6–7 war is set to music.[849] The implication is that by singing and praising the Israelites will overcome. To execute vengeance on the nations is meant to show the Israelites that it "was not God's weakness but their own sins that consigned them to subjugation."[850] Theodoret says that "conquest in war is not inconsistent with repose; in these words, then, he foretells the Maccabees' valor, exercised by them in

---

843. Cyril, "Catechetical Lectures," 140.

844. Jerome, *Homilies*, 424.

845. Cassiodorus, "Explanation of the Psalms," 458.

846. Gregory, "Select Orations," 336.

847. Jerome, *Homilies*, 426.

848. Sulpitius Serverus, "The Doubtful Letters," 56. Sulpitius Serverus (c. 360–420) devoted himself to monastic retirement.

849. Chrysostom, *Commentary*, 378.

850. Ibid., 379.

subduing neighboring peoples and struggling against the Macedonians."[851] Theodoret also says, "What they did in justice against [the enemies] was written down and to this day remained their unforgettable glory."[852]

Turning to a Western father of the Alexandrian school, Jerome makes a connection between the double-edged sword in the saint's mouth and the one in Jesus' mouth in Rev 1:16.[853] The two-edged sword that the Lord gives his disciples is his teachings, both historical and allegorical, which slay adversaries and protect his faithful. Jerome makes a distinction between punishment on the people and punishment on the leaders; the former is not the object of the punishment, but of the latter Jerome says, "that I might be able to kill Arius, Eunomius, Manichaeus, and destroy every last heresy!"[854] The monk Cassiodorus understands the two-edged sword as the "word of the Lord Saviour who said in the gospels that he came not to send peace but a sword (Mt 10:34)."[855] For Cassiodorus "There is one sword, but two ways of cutting which He grants to the chosen peoples at various selected moments of time."[856] But essentially the sword symbolizes the future judgment which the blessed ones will participate in: "To execute vengeance on the nations truly takes place when they shall judge in company with the Lord."[857]

Psalm 149 in Augustine

Given the hymnic nature of the psalm and Augustine's figural reading there is nothing noteworthy to record about the context for this investigation.

Meaning of the response

Augustine suggests the "new song" is the song of peace and charity to be sung by "those in whom eternal life is begun."[858] Further, for Augustine one's deeds determine whether one is really singing a new song.[859] The true Zion (the true Jerusalem) is the assembly of saints in heaven and on earth and

---

851. Theodoret, *Commentary on the Psalms*, 371.
852. Ibid.
853. Jerome, *Homilies*, 427.
854. Ibid.
855. Cassiodorus, "Explanation of the Psalms," 460.
856. Ibid.
857. Ibid.
858. Augustine, *Exposition, Vol. 6*, 492.
859. Ibid., 493.

"Christ is our creator, our king, our priest, and our pure sacrifice."[860] King Jesus fought for us and appeared to lose but in actuality he won.[861]

As expected, Augustine interprets figurally the double-edged sword in the hands of the saints (v. 6). The double-edged sword is the word of the Lord.[862] One side refers to temporal matters and the other to eternal matters. He illustrates through the example of Mt 10:34 how the sword brings dissention within a family.[863] From v. 7 Augustine suggests there will be slaughter, glorious battles and victory, with vengeance being wreaked upon the nations every day by speaking out.[864] He uses Babylon as an example and quotes Rev 18:6, "Repay her twice over for what she has done."[865] He explains how Babylon received a twofold punishment. When Babylon (Rome in Augustine's example) persecuted Christians, bodies were killed but God was not destroyed. Now pagans are being killed by becoming Christians and idols are being smashed, "But you must not think of people being literally struck with swords or of blood being spilt or of wounds in the flesh."[866] In the *Confessions* Augustine translates the slaying of the wicked with a slightly different emphasis: "Oh, if Thou wouldest slay them with Thy two-edged sword, that they be not its enemies! For thus do I love, that they should be slain unto themselves that they may live unto Thee."[867]

For Augustine the kings in fetters and the nobles in chains of iron (vv. 8–9) are also allegorical.[868] The kings in fetters represent rich people who have accepted fetters to hold them back from unlawful deeds,[869] whereas the iron symbolizes fear.[870] The "judgment written" refers to the events which "were described long ago but are being fulfilled now."[871]

---

860. Ibid., 496–497.
861. Ibid., 497.
862. Ibid., 501.
863. Ibid.
864. Ibid., 502.
865. Ibid.
866. Ibid., 503.
867. Augustine, *Confessions*, 180.
868. Augustine, *Exposition, Vol. 6*, 205.
869. Ibid., 504.
870. Ibid., 505.
871. Ibid., 506.

John Calvin

Suffering

Calvin interprets Ps 149 as God speaking of his benefits to the Church exclusively.[872] The psalm was composed at the time of the early restoration and the object of the Psalm was to encourage them to expect complete and full deliverance.[873] However, it was also a remedy for evils which would follow under the cruel tyranny of Antiochus.[874] A "new song" is meant to convey a rare and unusual benefit.[875] The term 'nwym (v. 4) meaning "poor and afflicted ones" describes the exiles; bodily afflictions have a tendency to subdue pride.[876]

Meaning of the Response

Calvin offers an impressive explanation of the images of violence in vv. 8–9. The praise connected to the image of the sword is meant to suggest that the deliverance of God had been remarkable. The symbol of couches is meant to highlight the extent to which the returnees will be secure in the land, that is, they will even subjugate the kings and enemies who formerly ruled over them.[877]

Calvin notes that the idea of executing vengeance during and immediately following the exile seems incredible, and that this did not take place before the advent of Christ.[878] The Jews, who were greatly reduced in number, were called to exercise faith in God's promise.[879] Calvin says,

> The vengeance spoken of is such as the Israelites would take, not under the influence of private resentment, but by commandment of God; and this we mention that none may infer that they are allowed to take vengeance for personal injuries.[880]

---

872. Calvin, *Commentary*, 310.
873. Ibid.
874. Ibid., 311.
875. Ibid.
876. Ibid., 313.
877. Ibid., 314.
878. Ibid.
879. Ibid.
880. Ibid.

Calvin translates the mention of the kings and nobles in v. 8 as an amplification of v. 7. This was fulfilled in only a very slight way at the time of the Maccabees, but only fully in the advent of Christ.[881] Verse 9 qualifies what the psalmist has written about the previous verses.[882] At first Calvin thinks it strange that the "merciful ones of God" should be sent out to "commit slaughter and pour out human blood."[883] However, the meaning, Calvin says, is that "When God himself is the author of the vengeance taken, it is just judgment, not cruelty."[884] This judgment that was written (v. 9) is the divine mandate for the Jews:

> not to proceed under the influence of private resentment, and to throw a rein over passion; saying upon the matter, that God's children may not execute vengeance but when called to it, there being an end of all moderation when men yield themselves up to the impulse of their own spirits.[885]

Yet Calvin is not unaware of the tension that the violent images present with Jesus' meek manner. In response, Calvin says, "Christ is also armed with an iron sceptre, by which to bruise the rebellious, and is elsewhere described as stained with blood, as slaying his enemies on every side, and not being wearied with the slaughter of them (Isa 63:2)."[886] Calvin does note that this is not surprising since the world despises mercy.[887]

Furthermore, the physical violence was permissible to the Jews alone and not to Christians, "except, indeed, that rulers and magistrates are vested by God with the sword to punish all manner of violence; but this is something peculiar to their office."[888] For the Church the sword comes now to symbolize the "word and spirit; that we may slay for a sacrifice to God those who formerly were enemies, or again deliver them over to everlasting destruction unless they repent (Eph 6:17)."[889]

Calvin's concluding comments on how the images of violence are to be appropriated by Christians are given in his own words:

---

881. Ibid., 315.
882. Calvin, *Commentary*, Vol. 5, 315.
883. Ibid.
884. Calvin, *Commentary*, 315.
885. Ibid., 316.
886. Ibid.
887. Ibid.
888. Ibid.
889. Ibid. Calvin also quotes Isa 11:4 in the following verses.

An Exegetical and Historical Study of Psalms 110, 119, 129, 137, 139, and 149   173

> If believers quietly confine themselves within these limits of their calling, they will find that the promise of vengeance upon their enemies has not been given in vain. For when God calls us, as I have said above, to judgement written, he puts a restraint both upon our spirits and actions, so as that we must not attempt what he has not commanded.[890]

Finally,

> Most men give vent to fury and rage, under the idea that the only way to defend their life is by showing the savageness of wolves. Although God's people, therefore, have nothing of the strength of the giant, and will not move a finger without divine permission, and have a calm spirit, the Psalmist declares, that they have an honourable and splendid issue out of all their troubles.[891]

Comparison with Exegetical Findings of Psalm 149

Once again, the purpose here will be to allow the historical findings to supplement my exegesis. One of the challenging aspects of interpreting Ps 149 is that the immediate adversity of the post-exilic community has passed. In the background stands the suffering of the exile and so the desire to exact vengeance on the nations is isolated in its purist form. In a straightforward historical reading, the Israelites have suffered greatly at the hands of the Babylonians, but that is over and now it is their turn to exact revenge.

One area which was not looked into independently in my exegesis was the term in v. 1, a "new song." However, its connection with Revelation is quite revealing. Of the three uses of the term ᾄδω "sing" in Revelation, one occurs in the context of an allusion to Ps 139:14 and the other two (Rev 5:9 and 14:3) occur in the context of an allusion to Ps 149:1. The term a "new song" whether it occurs in the OT or NT always expresses God's impending judgment or victory over the enemy (so Beale and Bount). In Revelation it is Jesus who is acclaimed with this position of judge. Rev 14:2–3 seems to celebrate God's universal rule seen in the judgment of enemies and the redemption of those who witness to it. Many of the commentators in this study comment on this "new song." Cyril of Jerusalem sees the "new song" as indicating the new Churches of Christ. Jerome sees the new song being indicative of a new people with a new king, Christ. Augustine also sees the

890. Ibid., 317.
891. Ibid.

"new song" as a song of peace and charity for the redeemed, and Calvin sees it as meant to convey rare and unusual benefits.

I argued in the exegesis that the theme of praise is a central theme in the psalm, and that the author has edited his psalm to show an intentional unity between the themes of judgment and praise. Praise and judgment are also linked by Sulpitius Severus, who has v. 5 being spoken by David at the last judgment when Christ returns. Chrysostom notes that the psalm sets war to music, "implying that by singing and praising they will overcome."[892] Chrysostom relates this song to the remarkable song of the victories of the Maccabees.

An image of importance in interpreting the violent intent of the psalm was the "two-edged swords." Jerome makes the connection between the double-edged sword in Jesus' mouth (Rev 1:16) and the double-edged sword in the mouths of the saints. But for Jerome the two-edged sword in the NT is the teaching, historical and allegorical, which slays adversaries and protects the faithful.[893] In this context, Jerome would very much like to figuratively slay the heretics of his time. Augustine, as well, gives a figural meaning to the double-edged sword. He illustrates through Mt 10:13 how Jesus' words as "the sword" can bring dissension. On the other hand, Cassiodorus interprets the double-edged sword and the exacting of revenge by the saints as referring to a future judgment in which they will participate with Christ. The poor will pass judgment on the princes of the earth.

In the exegesis the question was raised as to whether the meaning of the song allowed for its use in motivating a just war. Of the commentators which I examined none allowed it to be used as such. The literal interpretation by Theodoret was descriptive in nature, telling about what the Maccabees had done. Calvin clearly indicates that violence was permissible to the Jews alone and not to Christians. The many different figural interpretations attempt to bridge the gap between the images in Ps 149 and the calling of the Christian, which, as Calvin suggests, is to the restraints on spirit and action as given in "the judgment written."[894] Important, though, is how the "new song" and the praise elements interwoven with the violent images are also captured in the allusions to the Book of Revelation. The connection with Revelation 5:9 stresses Jesus as the worthy judge and with Rev 14:3 stresses in particular to the 144,000 and represents God's victory over the enemy. Jerome's observation of the connection between the double-edged sword and Rev 1:16 and Cassiodorus' explanation of the sword as suggesting a

---

892. Chrysostom, *Commentary*, 378.
893. Jerome, *Homilies*, 427.
894. Calvin, *Commentary*, 317.

time of future judgment in which Christians will participate with Christ, all strongly suggest that Ps 149 has eschatological overtones. Given these parameters it seems that Caspar Sciopius and Thomas Müntzer attributed to the meaning of the text a function which was not understood or suggested by any of the commentators in this study.

Chapter 3

Towards Developing an Understanding of the Language of Enmity as Prayer and God's Just Dealings with His People

ANALYSIS OF FINDINGS

Suggesting an Appropriate Way to Understand the Images of Enmity

WITH THE EXEGESIS AND the historical survey completed, our next task is to understand the meaning of these psalms as prayer and to move towards developing a theology of God's just dealings with his people. One of the basic assumptions of this study was that form criticism had limited the understanding of the responses of enmity in the psalms because violent images are found in more than just lament psalms of the individual. It was postulated that if images and motifs of enmity can be examined in the larger context of other responses to suffering at the hands of an enemy, then a more accurate picture may be obtained as to what they have to say about how the psalmists perceive justice. In this section I will attempt to compare the responses to distressing situations in Pss 110, 119, 129, 137, 139 and 149 in order to determine a more adequate understanding of the images of enmity. In the next section I will seek to understand the meaning of the findings as normative prayer. Following this explanation, I will examine the relationship between the psalmist, the enemy and God in a canonical context from the perspective of the modern pray-er. It is at this point as prayer reflecting the nexus of relationships between God, psalmist and enemy that a beginning towards contributing to a theology of God's just dealing with his people can be offered. In an ideal study all three elements would be investigated and commented on at the same time, synchronically, because they each simultaneously contribute to an overall understanding of these psalms. However, the following approach will allow their meaning and use as prayer to be more easily comprehended.

A Comparison of the Different Responses to Adversity in Pss 110, 119, 129, 137, 139 and 149

The goal of this study is to understand how psalms that contain images of enmity can function as prayers in the life of faith, and to make some proposals in explaining God's just dealings with his people. In other words, an accurate understanding of how the psalms portray justice is dependent on the psalms as forms of prayer, which disclose the psalmist's thoughts on the relationship between victim, perpetrator and God. It will be the goal of this section to understand the meaning of the responses of enmity in greater detail as they are key to understanding the psalmist's perspective on God's justice in dealing with people and, in particular, his people. The following table provides a useful summary of the pertinent results of the exegesis and historical survey. For more detailed information on which the discussion is based the reader is referred back to the specific psalm sections in the exegesis and the historical survey.

	Ps 110	Ps 119	Ps 129	Ps 137	Ps 139	Ps 149
Form	Royal (Messianic Prophecy)	Mixed Genre (lament, wisdom, hymn, thanksgiving)	Communal lament	Communal lament	Royal/Petitionary (Protective Psalm of the king)	Eschatological hymn
Response to moral adversity	Oracle and Oath formulas.	Meditation on Torah (precepts)	Agricultural Imprecation	War Imprecation	Capital Imprecation	Praise (hymn)
Image of enmity prayed for	Heap up corpses; shatter heads over the wide earth	N/A	Like dead grass which is depleted in substance, quantity and time	The shattering of little ones against the rock	That *ĕlôah* (God) would slay the wicked; bloodthirsty men depart from me; perfect hatred for those who hate the Lord	A two edged sword in their hands; to execute vengeance; to bind their kings and nobles; to execute the "judgement written"
Desired outcome	Complete subjugation of all enemies on a cosmic level	Yahweh's relational presence through Torah means injustice cannot exist	Complete elimination of the wicked	Complete elimination of evil represented in Babylon	Elimination of psalmist's enemies	Complete subjugation of all enemies on a national level (*nqmh* "vengeance")
Theological focus	Eschatological	Torah as pathway to relation with Yahweh	Eschatological	National removal of evil	Individual removal of evil. Perhaps eschatological	Eschatological

	Ps 110	Ps 119	Ps 129	Ps 137	Ps 139	Ps 149
Characterization of the enemies	Kings, nations and "heads"; recalcitrant aggressors. They surround Zion. Demonic source	Internal and external. Six different terms used. Far from Yahweh's Torah. Despise psalmist because they despise Torah	Outside the covenant (internal and external). Irrationality in their "hatred of Zion"	Treachery of Edom and great atrocities of war perpetrated by Babylon. Mocking of Yahweh (songs of Zion)	"Bloodthirsty," i.e., murderers. Defined as enemies of God; will continue in greater boldness (v. 20) if not opposed	Kings and nobles of the nations. Resist Yahweh's sovereign rule to the end
NT perspective	Judgment pertaining to one's understanding of who Jesus ("lord") is. Subjugation of enemies has begun but not completed. Violent images of judgment on recalcitrant enemies found in the New Testament.	Rev 16:5, 9; 19:2 Yahweh's righteous character and his actualized judgments on the earth are inseparable	NT uses agricultural images to reflect a severe form of judgment. Grass is symbolic of human lifespan	Jesus used the images in his acknowledgement of the historical judgment on Jerusalem for rejecting him and putting him to death. Use of Babylon in Revelation as the epitome of evil	"New song" connected with Rev 15:3. Praises are the realization of God's rule through judgment/jutice	New song in Rev 1: 6; 5:9; 14:3. Jesus as worthy judge over the whole earth. Victory over the enemy.

	Ps 110	Ps 119	Ps 129	Ps 137	Ps 139	Ps 149
Sacred nature indicated in the text	War and Priesthood joined through the liturgical modification of the prophetic oracle, n^eum yhwh "An oracle of the LORD." Lack of historical markers.	ʾašrê "Blessed formulas." Synonym for Torah in all verses except v 122. All verses address Yahweh except vv 1–3 and 115. Yahweh occurs 22 times—the poem has 22 strophes	V 8, the formulaic blessing formulas $b^e r\bar{a}k\hat{a}$ and $b\bar{a}ruk$ attached to the end of the imprecation. Hapax legomenon phrase, "those who hate zion"	Blessing formulas, ʾašrê accompany imprecations. The use of the term Zion. ʿôlālîm "little ones" differs from patterns of use in war oracles.	The direct address to ʾĕlôah. Yahweh orientated formulation of justice.	Unified themes of praise and judgment. Eschatological theme of Yahweh's reign over the whole earth. String of jussives. Hallelujah superscript and postscript.

Table 5. Summary of the pertinent information of Psalms 110, 119, 129, 137, 139, and 149.

Despite the clear differences between the psalms as indicated in the chart, they share a unified perspective in their portrayal of the object of and motivation for the enemies' hatred. The situation in Ps 110 begins by depicting the foes surrounding Zion and as the battle sequence progresses in vv. 5–7, the corpses are heaped up indicating the enemies were actively engaged in battle until the end. In Ps 119 the enemies despise the psalmist because he lives out Torah and so they despise Torah. They are also portrayed as those who are far from Yahweh's precepts. In Ps 129 the enemies are referred to as those who "hate Zion" and are thus portrayed by Augustine as irrational. In Ps 137, besides the atrocities committed against Jerusalem, there is an implicit challenge of Yahweh's authenticity as sovereign God in the taunts for the captives to sing songs of Zion. In Ps 139 the bloodthirsty are indicated as those who hate Yahweh and who challenge his inherent right as the creator of each individual. The binding of the kings and nobles in Ps 149 also speaks of active engagement in battle by the enemies. The *inclusio* between Ps 149 and Ps 2 reinforces the antagonism of the enemies. A unifying theological perspective is that in some way the adversity against the psalmist has its roots in adversity towards Yahweh or against what Yahweh stands for. Even in the case of Ps 119, the enemies may have been ostensibly concerned with the psalmist, but in actuality the reason they despised the psalmist was his close identification with Yahweh as is expressed through his meditating on and living out the Torah.

Yet there is another similarity that these psalms share, which is the desired outcome for the enemies in the response to their adversity. In Ps 110 the psalmist portrays the complete subjugation of all enemies on a cosmic level, "over the wide earth." In Ps 119 the psalmist desires the presence of Yahweh because he knows the enemies cannot co-exist with Yahweh. In Ps 129 the psalmist hopes for the complete elimination of the wicked in substance, quantity and time. In Ps 137 the psalmist hopes for the effective dissolution of a nation. In Ps 139 it is the ending of the life of those who have committed murder and hence the removal of the source of wickedness which is hoped for.[1] Finally, in Ps 149, we have the complete subjugation of the enemies on a national level. What all the images of enmity, including Ps 119 as a non-violent response and Ps 149 as hymn, share in common is a desire for the absolute removal of wickedness as represented in the characterization and activities of the foes. Perhaps this absolutism has developed out of wisdom literature where good and evil are portrayed in absolute categories. However, approached theologically, the absolutism seems to derive

---

1. As indicated in the survey of the commentators, the question of hyperbole cannot be answered for certain. However, the image is that of the ending of life and hence the absolute removal of the source of wickedness.

from depicting the enemies as aggressors towards Yahweh, which leaves no room for a moral middle ground. Given the utter hopelessness of the enemies' cause, one might find their stance implausible, yet this irrationality is one of the characteristics which defines the enemies, as Augustine keenly observed when commenting on Ps 129.

In keeping with the premise that the meaning of the OT finds its fulfilment in the life, words and witness to Jesus Christ, it will be worth noting some similarities which exist among the NT allusions in the different psalms. Again, I realize that the validity of these intertextual connections and the criteria to determine associations is open to debate, but I will proceed on the basis of the observations I have made in this study. It cannot be coincidental that all of the texts have some form of allusion to the final judgment. Given the severe images of enmity in some of the psalms (Ps 110, 137, 149) one might expect to find a reciprocal connection to the violent images of judgment in Revelation. Surprisingly, Ps 119, a non-violent image of response, has a connection with Rev 16:5, 9 and Rev 19:2. The implication is that Yahweh's righteous character and his judgments on earth are inseparable. Ps 129 was thought to represent a mild form of imprecation because it depicts grass dying. However, in the NT, agricultural images were used to depict a severe form of judgment. The chaff of Mt 3:1–12 is burned in an unquenchable fire. The fig tree which is cursed by Jesus in Mt 21:1--21 will never bear fruit again. Further, grass is symbolic of human lifespan and grass dying is also used to depict judgment.[2]

In Lk 19:44, Jesus quotes Ps 137:9 as prophetic judgment against Jerusalem for rejecting and murdering him. Notwithstanding the question of agency, Jesus was asserting that such violence could be a form of divine judgment. Further, Ps 137 finds a strong connection with judgment in the book of Revelation through the use of "Babylon" which by NT times had come to symbolize the epitome of evil. Ps 139 finds a connection with Rev 15:3 and 2:6. The former passage is associated with the "new song" and related to the defeat of the beast while the latter picks up Jesus commending the Church in Ephesus for hating the practices of the Nicolaitans. In Ps 149 there is also connection with Rev 5:9 and 14:3 through the "new song." Here the "new song" expresses praise for God's victory over the enemy. Each of the NT allusions or verbal parallels depicts an aspect of judgment and each has an eschatological element. Perhaps we can conclude two points from these comparisons. The first is that the images of enmity are also images of judgment, and secondly that judgment, even if it is a present phenomenon,

---

2. As noted in the exegesis of Ps 129, death is a form of judgment regardless of what age it occurs.

has an eschatological element to it. One psalm was not included in the above comparison because its importance in understanding the images of enmity deserves further mention.

In early Church history, Ps 110 became a central Christological text which was used to defend the orthodox position on the nature of Jesus and the Trinity. In understanding images of enmity and their connection to God's just dealing with his people, in my opinion, it should also occupy a central place. This is so for several reasons. First, Ps 110 betrays its importance as a bridge between the OT and NT by being the most quoted psalm in the NT.[3] Second, it clarifies Jesus' role as judge. In the quotations of Ps 110:1 in the gospels (Mk 12:36; Mt 22:44; Lk 20:42–43) and Acts (2:34–35), Jesus claims the right to judge based on one's understanding of who he is. Third, it clarifies the time frame in which judgment will occur. The chronological context for the universal reign of the "lord" is portrayed in an eschatological framework as having been inaugurated but not yet fulfilled through the bringing together of Ps 110:1 and Ps 8:4–6 in Hebrews 2:8–9. Fourth, the allusion to Ps 110 in Heb 10:13 shows that Jesus' session as the Melchizedekian priest provides the basis for mercy to be shown to those of the New Covenant.

To summarize, several observations have been suggested based on the comparison of the different images of enmity. First, the motivation for the enemies' animosity towards the psalmist is really an animosity towards Yahweh. Secondly, there seems to be a consensus among the hoped-for outcomes towards the enemy. The psalms portray a hope for the absolute removal of evil. Thirdly and tentatively, according to the NT, but not exclusively, there appear to be themes of judgment and eschatology associated with each of the psalms. So, we may conclude that in these prayers, the one who prays them is praying for God's judgment on the wicked. Before we move to investigating the images of enmity as prayer, we will discuss this judgment.

Images of Judgment

Given that we have established that the images of enmity are images of judgment on a recalcitrant enemy and having established the time frame by which to understand Christ's universal rule, we now turn to understanding judgment as it is portrayed in these psalms.

It will be noted that we have touched on the themes of judgment and eschatology in Ps 110 which are also characteristic of the other NT

3. The Psalms represent two-thirds of all OT quotations in the NT.

connections with the psalms in this investigation. If the images of enmity are only part of an eschatological judgment, then the praying of these images of enmity presents no real challenge for the Christian.[4] However, if they are not, and if Christians are engaging in prayer for God to judge evil in the present, then what type of judgment are they praying for? The Ante-Nicene and Post-Nicene Fathers, along with Augustine, are helpful in seeing how the text applies to the spiritual conversions of the enemies of Christ into followers of Christ.[5] However, besides Theodoret and a few others in the Antiochene school of exegesis, none of the early commentators in this study discusses how God judges recalcitrant evil in the present.

This is not the case with Luther and Calvin, who comment on present judgment in their commentaries on Ps 110. Luther sees two aspects to the extension of the Kingdom of God. The first is a metaphorical battle where the field is full of corpses, which describes the power of Christ's Word.[6] But the other deals with recalcitrant enemies whose source is the devil. For Luther the subjugation of all enemies is done in a secret way.[7] He believed that Yahweh alone subdues the enemies under the "lord's" feet without the assistance of Christians or physical power.[8] Luther gives historical examples to show how God can use violence and warfare on those who oppose the "lord." Calvin likewise divides people into two groups, those who will partake in God's glory and those who are the true enemies and remain lost forever, the reprobate. Calvin does not expound on the present working out of judgement as opposed to its eschatological working out in Ps 110. However, in Ps 119:52 Calvin comments that God carries out judgments daily, but these are hidden and not perceptible without God's help.[9]

If we follow Calvin and Luther that God's judgment is a realized eschatology, then the images of enmity used as prayer may be efficacious in God carrying out his judgment. That is, the prayers are part of the agency of God working to enact punishment on evildoers before the end time, but this remains hidden to a certain degree. One criticism against those who want to

---

4. Hilary and Cyprian often encourage believers to patiently bear under suffering by the prospect of seeing God's wrath on their enemies. Hilary apparently took the imprecations in the psalms literally. For Hilary the memory of the persecutions were still "within the memory of living men" and his conflict with heretics undoubtedly spurred him on. Further, "it was a Christian duty and privilege to rejoice in the future destruction of his opponents" (Watson, "Introduction," 90–91).

5. Once again, I refer the reader to the exegesis for details.

6. Luther, "Psalm 110," 342.

7. Ibid., 242.

8. Ibid., 255.

9. Selderhuis, *Calvin's Theology*, 157.

allegorize or who refuse to pray these psalms is that in doing so they mitigate the reality of evil in all its various expressions. The English cliché "out of sight out of mind" does not apply to the reality of evil. Further, they must construe a world where God is active in rectifying injustice in a way which removes the Church from the concrete reality of evil. If the reality of evil is lost, the Church's solidarity with victims of evil becomes elusive. Such a sanitized world is coloured so that both goodness and evil become blended into an indeterminate gray. Perhaps those who wrote wisdom literature with its absolute characterization of good and evil had a clearer understanding about the nature of evil than moderns. It is not enough for the Church to identify with abstractions of evil using generic terms. These prayers are formulated sacred prayers, but they do it in all the textures of the language of enmity. The true nature of the Kingdom of God does not deny the reality of evil as expressed in these images of enmity because the symbols themselves are an accurate representation of evil.[10]

One of the goals of praying the psalms with language of enmity is to call for God's judgment on evil. It was observed in the exegesis of Ps 119 and confirmed by Augustine and Calvin that the notion of judgment brought great delight and comfort to the psalmist. That is, as the psalmist meditated on the Law he understood that evil and the presence of Yahweh were incompatible. In his seventh exposition on Psalm 119, Augustine gives a definition of justice and retribution. For Augustine there are four types of retribution: evil retribution for evil; good for good; evil repaid with good; and good may be repaid with evil.

> Of these four types of retribution two are manifestations of justice, in the recompense of evil with evil and of good with good. The third is a manifestation of mercy, when good is rendered for evil. The fourth is alien to God, who has never repaid anyone with evil in return for good. The one I mentioned in the third place necessarily has priority, because if God did not repay evil with good there would never be any good people to whom he could render good for good."[11]

---

10. One has only to look to the Bibighar Massacre at Cawnpour (now Kanpur) in the mid-nineteenth century or the Nazi concentration camps of the twentieth century to see a literal picture that what happened to the little ones in Ps 137:9 was not just an ancient practice. News is presently leaking out about the atrocities being committed in Syria and Iraq and historians are undoubtedly going to find that the atrocities committed in the present age rival the atrocities of any ancient warfare.

11. Augustine, *Exposition*, Vol. 5, 369.

Furthermore, judgment is the working out of the virtue of justice. In this regard, justice is never an abstraction of philosophical ideas but directed towards a perpetrator.

Judgment therefore has two purposes in the Scriptures. Ps 110 is a pivotal psalm in this regard because, understood in the context of the NT, it correlates to the session of Christ and his universal rule as already but not yet fulfilled. As many commentators in the historical survey noticed, all people stand as enemies before God and under his judgment. God punishes or judges all forms of evil; this is something that is evident in the experiences of the psalmist (Ps 119) and the exile of Israel (Pss 129, 137, and 149). None escapes judgment; even the elect merely avert it to the type of the Melchizedekian Priest, Jesus Christ. God will and, according to his nature, must punish all evil. Death itself is the final form of judgment for all people and is a form of God's wrath (see Ps 129). In a certain sense, the imprecations which contain images relating to the death of the reprobate are variations of this judgment. It is Christ who has changed this equation. So Zenger is correct in commenting that one of the purposes of judgement is to lead towards repentance: "Judgment is the way God helps human beings to self-discovery; it is liberation from the delusion of innocence, awakening from the sleep of conscience, release from life's lie."[12] So in one sense praying these images is really seeking for judgment in the way Augustine explained as rendering good for evil. Probably this is why Augustine and the others could associate Ps 119 with the behaviour of the martyrs. This form of repaying evil with good is what Christians are exhorted to do in the face of evil (Rom 12:14; Mt 5:44; Lk 6:28; 1 Cor 4:12; 1 Pet 3:9). The other form of judgment on the reprobate is both a present and an eschatological reality with the purpose of restoring everything as it should be (Ps 149) and giving the wicked what they, in their delusional state, desire.

UNDERSTANDING THE LANGUAGE OF ENMITY AS NORMATIVE PRAYER

Prayers as Normative Scripture

One of the ways of avoiding the images of enmity in the Psalms is to assume a Marcionite-type view towards the OT as scripture and disregard them as reflecting an inferior religion.[13] Yet within the OT there seems to be a tension between an ethic which guards the sacredness of life and the value of

---

12. Zenger, *God of Vengeance?*, 68.
13. Ibid., 13–22.

one's neighbour and its extreme opposite reflected in "dashing little ones against the rock." The sixth Commandment says "Thou shalt not murder," and the codified law in Leviticus speaks about loving one's neighbour (Lev 19:34). Yet, each of the psalms with language of enmity either describes the taking of life or wishes for it. Since we are dealing with the psalms as prayer texts,[14] one way to deal with this ethical tension is to assume that Israel did not distinguish between the sacred and the profane.[15] However, I will argue below that the sacred[16] use of language in the psalms with images of enmity in this study, even in a theocratic society, indicates a distinction between the common use of language and the cultic or sacred use. Understanding the message of these "sacred" psalms and how they function as prayer forms a basis towards using them in the life of faith and constructing a perspective about God's justice in dealing with people and, in particular, his people. As Le Moen suggests, the patterns of *lex orandi*, *lex credendi* and *lex agendi* (prayer, belief and action) are tightly interwoven.[17] The prayers come to us as scripture and so the present task is to explain how these images of enmity as normative revelatory scripture function as prayer.

Zenger suggests that "the Bible is not revelation in the sense of an immediate, verbal communication from God, but is 'the word of God in human words.'"[18] To clarify what he means Zenger provides several examples from the NT and OT. In his example using Deuteronomy 7, he insists that according to a fundamentalist view of revelation "one would have to refuse the name 'revelation' to many texts about war and destruction in the Old Testament."[19] Zenger sees the revelatory normativeness of the psalms in that "God in person confronts us with the fact that there are situations of suffering in this world of ours in which such psalms are the last thing left to suffering human beings—as protest, accusation, and cry for help."[20] Zenger also makes the point that a revelatory dimension gives victims of violence a voice so as not to become speechless, and he leaves open the question of

---

14. The descriptive texts may require a different line of examination. I am merely speaking about the language of enmity as prayer.

15. Note Scheffler's ("War and Violence," 5) comments about war and violence in the OT: "The fact is that in ancient Israel generally no distinction was made between sacred and secular reality, especially when life and death issues were at stake." This statement frames the issue from a modern perspective that functions within a dual church and secular/state mentality.

16. The term "sacred" embraces not only cultic use, but its present use as prayer.

17. LeMon, "Saying Amen to Violent Psalms," 93.

18. Zenger, *God of Vengeance?*, 81.

19. Ibid.

20. Ibid., 85.

God's involvement in helpless situations.[21] These are all important and helpful functions of the imprecatory psalms and Zenger correctly points out that victims can benefit greatly from using these psalms, but he does not explain why victims have the right to pray these violent images. Further, to say that the imprecatory psalms as revelation only speak by giving voice to victimization reduces their function or at least the scope of their function. Part of how these psalms function as normative prayer remains unanswered. Bosma has argued *pace* Von Rad's suggestion that the psalms are Israel's response to Yahweh's deeds, that in the psalms there is also the voice of God, the voice of the enemy, the voice of God's ministrants and a canonical voice especially indicated through the placement of Torah psalms by the editors of the Psalter.[22] In the end, Zenger's focus on the victims' plight, although helpful, leaves one with the feeling that these psalms function as the words of people to God, but not as the words of God to people.

A more helpful but also incomplete approach to understanding the images of enmity as normative scripture is the approach taken by Nancy de Claissé-Walford. De Claissé-Walford argues that the communities of faith incorporated imprecatory psalms into the canons of scripture because the leaders acknowledged the importance of these texts.[23] By their inclusion into the canon they have now been transformed from words of the faithful to God into words from God to the faithful.[24] Wallace takes this one step further and has argued from a survey of the use of the psalms in Church history that the psalms have been understood as words to God and words from God which Christians can receive as gift and offer back to God.[25] The key to understanding the images of violence as prayer starts with the realization that these prayers are unique. So it is as unique prayers given by God to be prayed to God that we must understand the images of enmity as normative scripture.

TOWARDS A SPIRITUAL UNDERSTANDING OF THE IMAGES OF ENMITY

The question becomes, what is being prayed for when the modern worshipper prays these particular images? If we refuse to pray with the language of enmity are we merely returning to the notion of the psalms as reflecting

21. Ibid.
22. Bosma, "Discerning the Voices," 127–170.
23. De Claissé-Walford, "Theology of Imprecatory Psalms," 80.
24. Ibid.
25. Wallace, *Words to God*, 3–15.

a belief that for the ancients there was no difference between the sacred and profane? even if the profane for the ancients was part of a theocratic world-view. Or that the psalms are only human words to God? One of the conclusions from the comparison of the psalms used in this investigation was that the meaning behind the images of enmity is the call for the complete removal of evil. In other words, there was a deeper spiritual meaning behind the ostensible images of enmity. But are there any indications within the individual psalm texts in this study that those who composed them understood a different or deeper spiritual meaning to these images?

In order to address this question we will have to look at the distinctiveness of the language of these psalms. I suggest that in the psalms with images of enmity in this study there was a distinction made between the non-cultic use of these images and their sacred or cultic use. In making this distinction, I am making a theological claim which is supported by anthropological and sociological definitions of religious language.

> [An anthropological study of religious language] concerns linguistic practices that are taken by practitioners themselves to be marked or unusual in such a way as to suggest that they involve entities or modes of agency which are considered by those practitioners to be consequentially distinct from more 'ordinary' experience, or situated across some sort of ontological divide from something understood as a more everyday 'here and now'.[26]

This difference is also recognized in a sociological approach to religious language:

> Members of any socioculture, or, at least, those who have been fully enculturated and socialized into speech-community, can and do differentiate between religion and non-religion . . . No matter how difficult it may be for outsiders . . . to find the exact boundaries."[27]

---

26. Keane, "Language and Religion," 431.

27 Fishman, "Decalogue," 14. I am not framing my argument from either an anthropological or a sociological perspective. I am merely commenting that two different disciplines understand religious language and secular language to be different. An ancient theocratic society might not be described in such terms as sacred and religious, but there is no reason to assume that a difference did not exist between the cultic use of language and its use in non-cultic contexts. I am not necessarily interested in explaining how the denotative meaning of language can describe the ontological as much as I am in showing how the language in the psalms I am looking at combines images and rhetoric in a peculiar way, as cultic language, that can be defined as sacred or religious.

By using the term "sacred" I mean the cultic or religious use of language in contrast to how it may have been used and understood in a non-cultic setting. Of course moderns speak of the sacred and the profane in a way which would not have been comprehensible to an Israelite with a theocentric worldview. Nevertheless, those who composed the psalms composed them as prayer or liturgy, which they realized carried a different inherent meaning than the use of such language in a non-cultic setting. What this "sacred" meaning is will be different for each psalm, but the meaning does not need to be limited to how it might have been understood in a non-cultic setting.[28] If the above proposal about the relationship between meaning and function of language is valid, the sacred perspective should be detectable regardless of the specific approach moderns take to study the psalms—allegorical, historical-critical, form-critical, cult-critical, or literary and canonical. In other words, the "sacredness" comes from its function as cultic or religious language. In the most recent movement in Psalm studies, Mays, in his inaugural address regarding reading psalms in their literary context, suggested that in the Psalms given settings changed, patterns and vocabularies took on new significance and the Psalms changed on the basis of changing conditions.[29] I suggest that the same observation could be applied to the original composers of the psalms who took common language such as warfare and violence and by incorporating it into cultic worship endued it with further meaning by the use of particular vocabulary and/or rhetoric structures. In other words, those who composed these psalms understood that they were composing liturgy and infused this liturgy with distinct meaning.

The following examples from the psalms in this investigation seem to indicate that the language of enmity in these prayers may function differently from a non-sacred use.[30] First is the placing together of priest and king

28. In his proposal for the Psalms to be read according to the typology of function, Brueggemann ("Psalms and the Life of Faith," 8–9) comments that form criticism (i.e., Gunkel) could not deal with the interrelatedness of various psalms and actual human experience and that Mowinckel's proposal was too speculative. My approach sees a sacred reality in the language of the text which was part of the text's original typology of function.

29. Mays, "Question of Context," 14–15.

30. I am not trying to work out general parameters for such a procedure. Such parameters would involve the investigation of cultic and non-cultic texts both from Israel's tradition and its ANE neighbors. For this investigation I merely wish to point out some observations from the texts under consideration rather than being exhaustive. If the Psalms are carefully composed documents from a literary standpoint (see Ps 139), then is it assuming too much that the content, with its capacity for nuanced meaning, was also selected carefully. It seems to me that the very notion of having a cult to worship a deity inherently suggests a difference between cultic and non-cultic

in Ps 110, something which has led to much polemical writing for those who hold that David is the "lord." Further, the language of war is merged with the sacred language of the Melchizedekian priest through a liturgical modification of the pure prophetic oracle, n^e'um yhwh "an oracle of the LORD." In addition, the time frame established in Ps 110 and the focus on the utter defeat of the enemy, along with a lack of historical markers, may also be indicative of a "spiritual" language. In Ps 119 we have the 'ašrê "blessed" formulas (vv. 1, 2) which act as an introduction and are part of the hermeneutical key to understanding the whole psalm. Furthermore, there is only one verse (v. 122) which does not mention a synonym for God's revealed Torah. And besides the hermeneutical key (vv. 1–3) and v. 115, the voice of the psalmist addresses Yahweh. Further, the term yhwh occurs 22 times in the poem of 22 strophes. In Ps 129, once again we have blessings in the form of benediction formulas b^erā<u>k</u>â and bāra<u>k</u> attached to the end of the imprecatory portion of the prayer. Moreover, the enemies are characterized by the *hapax legomenon* phrase "those who hate Zion" which has eschatological overtones.

In Ps 137:9 there are again covenantal blessing formulas 'ašrê (vv. 8 and 9) which accompany the violent imprecations. There cannot be any doubt that attaching these covenantal formulas to images of enmity adds a new dimension of meaning. The term Zion also has significance related to the character of Yahweh. Further, the use of 'ôlālîm "little ones" in Ps 137:9 differs from the pattern of its use in war oracles in the prophetic literature. In Ps 139 there is the direct speech to God, with the use of the term ĕlôah "God." Comment was made on whether the absolutism of the "hatred" statements reflected hyperbole or wisdom leanings. Moreover, the psalmist is content not to formulate the agency of justice in his prayer. He merely develops a Yahweh-oriented perspective. In Ps 149 we have the carefully unified themes of praise and judgment.[31] In narrative war portions of Scripture, it is not common for authors to record specific shouts of imprecations or praise to God. After walking around Jericho for seven days, Joshua and the people "shout," but we are not told what they shout. Hebrew war narrative does not seem to be concerned with the verbal development of plot, theme or characterization. Further, there is the "written" source of

---

communication with that deity

31. Once again, that the theocratic world-view of the Israelites did not separate religious and common life as it is today is undoubted. But this is different than saying that the Israelites had no capacity to make a distinction between the sacred and non-sacred use of language. It is we moderns who read our secular-religious assumptions into the text thereby missing any nuances the ancients may have had between the cult and not-cultic use of language.

revelation, the eschatological theme of Yahweh's rule over the whole earth, and the hymnic nature of the psalm noted in the string of jussives and the hallelujah superscript and postscript. In making these observations we are going beyond recognizing the psalms as poetry. The psalms as poetry and song do help us to inhabit and celebrate the psalmist's worldview,[32] but it is not poetry alone that accounts for the distinctness of the psalms. Roughly two-thirds of the OT is poetry.[33] Rather it is their nature as prayer offered up to God that contributes to their distinctiveness.

It is not just as spiritual texts as opposed to secular texts that the psalms distinguish themselves. They also stand unique within the whole range of genres in Scripture. This is not to say that the psalms only address spiritual matters as opposed to historical or political matters, something which Kraus suggests is not true.[34] But it is to recognize the capacity for a possible distinctness in meaning of the language which is dependent on the original function of language.

Once again, according to Wallace commentators such as Athanasius, Calvin and Luther maintained a balance between the two traditions of seeing the psalms as the words of man and the words of God.[35] The balance was also seen in the "complementary approaches of the cathedral and the monastic traditions."[36] In fact, the dual nature of the psalms is reflected in the incarnational nature of God's word proclaimed in Scripture and in the divine Word come in human flesh.[37] In one regard, the whole Bible may be regarded as a religious text. However, even in this context the psalms have a unique role and function.

What the meaning of this spiritual language is will depend on each psalm. Brown has noted that scholars have overlooked the Psalter's use of imagery at great cost.[38] What I mean by sacred language in this instance is not necessarily dependent on a metaphorical or allegorical interpretation. What modern Christians are doing when they pray these psalms is spiritualizing these prayers, but not in the same way that the Church Fathers did, and in this regard Houston's criticism of the early Church Fathers is justified, namely, that the practice of allegory as exemplified in Origen, Jerome, Hil-

---

32. So Wright, *Case for the Psalms*, 21.

33. Perhaps saying a large portion of OT scripture is poetry will suffice for this study; one-third to two-thirds depending on how one defines Hebrew poetry.

34. Kraus, *Theology*, 16.

35. Wallace, *Words to God*, 14.

36. Ibid.

37. Ibid., 15.

38. Brown, *Seeing the Psalms*, ix.

ary of Poitiers and Chrysostom is orthodox in theology but unorthodox in methodology.[39] Metaphor signals the transference of meaning from something familiar to something new.[40] Nevertheless, metaphor and allegory assume a disconnection between the target and the source domains regardless of the common ground of understanding. It is rather the distinct meaning of the language as it took on a particular cultic function which provides the bridge or connection with the modern worshippers use of language. In particular, the language of enmity, I suggest, maintains this connection with the referent through the universal unchanging nature of evil.

This is not a novel way of understanding the text. The "sacred" understanding of the text by the earliest canonical communities could not have been limited to only a literal understanding of the images of enmity, especially if the editors intended the setting of Book V to be understood as occurring in the beginning but not yet completed restoration. The rhetorical feature which most closely describes how the language of enmity may be understood in these psalms is synecdoche. Synecdoche states that the part stands for the whole or the whole stands for the parts. So there is a connection between the source and target domains. Brown has rightfully noted that the Psalms are performative in nature and that they find their relevance primarily in what they invoke.[41] His purpose was to highlight the role of metaphor, but this is true of the rhetoric of synecdoche as well.

The Language of Enmity

But why would Christians need to use these images praying from this side of the Cross? One reason is that they represent the unchanging and true nature of evil: aggressive and recalcitrant (Ps 110); despising of Yahweh to the extent that they despise those who follow his laws (Ps 119); excessively brutal, proud, irrational (Ps 129); mocking, treacherous, and perpetrating war atrocities (Ps 137); bloodthirsty murderers and progressively more evil if not restrained (Ps 139); and defiant in a collective (national) way (Ps 149). The language used to describe the enemies and their actions in the psalms is what can be described as the "language" or "grammar" of evil. Blood and violence, war atrocities such as the killing of little ones, murder, hatred, battlefields and corpses heaped up are part of this language. Praying the language of enmity is really praying the "language" or "grammar" of evil. When Christians pray these "sensational" images, they are merely reflecting

39. Waltke and Houston, *Pslams as Christian Worship*, 7.
40. Brown, *Seeing the Psalms*, 5.
41. Ibid., x.

back to God what he already sees and knows about the wicked. Brueggemann suggests that the psalms capture the rawness of human experience.[42] Perhaps we can go further and say that these psalms capture in language the rawness of evil in human experience, which has now become embedded in the language of the psalms, the gift of the psalms as God's word offered back up to God. Brueggemann also comments that when praying, Israel prays God's character back to God.[43] If this is the case, then praying the language of enmity is praying back to God what should not be, and what God has an obligation to rectify. The language of enmity is not vague descriptions of evil, but its pointed reality. The language may reflect a particular place, time and worldview. However, the nature of evil reflected in this language has not changed. These psalms pray for the annihilation of evil, the presence of which is incompatible with Christ's rule, and they do so using real images of evil.

Psalm 137 as an Example

Perhaps a clearer way of seeing this can come through the example of Ps 137. To begin with, the attaching of the *'ašrê* "blessed formula" to the imprecation of shattering little ones against the rock indicates that the imprecation has a "sacred" meaning. The "blessed formula" draws God into the psalm and prayer. "Blessed" assumes that such actions will be effected and commended by God. A sacred meaning does not mean an allegorical meaning, although many early Church commentators allegorize the imprecation of the shattering of the little ones against the rock to mean sinful thoughts. Augustine, for example, says that the little children are evil desires and the rock is Christ.[44] In this way the denotative force of the evil images of the children being dashed against the rocks is muted. Further, there is nothing that connects the psalm to the larger issues of justice, which seems to be what those who composed the psalm were looking for. In other words, an allegorical interpretation becomes a pietistic interpretation that looks inward.

I suggested in the exegesis that shortly after the fall of Babylon the language of enmity would have been understood as a metaphor for the complete elimination of the government of Babylon and hence the dissolution of the nation. That the dashing of little ones never seems to have occurred in Babylon's overthrow suggests that there was more to this image than a literal interpretation of *lex talionis*. However, if the fall of Babylon is considered

---

42. Brueggemann, *Praying the Psalms*, 64.
43. Brueggemann, "Psalms as Prayer," 47.
44. Augustine, *Exposition, Vol. 6*, 240.

the fulfillment of this prayer, then Yahweh goes beyond the principle of *lex talionis*, which was meant to limit the extent retributive justice could take within particular historical communities. He is not bound by this principle.

The principle of *lex talionis* acts as a mirror in reflecting the evil perpetrated. The psalmist holds up the graphic detail of the specific war atrocity of murdering little ones and prays that Yahweh would repay Babylon in kind. Yahweh's response is to put an end to the functional existence of the nation and hence any capacity for the perpetrators to commit any further evil. In other words, the answer to this imprecation goes beyond the confines of the normal retribution which is asked for. Moreover, the synecdochal meaning and use suggests that the most extreme case of physical violence and vengeance then embraces all other forms of violence. The Israelites had suffered great atrocities at the hands of the Babylonians. Their prayer uses the language of these atrocities because it is an accurate reflection of the evil committed against them. Such evil still occurs today in a literal way[45] but also in many different shades. The deeper "sacred" meaning, as with all of the psalms in this investigation, is for the annihilation of evil. In other words, all acts of violent atrocities stand linked through the nature of the evil. I now turn to a brief look at how these psalms contribute to a theology of God's just dealings with his people in the context of their use as prayer.

THE CANONICAL CONTEXT AND GOD'S JUST DEALINGS WITH HIS PEOPLE

Psalmist, Enemy, and God and the Developing of a Theology of God's just Dealings with his People

In this section I will attempt to move towards contributing to a theology of God's just dealing with people and his people in particular. I emphasize the word "towards" because the discussion of Pss 110, 119, 129, 137, 139, and 149 in their immediate context of Book V or even the Psalter itself gives only a partial understanding of a theology of God's just dealing with his people. Psalms as prayers speak about a nexus of relationships between the

---

[45]. I have already made reference to nineteenth century Cawnpour (Kanpur) and the 20th century Nazi concentration camps as literal examples of the violent atrocities mirrored in Ps 137:9. There are so many other atrocities that mirror these literal atrocities, such as what occurred at Nanking, and in the Korean War, that I cannot give recognition to all the voices of even the twentieth century. As mentioned above, if news stories from Syria and Iraq are an indication of the type of atrocities that have been committed in the first fourteen years of the 21st century, then as is consistent with the unchanging nature of moral evil, these violent atrocities of war continue unabated.

psalmist, the enemy and God and hence developing a theology of God's just dealing with his people should recognize these relationships.

The central issue when talking about God's just dealing with his people is God's ostensible absence or silence in the midst of suffering of which the suffering in itself is offered as proof.[46] Brueggemann frames the question of injustice as one of theodicy or God's abandonment.[47] There appears to be incongruence between God as creator, sustainer and covenantal partner dedicated to the well-being of his people and a world where evil can and does flourish with all its horrendous consequences. But more specifically, the context of suffering can be discussed according to suffering that is intrinsic to life in creation and suffering that arises from embracing evil.[48] This thesis is concerned with the latter problem of moral evil and does not attempt to address suffering in the context of natural world order.[49] Furthermore, as Lindström has noted in his study of theodicy in the Psalms, "Suffering is not a theoretical problem but an experienced reality."[50] In an earlier work, Brueggemann noted that the issue of theodicy has been approached by modern theologians mainly by justifying the ways of God to man, but "in Israel what is called theodicy is not explanation but protest."[51]

Kraus refers to the notion of God's absence in the suffering and unjust treatment of the innocent as one of the "great questions of life" and suggests that "we should not raise the problem of a general theodicy, but should ask the question that forms the appropriate starting point for understanding the trouble of the psalmist."[52] Kraus's approach is to follow the line of argument in each individual psalm because "Only in this way can we learn how individuals in Israel formulated the great problems of life and in the depths of torment sought to deal with them."[53] To a large extent, the exegesis in this study followed Kraus's method in investigating each individual psalm to

---

46. According to Crenshaw ("Theodociy to Anthropodicy," 4) there are at least eight means of reconciling undeserved suffering with belief in order and purpose. Suffering is understood as retributive, disciplinary, revelational, probative, illusory, transitory, mysterious, or denying the possibility of discovering any meaning behind innocent suffering.

47. Brueggemann, "Psalms as Prayer," 59.

48. Provan, *Seriously Dangerous Religion*, loc. 2112.

49. So Lindström's ("Theodocy in the Psalms," 258) contention that the distinction between moral evil and natural evil is seldom obvious in the Psalms will not be investigated.

50. Ibid., 256.

51. Brueggemann, *Theology*, 739.

52. Kraus, *Theology*, 168.

53. Ibid., 168–169. His specific example is Psalm 73.

determine the meaning of the response to suffering that had arisen from adversity at the hands of the enemy. But there are two general questions about moral evil at the hands of an enemy that we will explore here. Lindström gives them as 1) How does God engage with evil and what does he do to overcome it? and 2) Must evil at its root and essence remain irrational and mysterious?[54] This second question can be rephrased in the context of this investigation as What can be known about moral evil?

To develop a theology of God's just dealing with his people we begin by investigating the psalms as prayers in their original context. The prayers of the psalmist or congregants are addressed to "You,"[55] which affirms that the source and ground of life lies outside themselves and hence ourselves.[56] I would qualify this to suggest that regardless of the voice of the psalmist in the psalm, for the modern pray-er the psalm is a communication with the "You" (see Introduction). In contrast, the enemy is defined by the absence of a relationship with the "You" (see the description of the enemy in Ps 119) and, as was seen above, the enemy is against everything which Yahweh stands for. Injustice from a theological perspective is always relational regardless of its categorization (e.g., distributional, retributive, penal, etc.) because even in its most reduced form it involves God. Prayer is the relational means through which the psalmist asks God to remember that certain relationships exist between himself, God and the enemies.

Developing a theology of God's just dealing with his people moves beyond the original constraints of the psalmist's prayers and involves investigating the psalms as prayers of the modern worshipper. Recent proposals for doing a theology of the psalms suggest placing emphasis on an interpretive community of many voices in a multicultural, multivoiced world.[57] Thus, the reader as pray-er is integrally involved in constructing a theology of the psalms of enmity. The basis for this present investigation is not so much the cultural context that the reader brings to the text, but rather the idea that, through the reader approaching the psalm texts as prayer, the texts become canonical texts of Scripture.

Furthermore, in praying the psalms the pray-er inhabits and celebrates a worldview where God's time and the worshipper's overlap and intersect

---

54. Lindström, "Theodicy in the Psalms," 268.

55. The "You" is meant to reflect the nature of Israel's relationship with God. The term has been made popular by Martin Buber (see Kraus' introduction [*Theology*, 11–16]).

56. Brueggemann, "Psalms as Prayer," 35.

57. Tanner, "Rethinking the Enterprise," 140–142. See also Braulik for a discussion of reception aesthetics ("Psalms and Liturgy," 313–316).

and God's space and the worshipper's overlap and interlock.[58] To expand on this slightly, the words of the psalmist as God's gift means that the psalmist, God, and modern pray-ers occupy the same sacred time and space. Part of the contribution to this overlapping is the eschatological nature of these psalms, which suggests that for both the psalmist and the modern worshipper the psalms have an "already but as of yet unfulfilled" perspective. This perspective links the psalmist and the modern worshipper to God's time. As a result, in what follows I will investigate God's just dealing with his people from a canonical perspective within the context of the findings in this investigation.[59] For the details behind this discussion, readers are again directed to the respective psalms in the exegesis, the historical survey and the comparative approach above. To a certain degree, there will be some restatement of the findings. However, in what follows, I will attempt to note some salient features from the individual psalms themselves as canonical prayer and allow the psalms to dictate the issues that arise (so Kraus).

Psalm 110: Unrestrained evil and Yahweh's "lord"

The pray-er enters Psalm 110 through the voice of the prophet, whether David or some other. The whole psalm maintains the nature of this prophetic speech, although the voice of the speaker changes.[60] The time frame inhabited by the pray-er is outside of the Aaronic covenant and there is a lack of pre-exilic land markers. The effect is to focus the conflict on the hostility of the enemies towards the "lord," and their impending defeat. The problem of evil is formulated from the perspective of the "lord" who is the recipient of Yahweh's oracle and oath and the recipient of the enemies' aggressive behavior. In the first strophe, the enemies surround Zion where they aggressively challenge the "lord's" divinely given mandate to rule. In the second strophe, after the Melchizedekian oath, the enemies appear as unjust aggressors who have battled to the last man against the "lord" (vv. 5–6).[61] The situation here is not Yahweh's absence in the midst of suffering violently at the hands of an unjust enemy.

---

58. Wright, *Case for the Psalms*, 21.

59. As is clear from Braulik's ("Psalms and Liturgy,") study, a Protestant canonical context differs from a Roman Catholic canonical context. However, even within the Protestant tradition there are different views on the role of the interpretive community. LeMon ("Saying Amen to Violent Psalms," 105) believes the community is needed to adjudicate the propriety of individuals praying the violent psalms.

60. See exegesis footnote to Ps 110:3.

61. See the exegesis for other positions on who the subject of vv. 5–7 is.

This is not the normal pattern of hostility in the complaints of the individual, where the dishonored human exists in a sphere that is hostile to both man and Yahweh.[62] Rather, historical realities fade and Yahweh is portrayed as the real source behind the "lord's" victory over a recalcitrant and aggressive enemy. The images here reveal how Yahweh deals with his enemies and the true nature of the enemies. He meets their utter evil with complete victory through the agency of his "lord."

The modern pray-er adds several canonical dimensions to this picture. First, there is the working out of the complete defeat of the enemies in a particular time frame. Second, Jesus Christ is identified as the "lord" and type of the Melchizedekian priest. Third, all people are identified as enemies of God at some point in their existence, the elect and reprobate. Fourth is the pray-er's participation through prayer in the agency of Yahweh's defeat of the enemies.

War is a sophisticated form of organized and planned evil. This prayer for Christ's rule accurately reflects the capacity for evil of all those who are enemies of Christ. Their natures have become so calcified in evil and their thinking so delusional that they not only despise the "lord" but think they can defeat Yahweh. Perhaps the singular *rōš* "head" which is interpreted grammatically as a collective whole is symptomatic of a synecdochal understanding of the images. Some commentators who understood the term as referring to Satan as the chief enemy of God may have perceived this connection. The language of enmity epitomizes the rebellion against the "lord" and accurately reflects all other latent forms of evil that are only temporarily disguised. For the Christian, the murder of Yahweh's "lord" has historical precedent.[63] In an eschatological framework evil comes to full bloom in the final battle also depicted in the book of Revelation. There appears to be no restraining grace to limit its potential at that time. In short, the images of battle merely depict the "lord" giving to the enemies what they irrationally pursue.

Psalm 119: Torah as Yahweh's Presence and Judgment

In Psalm 119 the psalmist begins his long acrostic prayer by presenting a hermeneutic key which affirms what the true nature of dedication to the Law means. The two *'ašrê* "blessed" formulas in vv. 1–2 draw Yahweh into the psalmist's prayer since Yahweh is the one who effects the "blessedness." The psalmist's expressions about Torah (1b), about sin (3a) and about walking

---

62. So Lindström, "Theodicy in the Psalms," 264.
63. Theologically, Christians are the pardoned culprits.

in Yahweh's ways (1a and 3b) are expressions of the psalmist's desire for the presence of Yahweh (2b) epitomized in the last verse of the "aleph" א strophe (v. 8) that Yahweh not utterly forsake him. For the psalmist, seeking after Yahweh is reinforced throughout the psalm (*lēḇ* "heart" occurs 14 times in 176 verses; Yahweh occurs 22 times).[64]

In the midst of the psalmist's pursuit of Yahweh through Torah-dedication the psalmist encounters a world filled with enemies and conflict which challenges his pursuit and understanding of Yahweh's presence. He identifies his antagonists as *the insolent, princes, kings, the wicked, enemies, and foes*. The enemies are external to the nation, being found all over the earth (v. 119), but also found within the nation itself. However, the psalmist more specifically defines them as those (*kings*, v. 46) who do not know the *'ēḏût* "statutes" (NIV) or those (*enemies*, v. 98) who do not have the *miṣwōṯ* "commandments" of Yahweh. They are also those who forsake Yahweh's Torah (*wicked*, vv. 53, 155) and those who stray from the *ḥuqqîm* "decrees" (NIV). They are even described as those who "forget" the *dᵉḇārîm* "words" (v. 139) of Yahweh. The psalmist is not merely contrasting the enemies with himself but identifying the enemies in relation to Yahweh.

The enemies stand in relation to Yahweh as those who are unaware of his Law or who wilfully reject it. However, in terms of the suffering of the psalmist the enemies are presented as responsible agents. They plot against the psalmist (v. 23), deride him (v. 51), ensnare him with cords (v. 61), smear him with lies (v. 69), subvert him with guile (v. 78), dig pits to trap him (v. 85), lie in wait to destroy him (v. 95), set a snare for him (v. 110), persecute him without cause (vv. 157, 161) and oppress him (v. 122). The psalmist is afflicted (vv. 50, 92, 153, 107) severely (v. 107) and suffers from human oppression (v. 134). Moreover, as Augustine noted, meditating on the law is a form of repaying evil with good.[65] As per Bede, Chrysostom, Augustine and Calvin, meditation on the law contains within it ethical implications which are relational and so we have the principle of *lex orandi, lex credendi*, and *lex agendi*. So the evil of the enemies here is not an abstraction but has a focus in despising the psalmist.

The psalmist presents to Yahweh his understanding of Yahweh's involvement in his suffering from three different perspectives. He feels abandoned by Yahweh (vv. 8, 19). He feels frustrated at not being able to live

---

64. According to Lindström ("Theodicy in the Psalms," 259, 265) the view of life which was developed in the monarchical period and focused on the first temple suggests that Yahweh's area of power is symbolized by the sanctuary. The notion of Torah would then be a later development of the sphere where Yahweh's presence and hence protection lay.

65. Augustine, *Exposition*, Vol. 5, 380, 381.

up to the ideal of the Law (vv. 4, 176), and in some manner he feels that God has been responsible for his affliction (v. 75). That is, he recognizes in some mysterious way that God is involved in his suffering, although he does not formulate the nature of this involvement. Furthermore, the psalmist expresses his devotion to the Law, not as motivation for answer to his prayers, but rather his suffering has led to his Torah-renaissance (vv. 67, 71, 75). For the psalmist to meditate on the Torah of Yahweh is to seek Yahweh. However, the law has an elusiveness to it and the psalmist is beset by the injustice of his enemies.

The psalmist does respond by cursing the insolent, but only once in v. 78, where in the same verse he offers his other response to the guile of the insolent, which is to affirm to Yahweh that he will meditate on Yahweh's *piqqûdîm* "precepts." The psalmist knows that meditating on the precepts of Yahweh brings him into the way of Yahweh, which is devoid of the *šeqer* "deceit" (*NIV*) of the insolent (vv. 29, 104, 128 and 163). Imprecating against the insolent is the psalmist's way of calling on Yahweh to bring the psalmist's enemies in line with the way of Yahweh which entails judgment (v. 118). The psalmist's attitude towards meditating on the Torah is not ambiguous or capricious.

The psalmist is also resolute about his commitment to the Torah in the midst of persecution (vv. 95, 110, 87, 92, 23, 61). The Law is the psalmist's delight in affliction because in the Law is the notion that Yahweh is just in exonerating the innocent and punishing the wicked. Curses as a means of seeking justice turn outwards towards the enemies through prayer to Yahweh, but meditation on the Law focuses the psalmist to turn towards Yahweh alone. Two things happen: one is that evil is placed in perspective in relation to Yahweh. Second, the psalmist understands that the wicked cannot coexist with Yahweh and so perceives suffering as the absence of Yahweh. The psalmist continues to seek Yahweh through the Law because it is not only the means of relationship with Yahweh, but in the Law is a disclosure of Yahweh's character which provides much comfort to the psalmist.

The modern worshipper who joins in with the psalmist in this prayer carries also the fuller canonical understanding of the New Testament witness. The modern pray-er takes confidence in the fact that the revelation of God through the Law (Ps 119) and through the gospel (Rom 1:16) is utterly trustworthy. Jesus understood that the Law pointed to himself (Mt 5:17–18; Lk 24:27; Jn 5:39, 46). Furthermore, the modern worshipper knows that Yahweh's disclosure in the Law as righteous is inextricably linked to the nature and actualization of his judgments upon the earth, which are true and just (Rev 16:5, 7 and 19:2).

The very act of presenting prayer about one's dedication to Torah is a reminder to Yahweh of his obligation that his character and judgments become inseparable. The modern worshipper formulates the problem of suffering then in terms of Yahweh's character. Prayerfully meditating on the true Law is not only relational but removes the question as to why God allows suffering. God and injustice cannot coexist. Yahweh has no option but that, on the basis of his character, he must eliminate injustice. His latency in actualizing his character through judgment has an eschatological perspective to it, the working out of which has become clarified through Ps 110 and its delineation in Hebrews.

The prayer, however, is not a pleading for a pietistic experience. The psalmist and the modern Christian are seeking for Yahweh's presence in the governance of their affairs, which involves a response to the adversity of the enemies. With such a presence, evil cannot exist. So the modern worshipper in seeking after Yahweh is presenting to Yahweh his role as the rectifier of injustice, not something which is disassociated from him as is sometimes inferred through the use of political or penal metaphors, but is a threat to his very revelation which is trustworthy. To conclude, perhaps besides the many benefits to the believer of meditating on the Law (see especially Calvin), praying this psalm about meditating on the Law rather than cursing their enemies recognizes the innate concept of how the Law can be used wrongly. As the author of the *Constitutions of the Holy Apostles* put it, "He that forbade revenge, now commands longsuffering, not as if just revenge were an unrighteous thing, but because long-suffering is more excellent."[66]

Psalm 129: Yahweh's Righteousness, Agency, and Agricultural Imagery

In Psalm 129 the psalmist presents Yahweh with the history of Israel from the time of its youth in the Exodus wanderings and progresses through the exile to the restoration and into the present and future. The people stand in a situation of suffering at the hands of an excessively cruel enemy. But Yahweh has "cut the cords of the wicked" and so the people have been liberated by Yahweh and restored from the exile. The enemies are those who "hate Zion" and Zion entails in its meaning identification with Yahweh. In presenting the panorama of Israel's suffering at the hands of its enemies, the psalmist establishes in the history of Israel's relationship with its enemies and Yahweh that the past is a basis for understanding the present and the future. In

---

66. "Book VI," 460.

Yahweh's battle with evil he is focused here on his covenantal people and goes back to the beginning. Evil directed towards the Church is inevitable.

In this prayer to Yahweh the "cords" are not only symbolic of the oppressiveness of the enemies at the time of exile, but an indication of the divine judgment of Yahweh on the Israelites. It might be tempting to think that the psalmist was singularly focused on Yahweh's deliverance. However, the language of the psalm alludes to the exile as being a judgment from Yahweh. Biblical precedent has Ephraim put under the "yoke" (cords) of the nations as a judgment for its wickedness and injustice (Hos 10:11; Deut 28:48; Isa 9:3). The image of the withering grass depicts the devastating effects on the victims of military aggression that can refer to the exilic military aggression against Israelites (2 Kgs 19:26; Isa 37:27; see exegesis). Again, the imprecation begins with the wish that all those who hate Zion be put to shame and turned back. However, the nation of Israel experiences shame and is "turned back in defeat" because of its sin (Isa 42:17).

The acclamation that "Yahweh is righteous" in v. 4, the *Janus* verse in the psalm, indicates Yahweh is equitable in his judgments. The "righteousness" of Yahweh is always manifested as a relational concept, not as an absolute, ideal, ethical norm.[67] Kraus sees the notion of punishment as a secondary emphasis of God's justice, whereas the primary work of God's justice is "the bringing of assistance, deliverance, and loyalty to those who are victims of injustice, persecution, and false accusations."[68] The judgment upon the elect and the reprobate may have different purposes, but Yahweh's covenantal loyalty (blessed formulas) to Israel even when it means their exile is the basis for which they can pray the imprecations on their enemies. If he had punished them, how much more would he punish the foreign enemies!

In this mystery of Yahweh as both punisher and deliverer, which is clearly reflected in Hezekiah's prayer (2 Kgs 19; Isa 37), there are several points to note. First, the enemies have not been able to overcome Israel. That is, there is a restraining limit to the extent of devastation which the enemies can carry out. Secondly, the enemies are oblivious to the plan of Yahweh. That is, the enemies act in their own agency of wickedness, although in some mysterious way Yahweh uses such an agency in the working out of his "righteousness" which as mentioned above is relational. The psalmist does not ask Yahweh how is it possible, but at the same time he does not avoid the mystery involved in Yahweh's agency. Israel is not spared in its disobedience, but the enemies are portrayed as those who are aggressive and who will ultimately be annihilated. What makes this even more difficult to

---

67. Kraus, *Theology*, 43.
68. Ibid., 43.

perceive is that the enemies are guided by an irrational thought process. For the community, though, Yahweh is righteous and so the suffering aroused through disobedience is given perspective. In the main narrative in Ps 129, the progression is that the enemies are not able to prevail, Yahweh delivers Israel, and then there is an imprecation for the enemies to be reduced to non-existence. In a parallel hidden narrative the enemies acting in their own agency become the means by which Yahweh punishes a disobedient nation and then whom Yahweh judges to deliver Israel from the exile.

The jussive forms make it clear that the psalmist sees the Israelites participating in the demise of the enemies which occurs through the agency of Yahweh's active judgment. The desired outcome on those who hate Zion is wished for through an agricultural metaphor. The prayer for the enemies to be like the withering grass implies their removal in substance, quantity, and time. By using the benedictory formulas in v. 8 the psalmist draws Yahweh into the process of judgment on the enemies. Such a sacred blessing would only be effected and conferred by Yahweh. The prayer is for the complete defeat of the enemies to the point where they no longer exist.

Modern worshippers who enter into this agricultural world may think they are dealing with less harsh images of judgment. However, the use of agricultural images to depict the judgment of God can be quite severe in both the OT and the NT (see exegesis). In pre-industrialized societies one would expect agricultural imagery to play a central role in people's lives. Yet what made agricultural imagery so effective was the double nuance it carried, having its own life cycle as well as being essential for human sustenance. Famine meant widespread death. Furthermore, flourishing agriculture was an image used for the righteous alone (so Ps 1). As Claudia Sticher has observed from her investigation of Pss 92 and 37, even when the evildoers (*Übeltäter*) seem to have stretched out their roots, they will not endure because the wicked are like grass.[69]

The modern worshipper enters into the psalmist's world which stretches into the worshipper's time frame and beyond into the future, through the eschatological images. In praying these agricultural images the worshipper is seeking for the complete removal of all enemies of the Church in manner, substance, and time. The true Church has existed as a continuum from the earliest of times and today has enemies that are no less oppressive than those of the past.

---

69. Sticher, "Die Gottlosen," 268.

Psalm 137: Memory, Violence and the Extent of Judgment

In Psalm 137, the psalmist begins his prayer by reminding Yahweh that the mocking of the captors is really a form of humiliation which is directed at Yahweh's character. That is, in their asking for songs of Zion, the captors were asserting the falsehood of Yahweh's intimate relationship to Zion. Further, Zion in Ps 137 is a symbol for everything Yahweh stands for. The pathos of vv. 1–3 also relates to Yahweh not only the suffering that the Israelites experience at the hands of their captors, but, just as significantly, their recognition that the hand of the living God was upon them in the form of punishment (see Ps 129 above). The psalmist appeals to Yahweh in his longing for Jerusalem through oath formulas. His hope is for the restoration of Jerusalem, which is a visible sign of the presently hidden reality of Zion. Memory also sets off the imprecation against Edom.

There is irony in the psalmist presenting to Yahweh Edom's calls of treachery "Tear it down!" This is something which Yahweh knows; there is no need for an outside objective witness. The psalmist appeals to Yahweh with the principle of *lex talionis* in the imprecation. This is how the psalmist believes the atrocities of Babylon will be rectified. However, with the dissolution of Babylon the imprecation signifies the complete removal of the functional existence of this nation and its capacity for any evil. Yahweh goes beyond the principle of *lex talionis* which was meant to limit the extent retributive justice could take within particular historical communities. He is not bound by this principle, but the psalmist is. Yahweh addresses the real source of the evil and incapacitates it. The reader is referred above for an explanation of how the sacredness of the language functions as synecdoche.

Memory plays a key role in the relationships in this psalm. As Chrysostom noted, when we remember God we choose good things but when God remembers we accomplish them.[70] On the one hand Babylon ceases to exist as a nation and so it cannot create any more memory. However, its memory lingers on for the Christian and becomes the symbol of the epitome of evil portrayed in Revelation. Jesus remembers as well, not as static historical fact but as bearing on the unbelief of Jerusalem in his day, and he uses Ps 137:9 in a judgment speech. Those who enter into the psalmist's world in prayer are able to understand more deeply that God's final goal for recalcitrant perpetrators of evil is never merely retributive or penal, but the complete removal of any capacity to commit evil.

---

70. Chrysostom, "Homilies on the Epistle to the Hebrews," 484–485.

Psalm 139: Creator and Sustainer of all People and Avenger of Blood

In Psalm 139 the psalmist stands in the midst of or just before danger (protective psalm, so Mowinckel) among substantial enemies.[71] The psalmist skilfully holds up to Yahweh His role as the omniscient, omnipresent, and omnificent God, or in common parlance the creator and intimate sustainer of all life.[72] However, God's active and relational presence stands in contrast to the hostile reality that the psalmist faces (vv. 18–19). Both the psalmist and Yahweh stand in relation to the enemy as signified in the phrase *'anšê ḏāmîm* "blood thirsty." The psalmist's solidarity with Yahweh is further emphasized in the identification of the enemies as Yahweh's enemies. The psalmist is the recipient of the attacks of the bloodthirsty and responds by presenting Yahweh with a plea to slay the "bloodthirsty." In v. 14 the intricacy of Yahweh's deeds of creation are great, but as the psalmist moves into vv. 19 and 20 the question to Yahweh becomes how he can let his wonderful deeds of creation be so wantonly destroyed. After all, Yahweh is the *ḏōrēš dāmîm* "the avenger of blood" (Ps 9:13). Bloodshed pollutes the land and atonement cannot be made for the land on which blood has been shed except by the blood of the one who shed it (Num 35:33; Ps 106:38). The psalmist is implicitly formulating the problem of God's just dealings with his people. How can those who are enemies stand if God is fulfilling his obligations?

The psalmist's approach to the enemy is twofold. He petitions (taking the particle *'im* in v. 19 as indicating the optative mood) for God "to slay" his enemies. By the use of the specific verb *qāṭal* "to slay," the psalm is most likely alluding to the treachery of Edom in the sack of Jerusalem. In the second petition the psalmist commands the "bloodthirsty" to depart from him. The two appeals are unified by the understanding that the removal of the enemies is a sign of God's presence. Therefore, in vv. 1–18 the psalmist has related to Yahweh as one with anxious or disquieting thoughts. Yahweh discerns the psalmist's thoughts from afar (v. 2a) and Yahweh, whose thoughts are precious to the psalmist (v. 17a), is intimately present in the psalmist's existence.

The psalmist turns from Yahweh's obligations in vv. 19–20 to his own. Like Jeremiah, the psalmist realizes that the heart is evil and seeks to see if there is sin in his life. The reality of the enemies' assault and Yahweh's obligation as the avenger of blood brings the psalmist to a crisis of understanding

---

71. According to Lindström ("Theodiciy in the Psalms," 295) Ps 139 belongs to the wisdom tradition, which is the youngest theological tradition in the Book of Psalms.

72. The use of these terms omniscient, omnipresent, and omnificent is not meant to depict a static view of God.

God's just dealing with his people. So, the psalmist turns to his own life to make sure that there is no hidden sin causing this incongruence he feels. In the end, the psalmist resolves the incongruence by committing himself to the "way everlasting." Perhaps in the psalmist's presentation of the enemies as hostile to God himself, the psalmist is alluding to an ultimate eschatological defeat of the enemies.

Those modern worshippers who use this psalm present to Yahweh his obligation as creator of all life. They are able to worship Yahweh for his "great deeds," which in Revelation 15:3 are associated with the "new song" and are also associated with the defeat of the beast. It was questioned in the exegesis as to whether the psalmist is using hyperbole in v. 19. However, as synecdoche, the whole refers to all the parts. The ultimate form of the degradation of humanity is murder, but there are many other forms in between. This image, whether viewed as synecdoche or hyperbole, contains all other forms of degradation. But it also brings to the forefront the characteristic of evil which Calvin noted, namely, that unchallenged the wicked become worse. There is no sense of restraint.

Praying this language presents to Yahweh his responsibility to rectify all injustices. Brown's comments are relevant here: "Personal creation is the divine charter of life and loyalty by which God becomes bound to a particular life, ensuring that the individual flourishes within the protective sphere of righteousness."[73] The modern worshipper enters into the time frame and space of the psalmist and Yahweh. Yahweh is not limited to the temple in this psalm, but as Paul writes in Rom 8:27 (cf. Ps 139:1) the Spirit of God searches and aids Christians in their prayer. Presence in Ps 139 is not a function of Temple or Torah, but rather God's relationship to all people as creator (Ps 139) and King of the nations (so the allusion in Rev 15:3). In this eschatological perspective, Yahweh maintains and upholds his relationship and hence obligation to all people.

Psalm 149: Praise, Violent Judgment and Universal Reign

The psalmist and congregation enter into Psalm 149 in the context of praising as a nation. "Israel's prayer life, in lament as in doxology, is saturated with the issue of justice."[74] The psalm unfolds to the significant grounds for praise in v. 4, "May the LORD take pleasure in his people; he adorns the lowly with salvation." Whereas Ps 139 dealt with the creation of the individual, Ps 149 takes as its premise the creation of the nation, his chosen

---

73. Brown, "Creatio Corporis," 124.
74. Brueggemann, "Psalms as Prayer," 61.

people. The use of the term *ḥăsidîm* "saints" in verses 1, 5 and 9 seems to mark this special relationship. The congregation understood the agency of Yahweh as occurring through the community of the faithful (v. 6). That is, they understood evil not as an abstract principle but as part of their historical reality. However, from the coordination of v. 9b with v. 8 as well as the eschatological markers in the text, it seems the community was more interested in the defeat of those who opposed Yahweh's rule rather than in gratuitous violence. Comparison of the "book" which deals with the individual in Ps 139:16 and the "judgment written" in Ps 149:9 might suggest that the judgment in Ps 149 is on a national level.

So this prayer seems to be against the nations, suggesting that culpability is not just on an individual level, but on a national level, which was also the conclusion of Ps 137.[75] Furthermore, *nᵉqāmâ* "vengeance," always refers to nations in its five uses in the Psalms. The overall image of judgment goes beyond the immediate enemies experiencing a reversal of fortune. The symbol is of the utter defeat of the nations. If the use of *nᵉqāmâ* was only meant to symbolize pay back for hostility in the sense of *lex talionis* then the prayer would merely seek to punish the specific nations that had harmed the Israelites. But once again it is the complete universal rule of King Yahweh over all nations that is prayed for and celebrated. In this sense *nᵉqāmâ* can be understood in the sense of re-establishing the created order as it was meant to be under Yahweh's rule. The acts of the nations, Babylon included, portrayed in their hostility to Israel were acts against God's sovereign rule over the earth. The exile revealed Israel's failure to submit to Yahweh. Israel's reversal in fortune becomes a picture of the nations' (*gôyīm*) failure to submit to Yahweh's rule.

For the modern worshipper, the issue is not of practice here.[76] The expansion of the Kingdom of God through the agency of the Church has no political motives and is not accomplished through military means. What is the Christian doing when he or she joins in the praise and hope for judgment depicted in this psalm? On one hand the modern pray-er is offering praise as a normative response to Yahweh's deliverance and his reconstitution of the created order. On the other hand, he or she is holding national

---

75. Could Abraham Lincoln's (Second Inaugural Address, March 4, 1865) understanding of the Civil War as a type of judgment on the nation be indicative that previous generations of Christians understood this aspect of judgment more clearly than the modern individualist societies of the West?

76. Besides the findings in this study, the conclusion that Firth (*Surrendering Retribution*, 139–142) reaches in his study *Surrendering Retribution in the Psalms*, suggests that in the laments of the individual, the psalmist rejects the right of human retribution and stays within a limitation of what violence can be asked for from God.

enemies before Yahweh. The images of sword and fetters and chains of iron reflect the recalcitrant nature of these enemies. Such images do not represent the conditions of surrender. Thus, as the morally evil so wish, there will be no submission, only defeat.

The sword remains an appropriate symbol in prayer for the Christian because it reflects the true nature of evil, not the violent capricious tendencies of those who composed the psalm. The hope is for the restoration of Yahweh's created order at the national level. So the sword is a synecdoche of the evil perpetrated by nations against Yahweh's people. Once again with Ps 110, warfare is the most organized and sophisticated form of rebellion. In the end, judgment of evil should always lead to rejoicing by those who are the people of God. The praise is directed towards Yahweh and not to the punishment of the enemies. It is the glory of the saints to usher in Yahweh's universal rule over all nations through the agency of praise and prayer.

Christians who use this psalm join in with the "new song" alluded to in Revelation 5:8 and 14:3, which in both the OT and NT express God's victory and judgment over the enemy. The prayers in Rev 5:8 appear to be a call for God to act in judgment and vindication.[77] The content of the "new song" is the worship given to Jesus for his crucifixion and the priesthood he has conferred on the people he has redeemed along with their reign over all the earth. The worshipper who prays this psalm enters into the time and space of the psalmist, God and all the saints. The modern pray-er of this psalm, like the psalmist, celebrates the universal reign of Jesus in all of its eschatological overtones.

How God Engages Moral Evil and its Nature

Before summarizing the results of the answers to these two questions, I will add a caveat to moving towards a theology of God's just dealings with people which has arisen from this study. In my opinion, a theology of God's just dealings benefits from taking into consideration the role of the sinfulness of God's people and the agency of the wicked as part of God's plan. This complex notion is not commented upon in some theodicies of the psalms because God's presence and absence are understood as unrelated to the sinfulness of the psalmist.[78] Psalms 129 and 137 as communal laments are help-

---

77. Blount, *Revelation*, 113.

78. Lindström's ("Theodicy in the Psalms," 291) conclusion for national complaint psalms, which suggests that in these psalms there is a refusal to accept the sin-punishment idea as an explanation of the misfortune, does not seem to reflect the content of Ps 137. Lindström (Ibid., 219), however, does not include Ps 137 in his study and refers

ful in this regard. Yahweh engages evil equitably and righteously, regardless of the perpetrator, which in the case of Ps 137 is his chosen people and Babylon. This is what the exiles had known and then sought to preserve in these psalms. Yahweh's agency of removing evil involves evil nations themselves. In this case, as Luther commented, Yahweh uses one rogue nation to punish another. However, Yahweh also punishes the rogue nation. The punishment is not for carrying out the judgment decreed, though. The rogue nation's act of hostility towards another nation is symptomatic of its own evil intentions. Yahweh is merely using the tendencies of the rogue nation itself. There is a limit to humanly penetrating this mystery, but at its core Christians are confronted with their own self-identification as enemies of the "lord" at one time and the necessity of priestly grace.

Theologians usually define the issue of unjust suffering within the framework of God's absence. In Psalms 119 (Torah) and 139 (Creator) the absence of God's presence is given as a reason for the psalmist's suffering at the hands of enemies. However, we must further define the relationship between unjust suffering and God's presence in the context of the findings of Ps 139. In Ps 139 the psalmist makes clear that the conception of God's absence is not an ontological absence. Therefore, the absence in the midst of injustice which the psalmist refers to is Yahweh's failure to engage the enemies accordingly. That is, the language of enmity is not a response to God's absence from the worshipper, but his failure to engage the wicked. God's just dealings with his people is, therefore, conceived of as his activity in overcoming the enemies and restoring the created order to being as it should be. The language of enmity, as trusted and canonical prayer, plays a role.

These texts with language of enmity have been helpful in understanding the nature of recalcitrant moral evil.[79] For example, the activity of the enemies is isolated from historical markers in Ps 110 to give a picture of the true unrestrained nature of moral evil. Moral evil in its causes can be sophisticated and determined as is evident in the gathering of armies to wage war. In Ps 137 the principle of *lex talionis*, besides defining a retributive principle, also acts like a mirror, accurately reflecting evil deeds. In his comments on Ps 129 Augustine brilliantly penetrates the irrationality of moral evil. Ps 139 makes clear that moral evil directed towards another person is

---

to it as lacking both praise and complaint. See comments in the exegesis on Ps 137:1–3 in which I take a different view. It is also interesting to note that allowing for some suffering to result from sin leads to the same conclusion as suggesting that suffering is unexplainable; "evil is given its (proper) place as an inferior opponent to God's rule, but still not a harmless influence on human life" Lindström (Ibid., 293).

79. Readers are also referred back to section *The Language of Enmity* above.

really an affront to Yahweh, who is creator of both victim and perpetrator. In the case of the psalmist in Ps 119 we noted that the ethical connection between knowing the Law and living out the Law was grounds for the animosity of the wicked. In the case of the disobedience of the Israelites and the moral agency of Babylon, there are apparently no such ethical grounds. Real evil not only wishes to destroy the good, it wishes to destroy everything. The language of evil accurately represents the deeds of the enemies at the level of the individual (Ps 139), the nation (Pss 137 and 149) and all humankind (Pss 110 and 149). In short, moral evil is delusional and, if unrestrained, ever expanding in an aggressive manner.

Chapter 4

Conclusion

SUMMARY OF INVESTIGATION AND FINDINGS

IN THE FIRST SECTION of this study I argued through the technique of *inclusio* that the editors of Book V intended its context to be understood as the beginning-but-not-yet-completed restoration.[1] This open-endedness most likely contributes to the eschatological emphasis of some of the psalms. However, such an investigation was not part of the undertaking in this study. I then went on to exegete six psalms as individual independent units, attempting to understand the context of the psalmist's suffering and the meaning of the response to that suffering. The genre, those elements a reader sees as common to certain texts,[2] was defined broadly as prayer (Pss 1–150) and then more specifically as six psalms where the psalmist responds to some form of perceived suffering. Another defining feature of these psalms was that, except for Ps 119, they all used language of enmity in their response to the adversity.[3] Furthermore, none of the psalms was classified as a pure lament or complaint of the individual.

I then moved on to a limited historical survey to determine how these salient elements of suffering and the meaning of the response (language of enmity) had been interpreted. The historical survey added to the exegesis,

---

1. This is not the only perspective the editors wished to draw attention to.
2. So Nasuti, *Defining the Sacred Song*, 52.
3. Although Ps 119 was investigated for its unique response to adversity, it still contained one imprecation of shame.

as in the case of Augustine's insight into the enemies in Ps 129 and Calvin's understanding of the nature of evil from Ps 139. Another example of added insight was the notion of judgment contained in the Torah in Ps 119. An example of how the survey acted as a correction was seen in the confirmation of the enemies as being both external and internal to the kingdom in Ps 129.

It was hoped that by investigating psalms beyond the category of the lament of the individual (so all the psalms in this study) and by including responses to adversity that did not contain images of enmity (so Ps 119) that a better understanding could be determined as to what was occurring behind the use of these images. The images of enmity themselves varied: Ps 110 violent warfare, (Ps 119 meditating on Torah), Ps 129 agricultural imprecations, Ps 137 war atrocities, Ps 139 killing, Ps 149 violent warfare. By comparison of the psalms the following conclusions were made. All the psalms had as their basis the understanding that the enemies' hostility was actually directed towards Yahweh or what Yahweh stood for. Further, the complete removal or annihilation of evil was hoped for in these psalms. This was often formulated in the context of Yahweh's presence (Ps 119, 129, 139). Controversial but consistent despite any pre-conceived expectations of the writer, all the psalms in this study had New Testament inter-textual connections which suggested that the images of enmity are images of judgment and that there was an eschatological element to this judgment.

It was noted in the exegesis and exemplified in the jussive form of the imprecations that the agency of judgment occurred through prayer and was dependent upon Yahweh.[4] Further, the epitome of this judgment could be seen in Yahweh acting through his "lord" in Ps 110. In short, prayer suggests that one is praying these judgments into actualization, whereas prophetic judgment oracles merely state that judgement will occur (see Luc's proposal).[5] From here I moved on to examining the language of enmity as normative prayer. In this capacity, I noted that there were some shortcomings in limiting the function of the prayers to victim responses, as helpful as such an approach is. I suggested that the unchanging nature of evil was an important emphasis behind the language of enmity and that the use of such language merely reflected back to Yahweh what was true about the character and actions of the wicked.

It was also noted that the language of these psalms reflected a sacred use of language distinct from its ordinary use. The closest rhetorical device to explain the language of enmity, I suggested, is synecdoche. In synecdoche

---

4. My argument in the Introduction for prayer as the basis of genre implies that all the psalms can be offered as prayer.

5. Luc, "Interpreting the Curses."

the parts stand for the whole or, in the case of the psalms, the images of enmity are a whole which stand for the parts. The evil relayed in the dashing of little ones against the rocks covers all forms of evil which are expressed in violent atrocities. What I am proposing goes beyond understanding the psalms as documents which reflect the emotional experiences of human life. The Israelites may have been more able than moderns to understand evil and its capacity for destruction. The language they prayed was not a reflection of their immoral pre-Christian beliefs. Rather the language reflects an accurate understanding of evil. They understood that justice meant the removal of evil, and they prayed for it.

I then proceeded towards developing a theology of God's just dealing with people and in particular his people. In this regard, I built on N.T. Wright's observation about prayer and the psalms, and I utilized Kraus's methodology which insists that the individual psalms themselves should pose the questions for any investigation into unjust suffering. The nexus between God, enemy, and psalmist(s) then becomes the vehicle for the modern pray-er who enters into this world to understand what can be known about moral evil and how God engages with moral evil to overcome it. Besides the individual findings of each psalm which contributed to a better understanding of these questions, two salient features are worth repeating. First, a theology of God's just dealing should be able to incorporate the questions posed in Ps 129 and 137 about the sinfulness of God's people as well as the agency of the wicked as part of God's plan to rectify injustice. Second, the absolute absence of God's presence is not the defining characteristic of suffering in the face of moral evil, but, as Ps 139 makes clear, the absence of God's engagement is. In short, the genre of prayer as the method of investigation in this study is also the central answer to the question, "How does God engage and overcome moral evil through the agency of his Church?"

Implications of this Study

It is hoped that the above study of the language of enmity in Psalms 110, 119, 129, 137, 139 and 149 as canonical prayer contributes to the understanding of the nature of moral evil and its eradication. In this respect, I have not focused on the poetry of the psalms outside of the rhetoric of synecdoche. Zenger and Brueggemann have written extensively of the poetry in these types of psalms and the therapeutic effect it has on the pray-er. I have tried to get at the spiritual realities behind the text and have found synecdoche the most helpful rhetorical device for this.

Miller in his OT survey on prayer makes the following comment:

The mode of overcoming, God's self-giving and suffering love in Jesus Christ, means that the curse prayers do not finally teach us how to pray or stand as models of prayer for us. They may give expression to the thoughts and words and feelings that we cannot let go except as they are let go to God in prayer.[6]

Behind these sentiments Miller is alluding to Rom 12:14 and Mt 5:44. In contrast, the exegesis and historical survey of Ps 110 suggests that the cross of Christ teaches that without the love of God and his restraining grace in general, I would be an aggressive and recalcitrant foe on the battlefield arrayed with the other enemies despising the "lord" and what he stands for. The cross is how the "lord" has made known his universal mandate to rule and the means by which punishment on the repentant enemies is averted. The cross is also a testimony to the desire of all enemies to destroy the "lord" and prevent his rule.

Central to the perspective of this study is that God's judgment on moral evil occurs through the agency of God's people praying. God responds to the prayers of his people both explicitly and implicitly. The former falls under the hidden wonders of God's working but the latter is a result of Yahweh's relation to his people and all he has created. When Yahweh's people seek after him, he is found and his engaging presence precludes evil. Yahweh's judgment on evil either leads to salvation or to the annihilation (complete removal) of evil. There is no middle ground.

Nevertheless, Jesus showed that believers are not to be engaged in any violent establishing of the Kingdom of God. Even so, God reserves the right to meet evil in its own arena and on its own terms. The outcome hoped for in these psalms goes beyond the principles of *lex talionis*. It is the absolute removal of evil that is at stake. However, the annihilation of evil does not necessarily mean the annihilation of people, as can be seen from Ps 137. Here judgment leads to the permanent incapacity of moral evil. The language of evil accurately represents the deeds of the enemies and God's obligation at the level of the individual (Ps 139), the nation (Pss 137 and 149) and all humankind (Pss 110 and 149). God, so to speak, in the issuing of justice gives the reprobate what they will for themselves.

The conclusion of this study is that the psalms with language of enmity are an important resource to be used as prayer in the church and in my opinion should remain unaltered, because the issue of praying for God's justice in the form of judgment is risky business. The language is not an end in itself because, as the exegesis has shown, beneath the harshness of the language exist deeper spiritual realities of a desire for justice. The language

---

6. Miller, *They Cried to the Lord*, 9.5.

itself reflects the "grammar" of evil. Blood and violence, battlefields full of corpses, and the killing of the innocent young are all part of this grammar. The deeper spiritual language embedded in these psalms suggests that the language of enmity can be understood as representing all forms of similar evil. In this regard, the rhetorical feature of synecdoche is fitting. Enemies of the "lord" have expressed themselves in the grammar of evil from the earliest times.

The feelings I bring to the issue of responding to injustice are tainted with my own understanding and how I have been conditioned to understand moral evil on a personal and larger scale. The language of enmity in these psalms as normative scripture acts to counter this bias. The psalms with language of enmity take the personal or public sentiments of rage, anger, and fear and filter these feelings and dispositions through these prayers. The modern pray-er enters into the psalmist's world and God's world and what is skewed in one's perception of wrongs committed, or perhaps is unbalanced by unrequited desire for vengeance, is filtered through these prayers and the just worldview they represent. The unhealthy and unjust sentiments are mitigated. The reason is that within the text lies the reality of God's revealed justice. This is not to say that justice is impersonal; the very nature of the psalms as poetic prayers shows that it is very personal. But beyond this personal and therapeutic aspect are spiritual realities behind these psalms expressed in the language of enmity, that God restrains himself according to what reflects his righteous character as he has revealed himself in his word (Ps 119). When we pray these psalms we need not fear the consequences for those who use them wrongly.[7] Those who pray for selfish gain or for unrequited revenge will not be praying at all. Or they and their prayers will be transformed into genuine expressions of seeking justice. The result will be all the benefits of such a therapeutic experience.

As the theological discussion of Ps 139 made clear, the question of theodicy in relation to moral evil is not really one of God's absolute absence, but rather of his engagement with moral evil and so also the Church's. Brueggemann was right when he said that the church would lose its voice for justice if it removed lament from its worship. Evil is real and speaking of evil even in a religious context benefits those who use this language because it allows the community to maintain solidarity with individuals and communities which are experiencing this evil. Without doing so, the

---

7. I came across an article (a google search will bring up specific examples of this type of wrong-headed-practice) which mentioned a pastor who was using the imprecatory psalms to pray for the death of the President. Not only in modern times, but Calvin in his commentary on Ps 109 mentions a monk who was hired by a wealthy lady to pray against her son.

Church loses sight of what evil really is. Consequently, the Church fails to participate in the issuing forth of God's justice and so the establishment of the Kingdom of God. Perhaps Ps 110 will stand as the vanguard psalm for the Church's response to injustice. It was used by the early Church to address the pressing need to define who Christ was and maybe it will occupy a defining place in the issue of establishing the "lord's" justice through prayer.

The final question remains as to how to appropriate these psalms. All I can do is offer one possible way in which they may be appropriated in public worship. The leader can begin with a short introduction to place the psalm in context and note the most troublesome parts of the language of enmity, which may also include a brief explanatory statement about synecdoche. After this the leader might proceed, "Dear heavenly father who knows the thoughts, words and deeds of all people. In keeping with the exhortations in your holy word, 'Love your enemies and pray for those who persecute you' and 'Bless those who persecute you; bless and do not curse for it is written, "it is mine to avenge and I will repay,"'[8] we pray the following prayer asking for your justice to issue itself through the relational righteousness of the Lord Jesus Christ, that there would be genuine healing for the victim, repentance of the perpetrator, the appropriate punishment,[9] restoration and healing. However, for those who are recalcitrant, may your issue of justice give them what they deserve, even what they truly will. We commit the following circumstances..." (situations of injustice can be mentioned). Following this the appropriate psalm is recited as communal prayer.

In short, formulating prayers with my own language of enmity is risky because instead of asking for God's will to be done, I may be asking for my will. Instead of God's kingdom to come, I may be asking for my kingdom. Instead of asking for strength to forgive others, I may be harbouring unforgiveness. Instead of entreating to be led not into temptation, I may be leading myself into such. Instead of being delivered from evil, I may be perpetrating evil. It may be that I am looking for my kingdom and glory rather than God's. Hidden in these psalms which call for the created moral order to be restored to its proper state is the mystery of grace.

---

8. Once again according to Augustine's definition of justice, praying the language of enmity might be a blessing to the perpetrator.

9. See footnote in Calvin's understanding of Ps 110. I have not tried to explain how God uses the state to punish moral evil. Such would go beyond the scope of this paper. But its inclusion in this prayer recognizes that God does use different agents in carrying out justice.

Bibliography

Aejmeleus, Anneli. *The Traditional Prayer in the Psalms*. Berlin:Walter de Gruyter, 1896.
Ahn, John. "Psalm 137: Complex Communal Laments." *JBL* 127 no 2 (2008) 267–89.
Ackroyd, Peter, R. *Exile and Restoration*. Philadelphia: Westminster, 1968.
Aland, Kurt, et al., eds. *The Greek New Testament*. 3rd corrected edition. Stuttgart: United Bible Societies, 1983.
Allen, Leslie, C. *Word Biblical Themes: Psalms*. Waco: Word Books, 1987.
———. *Psalms 101–150*. Rev. ed. WBC 21. Nashville: Thomas Nelson, 2002.
Allison, Dale C. "Rejecting Violent Judgment: Luke 9:52–56 and Its Relatives." *JBL* 121 no. 3 (2002) 459–78.
Alter, Robert. *The Art of Biblical Poetry*. New York: Basic, 1985.
Ambrose. "Letter 40: To Theodosius as to the Burning of a Jewish Synagogue." Pages 440—45 in vol. 10 of *The Nicene and Post-Nicene Fathers* of the Christian Church, Series 2. Edited by Philip Schaff and Henry Wace. 1886–1889. 14 vols. Repr. Grand Rapids, MI: Eerdmans, 1989.
———. "Letter 82." In *Psalms 51–150*. Edited by Quentin F. Wesselschmidt. OT vol. 8 of *Ancient Commentary on Scripture*. Edited by Thomas C. Oden. Downers Grove, IL: InterVarsity, 2007.
———. "Two Books Concerning Repentance." Pages 327–359 in vol. 10 of *The Nicene and Post-Nicene Fathers* of the Christian Church, Series 2. Edited by Philip Schaff and Henry Wace. 1886–1889. 14 vols. Repr. Grand Rapids, MI: Eerdmans, 1989.
Amir, Y. "Psalm 119 als Zeugnis eiines protorabbinischen Judentums." Pages 134 in *Studien zum Antiken Judentum* Edited by Y. Amir. BEATAJ, 2. Frankfurt and New York: Peter Lang, 1985.
Anderson, Albert A. *Psalms 73–150*. Vol. 2 of *The Book of Psalms*. Grand Rapids: Eerdmans, 1972.
Arndt, William F., and F. Wilbur Gingrich, trans and eds. *A Greek-English Lexicon of the New Testament and Other Early Christian Literature*. 2d edition revised and augmented by F. Wilbur Gingrich and Fredrick W. Danker from Walter Bauer's 5th edition, 1958. Chicago: University of Chicago Press, 1978.
Athanasius. "Discourse against the Arians." Edited by Quentin F. Wesselschmidt. OT vol. 8 of *Ancient Commentary on Scripture*. Edited by Thomas C. Oden. Downers Grove, IL: InterVarsity, 2007.
———. "Sermon 250.2." In *Psalms 51–150*. Edited by Quentin F. Wesselschmidt. OT vol. 8 of *Ancient Commentary on Scripture*. Edited by Thomas C. Oden. Downers Grove, IL: InterVarsity, 2007.

Auffret, Pierre. "Note sur la Structure Litteraire du Psaume 110." *Semeia* 32 (1982) 83–88.

Augustine. *The City of God against the Pagans*. New York: Penguin, 1972.

———. "Confessions: Chapter XIV, Of the Depth of the Sacred Scripture, and Its Enemies." Pages 176–89 in vol. 1 of *The Nicene and Post-Nicene Fathers*, Series 1. Edited by Philip Schaff. 1886–1889. 14 vols. Repr. Grand Rapids, MI: Eerdmans, 1988.

———. "Explanations of the Psalms 129.2." In *Psalms 51–150*. Edited by Quentin F. Wesselschmidt. OT vol. 8 of *Ancient Commentary on Scripture*. Edited by Thomas C. Oden. Downers Grove, IL: InterVarsity, 2007.

———. "Explanations of the Psalms 129.5." In *Psalms 51–150*. Edited by Quentin F. Wesselschmidt. OT vol. 8 of *Ancient Commentary on Scripture*. Edited by Thomas C. Oden. Downers Grove, IL: InterVarsity, 2007.

———. *Expositions of the Psalms 99–120*. Vol. 5 of *Expositions of the Psalms*. Translated from the Latin by Maria Boulding. The Works of Saint Augustine for the 21st Century, III/19. Hyde Park, NY: New City, 2003.

———. *Expositions of the Psalms 121–150*. Vol. 6 of *Expositions of the Psalms*. Vol 6. 121–150. Translated from the Latin by Maria Boulding. The Works of Saint Augustine for the 21st Century, III/20. Hyde Park, NY: New City, 2004.

———. "The Letters of St Agustine: To Proba." Pages 469–70 in vol. 1 of *The Nicene and Post-Nicene Fathers*, Series 1. Edited by Philip Schaff. 1886–1889. 14 vols. Repr. Grand Rapids, MI: Eerdmans, 1988.

———. "On the Trinity 2.5.7." In *Psalms 51–150*. Edited by Quentin F. Wesselschmidt. OT vol. 8 of *Ancient Commentary on Scripture*. Edited by Thomas C. Oden. Downers Grove, IL: InterVarsity, 2007.

———. "Our Lord's Sermon on the Mount According to Matthew." Pages 3–63 in vol. 6 of *The Nicene and Post-Nicene Fathers*, Series 1. Edited by Philip Schaff. 1886–1889. 14 vols. Repr. Grand Rapids, MI: Eerdmans, 1979.

———. "Sermon 322." In *Psalms 51–150*. Edited by Quentin F. Wesselschmidt. OT vol. 8 of *Ancient Commentary on Scripture*. Edited by Thomas C. Oden. Downers Grove, IL: InterVarsity, 2007.

———. "A Treatise on the Merits and the Forgiveness of Sins, and the Baptism of Infants. Pages 44–68 in vol. 5 of *The Nicene and Post-Nicene Fathers*, Series 1. Edited by Philip Schaff. 1886–1889. 14 vols. Repr. Grand Rapids, MI: Eerdmans, 1987.

BAGD. A Greek-English Lexicon of the New Testament and Other Early Christian Literature. (See Arndt & Gingrich, 1978).

Barré, Llyod. M. "Halëlû yäh: a broken inclusion." *CBQ* 45 (1983) 195–200.

Barth, Karl. 1995. The theology of John Calvin. Translated from the German by Geoffrey Bromiley. Grand Rapids, MI: Eerdmans, 1995.

Basil. "Homilies on the Hexaemeron 9.6." In *Psalms 51–150*. Edited by Quentin F. Wesselschmidt. OT vol. 8 of *Ancient Commentary on Scripture*. Edited by Thomas C. Oden. Downers Grove, IL: InterVarsity, 2007.

———. "Homilies on the Psalms 17.8." In *Psalms 51–150*. Edited by Quentin F. Wesselschmidt. OT vol. 8 of *Ancient Commentary on Scripture*. Edited by Thomas C. Oden. Downers Grove, IL: InterVarsity, 2007.

———. "On the Spirit." In *Psalms 51–150*. Edited by Quentin F. Wesselschmidt. OT vol. 8 of *Ancient Commentary on Scripture*. Edited by Thomas C. Oden. Downers Grove, IL: InterVarsity, 2007.
BDB. *The New Brown-Driver-Briggs-Gesenius Hebrew and English Lexicon* Hebrew-English Lexicon. (See Brown et al., 1979).
Beale, Gregory K. *The Book of Revelation: A Commentary on the Greek Text*. NIBTC. Grand Rapids, MI: Eerdmans, 1999.
Beale, Gregory K. and Sean M. McDonough. "Revelation." Pages 1081–1161 in *Commentary on the New Testament Use of the Old Testament*. Edited by Gregory K. Beale and Donald A. Carson. Grand Rapids: Baker Academic, 2007.
Bede. "Homilies on the Gospels 2.5." In *Psalms 51–150*. Edited by Quentin F. Wesselschmidt. OT vol. 8 of *Ancient Commentary on Scripture*. Edited by Thomas C. Oden. Downers Grove, IL: InterVarsity, 2007.
Beyerlin, Walter. *Die Rettung der Bedrängten in den Feindpsalmen der Einzelnen auf institutionelle Zusammenhänge untersucht*. Göttingen: Vanderhoeck und Ruprecht, 1970.
BHS. *Biblia Hebraica Stuttgartensia*. Stuttgart: Deutsche Bibelgesellschaft Stuttgart, 1967/77.
Blomberg, Craig L. "Matthew." Pages 1–109 in *Commentary on the New Testament Use of the Old Testament*. Edited by Gregory K. Beale and Donald A. Carson. Grand Rapids: Baker Academic, 2007.
Blount, Brian K. *Revelation: A Commentary*. The New Testament Library. Louisville: Westminster John Knox, 2009.
Booij, Th. "Psalm CX: Rule in the Midst of your Foes." *Vetus Testamentum* XLI, no. 4 (1991) 396–407.
———. "Psalm CXXXIX: Text, Syntax, Meaning. *Vetus Testamentum* LV (2005) 1–19.
Book of Common Prayer. Available online at http://www.bcponline.org/ p. 795.
Book of Common Prayer (Canada, 1962).
Bosma, Carl J. "Discerning the Voices in the Psalms: A Discussion of Two Problems in Psalmic Interpretation: Part 2. *Calvin Theological Journal* 44 (2009)127–170.
Botha, Phil J. "Interpreting 'Torah' in Psalm 1 in light of Psalm 119." *HTS Teologiese Studies/Theological Studies* 68, no. 1 (2012) Art. #1274, 7 pages. Available at http://dx.doi.org/10.4102/hts.v68i1.1274. s.l.:s.n.
———."A Social-Scientific Reading of Psalm 129." *Hervormde Teologiese Studies* 58, no. 4 (2002) 1401–1414.
Braulik, G. P. "Psalms and Liturgy: Their Reception and Contextualisation. Translated from the German by Friedl, H. *Verbum et Ecclesia* Jrg 24, no. 2 (2003) 309–332.
Brennan, Joseph P. "Psalms 1–8: Some Hidden Harmonies." *Biblical Theology Bulletin* 10, no. 1 (1980) 25–29.
Brenton, Lancelot C. *The Septuagint with Apocrapha: Greek and English*. Repr. Peabody, MA: Hendrickson, 1990.
Bright, John. *A History of Israel*. 3d edition. Old Testament Library. Michigan: Westminster, 1981.
Briggs, Charles A. and Emilie G. Briggs. *A Critical and Exegetical Commentary on the Book of Psalms*. New York: Charles Scribner's Sons, 1906.
Brongers, H. A. 1963. Die Rache und Fluchpsalmen im Alten Testament. Pages 21–42 in vol. 13 of Outestamentische Studien. Edited by P. A. H. de Boer. Leiden: Brill, 1963.

Brown, Francis, S. R. Driver, and Charles A. Briggs. *The New Brown-Driver-Briggs-Gesenius Hebrew and English Lexicon* (BDB). Peabody, MA: Hendrickson, 1979.

Brown, William P. "Creatio Corporis and the Rhetoric of Defense in Job 10 and Psalm 139." Pages 107–124 in *God Who Creates*. Edited by W. P Brown and S. D. McBride Jr. Grand Rapids, MI: Eerdmans, 2000.

———. *Seeing the Psalms: A Theology of Metaphor*. Louisville: Westminster John Knox, 2002.

Brueggemann, Walter. *The Message of the Psalms: A Theological Commentary*. Minneapolis: Augsburg, 1984.

———. *Praying the Psalms: Engaging Scripture and the Life of the Spirit*. 2d ed. Eugene, Oregon: Cascade, 2007.

———. "Psalms and the Life of Faith: A Suggested Typology of Function. Pages 3–32 in *The Psalms and the Life of Faith*. Edited by Patrick D. Miller. Minneapolis: Fortress, 2005.

———. "The Psalms and the Life of Faith: A Suggested Typology of Function." Pages 1–25 in *Soundings in the Theology of the Psalms: Perspectives and Methods in Contemporary Scholarship*. Edited by R. A. Jacobson. Minneapolis: Fortress, 2011.

———. *The Psalms as Prayer*. Pages 33–66 in *The Psalms and the Life of Faith*. Edited by Patrick D. Miller. Minneapolis: Fortress, 2005.

———. *Theology of the Old Testament: Testimony, Dispute, Advocacy*. Minneapolis: Fortress, 1997.

Burnett, Joel S. "A Plea for David and Zion: The Elohistic Psalter as Psalm Collection for the Temple's Restoration." Pages 95–113 in Diachronic and Synchronic Reading the Psalms in Real Time: Proceedings of the Baylor Symposium on the Book of Psalms. Edited by J. S. Brunett and W. H. Bellinger Jr. And D. Tucker,Jr. New York: T & T Clark, 2007.

Calvin, John. *Commentary on the Book of Psalms: Psalms 93–150*. Repr. Grand Rapids: Baker, 1989.

———. "Commentary on the Book of Psalms: Vol. 4 (93–118)." In vol. 6 in *Calvin's Commentaries*. Translated from the Latin by James Anderson. Repr. Grand Rapids, MI: Baker, 2003.

———. "Commentary on the Book of Psalms: Vol. 5 (119–150)." In vol. 6 of *Calvin's Commentary on the Book of Psalms*. Translated from the Latin by James Anderson. Repr. Grand Rapids, MI: Baker, 2003.

Cassiodorus. *Cassiodorus: Explanation of the Psalms*. Translated by P. G. Walsh. Ancient Christian Writers, 53. New York: Paulist, 1991.

———. "Expositions of the Psalms 128.2." In *Psalms 51–150*. Edited by Quentin F. Wesselschmidt. OT vol. 8 of *Ancient Commentary on Scripture*. Edited by Thomas C. Oden. Downers Grove, IL: InterVarsity, 2007.

———. "Expositions of the Psalms 128.6." In *Psalms 51–150*. Edited by Quentin F. Wesselschmidt. OT vol. 8 of *Ancient Commentary on Scripture*. Edited by Thomas C. Oden. Downers Grove, IL: InterVarsity, 2007.

Charette, Blaine. *The Theme of Recompense in Matthew's Gospel*. JSNTSup, 79. Sheffield: Sheffield Academic, 1992.

Childs, Brevard S. *Introduction to the Old Testament as Scripture*. Philadelphia: Fortress, 1979.

———. *Memory and Tradition in Israel*. London: SCM, 1962.

Clement of Rome. "1 Clement 28." In *Psalms 51–150*. Edited by Quentin F. Wesselschmidt. OT vol. 8 of *Ancient Commentary on Scripture*. Edited by Thomas C. Oden. Downers Grove, IL: InterVarsity, 2007.

———. "The First Epistle of Clement to the Corinthians." Pages 5–21 in vol. 1 of *The Ante-Nicene Fathers*. Edited by Alexander Roberts and James Donaldson. 1867–1873. American revised edition by A. Cleveland Coxe. 1895–1896. 10 vols. Repr. Grand Rapids, MI: Eerdmans, 1989.

Collins, John J. "The Eschatology of Zechariah." Pages 74–84 in *Knowing the End from the Beginning: the Prophetic, the Aapocalyptic and their Relationships*. Edited by L. L. Grabbe and R. D. Haak. London: T&T Clark, 2003.

Constitutions of the Holy Apostles. "Book VI." Pages 450–464 in vol. 7 of *The Ante-Nicene Fathers*. Edited by Alexander Roberts and James Donaldson. 1867–1873. American revised edition by A. Cleveland Coxe. 1895–1896. 10 vols. Repr. Grand Rapids, MI: Eerdmans, 1989.

Creach, Jerome F. D. *The Destiny of the Righteous in the Psalms*. St. Louis: Chalice, 2008.

Crenshaw, James L. "Introduction: The Shift from Theodicy to Anthropodicy." Pages 1–16 in *Theodicy in the Old Testament. Issues in Religion and Theology*. Edited by J. L. Crenshaw. Philadelphia: Fortress, 1983.

Croft, Steven J. L. *The Identity of the Individual in the Psalms*. JSOTSup, 44. Sheffield: JSOT Press, 1987.

Cyprian. "The Lapsed 27." In *Psalms 51–150*. Edited by Quentin F. Wesselschmidt. OT vol. 8 of *Ancient Commentary on Scripture*. Edited by Thomas C. Oden. Downers Grove, IL: InterVarsity, 2007.

———. "The Treatises of Cyprian." Pages 421–562 in vol. 5 of *The Ante-Nicene Fathers*. Edited by Alexander Roberts and James Donaldson. 1867–1873. American revised edition by A. Cleveland Coxe. 1895–1896. 10 vols. Repr. Grand Rapids, MI: Eerdmans, 1990.

Cyril of Jerusalem. "The Catechetical Lectures of Cyril: On the Words, and in One Holy Catholic Church, and in the Resurrection of the Flesh, and the Life Everlasting." Pages 134–143 in vol. 7 of *The Nicene and Post-Nicene Fathers*, Series 2. Edited by Philip Schaff and Henry Wace. 1886–1889. 14 vols. Repr. Grand Rapids, MI: Eerdmans, 1989.

Daglish, E. R. "The Use of the Book of Psalms in the New Testament." *Southwestern Journal of Theology* 27 (1984) 25–39.

Dahood, Mitchell S. *Psalms III: 101–150*. Garden City, NY: Doubleday & Company, 1970.

Davids, Peter H. *The Epistle of James: A Commentary on the Greek Text*. NIGTC. Grand Rapids, MI: Eerdmans, 1982.

De Claissé-Walford, Nancy L. "The Theology of Imprecatory Psalms." Pages 77–92 in *Soundings in the Theology of the Psalms: Perspectives and Methods in Contemporary Scholarship*. Edited by R. A. Jacobson. Minneapolis: Fortress, 2011.

Deissler, Alfons. *Psalm 119 (118) und seine Theologie: Eine Beitrag zur Erforschung der anthologischen Stilgattung im Alten Tetamentum*. Munich: Zink, 1955.

Delitzsch, Franz J. *Psalms*. 3 vols. Grand Rapids: Eerdmans, 1975.

———. *Psalms: Vol III*. Repr. Grand Rapids: Eerdmans, 1975.

De Wit, Willem J. "Your Little Ones against the Rock!: Modern and Ancient Interpretations of Psalm 137:9." Pages 296–307 in *Christian Faith and Violence 2*. Edited by D. Van Keulen. Zoetermeer: Meinema, 2005.

Docherty, Susan E. "The Use of the Old Testament in Hebrews: A Case Study in early Jewish Biblical Interpretation. WUNT, 2. Reihe, 260. Tübingen: Mohr Siebeck, 2009.

Driver, Godfrey R. "Studies in the Vocabulary of the Old Testament. 1." *Journal of Theological Studies* 31 (1930) 275–284.

Eaton, John H. *Kingship and the Psalms*. Naperville, IL: Allenson, 1975.

———. "Proposals in Psalms XCIX and CXIX." *Vetus Testamentum* 18, no. 4 (1968) 555–558.

———. *The Psalms: A Historical and Spiritual Commentary with an Introduction and New Translation*. London: Continuum, 2005.

——— *Psalms of the Way and the Kingdom: A Conference with the Commentators*. Sheffield: Sheffield Academic, 1995.

Erbele-Küster, Dorothea. *Lesen als Akt des Betens: Eine Reyeptionsästhetik der Psalmen*. WMANT, 87. Neukirchen-Vlluyn: Neukirchener, 2001.

Fiedrowicz, Michael. "General Introduction." Pages 13–66 in vol. 1 of *Augustine's Expositions of the Psalms*. Translated from the Latin by Maria Boulding. Hyde Park, NY: New City, 2000.

Firth, David G. *Surrendering Retribution in the Psalms: Responses to Violence in the Individual Complaints*. Nottingham: Paternoster, 2005.

Firth, David and P. S. Johnston, eds. *Interpreing the Psalms: Issues and Approaches*. Downers Grove, IL: Inter-Varsity, 2005.

Fishman, Joshua A. "A Decalogue of Basic Theoretical Perspectives for a Sociology of Language and Religion." Pages 14–25 in *Explorations in the Sociology of Language and Religion: Discourse Approaches to Politics, Society and Culture*. Edited by T. Omoniye and J. A. Fishman. Philadelphia: John Benjamins, 2006.

Fitzmyer, Joseph A. *The Aramaic Inscriptions of Sefire*. Biblica et Orientalia, 19. Rome: Pontifical Biblical Institute, 1967.

Flint, Peter. "The Book of Psalms in the Light of the Dead Sea Scrolls." *Vetus Testamentum* XLVIII (1998) 453–472.

Freedman, David N. "The Structure of Psalm 137." Pages 187–205 in *Near Eastern Studies in Honour of William Foxwell Albright*. Edited by H. Goedicke. Baltimore: John Hopkins Press, 1971.

Gerstenberger, Erhard S. *Der bittende Mensch: Bittritual und Klagelied des Einzelnen im Alten Testament*. WMANT, 51. Neukirchen-Vlluyn: Neukirchener, 1980.

———. *Psalms Part 1 with an Introduction to Cultic Poetry*. FOTL, 14. Grand Rapids: Eerdmans, 1988.

———. *Psalms Part 2 and Lamentations*. FOTL, 15. Grand Rapids: Eerdmans, 2001.

GES. *Gesenius' Hebrew Grammar*. Edited by E. Kautzsch. Translated by A. E. Cowley. Bible Works edition. 2005.

Gillingham, Susan E. "The Messiah in the Royal Psalms: A Question of Reception History and the Psalter. Pages 209–237 in *King and Messiah in Israel and the Ancient Near East: Proceedings of the Oxford Old Testament Seminar*. Sheffield: Sheffield Academic, 1998.

———. *Psalms Through the Centuries*. Vol. 1. Blackwell Bible Commentaries. Oxford: Blackwell, 2008.

Gingrich, Felix W. and Frederick W. Danker, eds. *Shorter Lexicon of the Greek New Testament*. 2d ed. Chicago: University of Chicago Press, 1965

GIND. Gingrich, Felix W. and Frederick W. Danker, eds. Shorter Lexicon of the Greek New Testament. 2nd ed. Chicago: University of Chicago Press, 1965.

Goulder, Michael D. "The Psalms of the Return: Book V, Psalms 107–150. JSOTSup, 258. Sheffield: Sheffield Academic, 1988.

Grabbe, Lester L. *Judaism from Cyrus to Hadrian. Volume 1: The Persian and Greek Periods*. Minneapolis: Fortress, 1992.

Grant, Jamie A. *The King as Exemplar: The Function of Deuteronomy's Kingship Law in the Shaping of the Book of Psalms*. Boston: Brill, 2004.

Greek New Testament. (See Aland et al., 1983).

Green, Joel B. *The Gospel of Luke*. NICNT. Grand Rapids, MI: Eerdmans, 1997.

Gregory of Nazianzus. "Select Orations of Saint Gregory of Nazianzen: The Last Farwell in the Presence of the One Hundred and Fifty Bishops." Pages 385–95 in vol. 7 of *The Nicene and Post-Nicene Fathers*, Series 2. Edited by Philip Schaff and Henry Wace. 1886–1889. 14 vols. Repr. Grand Rapids, MI: Eerdmans, 1978.

———. "The Select Orations of Gregory St. Nanzianzen: On the Arrival of the Egyptians." Pages 334–338 in vol. 7 of *The Nicene and Post-Nicene Fathers*, Series 2. Edited by Philip Schaff and Henry Wace. 1886–1889. 14 vols. Repr. Grand Rapids, MI: Eerdmans, 1978.

———. "Select Orations of Saint Gregory of Nazianzen: Oration 30." Pages 185–435 in vol. 7 of *The Nicene and Post-Nicene Fathers*, Series 2. Edited by Philip Schaff and Henry Wace. 1886–1889. 14 vols. Repr. Grand Rapids, MI: Eerdmans, 1978.

Gregory of Nyssa. "Dogmatic Treatises." Pages 33–247 in vol. 5 of *The Nicene and Post-Nicene Fathers*, Series 2. Edited by Philip Schaff and Henry Wace. 1886–1889. 14 vols. Repr. Grand Rapids, MI: Eerdmans, 1988.

Grisanti, Michael A. "Old Testament Poetry as a Vehicle for Historiography." *Bibliotheca Sacra* 161, Apr-Jun (2004) 163–178.

Grosse, B. "Le Psaume cxlix et la Reinterpretation Post-exilique de la Tradition Prophétique." *Vetus Testamentum* 54 (1994) 259–63.

Gunkel, Hermann. *Die Psalmen*. Göttingen: Dandenhoeck & Ruprecht, 1926.

———. "Psalm 149." Pages 47–57 in *Oriental Studies Published in Commemoration of the Fortieth Anniversary (1883–1923) of Paul Haupt as Director of the Oriental Seminary of the Johns Hopkins University Press*. Edited by C. Adler and A. Ember. Baltimore: Johns Hopkins University Press, 1926.

———. "Psalm 149: an Interpretation." *The Biblical World* 22, no. 5 (1903) 363–366.

Gunkel, Hermann and Joachim Begrich. *Introduction to Psalms: The Genres of the Religious Lyric of Israel*. Translated from the German by James D. Nogalski. Repr. Macon, GA: Mercer University Press, 1998.

Guthrie, George H. "Hebrews." Pages 919–995 in *Commentary on the New Testament Use of the Old Testament*. Edited by Gregory K. Beale and Donald K. Carson. Grand Rapids: Baker Academic, 2007.

HALOT. *The Hebrew and Aramaic Lexicon of the Old Testament*. Vol 1. 2001a. (See Koehler & Baumgartner, 2001).

HALOT. *The Hebrew and Aramaic Lexicon of the Old Testament*. Vol 2. 2001b. (See Koehler & Baumgartner, 2001).

Hayes, John H. "The Use of Oracles Against Foreign Nations in Ancient Israel. *JBL* 87, no. 1 (1968) 81–92.

Heine, Ronald E. *Reading the Old Testament with the Ancient Christian Church: Exploring the Formation of Early Christian Thought*. Evangelical Ressourcement:

Ancient Sources for the Church's Future. Grand Rapids, MI: Baker Academic, 2007.

Herrmann, Siegfried. *A History of Israel in Old Testament Times*. 2d ed. Philadelphia: Fortress, 1981.

Hidal, Sten. "Exegesis of the Old Testament in the Antiochene School with its Prevalent Literal and Historical Method." Pages 543–568 in *Hebrew Bible Old Testament: The History of its Interpretation. Volume 1, From the Beginnings to the Middle Ages (until 1300); Part 1, Antiquity*. Edited by M. Saebø, C. Brekelmans, and M. Haran. Göttingen: Vandenhoeck & Ruprecht, 1996.

Hilary of Poitiers. "Homily on Psalm 118." In *Psalms 51–150*. Edited by Quentin F. Wesselschmidt. OT vol. 8 of *Ancient Commentary on Scripture*. Edited by Thomas C. Oden. Downers Grove, IL: InterVarsity, 2007.

Hilber, John W. *Cultic Prophecy in the Psalms*. BZAW. Berlin: Walter de Gruyter, 2005.

———. "Psalm CX in Light of Assyrian Prophecies." *VT* 53, no. 3 (2003) 353–366.

Holladay, William. 2002. Indications of Jeremiah's Psalter. *JBL* 121, no. 2 (2002) 245–261.

Hossfeld, Frank-Lothar, and Erich Zenger. *Psalms 3: A Commentary on Psalms 101–150*. Minneapolis: Fortress, 2011.

Howard, David M. Jr. The Psalms and Current Study. Pages 23–40 in *Interpreting the Psalms: Issues and Approaches*. Edited by David Firth and P. S. Johnston. Downers Grove, IL: Inter-Varsity, 2005.

IBHS. *An Introduction to Biblical Hebrew Syntax*. (See Waltke & O'Connor, 1990).

Ignatius. "The Epistle of Ignatius to the Ephesians: Shorter and Longer Versions." Pages 49–58 in vol. 1 of *The Ante-Nicene Fathers*. Edited by Alexander Roberts and James Donaldson. 1867–1873. American revised edition by A. Cleveland Coxe. 1895–1896. 10 vols. Repr. Grand Rapids, MI: Eerdmans, 1989.

Jerome. *The Homilies of St Jerome: Vol 1: 1–59 on the Psalms*. Translated from the Latin by Marie Liguori. FC, 48. Washington, D.C.: The Catholic University of America Press, 1964.

———. "Letter 53.4." In *Psalms 51–150*. Edited by Quentin F. Wesselschmidt. OT vol. 8 of *Ancient Commentary on Scripture*. Edited by Thomas C. Oden. Downers Grove, IL: InterVarsity, 2007.

———. "The Letters of St. Jerome: From Epiphanius, Bishop of Salamis, in Cyprus, to John, Bishop of Jerusalem." Pages 83–89 in vol. 6 of *The Nicene and Post-Nicene Fathers*, Series 2. Edited by Philip Schaff and Henry Wace. 1886–1889. 14 vols. Repr. Grand Rapids, MI: Eerdmans, 1989.

———. "The Letters of St. Jerome: To Eustochium." Pages 22–41 in vol. 6 of *The Nicene and Post-Nicene Fathers*, Series 2. Edited by Philip Schaff and Henry Wace. 1886–1889. 14 vols. Repr. Grand Rapids, MI: Eerdmans, 1989.

———. "Treaties: To Pammachius Against John of Jerusalem." Pages 424–47 in vol. 6 of *The Nicene and Post-Nicene Fathers*, Series 2. Edited by Philip Schaff and Henry Wace. 1886–1889. 14 vols. Repr. Grand Rapids, MI: Eerdmans, 1989.

Jigoulov, Vadim. "Administration of Achaemenid Phoenicia: A Case for Managed Autonomy." Pages 138–151 in *Exile and Restoration Revisited: Essays on the Babylonian and Persian Periods in Memory of Peter Ackroyd*. Edited by G. N. Knoppers and L. L. Grabbe. London: T&T Clark, 2009.

John Chrysostom. "Against the Anomeans 1.24-25." In *Psalms 51–150*. Edited by Quentin F. Wesselschmidt. OT vol. 8 of *Ancient Commentary on Scripture*. Edited by Thomas C. Oden. Downers Grove, IL: InterVarsity, 2007.

———. "The Homilies on the Statues: To the People of Antioch." Pages 331–344 in vol. 9 of *The Nicene and Post-Nicene Fathers*, Series 1. Edited by Philip Schaff. 1886–1889. 14 vols. Repr. Grand Rapids, MI: Eerdmans, 1978.

———. "Homilies on 1 Corinthians: Homily 33." Pages 194–201 in vol. 12 of *The Nicene and Post-Nicene Fathers*, Series 1. Edited by Philip Schaff. 1886–1889. 14 vols. Repr. Grand Rapids, MI: Eerdmans, 1979.

———. "Homilies on the Gospel of John: 15." In *Psalms 51–150*. Edited by Quentin F. Wesselschmidt. OT vol. 8 of *Ancient Commentary on Scripture*. Edited by Thomas C. Oden. Downers Grove, IL: InterVarsity, 2007.

———. *Commentary on the Psalms*. Vol. 2. Translated by R. C. Hill. Brookline, MA: Holy Cross Orthodox, 1988.

———. "The Homilies of St. John Chrysostom on the Epistle to the Hebrews: Hebrews 11:20-22." Pages 481–86 in vol. 14 of *The Nicene and Post-Nicene Fathers*, Series 1. Edited by Philip Schaff. 1886–1889. 14 vols. Repr. Grand Rapids, MI: Eerdmans, 1989.

———. "Homily XIII." Pages 458–464 in vol. 9 of *The Nicene and Post-Nicene Fathers*, Series 1. Edited by Philip Schaff. 1886–1889. 14 vols. Repr. Grand Rapids, MI: Eerdmans, 1978.

Justin Martyr. "The First Apology." Pages 163–187 in vol. 1 of *The Ante-Nicene Fathers*. Edited by Alexander Roberts and James Donaldson. 1867–1873. American revised edition by A. Cleveland Coxe. 1895–1896. 10 vols. Repr. Grand Rapids, MI: Eerdmans, 1989.

Keane, W. "Language and Religion." Pages 431–449 in *A Companion to Linguistic Anthropology*. Edited by A. Duranti. Malden, MA: Blackwell, 2004.

Keele, Othmar. *The Symbolism of the Biblical World: Ancient Near Eastern Iconography and the Book of Psalms*. Winona Lake, ID: Eisenbrauns, 1997.

Kellermann, Ulrich. "Psalm 137." *ZAW* 90 (1978) 43–58.

Kidner, Derek. *Psalms 1–72*. TOTC, 15. Downers Grove, IL: IVP Academic, 1975.

———. *Psalms 73–150*. TOTC, 16. Downers Grove, IL: IVP Academic, 1975.

Kirkpatrick, Alexander F. *The Book of Psalms*. Cambridge: Cambridge University Press, 1921.

Kissane, Edward J. *The Book of Psalms*. Dublin: Browne and Nolan, 1954.

———. "The Interpretation of Psalm 110." *Irish Theological Quarterly* 21 (1954) 103–14.

Koch, Klaus. "Der Psalter und seine Redaktionsgeschichte." In *Neue Wege der Psalmenforschung*. 2d ed. Edited by K. Seybold and E. Zenger. Feiburg: Herder, 1995.

Koehler, Ludwig., Walter Baumgartner, and J. J. Stamm, eds. *Hebrew and Aramaic Lexicon of the Old Testament* (HALOT). Translated and edited under the supervision of M. E. J. Richardson. 2 vols. Leiden: Brill, 2001.

Kratz, Reinhard G. 2009. "The Relation between History and Thought: Reflections on the Subtitle of Peter Ackroyd's *Exile and Restoration*. Pages 138–151 in *Exile and Restoration Revisited: Essays on the Babylonian and Persian Periods in Memory of Peter Ackroyd*. Edited by G. N. Knoppers and L. L. Grabbe. London: T&T Clark, 2009.

Kraus, Hans J. *Psalms 1–59: A Continental Commentary*. Translated from the German by Oswald, H. C. Minneapolis: Augsburg, 1988.

———. *Psalms 60–150: A Commentary*. 5th ed. Translated from the German by Oswald, H. C. Minneapolis: Augsburg. 1989.

———. *Theology of the Psalms*. Minneapolis: Fortress, 1992.

Ladd, George E. *A Theology of the New Testament*. Grand Rapids: Eerdmans, 1993.

LeMon, Joel M. "Saying Amen to Violent Psalms: Patterns of Prayer, Belief, and Action in the Psalter." Pages 93–109 in *Soundings in the Theology of the Psalms: Perspectives and Methods in Contemporary Scholarship*. Edited by Rolf A. Jacobson. Minneapolis: Fortress, 2011.

Levenson, Jon D. "The Sources of Torah: Psalm 119 and the Modes of Revelation in Second Temple Judaism." In *Ancient Israelite Religion*. Edited by Frank M. Cross and Patrick D. Miller. Philadelphia: Fortress, 1987.

Lindström, Fredrick. "Theodicy in the Psalms." Pages 256–303 in *Theodicy in the World of the Bible*. Edited by Antti Laato and Johannes C. de Moor. Leiden, NLD: Brill, 2003.

Liturgy of the Hours Psalter. Available online at http://www.liturgies.net/Prayers/lohpsalter.htm#Psalm 13 Date of access: 11 Nov. 2014.

Louw, Johannes P. and Eugene A. Nida. , E. A., *Greek-English Lexicon of the New Testament Based on Semantic Domains*. 2nd ed. New York: United Bible Societies, 1988.

Luc, Alec. Interpreting the curses in the Psalms. *Journal of the Evangelical Theological Society* 42 no. 3 (1999) 395–410.

Lucas, Shirley. *The Concept of the Messiah in the Scriptures of Judaism and Christianity*. New York: T & T Clark, 2011.

Luther, Martin. "First Lectures on the Psalms II." Pages 414–534 in Vol 2 of Luther's Works. Translated by Herbert J. A. Bouman. Edited by Hilton C. Oswald. St Louis: Concordia, 1956.

———. "Psalm 110." Pages 228–348 in *Selected Psalms II*. Vol 14 of Luther's Works. Translated by H. Richard Klann. Edited by Jaroslav Pelikan. St Louis: Concordia, 1956.

Mason, Eric F. *You Are a Priest Forever: Second Temple Jewish Messianism and the Priestly Christology of the Epistle to Hebrews*. STDJ, 74. Leiden: Brill, 2008.

Mays, James L. "The Question of Context in Psalm Interpretation." Pages 14–20 in *The Shape and Shaping of the Psalter*. Edited by J. Clinton McCann. Sheffield: Sheffield Academic, 1993.

Melugin, Roy F. "Canon and Exegetical Method." In *Canon Theology and Old Testament Interpretation: Essays in Honor of Brevard S. Childs*. Edited by Gene M. Tucker, David L. Petersen and Robert R Wilson. Philadelphia: Fortress, 1988.

Methodius. "The Banquet of the Ten Virgins: Or Concerning Chastity." Pages 305–402 in vol. 6 of *The Ante-Nicene Fathers*. Edited by Alexander Roberts and James Donaldson. 1867–1873. American revised edition by A. Cleveland Coxe. 1895–1896. 10 vols. Repr. Grand Rapids, MI: Eerdmans, 1987.

Miller, Patrick D. "The End of the Psalter: A Response to Erich Zenger." *JSOT* 80 (1998) 103–110.

———. *They Cried to the Lord: the Form and Theology of Biblical Prayer*. 1994. Kindle edn. Available online at http://www.amazon.com.

Mitchell, David C. *The Message of the Psalter: An Eschatological Programme in the Book of Psalms*. JSOTSup, 252. Sheffield: Sheffield Academic, 1997.
Mowinckel, Sigmund. *The Psalms in Israel's Worship*. Vol 1. Translated from the German by D. R. Ap-Thomas. Oxford: Blackwell, 1962.
———. *The Psalms in Israel's Worship*. Vol 2. Translated from the German by D. R. Ap-Thomas. Oxford: Blackwell, 1962.
Moyise, Steve. *Jesus and Scripture: Studying the New Testament Use of the Old Testament*. 2010. Kindle edn. Available online at http://www.amazon.com
———. *The Later New Testament Writings and Scripture: The Old Testament in Acts, Hebrews, the Catholic Epistles and Revelation*. 2012. Kindle edn. Available online at http://www.amazon.com
Nasuti, Harry P. *Defining the Sacred Songs: Genre, Tradition, and the Post-Critical Interpretation of the Psalms*. JSOTSup, 218. Sheffield: Sheffield Academic, 1999.
NIDOTTE. *New International Dictionary of Old Testament Theology and Exegesis*. Vol. 1. Grand Rapids, MI: Zondervan, 1997.
NETS. *A New English Translation of the Septuagint and Other Greek Translations Traditionally Included Under That Title*. Edited by Al Pietersma and Ben G. Wright. New York: Oxford University Press, 2007.
Ogden, Graham S. "Prophetic Oracles against Foreign Nations and Psalms of Communal Lament: The Relationship of Psalm 137 to Jeremiah 49:7-22 and Obadiah." *JSOT* 24 (1982) 89-97.
Origen. "Against Celsus." Pages 395-670 in vol. 4 of *The Ante-Nicene Fathers*. Edited by Alexander Roberts and James Donaldson. 1867-1873. American revised edition by A. Cleveland Coxe. 1895-1896. 10 vols. Repr. Grand Rapids, MI: Eerdmans, 1979.
———. "De Principiis." Pages 239-384 in vol. 4 of *The Ante-Nicene Fathers*. Edited by Alexander Roberts and James Donaldson. 1867-1873. American revised edition by A. Cleveland Coxe. 1895-1896. 10 vols. Repr. Grand Rapids, MI: Eerdmans, 1979.
———. "Homilies on Genesis 12.1." In *Psalms 51-150*. Edited by Quentin F. Wesselschmidt. OT vol. 8 of *Ancient Commentary on Scripture*. Edited by Thomas C. Oden. Downers Grove, IL: InterVarsity, 2007.
——— "Homilies on Leviticus: 1.1.4." In *Psalms 51-150*. Edited by Quentin F. Wesselschmidt. OT vol. 8 of *Ancient Commentary on Scripture*. Edited by Thomas C. Oden. Downers Grove, IL: InterVarsity, 2007.
Pao, David W. and Eckhard J. Schnabel. "Luke." Pages 251-414 in *Commentary on the New Testament use of the Old Testament*. Edited by Gregory K. Beale and Donald A. Carson. Grand Rapids, MI: Baker Academic, 2007.
Perowne, John J. S. *The Book of Psalms*. 4th ed. Repr. Grand Rapids: Zondervan, 1966.
Peter Chrysologus. "Sermon 2." In *Psalms 51-150*. Edited by Quentin F. Wesselschmidt. OT vol. 8 of *Ancient Commentary on Scripture*. Edited by Thomas C. Oden. Downers Grove, IL: InterVarsity, 2007.
Prinsloo, W. S. 1997. Psalm 149: praise Yahweh with tambourine and two-edged sword. *Zeitschrift für die Alttestamentliche Wissenschaft* 109(3):395-407.
Provan, Iain. 2013. Seriously Dangerous Religion: What the Old Testament Really Says and Why it Matters. 2013 Kindle edn. Available online at http://www.amazon.com

Rendtorff, Rolf. The Psalms of David: David in the Psalms. Pages 53–64 in *The Book of Psalms: Composition and Reception*. Edited by Peter W. Flint and Patrick D. Miller. Leiden: Brill, 2005.

———. Zum Gebrauch der Formel n'um Jawe im Jeremiahbuch. ZAW 66 (1954) 27–37.

Scheffler, Eben. "War and Violence in the Old Testament: Various Views." Pages 1–17 in *Animosity, the Bible, and us: some European, North American, and South African Perspectives*. Edited by John T. Fitzgerald, Fika J. van Rensburg, and Herrie van Rooy. Atlanta: Society of Biblical Literature, 2009.

Selderhuis, Herman J. *Calvin's Theology of the Psalms*. Grand Rapids, MI: Baker Academic, 2007.

Seybold, Klaus. *Die Psalmen*. HAT, 1.15. Tübingen: Mohr Siebeck, 1996.

Sheppard, Gerald T. "Enemies and the Politics of Prayer in the Book of Psalms." Pages 61–82 in *The Politics of Exegesis: Essays in Honor of Norman Gottwald*. Edited by David Jobling, Gerald T. Sheppard and Peggy L. Day. New York: Pilgrim, 1991.

Smoak, Jeremy D. "Building Houses and Planting Vineyards: The Early Inner-biblical Discourse on an Ancient Israelite Wartime Curse." JBL 127 no 1 (2008) 19–35.

Soll, Will H. *Psalm 119: Matrix Form and Setting*. Washington: Catholic Biblical Association of America, 1991.

Stander, Hennie. Violence in Chrysostom's commentary on the Psalms. *Ekklesiastikos Pharos* 94 N.S. 23 (2012) 115–122.

Sticher, Claudia. „Die Gottlosen Gedheihen Wei Gras: Zu Einigen Pflanzenmetaphern in den Psalmen eine Kononische Lektüre." Pages 251–268 in Metaphors in the Psalms. Edited by Pierre van Hecke and Antje Labahn. Leuven, Belgium: Peeters, 2010.

Sulpitius Severus. "The Works of Sulpitius Severus: The Doubtful Letters of Sulpitius Severus." Pages 55–70 in vol. 11 of *The Nicene and Post-Nicene Fathers*, Series 2. Edited by Philip Schaff and Henry Wace. 1886–1889. 14 vols. Repr. Grand Rapids, MI: Eerdmans, 1986.

Tanner, Beth. "Rethinking the Enterprise: What Must be Considered in Formulating a Theology of the Psalms. Pages 139–152 in *Soundings in the Theology of Psalms: Perspectives and Methods in Contemporary Scholarship*. Minneapolis: Fortress, 2011.

Tebes, Juan M. "The Edomite Involvement in the Destruction of the First Temple: A Case of Stab-in-the-back Tradition?" JSTO 36, no. 2 (2011) 219–255.

Tertullian. "On the Resurrection of the Flesh." Pages 545–595 in vol. 3 of *The Ante-Nicene Fathers*. Edited by Alexander Roberts and James Donaldson. 1867–1873. American revised edition by A. Cleveland Coxe. 1895–1896. 10 vols. Repr. Grand Rapids, MI: Eerdmans, 1989.

The Liturgy of the Hours Psalter. Available online at http://www.liturgies.net/Prayers/lohpsalter.htm#Psalm 13. Date of access: 11 Nov. 2014.

Theodoret of Cyrus. *Commentary on the Psalms, 73–150*. Translated by Hill, R. C. FC, 102. Baltimore, MD: Catholic University of America Press, 2001.

———. "Discourse 1.39." In *Psalms 51–150*. Edited by Quentin F. Wesselschmidt. OT vol. 8 of *Ancient Commentary on Scripture*. Edited by Thomas C. Oden. Downers Grove, IL: InterVarsity, 2007.

TDOT. Theological Dictionary of the Old Testament. Vol 3. Grand Rapids, MI: Eerdmans, 1978.

Van der Wall, A. J. O. "The structure of Psalm CXXIX." *Vetus Testamentum* 38, Jul (1988) 364–367.

Van Rooy, Herrie. *The East Syriac Psalm Headings: A Critical Edition*. Piscataway, NJ: Gorgias, 2013.

———. "The Enemies in the Headings of the Psalms: A Comparison of Jewish and Christian Interpretation. Pages 41–57 in *Animosity, the Bible, and Us: Some European, North American, and South African Perspectives*. Edited by J. Fitzgerald, F. van Rensburg, and Herrie van Rooy. Atlanta: Society of Biblical Literature, 2009.

———. "Reading the Psalms Historically: Antiochene Exegesis and a Historical Reading of Psalm 46." *AT*, 2 (2009) 120–134.

Von Rad, Gerhard. Genesis: A Commentary. 3d ed. London: SCM, 1972.

Wallace, Howard N. "King and Community: Joining with David in Prayer." In *Psalms and Prayers: Papers Read at the Joint meeting of the Society of Old Testament Study and Het Oudtestamentisch Werkgezelschap in Nederland en België, Apeldoorn, August 2006*. Edited by Bob Becking and Eric Peels. Leiden: Brill, 2007.

———. "Words to God, Word from God." Hampshire, England: Ashgate, 2005.

Waltke, Bruce K. *An Old Testament Theology: An Exegetical, Canonical and Theological Approach*. Grand Rapids: Zondervan, 2007.

———. "Superscripts, Postscripts, or Both. *JBL* 10, no. 4 (1991) 583–596.

———, and James Houston. *The Psalms as Christian Worship: A Historical Commentary*. Grand Rapids: Eerdmans, 2010.

———, and Michael O'Connor, eds. *An Introduction to Biblical Hebrew Syntax* (IBHS). Winona Lake, IN: Eisenbrauns, 1990.

Watson, E. W. "Introduction." Pages i–xcv in vol. 9 of *The Nicene and Post-Nicene Fathers*, Series 2. Edited by Philip Schaff and Henry Wace. 1886–1889. 14 vols. Repr. Grand Rapids, MI: Eerdmans, 1979.

Watts, Rikk E. "Mark." Pages 111–249 in *Commentary on the New Testament Use of the Old Testament*. Edited by Gregory K. Beale and Donald Carson. Grand Rapids: Baker Academic, 2007.

Weiser, Artur. *The Psalms: A Commentary*. 5th ed. Translated from the German by Herbert Hartwell, OTL. London: SCM, 1962.

Wenham, Gordon J. "Prayer and Practice in the Psalms." Pages 279–295 in In *Psalms and Prayers: Papers Read at the Joint meeting of the Society of Old Testament Study and Het Oudtestamentisch Werkgezelschap in Nederland en België, Apeldoorn, August 2006*. Edited by Bob Becking and Erik Peels. Leiden: Brill, 2007.

———. "Towards a Canonial Reading of the Psalms." Pages 333–351 in *Canon and Biblical Interpretation*. Edited by Craig Bartholomew, Scott Hahn, Robin Parry, Christopher Seitz, and Al Wolters. Grand Rapids: Zondervan, 2006.

Westermann, Claus. *Praise and Lament in the Psalms*. Atlanta: John Knox, 1981.

Wilson, Gerald H. The Editing of the Hebrew Psalter. SBLDS, 76. Chico, CA: Scholars, 1985.

———. King, Messiah, and the Reign of God: Revisiting the Royal Psalms and the Shape of the Psalter. Pages 391–406 in *The Book of Psalms: Composition and Reception*. Edited by Peter W. Flint and Patrick D. Miller. Leiden: Brill, 2005.

———. "Shaping the Psalter: A Consideration of Editorial Linkage in the Book of Psalms." Pages 72–82 in *The Shape and Shaping of the Psalter*. Edited by J. Clinton McCann. Sheffield: JSOT Press, 1993.

———. "The Structure of the Psalter." Pages 229–246 in *Interpreting the Psalms: Issues and Approaches*. Edited by Philip S. Johnston and David Firth. Downers Grove: IVP Academic, 2005.

Wright, Nicholas T. *The Case for the Psalms: Why They Are Essential*. 2013. Kindle edn. Available online at http://www.amazon.com

Würthwein, Ernst. "Erwägungen zu Psalm CXXXIX." *VT* VII (1957) 165–182.

Young, Edward J. "The Background of Psalm 139." *Bulletin of the Evangelical Society* 8 no.3 (1965) 101–110.

Zenger, Erich. The composition and theology of the fifth book of Psalms: Psalms 107–145. *Journal for the Study of the Old Testament* 80 (1998) 77–102.

———. *A God of Vengeance? Understanding the Psalms of Divine Wrath*. Translated from the German by Linda M. Maloney. Louisville: Westminster John Knox, 1996.

Subject Index

Aaron, 162
  covenant, 198
  order, 34, 40
  pre-Aaronic, 27
  priesthood, 48
Abel, 98, 100
Abraham, 64, 79, 100, 116, 208
  Abram, 28–29, 34
Acrostic (poem), 52, 55, 199
Adam, 68, 120
Advent, of Christ, 171–72
Adversity, 2, 49, 55, 57, 59, 69, 72–75, 78–79, 82, 90, 93, 113, 120, 140, 160, 173, 177–78, 181, 197, 202, 212–13
Afflicted, 56, 83, 171, 200
Affliction, 56–57, 60, 68, 77–79, 171, 201
Agency, 112, 138, 162, 182, 189, 191, 202–4, 209, 213
  of agrarian curse, 90
  of Babylon, 211
  of the church, 209, 214
  of Cyrus and Darius, 125
  of God (Yahweh), 26, 90, 100, 110, 161, 184, 199, 203–4, 208, 210
  of God's people, 162, 215
  of the 'lord', 199
  of the wicked, 209, 214
Aggressive, of enemy, 98, 198, 203, 215
  of evil, 193, 211
  of recalcitrant, 49, 199
Agricultural, imprecation, 93, 178, 213

imagery, 10, 82–83, 93–95, 101, 179, 182, 204
  of judgment, 93, 204
  metaphor, 82–83, 85, 93, 204
  in NT, 95–96
  in *Ruth*, 92
Alexandrian, commentators/school, 9, 11–12, 41, 117–19, 143, 167, 169
Allegoria, 11
Allegorical, Christ-centered, 10
  interpretations, 41, 43, 47–49, 116, 124, 169–70, 174, 192, 194
  method, 9, 117, 119, 126, 161, 190
Allegory, 11, 46, 125, 192–93
  prophetic, 41
Amalekites, 161–62
Ammon, 31
Ammonites, 37, 62
Anabaptists, 45–46
Anagoge, 11
Antinomy, 92
Antiochus Epiphanes, 99, 171
Antiochene, commentators/school, 9, 11, 19, 41–42, 49, 66, 117–18, 143, 145, 167, 184
  interpretation, 9, 120, 168
Annihilate, 88, 203
Annihilation, of evil, 194–95, 213, 215
Apocalyptic, 40, 48
Apologist, 11, 40–41, 143
Arabs, at time of restoration, 37, 62
Aramaisms, 53, 135
Arameans, 88
Arian, 66, 119, 219
Artaxerxes, 37, 53, 62

Asaphites, 36
Ascension, 39–40
Assyrians, 88
  oracles, 26, 30–31

Babel, 94, 166
Babylon, 5, 102–16, 194
  charges against, 108–9, 164, 173
  crimes committed by, 114, 179, 195, 208
  epitome of evil, 115, 178
  festivals, 8, 135
  fixation in memory, 110
  gods of, 29, 127
  haruspicy, 135
  interpretation of by *ANPN Fathers*, 10, 117–21, 125, by Augustine, 121–22, 125, 170, by Calvin, 124–25
  judgment against, 110–11, 125, 194, 205, 210
  means of judgment, 164, 211
  in NT, 115, 126, 167, 170, 179, 182
  place of exile, 5, 105–6, 160
Babylonians, 62, 88, 107–8, 110, 164, 173, 195, cruelty of, 92
Beast, 142, 182, 207
  mark of, 167
Beatitudes, 66, 112
Benediction, 84, 92, 112, 191
Blessed, 50, 57, 65–67, 79, 104, 119–20, 169, 180, 191, 194, 199, 203
Blessing formula, 85–88, 92, 94
  with imprecations, 105, 112–13, 180, 191
  negative, 91, 93
Blood, 115, 136, 138–39, 157, 170, 172, 193, 216
  avenger of, 138–39, 142, 206
  bloodthirsty, 127, 130, 138, 140, 142, 144–45, 148, 152–53, 178–79, 181, 193, 206
  bloody, 120, 136, 145
  innocent, 139, 151
  men of, 134, 136, 138, 141–42, 145, 148
Book IV, 20

Book V, 9, 15–21, 23–24, 36, 43, 49, 89, 140, 154, 158–61, 164–65, 193, 195, 212
Book of Common Prayer, 127
Branch. *See* David, branch of.
Brutal, 111–12, 193
Burn, 43, 66, 95–96, 101, 144, 153, 182
Byzantine Empire, 45

Cain, 100
Canaanite, 28–29
Canonical, 4, 5, 9–10, 14–15, 20–21, 23, 61, 110, 161, 176, 188, 190, 193, 195, 197–99, 201, 210, 214
Canonical-messianic, 4
Cappadocian, 11, 119, 143, 168
Chaos, 35, 135
Chiasm, 104–5
Christological interpretation, 39
Coda, 16, 165
Commandments, 50, 52, 55, 58–59, 69, 70, 73, 75, 77, 200
Communal Lament, 2, 14, 22–24, 54, 85, 90, 132, 178, 209
Complaint, communal, 84, 90
  individual, 132, 199, 212
  psalms, 51, 132, 199, 212
Covenant, 17, 28, 34, 87, 116, 134, 179
  Aaronic, 198
  of eternal salvation, 73–74
  New, 39–40, 65, 151, 183
Covenantal, armies, 157
  blessing formulas, 93, 112–13, 191, 203
  community, 87, 112, 135, 162, 164
  enemies, 135
  festival, 7–8
  God, 18
  justice, 93
  language, 92, 104, 112, 134
  loyalty, 92
  mandate, 33
  name, 132
  partner, 196
  people, 162, 164, 203
  perspective, 19, 93
  pre-, 34

Creation, 98, 132, 135, 151, 166, 167, 196, 206, 207
  of person, 68, 131, 207
  of nation, 207
Creator, 17, 135, 138, 142, 163, 170, 181, 196, 206–7, 210–11
Cross, 77, 126, 168, 193, 215
Cult/cultic, 4–8, 14, 23, 30, 34, 51, 54, 61–62, 80, 89, 106, 112–13, 133–34,139, 155, 157, 159–61, 187, 189–91, 193
Cult-functional approach, 4–6
Curse, 2, 5, 60, 77, 81–82, 90–94, 96, 111, 124, 201, 215, 217
  of heaven, 100–101
  Jesus', 101, 182
  self-curse, 106, 114, 127
Cyrus, 29, 37, 61, 110, 120, 124–25, 160

Darius, 37, 61–62, 124–25
David, 10, 20–21, 25–26, 29–34, 102, 119, 150–51, 191
  authorship, 30, 146
  Book of, 8
  branch of, 36, 37
  dynasty, 34, 158
  psalms, 17, 72, 78, 102
  prophecy of, 122, 144, 168, 174, 198
  superscripts, 20, 127
Death, 38, 93, 101, 144, 187, 204
  of children, 111
  of enemies, 138
  of enemies of Christ, 45
  figural, 153
  form of judgment, 182, 186
  of Jesus, 116
  letter of, 69
  outcome of curse, 23–24, 82, 96, 141
  penalty, 47
  spiritual, 97
  violent, 41
Decian persecution, 144
Deeds, 70, 81, 115, 141, 144, 152, 163, 167, 169–70, 188, 206–7, 210–11, 215, 217
  bloody, 145

Destruction, of Babylon, 109–10, 125
  of enemies, 47, 90, 93, 96, 104, 172, 184, 187
  evil's capacity for, 214
  of Jerusalem, 52, 108, 116
  of Tyre, 125
  of ungodly, 77
  utter, 90, 99
Donatists, 68
Doxology, 16–17, 152, 165, 207

Earth, 25, 27, 29, 34–35, 45, 48, 55, 59, 63–64, 115, 129, 164, 166, 169, 174, 178–82, 192, 200–201, 208–9
  goddess, 135
  ruler, 44
Edom, 102–3, 105–9, 114, 118–24, 126, 138–39, 205–6
Egypt, 7, 45, 94, 99, 100
Egyptians, 88
Elamites, 62
Enarrationes in Psalmos, 43, 67
Enemy/enemies. See "Perceived Suffering of Psalmist" in individual psalms.
Enthronement, 30–31, 34,
Ephesus, 142, 182
Ephraim, 92, 203
Eradication, 3, 214
Eschatology, 36, 183–84
Eschatological, 32, 34–35, 38, 40–43, 47–49, 87, 89, 93, 98, 113, 140, 152, 157, 159, 160–62, 154–65, 175, 178, 180, 182–84, 186, 191–92, 198–99, 202, 204, 207–9, 212–13
Evil, moral, 3, 5, 23, 25, 55, 195–97, 209–11, 214–17
  natural, 4, 196
Evildoers, 44, 134, 138, 184, 204
Exile, 5, 10, 19, 20, 31, 36–37, 52–54, 56, 60, 87, 89, 92–94, 96, 105–8, 110, 114, 116, 118, 123, 125, 160, 163–64, 171, 173, 186, 202–4, 208, 210

Subject Index

Faith, 12, 13, 64, 67, 69, 72, 75, 97, 112, 118, 144, 171, 177, 187–88
Festival, Akitu, 8, 135
  Babylonian New Year, 8
Festival, Akitu *(continued)*
  Covenant, 7
  of African Martyrs, 68
  King's Enthronement, 31
  Pentecost, 51
  Pre-exilic Cult, 157
Footstool, 26, 33–34, 38–40, 43, 47
Form-criticism, 51, 78, 176, 190

Gehenna, 96
Genre, 4, 14, 16, 51, 159, 192
  definition of, 13, 212
  eschatological, 152
  mixed, 2, 23–24, 51, 54, 84, 132, 178
  as prayer, 12–13, 213–14
Gentile, 40, 69, 87, 97, 100, 168
Gesham, 62
Glory, 46, 67, 71, 81, 155–56, 162–63, 168–69, 184, 217
  future, 141, 184
  in the cross, 168
  of saints, 209
God the Father, 168
Godhead, 40, 168
Gospel, 39, 42, 44–45, 63, 65–67, 74, 76, 80, 96, 115–16, 143, 201
Grass. *See* "Withering Grass—A Symbol of Utter Destruction," 90–93
  image of judgment, 95, 96, 98, 100, 101, 178, 182
  in *LXX*, 95
  NT images of grass, 95, 98, 101
  spiritual symbol, 97
  symbol of pride, 98, 99
Grace, 69, 72–73, 75, 79, 148, 199, 210, 215, 217
Grammatico-historical interpretation, 4
Guilt, 77, 83, 109, 133

Haggai, 20, 32
Hallelujah, hymn, 17
  psalms, 17–19

superscript/postscript, 155–56, 180, 192
Hate, the blameless, 136
  perfect, 149, 153, 178
  sinners, 146
  sin, 147
  tension in, 153
  Yahweh, 130, 134–35, 181
  Zion, 84–85, 87, 89–90, 93, 94, 100–101, 180–81, 191, 202–4
Headings, 4, 10, 43, 145, 163
Heart, 29, 50, 56, 58, 60, 66–67, 69–70, 74, 78–79, 101, 130, 137, 139, 141, 144, 200, 206
Heaven, 39, 65–66, 100–101, 128, 132, 143, 163, 169, 217
Hell, 46
Heresy, 40, 169
Heretic, 77, 119, 145, 148, 153, 174, 184
Hezekiah, 92, 203
Holy Spirit, 39, 67, 69, 73, 75, 76, 80, 117, 141, 144, 151
Holy War, 26, 161, 164
Hur, 162
Hymnal, hymn, 2, 15, 16, 22–24, 51, 54, 132, 142, 154, 157, 159, 178, 181
  eschatological, 157, 161, 178
Hyperbole, 153–54, 181, 191, 207

Idols, 87, 121, 144, 170
  idolatry, 130, 133, 135
Imagery, agricultural, 10, 83, 93–95, 101, 202, 204
  children being dashed, 124
  deliverance, 94
  enemies, 49
  fleeing, 148
  general, 93, 113, 141, 192
  grass, 101
  war, 5, 25, 35, 83, 91, 112–13, 159–60, 162
Imprecatory, 2, 3, 22–23, 81, 89, 188, 191, 216
Incarnation, 168, 192

Inclusio, 16–21, 58, 84–86, 126,
  131–32, 136, 154, 156, 158–60,
  162, 165, 181, 212
Injustice, 49, 61, 78, 89, 92, 107, 138,
  178, 185, 196–97, 201–3, 210,
  214, 216–17
Insolent, 54–56, 59, 200–201
Interpretation, anthropological, 39
  Alexandrian, 11, 12, 41
  Allegorical, 192, 194
  Calvin's plain, 48
  Christological, 39
  Christian, 168
  Four hinge points of, 11
  Cult-historical, 6
  Eschatological, 140, 159
  Figural, 12, 101, 117, 121, 145
  Literal, 42, 120, 133, 144, 146, 153,
    161, 174, 194
  Liturgical, 68
  Messianic prophecy, 29
  Metaphorical, 44, 46, 124–25
  Papist, 73
  Pietistic, 194
  Post-exilic, 94
  Pre-Christian, 20
  Prosopological, 152
  Sacred, 21
  Spiritual, 42, 43, 46
Integrity, 15, 35, 75, 130, 149, 150, 152
Irrational, 98, 101, 179, 181–82, 193,
  197, 199, 204, 210
Israelite, 5, 26, 29, 31, 37, 55, 58,
  89–92, 112–13, 118, 126–27,
  157, 160, 162, 164, 167–68, 171,
  173, 190–91, 195, 203–5, 208,
  211, 214

Jehoiachin, 53
Jeremiah, 10, 28, 30, 52–53, 102, 110,
  124, 137, 139, 206
Jerusalem, self-curse, 106, 127
  self-cursing oaths, 112, 114, 123,
  126
Jews, 12, 40, 42, 48, 77, 98, 118, 120,
  171–72, 174
Joshua, 191
  ben Jehozadak, 36–37

Josiah, 118, 144, 153
Judaism, 40, 53, 61
Judge (noun), Christ as, 38–40, 43,
  94–95, 166, 173–74, 179, 183
  God as, 47b, 75, 80
  wicked blaspheme, 150, 153
  Yahweh as, 109
Judge (verb), of God, 75, 150, 153, 184
  of God's people, 169
  of Jesus, 183
  of Yahweh, 32–33, 63, 78, 101
Justice, according to Augustine,
  70–72, 81, 185–86
  retributive, 195, 205
  penal, 197, 202, 205

Kingdom, 7, 45, 48–49, 126, 213, 217
  of Jesus/Christ, 39, 44, 46–49, 126
  of God, 45–46, 126, 139, 157,
    184–85, 208, 215, 217
  of heaven, 65

Lament, 1–3, 6, 21, 51–52, 54, 57, 60,
  62, 105, 114, 133, 154, 159, 165,
  176, 178, 207, 216
  communal, 22, 24, 54, 85, 90, 132,
    178
  individual, 1, 2, 14, 21, 22, 23, 25,
    54, 59, 133, 212, 213
Land, 5, 10, 29, 35, 58, 61–62, 92, 97,
  103–4, 114, 117, 138, 141, 163,
  171, 198, 206
Lex agendi, 1, 187, 200
Lex credendi, 1, 187, 200
Lex ordandi, 1, 187, 200
Lex talionis, 109, 111, 115, 164, 194,
  195, 205, 208, 210, 215
Liberation, 89, 186
Literal meaning. *See* interpretation
Liturgical, 2, 5, 8, 14–16, 30–31, 36,
  62, 68, 114
  modification, 30, 180, 191
  Roman Catholic 8, 12–13
Liturgy, 190
  Liturgy of Hours, 23, 127
  Post-exilic, 51
  Roman Catholic, 8, 22, 24, 197–98

Subject Index

lord, 23, 25–26, 31–33, 35–36, 38, 40, 45–46, 49, 81, 135, 179, 183–84, 191, 198–99, 210, 213, 215–16
Lord, 18, 27–29, 31–32, 37, 41, 45, 63, 65, 69, 70, 75, 77, 79, 83–86, 97, 103, 110, 127, 134–35, 139, 145, 155–56, 158, 168–70, 178, 217
Love, active through faith, 72
  adulterous, 119, 121
  for brother/neighbor, 64, 80, 144
  of commandments/law/word, 59, 64, 69, 71, 74, 76, 80
  for enemy, 118, 127, 147, 149, 153, 170, 217
  first, 142
  God's, 59, 80, 126, 215
  for God, 68, 80, 126
  justice, 70, 72
  just deeds, 81
  qualities of, 146
  steadfast, 16, 87
  suffering of Christ, 215
  theme of, 81
  of things, 121
  of virtue, 146

Maccabees, 10, 167–68, 172, 174
Martyrs, 65, 68, 71, 79, 97, 186
Meditation, as a classification, 133
  resulting in fear of God, 149, 151
  king's, 136
  on law/*torah*, 59, 61, 63, 66–67, 71–74, 78, 80, 178, 200–201
Melchizedek, 25, 27, 28–29, 34, 39–40, 44, 48, 183, 186, 191, 198, 199
Memory, of persecutions, 184
  in Ps 149, 163
  theme of in Psalm 137, 102–3, 105–10, 112–13, 115, 117, 121, 122, 125–26, 205
Mercy, 39, 69, 71, 172, 183, 185
  merciless, 87
Merism, of prophetic war oracles, 110
  of Yahweh's knowledge, 132
Messiah, 27, 29, 31, 33–35, 38, 40
Messianic, pertaining to Ps 110, 28–30, 34, 38, 40, 93, 178

pertaining to Ps 149, 159
Metaphor, agricultural, 82–83, 85, 204
  critique of, 124–25, 82, 192–94
  cruelty of warfare, 108, 110
  of dashing children, 111
  destruction of enemy, 93, 96
  distress, 82
  furnace, 96
  of (withering) grass, 83, 88, 90–91, 93
  military, 47, 89
  of plowman, 83, 88–90
  shepherd, 47
  of singing, 142
  of youth, 88
Metonym(y), 57–58, 107, 133
Midrashic, 10, 109
Military, 14, 26, 29, 31, 34, 47, 87, 89, 91, 93, 100, 107, 110, 116, 133, 163, 203, 208
Modus Operandi, of God, 44
Mohammed, 45
Moses, 67, 76, 98, 142, 149, 162

Nativity, 168
n^eum yhwh, 29, 30, 34, 138, 180, 191, 198
New Song, 17, 142, 155, 161, 166–69, 171, 173, 174, 179, 182, 207, 209
Nicolaitans, 142, 182

Oath, Melchizedekian, 198
  psalmist's (formula), 68, 114, 118, 205
  YHWH's (formula), 28, 30, 178, 198
Oracle(s), Assyrian, 26, 30
  divine, 22, 29
  formula, 28, 30, 32, 178
  prophetic, 2, 28, 30–31, 213
  use of, 36
  war, 110, 180, 191
Orthodox, 10, 29, 40, 183, 193
  unorthodox, 193

Pagan, myths, 135
  nations, 163
Pagans, 42, 48, 170

Subject Index

Papist, interpretation, 73
Parallelism, 17, 19, 57, 68, 102–3, 110, 129, 130, 158, 160, 162–63
Paul, 63–66, 69, 74, 79, 81, 168, 207
Peace, 35, 64, 117, 169, 174
Pentecost, 51
Perpetrator, 3, 109, 177, 186, 195, 205, 210–11, 217
Persecution, 52, 56, 60, 65, 68, 71, 77, 97, 98, 100, 121, 144, 184, 201, 203
Pesher, 10
Pharisees, 39, 64, 95–96, 115
Philistines, 88
Pietistic, 77, 194, 202
Piety, 57, 74, 144, 147
  impiety, 42
Prophecy, 9, 30, 116, 125, 167
  of David, 122
  messianic, 28–30, 44, 46, 178
  royal, 28, 31, 178
  spiritual kingdom of Christ, 46
Polemic, 40, 68, 132, 135, 191
Poor, 83, 138, 171, 174
Postscript, 180, 192
Prayer, 1–4, 7, 12–15, 21–23, 25, 51–52, 57, 83–84, 87, 90, 92, 93, 97, 100, 102, 105, 118, 122–23, 127, 138, 141, 145, 147, 152, 154, 161, 166
  see Chapters 3 and 4
Presence, of enemies, 137, 148
  of evil, 194
  of God, 41, 59, 92, 136, 138–39, 206–7, 209–10, 214
  of Yahweh, 58, 60–62, 78–81, 128, 137, 139, 178, 181, 185, 199–200, 202, 213, 215
Priest, 8, 27, 31, 32, 34, 37, 62, 84–85, 144, 153, 190
  of Christ, 38–40, 42–43, 46, 170
  Melchizedekian, 25, 27, 29, 34, 39–40, 44, 48, 183, 186, 191, 199
Priesthood, Aaronic, 27, 34, 39, 40, 48, 180
  of Christ, 42, 39
  conferred by Christ, 166, 209

Priestly, of Aaronic, 40
  blessing, 85
  endowment, 34
  function, 37, 43
  grace, 210
  group, 84
  requirements, 36
  theme, 36
  title, 29
Prodigal Son, 147
Prophecy, 9, 30, 44, 46, 122, 125, 167, 178
  royal/messianic, 28–31
Prophetic, 10, 26, 29, 30, 41, 76, 116, 141, 198
  allegory, 41
  literature, 7, 110, 163, 191
  oracles, 30–31, 180, 191
  judgment, 38–39, 95, 116, 126, 138, 182
  judgment oracles/speeches, 2, 22, 24, 28 82, 213
  vastanda, 104
Prosopological, 26, 120, 145, 152
Proud, 43, 77, 95, 148, 193
Providence, 73, 79, 127, 150
Punishment, 24, 41–43, 48, 63, 70, 77, 100–101, 107–8, 111, 114–15, 120, 125, 147, 155, 163, 169–70, 184, 203, 205, 209–10, 215, 217

Qumran Hypothesis, 15

Recalcitrant, 35, 40, 42, 45, 48–49, 98, 179, 183, 184, 193, 199, 199, 205, 209–10, 215, 217
Redeemed, 18, 158, 166–67, 174, 209
  of Zion, 157
Redemption, 167, 173
Rehum, 62
Reign, 34–35, 45, 62, 93, 166, 180, 183, 207, 209
Remnant, 100
Repentance, 39, 71, 75–76, 92, 117, 186, 217
Reprobate, 46–48, 75, 124, 184, 186, 199, 203, 215

Restoration, 9, 14, 19–21, 24, 36–38, 53, 61–62, 89, 94, 107–8, 140, 155, 160, 164–65, 171, 193, 202, 205, 209, 212
  of synagogue, 66
  of victim, 155, 217
Resurrection, 117, 141
  of Christ, 168
Retribution, 18, 57, 120, 158, 185, 195, 208
Rhetorical, 14, 131–32, 137–38, 141, 154, 193, 213–14, 216
  critical, 4
Right hand, 26–27, 32–33, 103, 128, 168
Righteous, 15, 50, 56, 60, 63, 65, 70, 75, 77, 80–81, 83, 89, 92, 94, 97, 99, 138, 147, 179, 182, 201, 203–4, 210, 216
Righteousness, 57, 64–65, 68, 72, 77, 144, 151–52, 207
Righteousness *(continued)*
  of God, 74–75, 80, 101
  of Yahweh, 92, 202–3
  of the Lord Jesus Christ, 217
Ritual, 7–8, 31, 107, 133, 135
Royal Psalms, 24–25, 29–30, 33, 34, 54, 87, 93, 139

Sacred, 21, 113, 154, 180, 185–87, 189–95, 198, 204, 213
Sacrifice, of Christ, 40, 48, 170
  cultic, 139
  of enemies (figural) 172
Sadducees, 95–96
Salvation, 17, 56, 73–75, 77, 142, 155, 157, 162–63, 207, 215
Sanballat, 37, 62
Satan, 35, 72–73, 79, 99, 199
Saviour, 169
Scepter, 26, 32–34, 41, 44, 46–47, 172
Scholasticism, 11
Sennacharib, 92
Serpent, 120
Session, of Christ, 38–39, 40, 42–44, 183, 186

Shame, 2, 23–24, 50, 59, 63, 65, 70, 73, 79, 82–84, 86–87, 91–92, 94, 107, 149, 203, 212
Sheol, 128, 132
Shepherd, 47, 49
Shethar-bozenai, 62
Shimshai, 62
Sin, 31, 57–58, 67, 69, 75, 81, 83, 92, 98, 117–18, 127, 133, 137, 139, 143–45, 147–48, 151–53
Sinners, 41, 83, 97, 99, 144–49, 153
Skopos, 10, 119–20, 143
Slay, 130, 132, 137, 140, 153–54, 169–70, 172, 174, 178, 206
Slaughter, 114, 126, 170, 172
Son of Man, 40
Song, 13, 14, 17, 51, 82, 84, 102–3, 107, 118, 142, 155, 157, 161, 166–69, 171, 173, 174, 179, 205, 207, 209, 212
Soteriological, 41–43
Sovereignty, 126
Spirit, of God, 73, 128, 141, 144, 148, 151, 172, 207
  evil, 115
  of the Lord, 29
  of man, 172–74
  rebellious, 47
Spiritual interpretation. *See* interpretation
Subjugation, 32, 34–35, 39, 41, 44, 47, 49, 89, 155, 164–65, 168, 178–79, 181, 184
Subscript. *See* postscript
Suffering. *See* "Perceived Suffering of Psalmist," in Chp 2.
Superscript, 15, 20, 180, 192
  see also headings
Statute, 2, 50, 52, 58, 63, 65–66, 70, 79, 200
Sword, 84, 91, 169–72, 174, 209
  double-edged, 17, 155, 164, 169, 17, 155, 164, 169–70, 174, 178
  blood, 157, 170
Symbol, Babylon, 205
  couches, 171
  demonic power, 115
  grass, 92, 101

Jesus weeping, 126
judgment, 100–111, 208
ruler, 38
scepter, 32–33
sword, 209
yoke, 93
Zion, 205
Synagogue, 66
Synecdoche, 3, 124–25, 193, 205, 207, 209, 213–14, 216–17

Targum, 8, 27, 103–4, 129, 130, 132
Tattenai, 62
Teachings, divine, 42
  of Jesus, 143
  Lord's 169
  NT, 126
  Origen's, 146
Temple, 4–5, 8, 14, 34, 36–37, 59, 61–62, 78, 80, 94, 106, 116, 200, 207
Temptation, 73, 122, 217
Theodicy, 196, 216
Theoria, 9, 11
Testimonies, 55, 58, 65, 67, 69–71, 77, 79
Thanksgiving, of psalms, 15, 54, 84, 133, 178
  for God's works, 150
  of the "new song," 166–67
  of song, 14, 51
Throne, of Yahweh, 40
Throne partner of Yahweh, 25, 27, 32–35, 38, 48
Tobiah, 62, 94
Torah. *See* exegesis and select historical survey of Ps 119, 49–81
Trinity, 145, 183
Tropological, 77
Turks, 45
Typology, 190

Ugarit, 83, 103, 135
Unjust, 1, 33–34, 62, 71, 75, 139, 196, 210, 214, 216

Vengeance, 1–2, 18–19, 22, 47, 75–76, 100–102, 123–24, 126, 150, 153, 155, 158–59, 163–64, 168–73, 178, 195, 208, 216
Victim(s), 3, 55, 87, 91, 154, 177, 185, 187–88, 203, 211, 213, 217
Vindication, 108, 151, 166, 209
Violence, categories in the Psalms. *See* "Selection of Psalms to be Studied," 21–24
Voice, as prayer. *See* "Prayer as the Basis for the Inclusion of Non-lament Psalms," 12–15
Vulgate, 129

Warrior, God, 26
  king, 26
  Yahweh, 26
Warriors, youthful, 27
Wealth, 121
Wisdom, of psalm elements/classification, 16, 51, 54, 62, 154, 178, 181, 185, 191
  Christ's, 70
  God's, 44, 143
  heretic's, 145
  readings, 56
  seek for, 67
  Torah, 51
  true, 58
  worldly, 74
Word of God, 3, 74–75, 78, 95, 98, 187
Words of God, 188, 192
Wrath, Christ's, 47
  day of, 41
  God's, 22, 24, 33–34, 41, 63, 71, 81, 91, 144, 184, 186
  Lord's 27
  plagues of, 142
  Yahweh's 18, 159

Xerxes, 37, 61

Yhwh, 18, 32, 85, 87, 90, 105, 108, 132, 135, 191
YHWH, 16, 51, 107, 157
Yoke, symbol of subjugation, 83, 89, 92, 203

Zechariah, 20, 35–37
Zurubbabel, 36–37

Ancient Authors and Personalities Index

Up until the sixteenth century

Ambrose, 65, 66, 79, 117, 119, 126
Arians, 66
   Anomoean Arians, 119
Arius, 169
Athanasius, 12, 25, 66, 79, 120, 143, 192
Augustine. *See* table of "Contents"

Basil, 120, 143, 144, 146, 151

Cassiodorus, 11, 97–98, 101, 145, 147, 153, 168–69, 174
Clement of Rome, 41, 119, 143
Constitution of the Holy Apostles, 81, 145, 153, 202
Cyprian, 65, 79, 144, 151, 184
Cyril of Jerusalem, 168, 173

Epiphanius, 146
Eunomius, 119, 169

Gregory of Nazianzus, 41, 97, 100, 101, 168
Gregory of Nyssa, 119, 126, 143

Hilary of Potiers, 8, 68, 79, 184

Ignatius, 66, 79

Jerome, 12, 27, 41, 48, 67, 80, 118, 120, 126, 128, 130, 146, 168–69, 173–74, 192
John Calvin. *See* table of "Contents"
John Chrysostom, 11, 12, 25, 42, 48, 66–67, 79–80, 117–18, 120, 125–26, 141, 143–44, 146–47, 151, 153, 167–68, 174, 193, 200, 205
Justin Martyr, 9, 41, 48

Manichaeus, 169
Martin Luther. *See* table of "Contents"
Methodius, 116

Origen, 12, 41, 67, 80, 116, 119, 120, 126, 146, 153, 192

Peter Chrysologus, 143, 151

Sulpitius Severus, 168, 174

Tertullian, 41
Theodoret of Cyrus, 9, 12, 42, 49, 97, 100, 118, 120, 143–47, 152–53, 167–69, 174, 184
Theodore of Mopsuestia, 8, 9, 10, 12, 94, 118, 166

Scripture Index

GENESIS
1:26	35
1:28	35
13:14–17	34, 38
14	28
22:16	29, 30
28:3	83

EXODUS
14	5
15	5, 142
17:8–16	162
17:14	163
32:11–13	149
32:26–28	149

LEVITICUS
19:34	187
23:43	7

NUMBERS
10:9	82
14:28	29
24:3	29
24:4	29
24:15	15
24:16	29
31:8	162
35:33	138, 206

DEUTERONOMY
2:4–6	123
4:20	96
5:11	130
7	187
16:3	7
16:12	7
20:13	163
20:16–18	163
25:17	163
28:48	92, 203
32	142
32:43	138
35	58

JOSHUA
10:24–27	162

1 SAMUEL
2:30	29

2 SAMUEL
23:1	29
23:2	29
24:8	105

1 KINGS
8:51	96
13:1–2	144, 153

2 KINGS

6:14	116
8:11	116
8:12	108
9:7	138
9:26	29
19	92, 203
19:26	91, 203
19:33	29
22:19	29

2 CHRONICLES

19:2	87, 135
34:27	29

EZRA

1:11	114
4:4–5	61
4:6—6:12	61
4:6	62
4:7:10	54
4:9	62
5:3	62
5:13–17	110
5:16	36
6:13–18	62
6:14	62
7	62
7:1	114
7:11–28	62
8:1	114
8:3	62

NEHEMIAH

2:19	62
5:1–15	62
6:5–9	37
6:5–7	36
6:12	62
6:14	62, 108
12:22	141
13:4–14	94
13:4	62
13:28	62
13:29	108

PSALMS

1–150	212
1–126	11
1–81	8, 10
1	5, 18, 57–58, 118, 158, 204
1:1	66
2	18–19, 33, 43, 45, 87, 93, 110, 139, 154, 157–58, 159, 181
2:1–3	19
2:1–2	18, 33
2:2	18, 159
2:3	18, 83, 158
2:5	33
2:6	158
2:9	18, 47, 158
2:10	18, 159
2:13	66
3	21
6:8	130
6:11	86
7	21
7:4	120
7:8	32
7:12–13	11
8	39
8:4–6	39, 183
9:3	87
9:8	32
9:13	206
9:15	103
12	22
14	22
16	135
17	21, 135
18	26, 163
18:48	163
19	5
21	26
21:2	135
22	11, 39
24	22
27	21
30	14
30:1	11
33:12	66
34	5, 15
35	15, 21
36:1	29

36:2	29
37	5, 58, 204
37:2	91
38	21
40:1	127
42–83	20
44	22
44:11	87
45:6	33, 44, 135
46	105, 107, 157
48	105, 107
49	5
51	11, 163
51:1	163
55	21
56	21
58	22
58:11	138
61:7	135
63	135
64	21
68:1	127
68:22	27
68:24	138
69	21
69:10	134
72:5	135
73	196
76:9	32
78	5
79	163
79:10	163
83	22
90:5	91, 95
92	21–22, 204
94	2
94:1	163
94:12	66
97:11	83
101	139
102:18	15
103–6	20
103	91
105	5
106	5
107	16–19, 154, 158–60, 165
107:2	18, 158
107:10	18
107:42	16, 18, 158
108–18	17
108–10	21
109	21–22, 43
110, *See* "Chapter 2,"	9, 12, 23, 49, 54, 87, 93, 113, 198–99
110:4	135
110:5–6	24
110:12	24
111	5
112	5
112:1	66
118	60
119, *See* "Chapter 2,"	23, 199–202
119:15	130
119:52	47
119:78	24
122	105
127	5
129, *See* "Chapter 2,"	10, 23, 113, 134, 202–4
129:7–9	24
132:1	109
132:17	36
132:18	22
136:1	29
136:2	29
137, *See* "Chapter 2,"	14, 22–23, 146–47, 154, 164, 205
138–45	17, 21
139, *See* "Chapter 2,"	21–23, 43, 161, 163, 206
139:14	166, 173
139:19–22	24
140	43
141:6	111
143	21
144	139
144:9	17
144:15	17
145–50	16
145	16–19
145:2	17
145:19–20	16
145:21	16–17
146–50	16–17

PSALMS (continued)

146–49	18
146–48	17
146	17–18
146:7	19
146:9	16
147	17
147:6	16
148	17
149, See "Chapter 2,"	12, 17–19, 23–24, 46, 142, 152, 207
149:5	18
149:6–9	14
149:6	17
148:7–8	19
149:7–9	18
149:7	14, 18
149:8	18
149:9	18–19
150	17–18, 165

PROVERBS

21:24	54
30:1	29
30:2	29

ISAIAH

2:3	41
3:1–4	26
3:7	130
5	164
9:3	92, 105, 203
10:5	33
11:4	172
13:16	110, 124
13:11	54
15:6	84
26:9	150
29:3	116
37	92, 203
37:27	91, 203
40:6–8	95
40:7	84
40:8	84
42:2	130
42:11	130
42:17	87, 92, 203
44	110
45	110
45:1	37
47:1–15	111
50:6	94
51:23	94
54:17	66
63:2	172

JEREMIAH

2:2	88
6	108
6:11	108, 110
8:13	95
9:1	116
9:20	110
11:14	96
13:14	110
17:9	137
22:5	30
22:28	110
23:5	30
26:18	89
28:17	141
31:18	73
31:31–34	151
32	164
33:15	30
43:2	54
44:7	110
48:10	124
48:12	110
49:7–11	109
49:7	124
49:13	30
50–51	110
50	110
51	110, 164
51:13	115
51:20	110
52:21	110
51:22	110
51:23	110
51:56	110

52	164
52:5	116

EZEKIEL

21:25–27	20
25:12	109
25:13	124
26	125
29:21	36
35:5	109

DANIEL

2:13	137
2:14	137
3:22	137
5:19	137
7:13	39

HOSEA

2:2	105
2:15	102
3:4	20
5:1–7	26
9:10	95
10:11	92, 203
10:14	108

AMOS

3:1–7	26

MICAH

1:3–7	26
3:12	89, 116

ZECHARIAH

3:8	36
4:6	36
4:9	36
6	36
6:12	36
6:13	37
13:7	20

MALACHAI

3:15	54
3:19	54

MATTHEW

1:11	115
1:12	115
1:17	115
3:1–12	95, 182
3	96
3:10b	96
3:12	94
3:42	96
5	79
5:3–10	66
5:8	66
5:10	65
5:17–18	64, 201
5:44	186, 215
6:12	69
7:19	96
10:13	174
10:18	63
10: 34	170
10:39	169
13:24–30	95
13:26	94
13:29	94
13:39	99
21:1–21	182
21:18–21	95
22:37–40	70
22:41–46	46
22:44	38, 183
23:1–39	39
23:13	64
23:23–24	64

MARK

1:3–8	95
3:29	39
4:12	39
7:6	39
7:10	39
8:17–18	39
11:12–14	95

MARK (continued)

11:20–24	95
12:36	38, 183
12:38–40	39
14:61–64	38
14:62	39

LUKE

3:2–17	95
4:5–6	41
4:21	10
6:28	120, 186
9:52–56	116
11:52	64
18:31–33	116
19:43–44a	116
19:44	115, 182
20:9–19	116
20:9–10	116
20:42–43	38, 183
20:45–46	39
22:48–53	126
24:26–27	116
24:27	64, 201
24:44–47	116
24:44–45	10

JOHN

5:39	64, 201
5:46	64, 201
13:17	66
14:6	66, 149

ACTS

2:17	151
2:34–35	38, 183
26:1–2	63
7:43	115

ROMANS

1:16	63, 201
2:1	81
3:27	69
4	64
7:14	67
8:16–17	65
8:17–18	141
8:27	141, 151, 207
8:28	68
9:12–13	122
9:32	64
10:4	74
12:14	186, 215

1 CORINTHIANS

3:9	74
4:12	186
13:4	146
15:25–26	45

2 CORINTHIANS

3:6	69
10:4	161
12:2	66
12:4	66
12:7	66
12:9	44

GALATIANS

3	64
6:14	168

EPHESIANS

6:10–20	33
5:12	79
6:17	172

2 THESSALONIANS

1:6–7	101

2 TIMOTHY

4:7–8	65

HEBREWS

1:2	10
1:3	39

1:13	39
2:8–9	39, 183
5:6	39
7:17	39
7:21	39
8:1	39
10:12–14	39
10:12	39
10:13	183
11:20–22	117
12:22	39

JAMES

1	101
1:10–11	95, 98, 101
5:1–6	95

1 PETER

1:24	95
5:13	115
3:9	186

1 JOHN

2:10	63–64, 80

REVELATION

1:5	166
1:6	179
1:16	169
2:6	114, 142, 152, 182
5:5–6	166
5:8	209
5:9	142, 152, 166, 173, 179, 182
6–14	142
13	167
14:2–3	167, 173
14:3	142, 152, 166–67, 173–74, 179, 189, 209
14:8	115, 167
14:11	167
15	152
15:1	141–42
15:2	142
15:3	141–42, 152, 166, 179, 182, 207
15:3–4	142
15:5–8	142
16:5	63, 179, 182, 201
16:7	63, 201
16:9	179, 182
16:19	115
17:5	115
17:14	40
18:2	115
18:6	115, 170
18:10	115
18:21	115
19:2	63, 179, 182, 201

www.ingramcontent.com/pod-product-compliance
Lightning Source LLC
Chambersburg PA
CBHW051633230426
43669CB00013B/2286